LEON EDEL has been active as a critic, writer, and teacher for more than a quarter of a century. His reputation as the foremost authority on Henry James was firmly established in 1962, when he won both the Pulitzer Prize for Biography and the National Book Award for Nonfiction for Volumes II and III of his life of James. Leon Edel is also known for his forays into literary history, his pioneering of literary psychology, and his editions of the works of Henry James, including THE COMPLETE TALES and THE COMPLETE PLAYS. Widely honored, he has been elected to the American Academy of Arts and Sciences, the British Royal Society of Literature, and the National Institute of Arts and Letters, which gave him an award for "creative writing in biography." New York University created its Henry James Chair of English and American Letters for him, and he is also Citizens Professor of English at the University of Hawaii. Mr. Edel is the author of HENRY DAVID THOREAU, JAMES JOYCE: THE LAST JOURNEY, LITERARY BIOGRAPHY, and THE MODERN PSYCHOLOGICAL NOVEL. With Edward K. Brown he is co-author of a biography of Willa Cather.

BY LEON EDEL

The Life of Henry James:

HENRY JAMES

THE MIDDLE YEARS: 1882—1895

LEON EDEL

 A DISCUS BOOK/PUBLISHED BY AVON BOOKS

Designed by Marshall Lee.

AVON BOOKS
A division of
The Hearst Corporation
959 Eighth Avenue
New York, New York 10019

First Discus Printing, August, 1978

DISCUS TRADEMARK REG. U.S. PAT. OFF. AND IN
OTHER COUNTRIES, MARCA REGISTRADA, HECHO EN
U.S.A.

Printed in the U.S.A.

The artist is present in every page of every book from which he sought so assiduously to eliminate himself.

Henry James

HENRY JAMES

THE MIDDLE YEARS: 1882—1895

Contents

BOOK SIX *The Dramatic Years*

1890 - 1894

BOOK SEVEN *The Altar of the Dead*

1894 - 1895

Illustrations

three quarters of an hour) a very pretty *small* pencil-drawing of me." *10 September 1886*

ALICE JAMES AND KATHERINE LORING IN LEAMINGTON

facing p. 289

From a photograph in the Houghton Library

KATHERINE DE KAY BRONSON

facing p. 352

From a watercolor by Ellen Montalba in the possession of Mrs. Bronson's granddaughter, Marchesa Nannina Fossi Rucellai. The pierced heart in the upper right was a favorite emblem of Mrs. Bronson's.

CASA ALVISI   *facing* p. 352

Mrs. Bronson's palazzetto in Venice, from a painting in the possession of Marchesa Nannina Fossi Rucellai

FENIMORE   *facing* p. 353

Constance Fenimore Woolson, from the photograph taken in Venice and found among James's albums, now in the Houghton Library. "I am rather devoted to profiles; it is the profile-view of a face that I notice first and remember longest."—*Miss Woolson*

HENRY JAMES IN CORNWALL 1894

facing p. 353

From a snapshot reproduced in Noel Annan's *Leslie Stephen* (1951). Standing behind the novelist are Mrs. Stephen (Julia Duckworth) and her son Adrian.

INTRODUCTION

IN THIS, THE THIRD VOLUME OF MY BIOGRAPHY OF HENRY JAMES, I tell the story of his life from 1882 to 1895. Cambridge has ceased to be "home." He has conquered London. His existence now becomes increasingly complex; for if England takes the place of Quincy Street, there is also a restless involvement with the Continent, and particularly with Italy. *The Middle Years* tells the story of this phase—of his social entanglements and his attachments, as well as of his evolution from chronicler of the "American girl" and "international" comedy, into an observer and recorder of English and Continental *mœurs*. And at the end of this period occurs his strange attempt to turn himself into a man of the theatre.

Above all, however, this volume tells the singular and intricate story of one attachment in Henry James's life which has hitherto remained wholly concealed. The record has been pieced together from such stray bits of evidence as life insists upon retaining in spite of all precautions. Inveterate burner of letters though James was, he remarked on one occasion that "there is no absolute privacy." And he went on to say that if artists are "well-advised to cover their tracks," there still exists a valid reason for "getting behind"—and the doing so, by a biographer and a critic, "may be a small affair compared with our [their] having really found something."

The "getting behind" in this instance, has cast light on a whole series of James's writings, from "The Aspern Papers" to *The Wings of the Dove* and from "The Altar of the Dead" to "The Beast in the Jungle." My task has not been easy, for James long ago described his determination to make the struggle between himself and his future biographer more equal than is usually the case in literary history. He recognized that the historian, coming late upon the scene, possesses a certain advantage over his powerless subject; understandably, it seemed to the novelist an unfair advantage. He argued, accordingly, that before death, the subject should do his utmost to assure the silence of the tomb. To leave evidence behind —say as George Sand and Alfred de Musset did, in full public glare —was to denude oneself in broad daylight. Every track covered, however—letters burned, or, even more, every letter "not written"— was a victory for privacy and silence: moreover this would serve to equalize the struggle by enraging the historian and spurring him on to use higher skills of deduction and more art; it would create a kind of parity between hunter and hunted. I have described this challenge in my book *Literary Biography* and in the preface to *The Selected Letters of Henry James*. Let it be said, however, that for every letter "not written," James wrote dozens; he created a false abundance, in which his "mere twaddle of graciousness" serves as a kind of biographical smoke screen.

Above all, Henry James issued an invitation to biographers to seek out the artist in "the invulnerable granite" of his art. I have accepted this invitation: for this is where the artist should be sought. The splendid Jamesian granite—as the man who quarried it well knew—contains however its secret doors and open passages. Otherwise the novelist would not have set down the words I use as epigraph for this volume, that the artist is present in every page of every book "from which he sought so assiduously to eliminate himself." Henry James was an intensely autobiographical writer. The biographer—the reader—cannot but be constantly aware of his presence, not only on every page, but in every turn of phrase. The novelist is sometimes enchanted with his own mastery of his form; his artistic ego controls and orders all that he does; his work makes demands on reader, critic, biographer: and we must recognize this, even though a younger generation of critics would prefer, it would seem, to retain the gentle avuncular presence, the elderly benign emasculate figure of the legend.

When Henry James used the title of "The Middle Years" for a tale written in his fiftieth year, and later planned to use it for a volume of unfinished reminiscences, he tried to suggest the "middle" span of an individual's life—from the late twenties to the late fifties—rather than what is spoken of as "middle age." The title is employed here, for biographical purposes, rather in the sense of Dante's *nel mezzo del cammin*. The "middle years" of my narrative are those of James's forties, the center of his life. At the end of this period he found himself in a dark wood; all was gloom and impenetrable mystery. He had no Beatrice to whom he could turn. More, he had no desire for a Beatrice. In his intense inner solitude, in the secret indirections of his existence, he had to make his way alone. The story of his faltering, but ultimately triumphal steps, belongs to my concluding volume. If I have titled the present pages *The Middle Years*, I should add that I have done so with the distinct feeling that they had, all the while, still another, a hidden title—*The Beast in the Jungle*.

LEON EDEL

Rome
March 1962

BOOK ONE

Terminations
1881=1883

HOMECOMING

IN HIS ROOM IN THE BRUNSWICK HOTEL, IN BOSTON, LATE IN NOVEMBER of 1881, Henry James found himself seated one day in front of a rather pretentious little marble-topped table, writing with an indelible pencil in a fat scribbler he had purchased some months before in London. The walls of the hotel room were white and bare; they shone in the flaring gaslight from a chandelier of imitation bronze, which hung from the middle of the ceiling and emitted a hissing brightness, flinging a patch of shadow across the page. When one extinguished the lights, illumination poured in through the transom over the double doors, flooded the bed, beat at one's closed eyelids. There was too much glare, too much scorching air from the heating system, too much ice water in the perpetual pitchers carried by waiters and bellhops. Henry's rooms in Bolton Street, as contrasted with these in Boylston Street, might have their English chill, but Henry had learned to accommodate himself to a fireplace and to candlelight; to adjust temperature and illumination to his needs. Nothing seemed adjustable in his hotel room. Henry was lonely and homesick. Cambridge and Boston had enclosed him, as always, in a possessive embrace. This act of writing in the fat scribbler was in itself a way of transporting himself out of his immediate American environment back to London—or to Venice. For what Henry was indelibly setting down was a statement unique among his surviving papers. It was a long retrospective summary of his six years abroad; a survey of his travelled cities and country visits, his new friendships and his Continental resources. He wrote in his light, rapid, characterizing manner, mainly a catalogue of sociabilities and impressions, as if to remind himself of all that he had seen and done, all that had been precious to him on the other side of the Atlantic.

He had returned to the old horizons, the house in Quincy Street, the Harvard Yard, with big square fresh buildings and slender elms reduced to spindles by the winter. Cambridge stretched away from the horizontal collegiate fence, low and flat, with vague featureless spaces. It looked like a clean encampment; the small wooden houses had a tent-like impermanence. There had been first a blaze of autumn; now the trees were profiles against high winter skies; the piled snow had come with Thanksgiving. In his two-sided Atlantic world, there were these contrasts—the horse-car and the gondola, the cultivated parks of London and Boston Common, the hierarchic world of England and the "tepid bath of democracy," in America. These were perhaps extremes. They reflected, however, a solemn fact. Henry was now an expatriate in his own land.

I

"Here I am back in America after six years of absence," he wrote at his marble-topped table, "and likely while here to see and learn a great deal that ought not to become mere waste material. Here I am, *da vero*, and here I am likely to be for the next five months." He was glad that he had returned. He had needed to see his family, to revive the "sense of the consequences that these relations entail. Such relations, such consequences, are a part of one's life, and the best life, the most complete, is the one that takes full account of such things. One can only do this by seeing one's people from time to time." Thus Henry assured himself that his journey had not been in vain. He added, however: "Apart from this, I hold it was not necessary I should come to this country."

What follows is a passage justly celebrated, for in it Henry reflected upon the choice he had made and the consequences it entailed. "My choice," he wrote, "is the old world—my choice, my need, my life. There is no need for me today to argue about this; it is an inestimable blessing to me, and a rare good fortune, that the problem was settled long ago, and that I have now nothing to do but to act on the settlement. My impressions here are exactly what I expected they would be, and I scarcely see the place, and feel the manners, the race, the tone of things, now that I am on the spot, more vividly than I did while I was still in Europe. My work lies there—and with this vast new world, *je n'ai que faire*. One can't do both—one must choose." He went on:

No European writer is called upon to assume that terrible burden, and it seems hard that I should be. The burden is necessarily greater for an American—for he *must* deal, more or less, even if only by implication, with Europe; whereas no European is obliged to deal in the least with America. No one dreams of calling him less complete for not doing so. (I speak of course of people who do the sort of work that I do; not of economists, of social science people.) The painter of manners who neglects America is not thereby incomplete as yet; but a hundred years hence—fifty years hence, perhaps—he will doubtless be accounted so.

The statement is not strange, but it is prophetic. Few Americans at the time would have understood it if they had been allowed to read it over Henry's shoulder. It was to remain unpublished for more than sixty years and thus was to be read in that future foreseen by the novelist. When it was written, most Americans were as oblivious of Europe as Europe was of them: the people on the great continent were preoccupied with their relations to their own land and each other, not their relations with the world. And Henry's statement was, as he himself saw, the statement of a novelist in search of subjects larger than those offered him by the scattered American scene. "My impressions of America, I shall, after all, not write here. I don't need to write them (at least not à propos of Boston); I know too well what they are. In many ways they are extremely pleasant; but," he added, "Heaven forgive me! I feel as if my time were terribly wasted here!"

II

When he had left Venice five months earlier, he could not have foreseen that he would thus be sitting, homesick, in a Boston hotel, indulging in a long reminiscence, offering himself the solace of the past for the inconveniences and nostalgia of the present. He had gone to Lake Como and then to Switzerland. He had felt a great relief as the coach mounted the Splügen into the Alpine air, out of the stifling cauldron of Italy. He remembered a certain glass of fresh milk which he drank that evening far up in the gloaming—a woman at a wayside inn fetched it from the cow. It was "the most heavenly draft that ever passed my lips." He went to Lucerne to visit Mrs. Kemble, but she had gone to Engelberg; he followed her to that "grim, ragged, rather vacuous, but by no means absolutely unbeautiful valley." One day he climbed the Trübsee toward the Joch pass. "The whole place was a wilderness of the alpine rose—and the Alpine stillness"; the beauty of the high cool valley, whose "great silver-gleaming snows overhang it and light it up," revived for Henry his memories of his old Swiss days. "I hadn't believed they could revive even to that point."

After Switzerland, he had returned to London to meet his sister. She had come abroad, frail and convalescent from the long illness she had suffered in 1878, accompanied by a Boston friend, Katherine Loring, a hearty woman who seemed to derive a genuine satisfaction in using her own vitality and strength to make life easier for her sickly friend. Henry recognized that Alice had become deeply attached to Miss Loring and seemed happy in her company and even dependent on her. The novelist spent a few days with his sister at Richmond, saw her afterwards at Kew and still later in Mayfair. It was quite clear that she was adequately companioned; she had her own itinerary, and was scheduled to sail for Boston before Henry would be ready to leave. Henry accordingly departed to pay a series of visits while the final chapters of *The Portrait* were at the printer's. He visited the Anglicized Russell Sturgises at Leatherhead, he went twice to Lord Rosebery's Mentmore, and on one occasion had as fellow-guest Mr. Gladstone; he also visited his publisher, Frederick Macmillan, at Walton-on-Thames. Above all he relished a visit to Somerset. "I think I have never been more *penetrated*—I have never more loved the land." He found a mellow and ancient feeling in the country and above all its houses— Montacute, Barrington, Ford Abbey and others. "These delicious old houses, in the long August days, in the south of England air, on the soil over which so much has passed and out of which so much has come, rose before me like a series of visions. I thought of a thousand things; what becomes of the things one thinks of at these times? They are not lost, we must hope; they drop back into the mind again, and they enrich and embellish it."

Then, as his sailing date approached, he had gone to Scotland, to Tillypronie, Cortachy, Dalmeny, Laidlawstiel. He remembered the drive from Kirriemuir to Cortachy—a commonplace road by daylight, as he later discovered, but in the twilight it was romantic to ford the river at the entrance to Cortachy and to drive through the dim avenues up to the great lighted pile of the castle, where Lady Airlie, hearing the wheels of the vehicle on the gravel, "put her handsome head from a window in the clock-tower." She asked if this were indeed Henry James and wished him a bonny good evening. Henry was in a Waverley novel.

III

Now, sitting in the uncomfortable hotel room, writing and remembering, Henry was confronted by things far removed from romantic novels. He had crossed the October Atlantic on the steamer *Paris* by the St. Lawrence route, so eager to get home that he disembarked with the mails at Rimouski and spent two days getting connections to Boston. He had gone directly to Quincy Street. His mother struck him as tired and shrunken: she had passed into old age while he had been away; his father was infirm and more lost than ever in his self-composed world. His Aunt Kate had come from New York to greet him. She found him "the same dear Harry who left us six years ago," but she also noted that he had become "a large, stout, vigorous looking man." Henry made friends at once with William's wife—the second Alice in Quincy Street—and saw his sister again: she had arrived but a few days ahead of him. There was also William's little boy, sufficiently articulate to boast shortly after Henry's arrival that he was "Uncle Harry's fascinating little nephew." He too had been named Henry —"the little Henri-*trois*," his uncle dubbed him. In the midst of so much "family," Henry passed almost a month before moving to the Boston hotel. He saw Howells almost immediately; his friend had just resigned the *Atlantic* editorship, and had been succeeded by the bland, sociable, gracefully verbal Thomas Bailey Aldrich. He saw his old friend T. S. Perry. He began to pay calls on Mrs. Gardner. He spent evenings with Grace Norton. He journeyed to Newport to see the Tweedys. Newport was charming; there were large light luxurious houses, planted with Dutch definiteness on the green of the cliff; the lawns touched each other without benefit of English hedge or fence; the ladies were brilliantly dressed and carried pretty parasols. The long lines of the far shore were soft and pure. All in all, the effect was quite delicate, "and anything that is delicate counts immensely over here."

But he was restless. His removal from Quincy Street to a Boston hotel had been designed to give him a feeling of his Bolton Street privacy; he wanted to resume his work. He found the hotel incompatible with literature. Early in December he went to New York to see what threads he could pick up there after his five-year absence from that city.

In Manhattan he stayed at No. 115 East Twenty-Fifth Street with Edwin Godkin, his former editor at the *Nation*, in the same neighborhood in which he had passed his long book-reviewing months of 1875. Manhattan was hospitable to its literary son— *The Portrait of a Lady* had just come out as a book and it had proved immediately popular. "I have been three weeks in New York," Henry recorded in his journal, "and all my time has slipped away in mere movement. I try as usual to console myself with the reflection that I am getting impressions. This is very true; I have got a great many." To Grace Norton in Cambridge he wrote: "I have seen many persons—but no personages; have heard much talk—but no conversation. Nevertheless the sense one gets here of the increase of the various arts of life is—almost oppressive; especially as one is so often reminded of it. The arts of life flourish—but the art of living, simply, isn't among them."

Henry went back to Quincy Street for Christmas. His younger brother, Wilky, increasingly an invalid, came from Wisconsin to be with the family, and with the exception of Robertson, the youngest son, the James family was briefly reunited. But somehow it was all rather melancholy. One gets a sense of sadness in the way in which, on the day after Christmas, in the old back sitting room, Henry gave himself over once again to his journal and to his memories—this time of his young manhood. "The freshness of impression and desire, the hope, the curiosity, the vivacity, the sense of the richness and mystery of the world that lies before us —there is an enchantment in all that which it takes a heavy dose of pain to quench and which in later hours, even if *success* have come to us, touches us less nearly. Some of my doses of pain were very heavy; very weary were some of my months and years. But all that is sacred; it is idle to write of it today."

In this passage he spoke of recovering "the vision of those untried years." Never, he wrote, "was an ingenuous youth more passionately and yet more patiently eager for what life might bring. Now that life has brought something, brought a measurable part of what I dreamed of then, it is touching enough to look back. I knew at least what I wanted then—to see something of the world. I have seen a good deal of it, and I look at the past in the light of this knowledge. What strikes me is the definiteness, the unerringness of those longings. I wanted to do very much what I have done, and success, if I may say so, now stretches back a tender hand to its younger brother, desire."

When Christmas was over, Henry did not linger in Cambridge. He returned to New York to attend "a gorgeous flowery banquet" given by Whitelaw Reid, whose Paris correspondent he had been. Here he met the just-retired Secretary of State, James G. Blaine. From New York he went to Philadelphia to pay a visit to Mrs. Wister and her husband. From Germantown he went on to Washington. He had never been there. In *The Bostonians* he was to make one of his ladies ask whether anyone had heard of "that little place," and to add that "they had invented it" while she had been abroad. Henry seems to have had this feeling as he stepped from the train one morning early in January, in streets filled with slushy snow, and looked at the single Dome and the single Shaft of the capital which then dominated the scene.

THE DOME AND THE SHAFT

HENRY FOUND THE STREETS OF WASHINGTON "ENORMOUS." THEY were lined with little red houses. Nothing seemed to pass save the tramway. Two sun-filled rooms were waiting for him at No. 720 Fifteenth Street; Henry Adams had reserved them; and in the same street the novelist had access to the Metropolitan Club. The first thing he did was to take a solitary walk to the Capitol. With the critical eye that had many times studied St. Peter's and the Florentine Duomo, surveyed the Invalides and the Dome of St. Paul's, he now appraised this great American dome, in the great democratic vista of a city that seemed to him still "too much of a village." False classic, white marble, iron, stucco. And yet it had a grand air. He went into the rotunda. It was a little like entering a railway station. There were no functionaries, no officers, no uniforms, no doorkeepers—not the least spot of color such as one found in the European seats of government. What was missing was some incarnation of the national conscience and the national dignity. He was to make a character remark that "this isn't government by livery"; however it is quite clear that Henry would have liked some livery in the vast expanse of marble, some relief from the labyrinth of spittoons.

He was to have later views of Washington, and to see the emergence of the designs over which Dome and Shaft now preside. His was the Washington which had recently buried President Garfield and was trying the assassin, Guiteau; in which the new President, Chester A. Arthur, moved in an easy intimacy, almost as a private citizen. The spittoons would recede and works of art would take over; but this was not, in effect, to change the artistic complexion of the place; Henry was to feel simply that the rotunda resembled "a stonecutter's collection of priced sorts and sizes." His first feeling, which he concealed, was that the Capitol was "repulsive." Later he was willing to concede that it embodied a kind of New World concept of space and air, of dominion and of power created *de chic*. His final picture was built on analogy—"the Washington dome is indeed capable, in the Washington air, of admirable, of sublime, effects; and there are cases in which, seen at a distance above its yellow Potomac, it varies but by a shade from the sense—yes, absolutely the divine campagna-sense—of St. Peter's and the like-coloured Tiber." Looking at it a quarter of a century after his first vision of it, he was to speak of the Capitol "as a compendium of all the national ideals, a museum, crammed full, even to overflowing, of all the national terms and standards, weights and measures and emblems of greatness and glory, and indeed as a builded record of half the collective vibrations of a people; their conscious spirit, their public faith, their bewildered taste, their ceaseless curiosity, their arduous and interrupted education."

This was a neat mixture of the flattering and the derogatory; for Henry had to reckon with American complacency. What he felt in 1882, and was to express no less succinctly in 1907, was that there wasn't in Washington "enough native history, recorded or current, to go round." He was also to echo a quarter of a century later Oscar Wilde's quip that "Washington has too many bronze generals." Describing the perpetual perspectives and converging avenues, the circles and crossways, the sense of great wide gardens, he was to have the feeling that given such ample measurements "the bronze generals and admirals, on their named pedestals, should have been great garden-gods, mossy mythological marble." The long vistas yearned for something more than the mere brief military or naval commemoration—they "waited for some bending nymph or some armless Hermes." Washington was an oddly scattered city, in which he got a general impression of high granite steps, light gray corniced colonnades, rather harmoniously low, contending for effect with slaty mansard roofs and masses of iron excrescences. It was all "a loose congregation of values." Much of the background seemed provisional, as if it could be unhooked and rolled up, like canvas scenery.

The city had two faces for Henry. There was official Washington, "the democratic substitute for a court city," and there was social Washington, harboring a society well organized, with its own tight codes and standards, that seemed to have little to do with politics. Henry marvelled at this, for in London he met Parliamentarians and lords everywhere, while in Washington he encountered chance legislators, in a society that seemed bent on excluding Senators and Congressmen rather than admitting them to its houses. There seemed to be passages of national life in which "the President himself was scarce thought to be in society."

Society seemed to operate in the foreground, and it used official Washington as its backdrop. It was a "City of Conversation"— and the conversation was mostly about itself. Moreover, elsewhere in America women were in control, and absentee husbands spent their days beside their ticker-tapes; in Washington there was "a re-committal to masculine hands of some share at least in the interests of civilization, some part of the social property and social office." It was all strange and entertaining; and looking upon it Henry wondered how the foreign diplomats, facing the phenomena of a capital that differed from, rather than resembled, the phenomena of other capitals and other societies, could cope with their task of "penetration and discretion." One supposes that Henry found it difficult to be discreet. He was hardly an "observant stranger" in his own capital. And the story which he began at this time and completed months later, "The Point of View," is indeed the most sharply critical of any which he ever wrote about his homeland. He may have concealed his opinions in it behind those of foreign visitors to New York and Washington, whose letters he created with craft and cunning, but his own "point of view" is unmistakable. One had to recognize, however, that much of Henry's vision of Washington was influenced by the spacious drawing room of No. 1607 H Street, in the tart reflections of his friend, the "Voltaire in petticoats."

I

"Thursday, Henry James put in an appearance; that young emigrant has much to learn here," wrote Clover Adams to her father on January 8, 1882. "He is surprised to find that he can go to the Capitol and listen to debates without taking out a license, as in London. He may in time get into the 'swim' here, but I doubt it. I think the real, live, vulgar, quick-paced world in America will fret him and that he prefers a quiet corner with a pen where he can create men and women who say neat things and have refined tastes and are not nasal or eccentric."

"I shouldn't wonder if the place were the most agreeable of our cities," Henry wrote to Grace Norton. "The Henry Adamses, who are my principal friends here, have a commodious and genial house and have been very kind to me. The pleasant thing here is the absence of business—the economy-empty streets, most of them rather pretty, with nothing going on in them. I am making the best of everything—so much so that I feel at moments as if I were rather holding my nose to the grindstone. It goes very well —but I will confide to you in strict privacy that in my heart of hearts I am woefully and wickedly *bored!* I am horribly homesick for the ancient world. *There* we needn't be always making the best of things. One may make the worst of them and they are still pretty good." To Henrietta Reubell he wrote: "Enormous spaces, hundreds of miles of asphalt, a charming climate and the most entertaining society in America." And to Godkin: "I have seen a good many people, chiefly under the influence of the Adamses and find the social arrangements and the tone of conversation, very easy and genial."

The Adamses constituted themselves Henry's guides and evaluators of all he reported to them from his social rounds. Mrs. Adams paraphrased Scripture to her father to describe the novelist's predicament—"And a certain man came down to Jerusalem and fell among thieves . . . and they sprang up and choked him." To which she added, "Henry James passed Sunday evening at Robeson's and dines tomorrow with Blaine." On his side Henry wrote to Godkin that the Adamses disapproved of the company he was keeping, "though I notice that they are eagerly anxious to hear what I have seen and heard at places which they decline to frequent. After I had been to Mrs. Robeson's they mobbed me for revelations; and after I had dined with Blaine, to meet the president, they fairly hung upon my lips." In the Adams house he was a constant visitor; Mrs. Adams seemed to have a perpetual tea party under way—two or three times a day—and frequent dinners at a little round table. Here Henry dined, early in his stay, with the new British Minister, Sir Lionel Sackville-West, fresh from his post in Spain where he had contracted his since-much-publicized alliance with Pepita, commemorated both by his descendant and by Virginia Woolf. "A rather dull (though amiable) personage," was Henry's verdict; however, he liked his "delightful little foreign daughter, who is the most perfect *ingénue* ever seen in America."

The Robeson of whom the Adamses disapproved was Congressman George Maxwell Robeson of New Jersey, whose wife of fifty Henry thought something of a "personage" although she was "fundamentally coarse." The Robesons were about to attain much notoriety by their sponsorship of Oscar Wilde during his visit to the capital. Newly-arrived from England, trading on his Gilbert and Sullivan reputation, Oscar had brought his aestheticism to New York and Philadelphia and now to Washington. The press talked largely of Bunthorne-Wilde. "The newspapers haven't got scent of Henry James yet," Mrs. Adams observed, and Henry managed to keep out of their way. However, he called on Wilde as a matter of courtesy. "Oscar Wilde is here—an unclean beast," he wrote to Godkin. He told Mrs. Adams he found him "a fatuous cad." But then Henry had admitted to Oscar he was homesick for London and Oscar adroitly implied that this was rather provincial of him. "Really! You care for *places?* The world is my home."

The Adamses approved of Henry's seeing Senator Thomas F. Bayard, member of an old Delaware family and brother of Mrs. Lockwood. Senator Bayard promptly sent Henry two invitations to dinner and offered him the use of a private room at the Capitol in which to entertain his friends. At Bayard's he met Horace Gray, a new Associate Justice of the Supreme Court. He goes to a ball at the British Legation; he dines with the Swedish Secretary; he chats with the Republican leader Wayne MacVeagh, and pleases him by remembering that Matthew Arnold considered him quite the pleasantest American he had ever met. To Mrs. Gardner Henry wrote that what he liked best in Washington society were certain girls, "very charming with a *désinvolture* rather rare *chez nous*." These included Miss Bayard and Miss

Frelinghuysen, daughter of the new Secretary of State, "happy specimens of the *finished* American girl—the American girl who has profited by the sort of social education that Washington gives." The Bayard girls were, he told his mother, "such as one ought to marry, if one were marrying." For the rest he was seeing "plenty of men, more than elsewhere, and a good many energetic types; but few 'accomplished gentlemen.'"

II

James G. Blaine, after meeting Henry in New York, invited him to his home to meet the twenty-first President of the United States, Chester A. Arthur. It was an elaborate dinner attended also by the British Minister, the Governor of California, Generals Sherman and Hancock, Senator Hale, Murat Halstead, Andrew Carnegie, the Hon. S. B. Elkins, and Allen Thorndyke Rice. The press called it a "small and noted company," and Henry James Jr. was described as "that eminent novelist and anglicized American." Henry observed the President's "well-made coat and well-cut whiskers," and enjoyed an intimate chat with him after dinner. President Arthur had known various members of the James family in Albany; he had even been present at the suicidal deathbed of a distant relative, Johnny James; and he had known Smith Van Buren, son of President Martin Van Buren, who had married one of Henry's aunts. Henry wrote to his mother that he "evidently believed me to be the son of Uncle William [the Reverend William James, elder brother of Henry's father] and wouldn't be disillusioned. This illusion was indeed apparently so dear to him, that I felt that if I had any smartness in me, I ought, striking while the iron was hot, to apply for a foreign mission, which I should doubtless promptly get." To Mrs. Gardner Henry wrote saying he thought the President "a good fellow—even attractive. He is a gentleman and evidently has that amiable quality, a desire to please."

At the end of January Henry was enjoying himself sufficiently to plan to remain until late February, and he had thoughts of visiting the South. He was finding the capital "genial and amusing." On January 27, however, his brother Robertson wrote that his mother had suffered an attack of bronchial asthma. On Sunday morning the 29th Henry wrote to her saying that it was "impossible almost for me to think of you in this condition, as I have only seen you hovering about the bed of pain, on which others were stretched." Late that evening, while he was dressing to go to a party, he received a telegram from William's Alice: "Your mother exceedingly ill. Come at once." There was no train until the next morning. Distraught and anxious, Henry rang the bell of the Adamses at 11 P.M. to inform them of his impending departure. He took the morning train to New York, and by that time Clover Adams had received an answer to a telegram of inquiry she had sent to Boston. She knew—what he did not—that Henry's mother was no longer alive.

· **MARY JAMES**

IN A DRIVING SNOWSTORM HENRY MADE HIS WAY FROM THE BOSTON depot to Quincy Street. Thirty-six hours had elapsed since he had been summoned home. He had arrived in New York at five the previous evening; at his cousin's Alice's telegram was translated to him: Mary James had died quite suddenly the previous evening, as she sat in the closing dusk with her husband and her sister— Aunt Kate—in the Quincy Street house. She had been recovering from the attack of asthma. Her heart had simply stopped in her seventy-first year.

Henry went to the Hoffman House to rest until he could take the night train to Boston. Here he spent the first hours of his grief. "I shall never pass the place in the future," he wrote in his journal, "without thinking of the wretched hours I spent there."

Now, in the early snow-reflected light, with the flakes swirling in the wind, Henry entered the north room of the house where his mother lay wrapped in her shroud. He found her "as sweet and tranquil and noble as in life." She seemed unchanged by death; there was much life—unendurably much—in her lifeless face. He later said he had never known how tenderly he loved her till he saw her lying there that morning. His death vigil was lonely —and triumphant: lonely, in that he had always felt a special tie between himself and his mother, as her favorite son; triumphant, in that he seemed to feel that with her death he came into full possession of her. In life he had had to share her with his father, with William, with his younger brothers and sister. Now, in the depths of his memory and imagination, she belonged only to him. He had felt this long ago when his cousin Minny died— felt the way in which she had been translated from "this changing realm of fact to the steady realm of thought." And this was why, when he wrote the long elegiac passage in his journal, commemorating all that his mother meant to him, he spoke of the "hours of exquisite pain." He was ready to thank Heaven that "this particular pang comes to us but once."

His father and Alice, by the time he talked with them, had begun to reconcile themselves to this break in their lives. Alice, frail as she was, seemed to have sufficient strength and courage for the occasion; and the elder Henry, infirm and tired, had his own philosophical way of taking the sorrows of life. Both were "almost happy." His mother still seemed to be there, in the house in which she had lived so long, "so beautiful, so full of all that we loved in her, she looked in death." Wilky arrived the next morning, a matter of hours before the funeral, from Wisconsin. Robertson had been in Quincy Street while Henry was in Washington. For the first time in fifteen years—and for the last—Mary James's four sons and her daughter were together under the family roof.

Wednesday dawned clear and cold. The storm had spent itself during the night. The sky was blue, the snow-shroud was deep, the air was brilliant and still. In the bright frosty sunshine the sons of Mary and the elder Henry carried their mother to her temporary resting place in a vault in the Cambridge cemetery. In the spring, a site would be chosen for the grave.

"She was the perfection of a mother—the sweetest, gentlest, most beneficent human being I have ever known," Henry wrote to his friends. "I was passionately attached to her," he told Mrs. Gardner. "She was sweet, gentle, wise, patient, precious—a pure and exquisite soul. But now she is a memory as beneficent as her presence." In the depths of his being, Henry possessed that memory.

AN EXQUISITE STILLNESS

A FEW DAYS AFTER HIS MOTHER'S FUNERAL HENRY JAMES MOVED from Quincy Street into Boston. "I wish to remain near my father," he wrote to a friend. "I do not wish however to be in Cambridge." He found rooms at No. 102 Mount Vernon Street, on Beacon Hill. They were bare and ugly, but comfortable. Here he reconstructed, as best as he could for this interim period, the conditions of Bolton Street. At first he felt that he should prolong his stay in America; his father was not well and Alice was not strong. William had his own family and his work. His other brothers were away. Of the sons of Mary James he alone was available. But as the weeks passed it became clear that Alice had for the time being found new strength in taking over her mother's role. She ministered to her father and ran the Quincy Street house without difficulty. The elder Henry insisted that his son return to his London tasks and to his own life. He therefore decided to maintain his original sailing date in May.

I

On the day after he moved into his rooms—February 9, 1882— he wrote the long passage in his journal on his mother's death, describing her as the "keystone" of the James family arch. The passage is eloquent in its subdued and self-conscious grief, and it reflects Henry's complete idealization of his mother. There is nothing comparable to it in the available writings of his brother; William, in all that he set down, said very little about Mary James, with whom he had so often been at odds. Henry's worship of her contains within it no suggestion that he ever imagined his mother as other than a creature of angelic tissue:

She held us all together, and without her we are scattered reeds. She was patience, she was wisdom, she was exquisite maternity. Her sweetness, her mildness, her great natural beneficence were unspeakable, and it is infinitely touching to me to write about her here as one that *was*. When I think of all that she had been, for years—when I think of her hourly devotion to each and all of us—and that when I went to Washington the last of December I gave her my last kiss, I heard her voice for the last time—there seems not to be enough tenderness in my being to register the extinction of such a life.

There were consolations. His mother's work was after all done; the "weariness of age had come upon her." He preferred losing her forever to seeing her begin to suffer. He thought "with a kind of holy joy of her being lifted now above all our pains and anxieties." Her death had given him "a passionate belief in certain transcendent things—the immanence of being as nobly created as hers—the immortality of such a virtue as that—the reunion of spirits in better conditions than these. She is no more of an angel today than she had always been."

He felt as if an "exquisite stillness" had settled around him. It was "but a form of her love. One can hear her voice in it—one can feel, forever, the inextinguishable vibration of her devotion." He rebuked himself for not having been tender enough with her at the end; he had been too blind to her sweetness and beneficence. He wished he had known what was coming "so that one might have enveloped her with the softest affection." And Henry went on to speak of her continued restlessness, her preoccupation with her children, her loyalty to her husband. "Summer after summer she never left Cambridge," he noted. His father was responsible for this—"it was impossible that Father should leave his own house." The passage is worth mentioning; under the guise of praising his mother's self-sacrifice he seems to criticize the elder Henry. "The country, the sea, the change of air and scene, were an exquisite enjoyment to her; but she bore with the deepest gentleness and patience the constant loss of such opportunities. She passed her nights and her days in that dry, flat, hot, stale and odious Cambridge, and had never a thought while she did so but for father and Alice. It was a perfect mother's life—the life of a perfect wife." It is difficult to see why Henry, in his sorrow, made this point; for there had been many summers spent away from Cambridge—in New England coastal resorts and even in Canada. Henry also seemed to glide over the fact that Alice had been seriously ill in recent years, and this, as much as the father's increasing infirmities, had kept his parents in Cambridge. In death as in life, Henry made himself his mother's champion against a kind of family oppression.

To bring her children into the world—to expend herself, for years, for their happiness and welfare—then, when they had reached a full maturity and were absorbed in the world and in their own interests—to lay herself down in her ebbing strength and yield up her pure soul to the celestial power that had given her this divine commission. Thank God one knows this loss but once.

It was inevitable that Henry should give to these words all the resonance of a funeral oration. In a touching manner he sought to pay his life-long debt in the most precious coin he possessed: in the power of language, the strength of imagery, the emotion carried by his pen. Mary James had been the central figure of all his years, and so she would remain. The strange thing was that on a deeper level of feeling, which he inevitably concealed from himself, he must have seen his mother as she was, not as he imagined and wanted her to be. She is incarnated in all his fiction, not as the fragile self-effacing and self-denying woman he pictured in his filial piety, spending her last strength for her children. The mothers of Henry James, for all their maternal sweetness, are strong, determined, demanding, grasping women—Mrs. Touchett or Mrs. Gereth, Mrs. Hudson or Mrs. Newsome. Sometimes these mothers have great charm and strength; sometimes they become the frightening figures of the governess or of Mark Ambient's wife. It is perhaps strange to juxtapose the mothers of Henry James's novels and tales beside the ideal mother of the commemorative tribute. Only in life was Henry prepared to create such a mother; in his fiction she is neither ideal nor ethereal.

Mary James had reared a family of five children. The younger brothers and the daughter had been crushed by the irrationalities and contradictions of the familial environment over which Mary had presided. The elder sons had surmounted them. Out of these tensions and emotions generated by the mother which played against the easy compliance of the father, there had emerged a novelist and a philosopher capable of expressing the very contradictions that had produced them—the one in brilliant fiction, the other in the lucid prose of rational thought.

II

"All those weeks after Mother's death," Henry was to write in his
journal, "had an exquisite stillness and solemnity." He kept his
London hours. In the mid-morning he would walk across the
Common and have his breakfast at Parker's. Then he would return to his rooms and write until four or five o'clock. In the
gathering winter twilight he would walk to Cambridge, "over the
dreary bridge whose length I had measured so often in the past,"
a mile of wooden piles, supporting a brick pavement with its
rough timber fence from which he looked at the frozen bay, the
backs of many new houses and a big brown marsh. And four or
five times a week he would dine in Quincy Street with his father
and sister. Then he would walk back to Boston in the clear
American starlight. "It was a simple, serious, wholesome time.
Mother's death appeared to have left behind it a soft beneficent
hush in which we lived for weeks, for months, and which was
full of rest and sweetness." Henry thought of her constantly as he
walked to Boston "along those dark vacant roads, where, in the
winter air, one met nothing but the coloured lamps and the far-
heard jingle of the Cambridge horse-cars."

His work interested him. He chose, during this period, to write
not the fiction to which he was addicted, but a play, the harbinger of his later siege of the theatre. He had written, in his youth,
three little skits or playlets, and published them; they had however relied neither on action nor on any particular characterization—had been simply little comediettas or farces sustained by a
certain conversational charm. Now, however, he set to work to
make a play of the least dramatic of his stories—"Daisy Miller."
It seemed to him that its success in the magazines and as a book
could be duplicated on the stage. In New York he had had
some preliminary negotiations with the Mallory brothers, who
owned the new Madison Square Theatre. They had encouraged
Henry and it was for them that he converted his light and airy
little tale into the concreteness of a dramatic action. To do this
he had to invent new "business." In the first place Daisy had

to survive; he could not kill her off; and she would marry Winterbourne. A villain was needed. Eugenio, the courier, was given this role and the foreign lady in Geneva, whom we never meet in the tale, now emerged as an *intrigante*, a *demi-mondaine* such as Henry had witnessed often on the stage of the Théâtre Français. Daisy recovers from her malaria, while the Roman Carnival is in full swing. The manager found it "beautifully written" but distinctly too literary. "It had too much talk and not enough action," he said. In his journal, James speaks of the Mallorys as behaving "like asses and sharpers." To Howells he wrote: "When we meet, I will tell you how those gifted brothers led me on protesting over the same path you trod to the same flowery pitfall, and with another play." Thus ended his first struggle—the first of a series—with theatre managers. Henry seems to have been naïve enough to think that in the world of the theatre managers were like magazine editors; he was master of the latter, he knew exactly how to deal with them. In the theatre, however, where direct business negotiation was involved wholly without the amenities and courtesies of the publishing world, he was usually baffled —and defeated. He had his play privately printed; he made an effort to get it accepted by the Boston Museum [Theatre], and he offered it to London managers. The verdict was always the same, and Henry finally sold it to Aldrich, for publication in the *Atlantic*, for $1,000. During this period he roughed out a first act for a drama founded on *The American*, planning here also to substitute a happy ending for Newman and Claire. The collapse of the "Daisy" negotiations led him to put it aside.

His preoccupation with play-writing during those snowy winter weeks may have betokened his inability, for the moment, to go on with his fictional work. The story he had begun in Washington lay unfinished in his portfolio, and play-writing filled in the time very well: moreover it fascinated him. It was like working out an elaborate puzzle. "My work interested me even more than the importance of it would explain—or than the success of it has justified," he noted. "I tried to write a little play and I wrote it; but my poor little play has not been an encouragement." It confirmed his convictions "as to the fascination of this sort of composition. But what it has brought [me] to know, both in New York and in London, about the manners and ideas of managers and actors and about the conditions of production on our unhappy English stage, is almost fatally disgusting and discouraging. I have learned, very vividly, that if one attempts to work for it one must be prepared for *disgust*, deep and unspeakable disgust."

The dramatic form seemed to him "the most beautiful thing possible," but "the misery of the thing is that the baseness of the English-speaking stage affords no setting for it." These reflections however belonged to a later time; at the moment he had only the joy of his creation, and when his play was written he carried his script to Mrs. Jack's and read it to her, during two long evenings. She was a sympathetic listener. Thus Henry had long ago imagined Benvolio, reading his plays to the irresistible Countess. He had, so to speak, had his private performance at the Court of Isabella.

III

The weeks passed; March came, and between bouts of homesickness and small Boston sociabilities, Henry managed to decrease the distance to his May 10 sailing date. How desperate he must have been we may gather from his writing a letter to William J. Hoppin at the American Legation, asking him for "a little parcel of London items." How was Mrs. Duncan Stewart? What was the latest news of her daughter, Mrs. Rogerson? He was homesick for London, "the full extent of my devotion to which I didn't know until I had put the ocean between us. My country pleases, in many ways, but it doesn't satisfy, and I sometimes wrap my head in my toga, to stifle (stoically) my groans." He told the First Secretary of Legation that when he next arrived at Euston Station, "I shall fall down and kiss the platform."

Mr. Hoppin dutifully pasted the letter into his diary: it is the only letter of any length he ever received from the novelist. On the same day that he wrote it, Henry also wrote to Henrietta

Reubell, thanking her for her budget of news from Paris—"your little whiff of the great Parisian hubbub seems to me the carnival of dissipation." To Mrs. Kemble he wrote that he smiled with derision at her suggestion that he might be "weaned" from "my London loves and longings by remaining over here." He was within a month of his sailing. "My father is much better than he was a month ago, and will not listen to my making any 'sacrifices' for his sake." He had heard from Mrs. Wister; he had had a letter from Mrs. Procter, "who writes as neatly as she talks, and from whose firm and brilliant surface the buffets of fate glance off." He was impatient to leave "and you are for a great deal in it."

Some time before he sailed his father and Alice took a small house in Mount Vernon Street, not far from his rooms, at No. 131. This represented the final breaking up of the house in Quincy Street, which had been the seat of the James family since the end of the Civil War. The house was too large for William's needs; and the elder Henry and Alice wanted something smaller and cosier. Henry saw them comfortably installed and was ready to sail with an easy conscience. Almost the last thing he did before his departure was to attend another funeral. On April 27 the bells of Concord had tolled for the death of Ralph Waldo Emerson and Henry made the familiar journey three days later to pay his respects to the old family friend, the benign figure of his childhood. The older generation was passing. Longfellow had died little more than a month before. It was a cool day in Concord and there was a threat of rain in the air. Regular and special trains brought a large congregation; others came in wagons and on foot to pay tribute to "the principal gentleman in the place." As a public funeral, Henry found it "curious, sociable, cheerful," a popular manifestation, the most striking Henry had ever seen provoked by the death of a man of letters. He was to attend more elaborate burials; nevertheless he cherished this memory of an almost rustic occasion, beside the new grave, near the grave of Hawthorne.

On the day before he sailed, his father wrote a long letter to him, to speed him on his journey: "My darling boy, I must bid you farewell. How loving a farewell it is, I can't say, but only that it is most loving. I can't help feeling that you are the one that has cost us the least trouble, and given us always the most delight. Especially do I mind Mother's perfect joy in you the last few months of her life, and your perfect sweetness to her. I think in fact it is this which endears you so much to me now. I feel that I have fallen heir to all Mother's fondness for you, as well as my proper own, and bid you accordingly a distinctly widowed farewell."

Henry was now his father's "angel" as he had been his mother's. "Goodbye then again, my precious Harry. We shall each rejoice in you in our several ways as you plough through the ocean and attain to your old rooms, where it will be charming to think of you as once more settled and at work." And he repeated: "A lingering goodbye, then, dearest Harry, from all of us! and above all from your loving Father, H.J."

A LITTLE TOUR IN FRANCE

HENRY CROSSED THE ATLANTIC ON THE "GALLIA" IN EIGHT DAYS AND nine hours. He left the ship at Cork. Eager as he was to return to Bolton Street, he wanted a glimpse of the land of his father's father. He spent a week in Cork and in Dublin and found both cities filled with constables and soldiers; otherwise he saw little but green fields and dirty cabins. He had no desire to become a sentimental tourist again, and if he had had any idea of turning his Irish visit into copy he abandoned it. On May 22 he was back in Bolton Street. Reclining on the sofa and awaiting him was an unexpected guest, his brother Robertson. On his desk was a pile of invitations. The London season was on with a vengeance. The city seemed oppressive, big, black and "actual." It was "a brutal sort of a place," he wrote to Godkin, and while he told him that he reverted to it with "a kind of filial fondness," somehow everything seemed changed. He was restless; he was bored. The death of his mother had, for the moment, drained life of all interest. The American episode was already fading away, and while he looked back at it with "a great deal of tenderness," he knew that Boston meant "absolutely nothing to me—I don't even dislike it," he wrote in his journal. He added: "I like it, on the contrary; I only dislike to live there." Much of his visit to his homeland seemed like a dream—"a very painful dream."

Nevertheless the nostalgia for his London life seemed to have evaporated as well. He went through the motions of participating in the "season," yet the London social world, into which he had plunged with such eagerness three years before, seemed to him "a poor world, this time; I saw and did very little that was interesting." And at the end of a brief journal note, he remarked: "I have gone in too much for society." To make matters worse he found himself invaded by editors and friends from the other side of the sea. At various times that summer Howells and his family, Osgood, Aldrich, Charles Dudley Warner, John Hay, Clarence King, whom he met at this time, were all in London, not to speak of certain ladies to whom he was indebted in various ways for hospitality, and whom he liked well enough in their own surroundings. Henrietta Reubell crossed from Paris; Mrs. Boit and her "merry laugh" reappeared; Mrs. "V. R." arrived and took rooms a few doors away from Henry's lodgings and made great advances into London society; Mrs. Wister came from Philadelphia to visit Fanny Kemble. In this "bewilderment of conflicting duties and pleasures" Henry was fretful. "All summer I had been trying to work," he wrote in his journal, "but my interruptions had been so numerous that it was only during the last weeks that I succeeded, even moderately, in doing something." This was when the season abated and the visiting Americans crossed to the Continent. Nevertheless he also remarks: "Shall I confess, however, that the evenings had become dull?" Even his election as an honorary member of the Athenaeum, where he had been proposed by Leslie Stephen, seemed now a routine matter. That he should possess two clubs in Pall Mall, side by side, and thus be on an equal footing as it were with England's political, literary, and religious world, now seemed to him less than significant. A process of disenchantment had begun. Indeed he found his evenings so dull that he sought out William J. Hoppin for company. Hoppin's journal of Sunday, August 25, 1882 records:

I had a long visit from Henry James last Sunday evening. He spoke of the neglect he had experienced in Boston when he was there last winter. One would have thought with the literary taste attributed to these people they would have feted him. But he got the privilege of the Union Club with some difficulty and was invited once to dinner. He spoke of all this without bitterness. Perhaps one should remember that he had just lost his mother and the Bostonians may have thought he did not care to be invited to parties. But they might have given him the chance of refusing.

I

To make Henry's restless summer complete, William suddenly decided to apply for a year's leave from Harvard with the double purpose of having a vacation and meeting some of his fellow-psychologists in Europe. Early in September the novelist found himself on his way to Euston Station to meet his brother's boat train. The strange thing was that William chose to take this leave a few months after the birth of his second son (who had been named William after his father and great-grandfather); at this moment of renewed paternity, he was planning to be away from his wife and infant for a year. He had done the same thing two years before, after his first-born had arrived; had rushed abroad for a summer's vacation, as if the presence of infancy in his house was more than he could bear. To be sure, his house, in which his mother-in-law and his wife's sister also lived, must at times have been a bedlam, and William could hardly have found peace there for the pursuit of his work. Perhaps the new child, like the first-born, may have also touched some chord of early memory in William and awakened an old anguish, that of little rivals invading *his* nursery—as Henry had done long ago. Shortly after arriving in Europe, he wrote a letter to his wife which might have given her pause, were she not so preoccupied: he described the German peasant women he had seen "striding like men through the streets, dragging their carts or lugging their baskets, minding their business, seeming to notice nothing in the stream of luxury and vice, but belonging far away, to something better and purer. . . . All the mystery of womanhood seems incarcerated in their ugly being— the Mothers! the Mothers! Ye are all one! Yes, Alice dear, what I love in you is only what these blessed creatures have." That sentence about "ugly being" and "ye are all one," if whimsical, nevertheless betrayed a singular state of feeling. And perhaps this was why William had, for the moment, put an ocean between himself and Cambridge. To Henry it seemed that William's timing was unfortunate. He used the word "abandoned" twice in writing to his sister-in-law. "With your husband in Venice and your eldest brother-in-law in these strange French cities [he was writing, later, from Bordeaux] you must feel rather bewildered and abandoned." But clearly he did not think of himself as the abandoner. "Your situation seems to me most unnatural, but I hope you bear up under it, and that you derive some assistance in doing so from your little Harry and William." And Henry returned to the charge: "Abandoned by your husband, you seem to me, dear Alice, very greatly to be pitied, and I assure you that I think of you with tender sympathy."

As William descended from the train at Euston Station he gave high proof of his temper to his brother. It was a vigorous monologue: "My!—how cramped and inferior England seems! After

all, it's poor old Europe, just as it used to be in our dreary boyhood! America may be raw and shrill, but I could never live with
this as you do! I'm going to hurry down to Switzerland and then
home again as soon as may be. It was a mistake to come over! I
thought it would do me good. Hereafter I'll stay at home. You'll
have to come to America if you want to see the family."

His eldest son, recording this many years later, remarked that
William was always under the spell of Europe when he was in
America—and was "most ardently American when on European
soil." The account continues: "The effect on Henry can better be
imagined than described. Time never accustomed him to these
collisions, even though he learned to expect them." Henry usually
ended by rushing William off to his Continental destination—
which was what he did this time, two days later—and, his nephew
added, "he remained alone to ejaculate, to exclaim and to expa-
tiate for weeks on the rude and exciting cyclone that had burst
upon him and passed him by."

II

This season of malaise was reflected in Henry's fiction. In Bolton
Street he completed the tale he had begun in Washington—"The
Point of View"—and its picture of American life comes to us as
in a series of folding mirrors, capturing in a bright critical light
the glittering weaknesses of the American democracy. What he
found was a country in which egalitarianism was diluting individuality; in which a thinness of history and a smallness of national
experience had to be reconciled with a continental grandeur and
a national sense of space and freedom. The repatriated American
gentlewoman, who has spent years in European pensions, complains that "there is no respect for one's privacy, for one's preferences, for one's reserves." The lady at Newport remarks on the
liberties given—and taken—by American youth and their deforma-
tion of the English language. "Of course, a people of fifty millions,
who have invented a new civilization, have a right to a language
of their own; that's what they tell me, and I can't quarrel with it.

But I wish they had made it as pretty as the mother-tongue, from which, after all, it is more or less derived. We ought to have invented something as noble as our country." She finds the men "better than the women, who are very subtle, but rather hard." The men are professional and commercial, "there are very few gentlemen pure and simple."

The girls are not shy, but I don't know why they should be, for there is really nothing here to be afraid of. Manners are very gentle, very humane; the democratic system deprives people of weapons that everyone doesn't equally possess. No one is formidable. . . . I think there is not much wickedness, and there is certainly less cruelty than with you. Everyone can sit; no one is kept standing. . . . The general good nature, the social equality, deprives them of triumphs on the one hand, and of grievances on the other. . . . You will say I am describing a terrible society,—a society without great figures or great social prizes. You have hit it, my dear; there are no great figures. . . . There are no brilliant types; the most important people seem to lack dignity. They are very *bourgeois.*

The emerging picture is of an easy democracy that breeds an easy mediocrity, in an atmosphere of advancing material civilization and chattering women. "The women listen very little—not enough. They interrupt; they talk too much; one feels their presence too much as sound. American women make too many vague exclamations—say too many indefinite things. In short, they have a great deal of nature. On the whole, I find very little affectation, though we shall probably have more as we improve."

This is one appraisal which America receives. The British M.P. surveys the same civilization good-naturedly, comments on the luxurious trains, and on the people, visits the schools and finds it extraordinary how many persons "are being educated in this country; and yet, at the same time, the tone of the people is less scholarly than one might expect." His impression is that children are better educated than adults. "The position of a child is, on the whole, one of great distinction."

Improved cooking-stoves, rosewood pianos, gas and hot water, aesthetic furniture, and complete sets of the British Essayists. A tramway through every street; every block of equal length; blocks and houses scientifically lettered and numbered. There is absolutely no loss of time, and no need of looking for anything, or, indeed, *at* anything.

The expatriated American aesthete complains at the absence of variety—"Everyone is Mr. Jones, Mr. Brown; and every one looks like Mr. Jones and Mr. Brown. They lack completeness of identity; they are quite without modelling." The French academician sees the women as engaged in a chase for a husband and American literature contains "no form, no matter, no style, no general ideas." The books seem written for children and young ladies. The newspapers contain no news, only stories about marriages and divorces "not in six lines, discreetly veiled, with an art of insinuation, as with us, but with all the facts (or the fictions), the letters, the dates, the places, the hours." His conclusion is that America is "the last word of democracy, and that word is—*flatness*." But Henry gives the last word to the Americans and largely to Marcellus Cockerell, who had had his fill of Europe. It is from his letter that Clover Adams culled the epigram most pleasing to herself, as it was to most Americans. "We are more analytic, more discriminating, more familiar with realities. As for manners, there are bad manners everywhere, but an aristocracy is bad manners organized."

The tale was published late in the year in the *Century Magazine*. Henry had predicted to his father that it would "probably call down execration on my head," and it did. The reviews were peevish; Henry's readers liked neither the sharpness of his observation nor the pointedness of his criticism. He was accused of being too severe in his treatment of the American national character. The tale tended to confirm the public image of the novelist as a chronic critic of the land of the brave and the free. James knew how "to play the harp of fiction," said one reviewer: but, he added, his harp didn't have enough strings. These remarks inevitably made James feel that Americans were thin-skinned. In the fullness of time, it is possible to observe that Henry James was saying nothing more to Americans about their land than what his fellow-novelists in France or in Russia or in England were saying to their own countrymen. They were functioning as artists, and by this process functioning as critics of life.

His disenchantment with English society emerged in a tale which was originally designed as a contrast between Anglo-American and French morality. It will be recalled that during his little journey of 1877 he had seen Dumas' *Le Demi-Monde* and had found it impossible to swallow the denunciation of the heroine "with a past" by a very moral young man who had been her lover. To "tell" on a woman, even if she were not the most moral creature in the world, seemed to Henry ungentlemanly; and he could not accept the high virtue made of this in the French play. In "The Siege of London," which he gave to Leslie Stephen for the *Cornhill*, he described the attempt of an American adventuress to obtain admission into London society. Nancy Headway wants to elbow her way to respectability in spite of her multiple divorces. She sets her cap at a stolid English baronet, Sir Arthur Demesne, under the observing eyes of a Secretary of Legation—a composite figure of Nadal and Hoppin, though somewhat more suave than either—as well as of a sophisticated American, rather like James himself. The society to which Mrs. Headway aspires is certainly "bad manners organized," and the lengths to which the mother of the baronet, Lady Demesne, goes to find out about Nancy's past embarrasses and finally irritates the sophisticated American. The tale is written in a rich vein of high comedy and its morality is the reverse of the French. Nancy gets her nobleman, and the American "tells" only when he knows it is too late to change anything. But in reality this tale is James's farewell to London society. He seemed to feel now that it was not much of an achievement to get into it—"poor world" that it was—indeed that anyone could do so with a little effort, as witness the case of Mrs. Headway. Even

New York would find her acceptable, once she became Lady Demesne.

The matter is put with some force by the Jamesian observer; his remarks show the road Henry had travelled since his talks with E. S. Nadal three years earlier. "I hate that phrase, 'getting into society.' I don't think one ought to attribute to one's self that sort of ambition. One ought to assume that one is in society—that one *is* society—and to hold that if one has good manners, one has, from the social point of view, achieved the great thing."

Perhaps Henry also felt the English had taken him up not because he had good manners and was a gentleman, but simply because they found him "entertaining." Nancy Headway proves to be a roaring success on the strength of her quaint Americanisms and her bold manner. "When she saw her audience in convulsions, she said to herself that this was success, and believed that, if she had only come to London five years sooner, she might have married a duke." This strong reaction to London society may have had some part in Henry's writing, at this time, his essay on "Du Maurier and London Society" which he published a few months later in the *Century*. He praised du Maurier for holding up "a singularly polished and lucid mirror to the drama of English society." He showed with what closeness he had studied the cartoons in *Punch* ever since his boyhood. And in a final passage Henry wondered, it seems, whether the conquest of London had been really worth while after all. Philistines were philistines, on either side of the Atlantic, and the artist was doomed always to be a stranger and an outsider anywhere in the world. Pondering du Maurier's Mrs. Cimabue Brown and his satire of aesthetes, Henry concludes that no revolution has occurred. The English were simply not an aesthetic people:

They have not a spontaneous artistic life; their taste is a matter of conscience, reflection, duty, and the writer who in our time has appealed to them most eloquently on behalf of art has rested his plea on moral standards—has talked exclusively of right and wrong. It is impossible to live much among them, to be a spectator of their habits, their manners, their arrangements, without perceiving that the artistic point of view is the last that they naturally take. The sense of manner is not part of their constitution. They arrive at it, as they have arrived at so many things, because they are ambitious, resolute, enlightened, fond of difficulties; but there is always a strange element either of undue apology or of exaggerated defiance in their attempts at the cultivation of beauty. They carry on their huge broad back a nameless mountain of conventions and prejudices, a dusky cloud of inaptitudes and gears, which casts a shadow upon the frank and confident practice of art. The consequence of all this is that their revivals of taste are even stranger than the abuses they are meant to correct. They are violent, voluntary, mechanical; wanting in grace, in tact, in the sense of humour and of proportion.

Art thus seemed to have no place either in an industrially-expanding America bent on equalizing everything, or in an England where the "conventions and prejudices," not to speak of "inaptitudes and fears," made him feel as if he were a freak of nature, or some curiosity, to be wined and dined and patted on the back without ever being truly appreciated or understood.

III

After Henry got William off to the Continent he paid a few country visits—this was one way of escaping from the London crowd and his fellow-countrymen—and crossed the Channel in mid-September to do a specific chore. A Harper editor had suggested to him that he write a travel book about France; this seemed to him a profitable thing to do. In spite of his large professional experience by this time, he did it without obtaining a definite commitment and Harper later backed out. Henry then sold the book to Osgood and, as *A Little Tour in France*, it was to serve successive generations of tourists in the château country and the Midi. Before starting his tour he paid his customary visit to Turgenev at Bougival, and this time found him quite seriously ill. They had some good talk nevertheless, and Turgenev wrote to Ralston: "Henry James has paid me a visit. He is as amiable as ever. But he has grown enormously fat."

Henry devoted all of October 1882 to his "little tour." He began it in the town of Tours, the birthplace of Balzac. Here he spent a week, joining Mrs. Kemble and Mrs. Wister who were holidaying there. Neither had the energy for much sightseeing, however. Mrs. Wister had her young son Owen with her, later to be celebrated as the pioneer of the "western" novel. Henry found him "attractive and amiable," but felt he was "light and slight, both in character and in talent." Mrs. Kemble was always her tragedienne self—"neither light nor slight," Henry remarked, and Mrs. Wister was now "a tragic nature, so much worn, physically, that I am sorry for her."

He found the châteaux interesting and the country around Tours "as charming as the essential meagreness of the French landscape will allow it to be." Leaving Tours and the Kemble-Wisters on October 8, Henry first travelled a small circle—Angers, Nantes, La Rochelle and Poitiers; then he went to Bordeaux, Toulouse, Carcassonne, Narbonne and Montpellier, and finally into the heart of Daudet's Midi—Nîmes, Tarascon, Arles, Avignon; after which he curved northward to Orange, Mâcon, Beaune and Dijon. By mid-October, when he was in the Midi, he wrote to William, who was in Venice: "I pursue my pilgrimage through these rather dull French towns and through a good deal of bad weather, and all my desire now is to bring it to a prompt conclusion. It is rather dreary work, for most of the places, I am sorry to say, are much less rich in the picturesque than I had supposed they would be." Decidedly the French provinces were not Italy. To Howells he wrote: "There is no more to my purpose at Bordeaux than there would be at Fitchburg, and I am not even consoled by good claret, as what I am given here is very much what you would get at F." He felt that France had preserved the physiognomy of the past less than England or Italy—that Napoleon had erased much of the pictorial and the "quaint." He experienced a revival of interest however when he came to the Roman towns; and certain of the cathedrals, as always, deeply absorbed his attention. In Avignon the Rhône was in flood, and he was pleased to get out of its watery streets and make a straight line for Paris. He had kept a journal during his little tour (apparently later destroyed), and from it he wrote his book a few months after. It is much less personal than his other travel writings, much more strictly a guidebook; and while it abounds in accurate and vivid descriptive passages, it leans a great deal on mere historic recital. The material was too architectural, and too historical; it lacked what he called the "human picturesque," and the book suffered accordingly. But it suffered too, it might be added, from the lack of his former freshness and from his general mood of fatigue and depression.

NOVEMBER PARTING

NOVEMBER HAD COME WHEN HENRY TRAVELLED FROM DIJON TO Paris, his little tour accomplished. He had seen more of France than he had ever seen before, and "on the whole" liked it better. The autumn was uncommonly wet. He put up at the Grand Hôtel and recognized once again that Paris had "a little corner of my complicated organism." He found the "same rather threadbare little circle of our sweet compatriots, who dine with each other in every possible combination of the alphabet—though none of their combinations spell the word satisfaction. That, however,"

he added to Mrs. Jack, "is the most difficult word in the language
—even *I* am not sure I get it right."

The pleasantest coincidence was to find John Hay at the Grand
Hôtel. Henry had never known well the man who had been Lincoln's assistant secretary and who combined a love of letters with
national duty in a way that was rare in Washington. But he respected him highly. With Hay was his friend Clarence King, author of the major governmental survey of the mineral resources of
the United States, and friend of Henry Adams. Like Adams,
James admired King's wit, his energy, his capacity for good talk,
his ceaseless interest in the world around him. The three breakfasted together, roamed the boulevards, prowled in shops. "He is
a delightful creature, and is selling silver mines and buying water-
colours and old stuff by the millions," Henry wrote to Mrs. Jack.
And to Howells he said: "King is a charmer. He charmed all the
bric-à-brac out of the shops." After his solitary journey in the Midi
it was a delight to come upon such congenial fellow-Americans in
the French capital.

He had exchanged notes with Ivan Sergeyevich, who continued
to be ill, and on November 17 went to see him at Bougival,
where the Russian had remained much later than usual, attended
by doctors, among them J. M. Charcot, who could not diagnose
what was wrong with him. More recently they had recommended
a milk diet, and when Henry found him he was astonished at the
change in his friend. His towering figure was stooped. His great
frame was shrunken. But he was as *accueillant* as ever. "He had
been ill, with strange, intolerable symptoms, but he was better,"
Henry later wrote, "and he had good hopes." Neither knew, when
they saw each other that day in November, when the trees at
Bougival were bare and the Seine was gray, what cruel months lay
ahead. Ivan Sergeyevich had cancer of the spine.

After a period of complete immobility, the Russian had begun
to go out again, and on that afternoon he had to go into Paris.
He did not want to take the suburban train, because he feared

he would find it uncomfortable; ordering a carriage, he asked
Henry to ride with him into the city. It was just seven years since
they had first met, when Turgenev used to mount with firm and
powerful tread the endless stairs that led to Flaubert's perch.
They rode through the thickening dusk, and for an hour and a
half Henry had his beloved friend to himself. Turgenev talked
constantly, and never better. He talked in English, and Henry
was to quote from this occasion a certain sentence to illustrate the
peculiar literary quality of Turgenev's use of that tongue—remembered phrases encountered in books. This gave a charming quaint-
ness and an unexpected turn to what he said: "In Russia, in
spring, if you enter a beechen grove"—these were the words
that came back to Henry from their carriage ride. What subjects
they touched upon he never recorded; but it was the same rich,
spontaneous talk which he had always cherished in his elder contemporary.

When they reached the city Henry left the carriage at an exterior boulevard. There was a little French fair going on in the chill
November air, under the denuded trees. The nasal sound of a
Punch and Judy show somehow became mixed with his farewell
at the window of the carriage. Then the vehicle rolled away.

A WINTER SUMMONS

HENRY HAD HARDLY RETURNED TO LONDON TO SETTLE DOWN AFTER
his ramblings, when word came from his sister and aunt that his
father was rapidly declining and did not have long to live. Al-

though he had left the United States barely six months before, he made immediate plans to return. William was at this time in Paris attending Charcot's clinics at the Salpêtrière. They agreed that Henry should sail, and William would come to London and stay in Bolton Street while awaiting further news. Henry obtained passage on the *Werra*, from Liverpool, leaving on December 12. The voyage was smooth and rapid. The ship reached New York on December 21, and waiting for Henry at the dock was a letter from Alice written the day before, a Wednesday.

Darling Father's weary longings were all happily ended on Monday at 3 P.M. The last words on his lips were "There is my Mary!" For the last two hours he had said perpetually "My Mary." He had no suffering but we were devotedly thankful when the rest came to him, he so longed to go, the last thing he said before he lost consciousness was "I am going with great joy!" The end of life had come for him and he went and I am sure you will feel as thankful as I do that the weary burden of life is over for him. I have no terrors for the future for I know I shall have strength to meet all that is in store for me; with a heart full of love and counting the minutes till you get here; always your devoted A—.

She told him that the funeral would be on Thursday morning. "There seemed no use in waiting for you, the uncertainty was so great."

His father, then, had been buried that very morning while his steamer was pulling into New York harbor. Henry reached Boston at eleven that night and was met at the station by his brother Robertson, who had come from Milwaukee for the funeral, and was leaving in the morning. In Mount Vernon Street Alice was resting. Aunt Kate, however, was up; they talked into the morning.

The elder Henry had died as he had lived, with an unflagging moral optimism; although his physical strength had failed him, he had turned his sickroom into a place of joy. He announced that he had entered upon the "spiritual life" and thereafter refused all food. The doctors spoke of "softening of the brain," but all the evidence indicates that until his last hours, he was in possession of his faculties. Francis Boott, who was in America that winter, came to see him a day or two before the end and they had a long talk. He lay facing the windows and refused to have them darkened. He slept a great deal. He was told that Henry was on his way. The news gave him pleasure, but he showed no sign of impatience—save to die. Toward the end, Aunt Kate heard him say, "Oh I have such good boys—*such* good boys!" Asked about funeral arrangements he said (Aunt Kate wrote this down):

That here is a man who has always believed in the only true spiritual life, a direct intercourse with God—and who leaves it as his dying wish that men should know and understand that all the Ceremonies usually observed in births, marriages and funerals are nonsense and untrue. The only true life is the spiritual one and this is only interfered with by these foolish words and doings that man has invented. [He further said] that he did not believe in individual salvation, but in the free personal intercourse of all men with God.

In long letters to William, conveying to him all the details as he gathered them, Henry said the father's passing had been "most strange, most characteristic above all, and as full of beauty as it was void of suffering. There was none of what we feared—no paralysis, no dementia, no violence." He had simply felt a great weakness; had swooned repeatedly; and after that had taken to his bed. Only the nurse and the loyal aunt were with him when he died. Alice had been increasingly ill and was being ministered to by Miss Loring. Thus ended the life of one of the most original of the earlier Americans, a strange, voluble, gifted man, who had led an unworldly life, out of the current of Transcendental thought. To an extraordinary degree he had given to his sons the vigorous qualities of his language, something of the bellicose Irishness of his nature, and the picturesqueness of his mind. "A little fat, rosy, Swedenborgiañ amateur," Ellery Channing had called him, "with the look of a broker, and the brains and heart of a Pascal." He had been, as Ralph Barton Perry said, a man with a mission dogged by a sense of futility—a frustrated writer who never quite conveyed his message in spite of his lively prose. In the fullest way in which any man may hope to be represented by his progeny, William and Henry James accomplished what their father had failed to do. If the world had not listened to him, with all the life and intensity of his being and his own idiosyncrasies of style and speech, it was to listen to them. They were to write themselves—and him—into the memory of the civilized world.

In the house in Mount Vernon Street, so recently animated by the presence of the elder Henry, a great silence reigned that Christmas. Alice, in a state of collapse, had been taken by Katherine Loring on the day after Henry's arrival to the Loring home at Beverly. Henry, deprived of his last glimpse of his father, developed one of his debilitating migraines and was ill for four days. Aunt Kate, sole survivor of the paternal group, who had dedicated her life to her sister, and her sister's husband and children, sat in silent meditation in the parlor, "not only without a Christmas dinner but without any dinner, as she doesn't eat, according to her wont."

The suddenness of Henry's jump from London to Boston had left him in a daze. He wrote to his publisher that he could touch the red brick houses opposite with his pen point and found himself wondering for the moment what had come over Bolton Street. "After I have been here two or three weeks I shall know pretty well where I am, and perhaps how long I shall be here."

"The house is so *empty*," he wrote to William. It was late in the evening and Henry had been down to the parlor to chat with his aunt. She repeated again and again that the father had "yearned unspeakably" to die. "I am too tired to write more, and my head is beginning to ache." He added: "All our wish here is that you should remain abroad the next six months."

A BLESSED FAREWELL

ON THE LAST DAY OF THE YEAR 1882, HENRY WALKED THROUGH THE
deep snow of the Cambridge cemetery where the previous spring
a family plot had been selected on a small rise in the land. Here
the mother had been committed to the earth. Now, in the silence
of the Sunday morning, Henry looked at the new grave, cut in
the cold ground ten days before. The elder Henry lay very close
to his wife. At some point during this visit the son took a letter
from his pocket and began to read it aloud into the wintry air,
addressing it to the graves. There was no eyewitness, so far as we
know, no one to record the quality of Henry's voice, or the way in
which he stood in the performance of this act. But its very nature
suggests a depth of feeling, a passion of tenderness. He seems to
have stood there alone, under a blue winter sky, in the piled snow,
within view of the distant field beyond the Charles.

What Henry read was a letter written by William to his father
on December 14, just after the elder son had arrived in Bolton
Street. It had reached Cambridge the day before, too late by a fortnight for the man for whom it was destined. Substituting his own
voice and presence for that of his brother, Henry now communicated it to the dead.

"Darling old Father," Henry read, "We have been so long accustomed to the hypothesis of your being taken away from us, that
the thought that this may be your last illness conveys no very
sudden shock. You are old enough, you've given your message to
the world in many ways and will not be forgotten; you are here
left alone, and on the other side, let us hope and pray, dear, dear
old Mother is waiting for you to join her. If you go, it will not be
an inharmonious thing. Only, if you are still in possession of your
normal consciousness, I should like to see you once again before
we part. I stayed here only in obedience to the last telegram, and

am waiting now for Harry—who knows the exact state of my mind, and who will know yours—to telegraph again what I shall do." Henry read on: "Meanwhile, my blessed old Father, I scribble this line (which may reach you though I should come too late), just to tell you how full of the tenderest memories and feelings about you my heart has for the last few days been filled. In that mysterious gulf of the past into which the present soon will fall and go back and back, yours is still for me the central figure. All my intellectual life I derive from you; and though we have often seemed at odds in the expression thereof, I'm sure there's a harmony somewhere, and that our strivings will combine. What my debt to you is goes beyond all my power of estimating,—so early, so penetrating and so constant has been the influence. You need be in no anxiety about your literary remains. I will see them well taken care of, and that your words shall not suffer for being concealed."

William promised his father that he would compile a volume of extracts from the elder Henry's writings, after the manner of the extracts from Carlyle, Ruskin and others. "I have long thought such a volume would be the best monument to you."

"As for us" [Henry continued to read]; "we shall live on each in his way—feeling somewhat unprotected, old as we are, for the absence of the parental bosoms as a refuge, but holding fast together in that common sacred memory. We will stand by each other and by Alice, try to transmit the torch in our offspring as you did in us." And so, after recognizing that he had at various times given his father trouble, and expressing the belief that in his own paternal role he would learn to understand his father's paternity, William ended:

"As for the other side, and Mother, and our all possibly meeting, I *can't* say anything. More than ever at this moment do I feel that if that *were* true, all would be solved and justified. And it comes strangely over me in bidding you good-bye how a life is but a day and expresses mainly but a single note. It is so much like the act of bidding an ordinary good-night. Good-night, my sacred old Father. If I don't see you again— Farewell! a blessed farewell!"

Henry had finished. He replaced the letter in his pocket. He had remained with his parents, in this solemn visit, a long time. He was certain, he told his brother, that the elder Henry had heard him "somewhere out of the depths of the still, bright winter air." And he also said: "As I stood there and looked at this last expression of so many years of mortal union, it was difficult not to believe that they were not united again in some consciousness of my belief."

The son and brother had performed his strange deeply-felt mystical act by the two graves. And now he could turn from the dead to the living. As he walked back, he stopped at William's house and sat with his brother's wife and her two children, admiring the infant William, "a most loving little mortal." Then he called on Francis J. Child, professor of English at Harvard, whom he had known from his own student days, and who had appeared to feel the elder Henry's death more than anyone outside the family. He received the condolences of Wendell Holmes, recently made a Judge of the State Supreme Court, and in writing all this to William he enjoined him not to come rushing home. Everything was being taken care of; moreover there was nothing William could do since the elder Henry's last will and testament had named his second son to be the executor. For the time at least Henry, the quiet "angel," assumed legally the administration of the James family affairs. Jacob had indeed supplanted Esau—and Esau at this moment was in a far-away land.

SON AND BROTHER

WILLIAM KEPT HIS WORD. WITHIN TWO YEARS—IN 1884—HE BROUGHT out *The Literary Remains of the Late Henry James*, a substantial miscellany of his father's writings with a long introduction by himself. His father's last book was, in a sense, William's first. Henry, receiving it, wrote to his brother on January 2, 1885 that it gave him "great filial and fraternal joy." He spoke of the "extraordinarily individual (some of them magnificent)" utterances in the volume. His father's religious system seemed intensely original and personal. "I can't enter into it (much) myself—I can't be so theological, nor grant his extraordinary premises, nor throw myself into conceptions of heavens and hells, nor be sure that the keynote of nature is humanity, etc. But I can enjoy greatly the spirit, the feeling and the manner of the whole thing, (full as this last is of things that *dis*please me too,) and feel really that poor Father, struggling so alone all his life, and so destitute of every worldly or literary ambition, was yet a great writer." Henry did his utmost to get the book noticed in England. Few seemed interested. And when the *Nation* did inadequate justice to it, Henry scolded Godkin. "I have a tenderness for my poor Father's memory which is in direct proportion to the smallness of the recognition his work was destined to obtain here below and which fills me with a kind of pious melancholy in presence of the fact that so ardent an activity of thought, such a living, original, expression of spirit may have passed into darkness and silence forever." The volume, with his brother's introduction, he told Godkin, seemed to him to have "a real literary importance."

I

Henry James the elder left an estate valued at $95,000. It consisted of more than $80,000 worth of land, houses and stores, in Syracuse, New York, yielding 7 per cent after taxes and maintenance, or about $5,000 a year. The remainder, largely money derived from the sale of the Quincy Street house, had been invested in prosperous railway stocks and bonds, with a yield per annum of $3,500. These latter were willed to Alice and provided adequately for an invalid spinster of that time. The estate was to be divided among the three brothers, William, Henry and Robertson. Garth Wilkinson James, the improvident and happy-go-lucky son, was omitted from the will because he had received his inheritance in advance. For some years he had been a constant drain on his father. Only a short time before, on declaring himself bankrupt, he had been given $5,000.

Wilky however was seriously ill; he had a rheumatic heart and other complications. He was crushed by his debts, and he had a wife and children in Milwaukee. Henry, from the outset, took the position that the will was "unfortunate," and proposed a re-division into four equal parts. Robertson, who had ample means, agreed; Alice, insofar as she was a party to the testament, also voted with Henry. William, thinking of his two sons, wrote from abroad that he was not at all certain a re-division would be equitable, given the large sums Wilky had squandered. He reminded Henry of the difference between the bachelor state and the responsibilities of paternity, and proposed re-division into fifths. He also worked out an elaborate breakdown into sixteenths, according to the population of the James family groups. Henry opposed this, and, as a matter of fact, had already moved for equal division, "assuming" William would agree. William's first impulse was to book passage early in February for home. What ensued was a strange and lively correspondence in which Henry threw all his weight into convincing William he must stay abroad—as if his very life depended on keeping his elder brother in Europe. In a 2,000-word letter he pointed out that William would have no place to stay in Cambridge, since part of his house had been sublet, and to live away from his family would engender gossip. He insisted that if William returned before his appointed time it would be "a melancholy confession of failure," a "sort of proclamation of want of continuity of purpose." William had made a point of going abroad because he needed rest and had work to do and "you were surely not altogether wrong." Cambridge itself was "barren" after London and Paris, Henry wrote, forgetting that this was his, not William's, feeling about the local scene. He peevishly said that William could be accommodated in Boston at the Mount Vernon Street house in the small guest room, where Aunt Kate had stayed, but "I won't offer to give up Father's room, because I lately made you a present of my rooms in London." And he argued there would be "a painful want of *form*" in William's returning to Cambridge "prematurely"—especially after having remained away during his father's illness and death.

William replied that Henry was meddling in his affairs; that however much Henry considered Cambridge "barren," these were not his feelings; and he expressed the wish that his brother should cease treating him as if he were a baby. However, he cancelled his passage, and after further negotiation, certain adjustments were made. A portion of the estate was set aside for Wilky's family, in a trust fund, with the net consequence that William and Henry would each receive about $1,300 a year. Henry travelled to Milwaukee in twenty below zero temperatures and a blinding blizzard for direct talks with the younger brothers, and later visited Syracuse to inspect the properties, which were located on James Street—the street named for the immigrant grandfather. William came home in March and Henry made over to him the general handling of the estate. His own income, he announced, was to go entirely to Alice —"this I desire always to be its regular destination. She assures me that she will have no occasion to use it—will save it and invest it for my benefit etc. But I wish her to have it, to cover all the contingencies of her new existence." Later, when William thought it his duty to keep Henry informed, he replied: "Never, I again beg you, take the trouble to tell *me* twice anything at all about my Syracuse dividend. I have made my income entirely over to Alice and take no further interest in it." Henry would continue to live by his pen.

II

He drove his pen on Beacon Hill during these months, and used to venture forth for walks in the snowy streets. He was to evoke, in a charming tale, "A New England Winter," written some months later, the familiar aspect of the long straight avenue airing its newness in the frosty day, with its individual façades, and their neat sharp ornaments, the large clear windows of the curved fronts facing each other "like candid, inevitable eyes." The picture of Beacon Street revives an earlier age of plate glass:

There was something almost terrible in the windows . . . how vast and clean they were, and how, in their sculptured frames, the New England air seemed, like a zealous housewife, to polish and preserve them. A great many ladies were looking out, and groups of children, in the drawing-rooms, were flattening their noses against the transparent plate. Here and there, behind it, the back of a statuette or the symmetry of a painted vase, erect on a pedestal, presented itself to the street, and enabled the passer to construct, more or less, the room within—its frescoed ceilings, its new silk sofas, its untarnished fixtures. This continuity of glass constituted a kind of exposure, within and without, and gave the street an appearance of an enormous corridor, in which the public and the private were familiar and intermingled. But it was all very cheerful and commodious, and seemed to speak of diffused wealth, of intimate family life, of comfort constantly renewed.

James became thoroughly familiar with the Boston winter scene —"the denuded bushes, the solid pond, the plank-covered walks, the exaggerated bridge, the patriotic statues, the dry, hard texture of the Public Garden for its foreground, and for its middle distance the pale, frozen twigs, stiff in the windy sky that whistled over the Common, the domestic dome of the State House, familiar in the untinted air, and the competitive spires of a liberal faith." In Washington Street, on a winter's afternoon, Henry trod the slushy thoroughfare, past the crawling horse-cars, the thronging pedestrians, the "sisterhood of shoppers" laden with satchels and parcels, the snow which thudded to the street from the sloping house-tops, the mounds of pulverized, mud-coloured ice on the sidewalks. The houses offered a jagged line of tall and short buildings, and there were staring signs, labels, pictures, familiar advertisements, a tangle of telegraph wires in the air. Every fifty yards there was a candy store. Behind the plate glass, behind counters, were pale, delicate, tired faces of women, with polished hair and glazed complexions. In Bolton Street, months later, Henry could recall it as vividly as if he had just seen it. He was struck by the "numerosity" of the womenfolk; there was a "deluge of petticoats." Henry felt he was in a city of women, a country of women, and it was this that determined him in the selection of the subject for his next novel. The talk, the social life—everything—seemed so completely in the hands of the opposite sex that he wondered whether he were not in a country stricken by war, with the men away on the battlefields.

"I feel strangely settled here for the present," he wrote to his publisher in London, "and shall probably remain for the summer. But after that—open thy bosom, London of my soul!" It was clear to him that he would not return again to America for a long time; there was no further reason for doing so. "My sister and I make an harmonious little ménage," he wrote, "and I feel a good deal as if I were married." He told Mrs. Kemble he had suggested to Alice that she come to England with him to set up a common household in London. His sister had, however, "shrewdly declined," he said, "for we are really both much too fond of our individual independence, and she has a dread of exchanging the comfortable *known* of Boston for the vast unknown of London." It was true that he and Alice, during this period, seemed to derive pleasure from their brother-and-sister household; it was the last holding together of the family, and Henry, in his father's room, and Alice, presiding over the house, must have felt a great deal as if they were re-embodying their parents. But if Henry spoke of Alice's "independence," he nevertheless noted the extent to which she leaned upon her powerful friend, Katherine Loring. Miss Loring had quite taken over the foreground of Alice's life; quite entered into her daily well-being and her nervous prostrations. Alice had

described Miss Loring shortly after meeting her in terms that
leave little doubt as to her role in their relationship: "She has all
the mere brute superiority which distinguishes man from woman,
combined with all the distinctively feminine virtues. There is
nothing she cannot do from hewing wood and drawing water to
driving runaway horses and educating all the women in North
America." Even before Henry had met Miss Loring he had remarked that "her strength of wind and limb, to say nothing of her
nobler qualities, must make her a valuable addition to the Quincy
Street circle." This had been during Alice's long convalescence
after her 1878 illness. He was to observe closely this relationship.
One might say that the figure of Olive Chancellor of *The Bostonians* had appeared upon the novelist's very doorstep.

III

Henry's productivity during the months he spent in America—in
spite of family preoccupations—was impressive. But, as after his
mother's death, he did not do much new work. He saw through
the press the dramatized *Daisy Miller* and he put together, for
J. R. Osgood, a volume containing three tales, "The Siege of London," "The Pension Beaurepas" and "The Point of View." He
assembled a volume of miscellaneous travel papers to which he
gave the title *Portraits of Places*, carefully editing those on England, to be certain not to offend his trans-Atlantic readers, and reminding them, in a special prefatory note, that the papers had
been written primarily for Americans. He included in this volume
also his old papers on Saratoga, Newport and Quebec, and here he
reminded both his American and English readers that these had
"only the value of history." Thirteen years had brought many
changes. He planned at this time to issue a volume of essays as
well, to be titled *Studies and Sketches* or perhaps *Impressions of
Art and Life*. However, he abandoned this plan, feeling that he did
not have a sufficient number of good essays. Four years later, when
the volume came out as *Partial Portraits*, it contained an almost
new table of contents. Henry reviewed all his American publishing

arrangements and pledged himself to produce a novel and a series of tales, giving J. R. Osgood not only the serial and American book rights but the English rights as well. This could only mean that he would receive more money from Osgood than he could realize by direct sale to Macmillan. The English publishing house, on its side, at this time proposed to Henry the issue of a small inexpensive pocket edition of his principal fiction to date. Henry welcomed the idea. Over and above the pleasure of having a collective edition on the market, he felt that this would give him an opportunity to establish himself in his new identity on the title page, to get rid of the Henry James "Jun." or "Jr."—the "mere junior"—now that his father was dead.

The Macmillan Edition was published late that year, in a series of attractive blue-bound volumes in small format. There were fourteen volumes in all. They sold for a shilling apiece, and the full set for a guinea. Henry had written to Macmillan, "I should like them to be *charming*, and beg you to spare no effort to make them so." The first three volumes were devoted to *The Portrait of a Lady*; then followed *Roderick Hudson* and *The American* in two volumes each, after which came *Washington Square*, *The Europeans* and *Confidence*, one volume each; leaving four volumes for the miscellaneous tales. These consisted of "The Siege of London" and "Madame de Mauves" in the volume devoted to international marriages; "An International Episode," "The Pension Beaurepas" and "The Point of View"—tales contrasting American and European manners; "Daisy Miller," "Four Meetings," "Longstaff's Marriage," and "Benvolio"—representing a subtle mixture, stories in which the heroine is frustrated or dies, save for "Benvolio" which portrays the ambivalent hero of these tales; and finally "The Madonna of the Future," "A Bundle of Letters," "The Diary of a Man of Fifty" and "Eugene Pickering." The groupings were as close as James could come to achieving congruity of theme; he could not altogether carry out his plan, because some stories were shifted in the interest of uniform volume-size.

In addition to seeing this edition through the press, Henry completed the greater part of his French travel sketches for Aldrich, in Boston, and wrote the first of the series of tales he had promised Osgood. This was "The Impressions of a Cousin," a story set in New York. The "impressions" are recorded by the cousin in her diary, which contains her account of the way in which an executor defrauds a young heiress, who will not prosecute him since she loves him—and how justice is quietly done. Henry thus drew vaguely on his recent responsibilities in family affairs. The tale is but half-heartedly written, a throwing together of miscellaneous observations of his American stay.

He was much more in the public eye during this winter than the previous year. This was due, in some measure, to a laudatory article about him which Howells had published the previous autumn in the *Century Magazine*, asserting that it was Henry who was "shaping and directing American fiction." Not many critics were prepared to accept this statement. With the article had appeared a rather meagre engraving of Henry by Timothy Cole, which suggests however his fine head, his clear-eyed gaze, and his general well-groomed and pleasant appearance. His lips are parted as if he is in the act of speaking, and beneath the picture is his large signature, full size, with the flourish that suggests but does not quite convey the about-to-be-withdrawn "Jr." Henry called it "a horrible effigy of my countenance." Howells's article was part reminiscence and part criticism. Now that he was no longer Henry's editor he could allow himself the liberty of expressing in public all the praise he had been obliged hitherto to bestow in private. He rightly recognized that the art—the technique—of fiction was becoming much more subtle than it had been in the era of Dickens and Thackeray, and he discussed in some detail Henry's gift for creating character. "Evidently it is the character, not the fate, of his people, which occupies him." Howells also said that a reader could find in Henry James's writings "a perpetual delight" in his way of saying things.

The effect of Howells's shrewd critical observations was not altogether what he expected. To some critics it seemed as if he were "puffing" the work of his friend; and in England certain journalists accused Howells and James of constituting an "American Mutual Admiration Society"—this in spite of the fact that Henry had never written about Howells save an anonymous review of an early novel. In a letter to Smalley, Henry referred to Howells's "ill-starred amiabilities to me." To Howells he remarked, a little ironically, that "articles about you and me are as thick as blackberries—we are daily immolated on the altar of Thackeray and Dickens."

Henry had been approached three times to give a reading in public, and finally he yielded. This was before a women's "Saturday Morning Club," where he read from a section of his "Little Tour" in France. The newspapers of the time reported that the rooms were crowded "by people of taste and fashion." Henry was introduced as the "Thackeray of America," and (said the reporter), his "English er-er-er" marred his utterance. He read in a monotonous manner, but the matter "more than made amends." At the conclusion of the reading, he was given a bouquet of white daisies surrounded by leaves of the homely seaboard plant known as "dusty miller." "I have hundreds of Daisy Millers here," said Henry, in a statement the ambiguity of which must have been lost on his preponderantly young female audience.

He made one other appearance, this one unannounced, and the testimony of it is to be found in the accounts of a meeting of the American Copyright League in New York. Henry had good reason to be interested in the work of the league; he had been pirated all too often. At a given moment he asked for the floor. "For ten or fifteen minutes," wrote Lawrence Hutton, "the speaker, known to every man present by his work, unknown in a personal way to most of his hearers, talked of things à propos of the matter in hand, in a manner absolutely to the point and carrying much weight. He made as great an impression as a speaker as he had ever made as a writer; and for the first time, after a long residence abroad, he was brought into intimate contact with the men of his own guild in his own country."

IV

He was in New York on April 15, 1883, in the city of his birth—and it was his fortieth birthday. Ten years before, when he became thirty in Rome, he had felt how short a distance he had travelled in his career; and if, during the decade that had elapsed, he had achieved his ambition, he was still dissatisfied. If anyone had told him that he could cease writing at this moment and remain a major figure in American fiction, he would have scorned the suggestion. Contemplating the advent of his fortieth year, he had written in his journal the previous autumn, on one of the days when he was in the Grand Hôtel in Paris: "I have hours of unspeakable reaction against my smallness of production; my wretched habits of work—or of un-work; my levity, my vagueness of mind, my perpetual failure to focus my attention, to absorb myself, to look things in the face, to invent, to produce, in a word. I shall be forty years old in April next: it's a horrible fact." The horrible fact had occurred. Having distinctly underestimated all his capacities, he had proceeded to offer himself some solace: "I believe however that I have learned how to work and that it is in moments of forced idleness, almost alone, that these melancholy reflections seize me. When I am really at work, I'm happy, I feel strong, I see many opportunities ahead. It is the only thing that makes life endurable. I must make some great efforts during the next few years, however, if I wish not to have been on the whole a failure. I shall have been a failure unless I do something *great!*"

These sentences may be taken as an accurate measure by Henry of himself. His first goal—success and a place in the world—had been solidly achieved. He had made himself into an author and a figure known on both sides of the Atlantic. The next step was to do more—"greatness" was a large word. In the meantime there remained almost half a year before he could see his way to return-

ing to England, to his own habitation and the ground of his real
work, since he wanted to remain for a while longer with Alice.
The record of these months is filled with small detail. He visited
Washington and was pleased by its aspect in the spring. He saw
his friends the Adamses again. In New York he met and befriended the Jewish poet Emma Lazarus, whose verses were to be
inscribed two years later on the Statue of Liberty. She was about
to go to London and he gave her an introduction to Mrs. Procter
and to the Smalleys. He was much preoccupied with Wilky, whom
he met in Washington on his return from Florida, and escorted
back to Cambridge. His brother's health had taken a turn for the
worse, and in Mount Vernon Street Henry sat up nights with him,
giving him what aid he could during his heart attacks. He paid
calls as usual on Mrs. Gardner, and he saw much of his old friend
Grace Norton.

To this period belongs the forging of those links of emotional
intimacy and attachment which were to make this one of the most
valued of all his friendships. It did not resemble his friendship
with Miss Woolson. Miss Norton was, after all, ten years older, and
she was a woman who asked for a kind of philosophical comforting which Henry could give her to the full, as he might have to
his mother. She was going through a bad phase at this time, a certain strain with her brother, a sense of isolation in the separate
home she had fashioned for herself in Kirkland Street, away from
Shady Hill, and Henry wrote to her always with great gentleness,
good humor and much feeling. Since he could no longer write the
letters of a son to his mother, he had found in Cambridge someone to whom he could offer his filial feeling—someone closer to
him intellectually than his mother had been. Some of his greatest,
his fullest and certainly his wisest letters were addressed to Grace
Norton, with a richness of detail and with the large pictures of
himself in the great world which he had of old given to Quincy
Street. To her he wrote a letter which embodies within it the very
heart of his philosophy and his attachment to reality—a kind of
simple stoicism based neither on looking backward nor forward:

I don't know *why* we live—the gift of life comes to us from I don't know what source or for what purpose; but I believe we can go on living for the reason that . . . life is the most valuable thing we know anything about and it is therefore presumptively a great mistake to surrender it while there is any yet left in the cup. In other words consciousness is an illimitable power, and though at times it may seem to be all consciousness of misery, yet in the way it propagates itself from wave to wave, so that we never cease to feel, though at moments we appear to, try to, pray to, there is something that holds one in one's place, makes it a stand-point in the Universe which it is probably good not to forsake.

And then, recurring to his frequent warning to his correspondent not to give herself too much to the world's woes and to the grief of others, he tells her:

. . . don't I beseech you, *generalize* too much in these sympathies and tendernesses—remember that every life is a special problem which is not yours but another's and content yourself with the terrible algebra of your own. Don't melt too much into the universe, but be as solid and dense and fixed as you can.

And with this, his admonition was that Miss Norton adopt his own kind of doggedness:

Don't think, don't feel, any more than you can help, don't conclude or decide—don't do anything but *wait*. . . . We all live together, and those of us who love and know, live so most. We help each other—even unconsciously, each in our own effort. . . . Sorrow comes in great waves—no one can know that better than you—but it rolls over us, and though it may almost smother us it leaves us on the spot and we know that if it is strong we are stronger, inasmuch as it passes and we remain. It wears us, uses us, but we wear it and use it in return; and it is blind, whereas we after a manner see.

A darkness, such as she was passing through, he said, was *only* a darkness—not an end, not *the* end. And so, arguing for acceptance of feeling, for opening oneself to it, James embodied here the concept of "living through" emotion until one has survived it. He argued equally for a certain kind of personal sovereignty in a world unfriendly to individualism.

Henry wrote this letter to Miss Norton within a month of his return to England. He took passage on the *Servia*, leaving Boston August 22; he filled in the intervening hot days by padding about in a state of undress in the Mount Vernon Street house and confining himself to lemonade and ice cream. He kept reasonably cool, and he kept up his work. Wilky had left for Milwaukee to rejoin his family. Henry must have known that this was their final parting. Alice spent the summer in a rest home, the Adams Nervous Asylum in Jamaica Plain where Henry occasionally visited her. He saw little of William, who went off to the mountains with his family.

Some weeks before his departure he spent a friendly week-end at Marion, Cape Cod, visiting Richard Watson Gilder, of the *Century*, and his wife, who was a sister of Mrs. Bronson. His impressions are incorporated in *The Bostonians*, where Marion is renamed Marmion. In a later story ("The Patagonia") he describes what must have been his general feelings on the empty summery Beacon Hill. Like its narrator, Henry had gone shortly before, for a brief visit, to Mount Desert—escaped to coolness and greenness—but he found it "as beautiful as a place can be in which the details are mainly ugly," adding, "I liked the whole thing extremely—and wish never to see it again." The Boston houses on these summer nights were dark and Beacon Street seemed a desert. The club on the hill alone emitted light from its cylindrical front, and the sound of billiard balls clicking within suggested the servants were passing the time in the empty place. The heat was insufferable. Henry thought with joy of the freshening breeze he would have on board ship.

The crossing was uneventful, and on August 29 he arrived in Liverpool where he stayed until September 1. He had been but forty-eight hours in Bolton Street when word reached him that Ivan Turgenev had come to the end of his sufferings at Bougival.

V

This loss, now but one of the series Henry had experienced, plunged him into renewed grief for his dead. One by one the fixed landmarks of his life were vanishing. "I am greatly touched by his extinction—I wanted him to live—mainly, I am afraid, because I wanted to see him again: for he had done his work," he wrote to the editor of the *Atlantic,* promising an article on the Russian. He followed with intense emotion the newspaper accounts of the final rites: the ceremonial at the station in Paris when the Russia-bound coffin was placed on the train and the farewell orations of Renan and About on behalf of the writers of France. It was with Renan's noble words that Henry began his own tribute, written little more than a month later, words which he himself rendered with great felicity from the French:

Turgenev received by the mysterious decree which marks out human vocations the gift which is noble beyond all others: he was born essentially impersonal. His conscience was not that of an individual to whom nature had been more or less generous; it was in some sort the conscience of a people. Before he was born he had lived for thousands of years; infinite successions of reveries had amassed themselves in the bottom of his heart. No man has been as much as he the incarnation of a whole race; generations of ancestors, lost in the sleep of centuries, speechless, came through him to life and utterance.

But if Renan spoke of Turgenev as impersonal, and if now it seemed, in Russia, the grief of the nation and the funeral pomp lifted Ivan Sergeyevich out of the range of familiar recollection, Henry set down, in his long paper for the *Atlantic,* the "personal" Turgenev: a simple record of his meetings with the Russian writer, his many recollections of him, his whole-hearted devotion to his work. The paper is both a series of reminiscences and a moving elegy; it reads as if it had been written at a single sitting and as if Henry had poured out all that he could remember, clinging to certain moments as to personal treasures—the Sundays at Flaubert's, the little breakfast-lunches on the boulevards, the aspect of Bougival, Turgenev's manner of speech, the last ride in the carriage, when they had parted on the exterior boulevard in front of a Punch and Judy show. "Intolerable pain had been his portion for many months before he died," Henry wrote. "His end was not serene and propitious, but dark and almost violent. But of brightness, of the faculty of enjoyment, he had also the large allowance usually made to first-rate men, and he was a singularly complete human being." He brought his long and deeply-felt account to an end with these words—they were almost an epitaph: "He was the most generous, the most tender, the most delightful, of men; his large nature overflowed with the love of justice; but he was also a rare genius." *

At the request of the *Century* he translated for it Daudet's reminiscences of Turgenev: this he did anonymously and only the survival of the two manuscripts, Daudet's and his own, testifies to this silent act on behalf of his friend and his old acquaintance of the *cénacle*. Daudet's article appeared in the November 1883 issue titled "Turgenev in Paris." Thus in two leading monthlies of America the passing of the Russian genius was eulogized through the agency of Henry James.

VI

Henry had barely posted his tribute to the *Atlantic* when he found himself writing a private tribute of quite another sort to his father's old friend, the English Swedenborgian, Dr. J. J. Garth Wilkinson. Wilky had been named for the doctor, and Wilky was now dead in Milwaukee at thirty-eight, the third member of the James family to die in two years, and the first of the children. He had been Henry's immediate junior; and if he had squandered his patrimony, it could be said that fate had squandered him. He had never had good health after his precocious service in the Civil War. When Henry got word that William had left for Milwaukee,

. . . .

* James altered this, in revising the essay for *Partial Portraits*, to read, "but he was also of the stuff of which glories are made."

summoned to Wilky's deathbed, he drew from among his possessions a little pencil drawing William had made many years before, when Wilky had been carried home from the battlefield, wounded after the assault on Fort Wagner. It is one of the early vivid sketches made by Henry's elder brother, the head alone of the wounded, rough-bearded soldier. Sitting in Bolton Street Henry looked at this drawing a long time. The time of the war came back to him. "It was taken," he wrote to Lizzie Boott, "at a moment when he looked as if everything was over, and is a most touching, vivid little picture. I say to myself as I look at it that it probably represents the dear boy now." With the aid of the past Henry sought to visualize the present. He was to publish the drawing years later in his autobiographies. "Peace be to his spirit," he wrote to Lizzie, "one of the gentlest and kindest I have ever known."

And so Henry had buried his dead. And now he was once more in his lodgings in London and at his large work-table by the Bolton Street window, looking out on Lord Ashburton's big house across the way. He had lived through a period of terminations; but, as he had written to Grace Norton, one could not continue to be engulfed by sorrow. He had said good-bye to his parents in their graves on the Cambridge hillock, and to his younger brother, dead before his time. The house on Quincy Street was no longer fixed in the orbit of his days. And he had once more quit America. His return to Europe was almost like another beginning of the career he had begun almost a decade before.

BOOK TWO

The Art of the Novel
1884=1885

THE LOST FRESHNESS

HENRY JAMES'S FIRST IMPULSE, ON HIS RETURN TO LONDON, WAS TO search for a house, where he could have light and air and all the amenities of a busy, sociable writing bachelor. His old lodgings had served their turn. Much as he was attached to them, they now seemed dingy and small. He began his search in St. John's Wood, where in the 1850's his father had brought his children from America, and where Henry remembered playing ball in a large garden in Marlborough Place with his Scottish tutor. Presently he discovered an ideal dwelling in Elm Tree Road. It had belonged to an artist and its large studio had been converted into a noble dining room. The place was commodious, and the garden charming. Henry discussed his plans for domestication with various London ladies, and corresponded about them with Grace Norton and Lizzie Boott. They assumed at once that he was contemplating marriage. "Sooner or later," he wrote to Lizzie in reply, "I shall take a house, but there is no hurry, and when I do a conjugal Mrs. H. is not among the articles of furniture that I shall put into it. I think, my dear Lizzie, that the human race is going crazy and am sorry to see that the madness has touched your gentle and luminous brain as well. Twenty people have spoken to me of late about renouncing my happy state—all save three or four taking upon themselves to urge it. Those three or four—the only wiseheads—have remarked 'Don't—don't—for heaven's sake!' and I never shall, my dear Lizzie, for I find life quite interesting enough as it is, without such complicated and complicating appendages." To Grace Norton he wrote: "I shall never marry; I regard that now as an established fact, and on the whole a very respectable one; I am both happy enough and miserable enough, as it is, and don't wish to add to either side of the account. Singleness consorts much better with my whole view of existence (of my own and of that of the human race), my habits, my occupations, prospects, tastes, means, situation 'in Europe,' and absence of desire to have children—fond as I am of the infant race." He had never regarded marriage, he said, "as a necessity, but only as the last and highest luxury."

And reflecting on his bachelor state, and the blessings of living in a section of London within walking distance of his clubs and the theatres, Henry had a "sudden sense of being very well off where I am." He told himself he would spend half his time on the roads riding the length of Regent's Park—and he broke off negotiations for the house. His Bolton Street rooms might be shabby but he had called them home for a long time. The right moment for becoming a householder had not yet arrived.

I

This brief flurry of house-hunting, which occurred within a month after Henry's return, was nevertheless symptomatic. Something had changed during his two crossings of the Atlantic, the loss of his parents, and his observation of American life. It was not only that he was now forty, and had made a further march into the country of "the lost freshness." He felt now that England was his true home; and he no longer need be an "observant stranger," or worry about offending his hosts; his re-publication of his long-ago English sketches at this moment in *Portraits of Places* was clearly a sign of this. What he felt distinctly, as he wrote his American friends, was that there was for him in London in any quarter of an hour, more *life*—he underlined the word—than he could experience in America in six months. And much as he "raged" against London Philistinism and often felt the oppressive largeness of the city, he nevertheless believed it to be the right place for him to live. It was now a matter of "learning to live there differently from what I have done hitherto."

One of the ways would be to find ultimately a more comfortable and spacious home. The other was to break away from London "society," and to go into it only at moments of his greatest ease. In the same way, he would bring to an end indiscriminate country visits. That "gilded bondage" he had equally outgrown. "I, at the age I have reached," he told his Cambridge confidante, "have purposes far too precious to put the rest of my years to, to be able to devote long days sitting about and twaddling in even the most gracious country houses." And so instead of superficial contacts with the British upper classes, Henry now began to form friendships of a more significant kind—and with the members of his own class, the writers and artists of London; to involve himself with their family life; to become godfather to their children and a genial visitor at their board. This period marks the beginning of his intimacy with the du Maurier household in Hampstead; the Edmund Gosses in Delamere Terrace; the Humphry Wards in Russell Square; the George Lewises in Portland Place. The list of his English friends and acquaintances was to grow and to remain largely in this easy stratum of society where he felt most at home, and where above all he could consort with men whose accomplishments were analogous to his own. His friendship with George du Maurier was a deeply attaching one; he found "something in him singularly intelligent and sympathetic and satisfactory." He liked walking to Hampstead from Piccadilly on a Sunday evening and sitting on a particular bench on the Heath with du Maurier where their conversation could roam over Anglo-French subjects with an ease and affection that never diminished. The bench became a symbol of something precious in his life. He had it photographed long after du Maurier was dead, and used it as a frontispiece in the New York Edition—as "Saltram's Seat," for the Coleridgean tale of "The Coxon Fund," in the volume of his "tales of the literary life." The marriages of the du Maurier sons and daughters and the career of Gerald du Maurier on the stage commanded his interest and loyalty. Some of his most charming non-literary letters are addressed to his du Maurier godson. Thus he could write to him, sending him an Association football, "I'm an awful muff at games," and invite his visit, offering "lots of breakfast and dinner and tea" and promising no questions about studies, "but if you think that is because I can't—because I don't know enough—I *might* get up subjects on purpose."

Mrs. Humphry Ward was to describe in her memoirs a characteristic domestic scene. During a visit paid by James to their house in Russell Square in the early 1880's on a day of languid heat, her youngest child, Janet, five, tiptoed into the drawing room and inspected the novelist. "He put out a half-conscious hand to her; she came nearer, while we talked on. Presently she climbed on his knee. I suppose I made a maternal protest. He took no notice and folded his arm about her. We talked on; and presently the abnormal stillness of Janet recalled her to me and made me look closely through the dark of the room. She was fast asleep." Mrs. Ward felt the childish instinct had divined "the profound tenderness and chivalry" of Henry James. There are numerous anecdotes of this kind, not least those of his imitating Sarah Bernhardt for the du Maurier children and making a brave entrance through two sliding doors, only to be suddenly arrested in the narrow aperture by his *embonpoint*.

II

His friendship with Edmund Gosse, at first rather casual (Henry thought him amiable but second-rate), became one of the most literary-gossipy friendships in Victorian annals. Gosse was gifted; he had a great facility as a writer, and was an assiduous and critical reader; he was also a great busybody of letters. He had rebelled against a sternly religious father, and had made his way by charm and ability from a lowly post in the British Museum to be translator to the Board of Trade. Later in life he became Librarian of the House of Lords. A writer of faded romantic lyrics, he was an indefatigable bookworm; he wrote easy and pleasant literary essays, and later critical and biographical studies of major importance. Sir Osbert Sitwell has aptly characterized his studies of minor Elizabethans as "impeccable in feeling, if not always, it appears, in fact." If Gosse was indeed guilty of scholarly slips, he nevertheless had a way of cutting through to essence, and in the end he became not only an important practitioner of the art of biography, but author of a classic autobiography, his study of his relationship to his religious-absolutist father. Henry found Gosse an endlessly amusing companion to break the solitude of some of his dinners at the Reform or the Athenaeum. Gosse had from the first cultivated literary men and painters. He had his finger in almost every literary pie in London. He wrote to his literary friends on subjects out of the daily press and thereby provoked answers; he was an eternal bee buzzing about friendly bookshelves; but with this he had grace of mind and a flair for gossip in a library. He knew the secrets of the literary generation, and he was an artful exchanger of confidences. If Henry praised a certain book he quietly passed the praise along to the author; if an author praised Henry, Gosse discreetly communicated the praise. Such procedures can be risky and yet Gosse seems to have handled them, on the whole, with high diplomacy. He made an art of flattery and a craft of gossip. It is posthumous publication that has betrayed him; as for example his telling Thomas Hardy that James admired *Tess*, even while James was denouncing the novel as "vile" to

Stevenson. This leaves us with the interesting question as to whether the duplicity was James's or Gosse's. However, so far as we know, James had no more reason for praising *Tess* to Gosse than to Stevenson.

The friendship, at any rate, for all of Gosse's artfulness, was genuine; and in the bourgeois sociabilities of Delamere Terrace, as well as in the later confraternity of the Royal Society of Literature, the two were faithful companions for the better part of four decades.

III

Thus by degrees Henry began to find substitutes for the lost anchorage of Cambridge. The process was slow and much of it hidden from himself, an intuitive search for footholds, attachments, dependencies, which had vanished in America. He might have more speedily achieved some form of contentment had not the life of the entire decade in England undergone so marked a change. The serenity of his own life, the triumphant time of his "Daisy Miller" period, had coincided with the greatest years of Victoria's imperium. Now the Victorian calm was being literally shattered by Irish dynamiters, anarchist violence, and the deep unrest of England's workers, in their starving despair of the early 1880's. "Nothing *lives* in England today but politics," he wrote to T. S. Perry. "They are all-devouring, and their mental uproar crowds everything out." England, he felt, was "on the edge of an enormous political cycle, which will last heaven knows how long." He added that he should "hate it more if I didn't also find it interesting. The air is full of events, of changes, of movement (some people would say of revolution, but I don't think that)." In the end his interest in English politics and public affairs was to help attach him "to this country and, on the whole, to its sometimes exasperating people." During the phase of his re-settlement in the British capital there were moments when he felt distinctly as if he were upon a heaving and boundless sea, without a rudder to steer him into a friendly port.

The ministry is still in office [he wrote to his former editor at the *Nation* in March 1885] but hanging only by a hair, Gladstone is ill and bewildered, the mess in the Sudan unspeakable, London full of wailing widows and weeping mothers, the hostility to Bismarck extreme, the danger of complications with Russia imminent, the Irish in the House of Commons more disagreeable than ever, the dynamiters more active, the income tax threatening to rise to its maximum, the general muddle, in short, of the densest and darkest.

If this was one of the most condensed sentences of current history ever penned by a man of letters, it was also Henry's way of describing the density and the darkness that had come into his life. What was clear to him now was that the day of his little "international" tales was virtually at an end. He could still write them but he believed he had worked that vein to exhaustion. He was moreover bored: and if "Pandora" and "Lady Barberina," written at this time, still have all the old power, the undimmed perception of international manners, they represent a terminal point. "Lady Barberina," as a study of an international marriage and a variant on the theme of "The Siege of London," is one of Henry's most successful tales: his picture of the transported English lady married to a New York doctor, living in splendor on Fifth Avenue, and of the Americans around her who cannot understand her boredom with the society of Manhattan, is written in a brilliant vein. The essence of the tale lies not in its critique of the two societies, but in James's grasp of the true incompatibilities between an aristocracy of blood and its inflexibilities, and an aristocracy of wealth and its pretensions. The whole genre was to prove prophetic: he had not only caught and mirrored a whole generation of "marrying Americans" and "marrying Britons," but life was to rewrite his story on a level beyond fiction.

Thus Henry turned to new subjects, only occasionally venturing back into the old in his shorter pieces. His novel of Boston, promised to Osgood, delayed for more than a year, had to be written; and after that he harbored in his imagination a spacious novel of London—actual London—that would mark his complete transplantation to the Old World.

CASTLE NOWHERE

IF HENRY'S ARTISTIC AND MENTAL LIFE HAD ITS COMPLICATIONS IN this period of private—as well as public—depression, his personal life seemed no less embroiled. He had not seen Constance Fenimore Woolson since the spring of 1881, when he had visited her apartment in Rome; she had remained on the Continent during his absence in America and had written him long—very long—letters. Now, however, in the autumn of 1883, and in spite of her protests that the English climate disagreed with her, she arrived in London, a bare month after Henry had unpacked his bags in Bolton Street. Certain sentences of an importunate nature, in one of her letters to Henry, show how far her state of feeling had gone in the interval. "You are never in Italy, but always in America," she had written the previous May; "just going; or there, or just returned. How many times have I seen you, in the long months that make up three long years? I don't complain, for there is no reason in the world why I should expect to see you." Fenimore complained in the very act of not complaining. Her appearance in London so soon after Henry's arrival seems to have been more than a coincidence. In her letters she had spoken of spending the winter in Algiers. She always said that she needed warmth and sunlight. Nevertheless, Henry reports to Lizzie on October 14,

1883 that "Costanza had just arrived in South Kensington," and in another letter to his Florentine friend he says that "the *Littératrice* is here and is really an angel of quiet virtue." Six months later he reports that "the Costanza is handy, in Sloane Street, and is to remain, I believe until August. But she is a most excellent, reasonable woman, absorbed in her work, upon whom I have not a single reflection to make. I like and esteem her exceedingly." It is possible that these veiled allusions are to some other lady writer; but they fit Miss Woolson. What we do know is that Fenimore did not go to Algiers, and that she braved English cold that winter, for she recorded in a letter of October 1884 that she had been in England for a full year.

I

In later years Miss Woolson and Henry agreed to destroy each other's letters; and still later Henry recovered those of his he had not had an opportunity to destroy. However, when the James papers were given to Harvard, four letters from Miss Woolson to Henry were among them. They belong to the period of his two trips to America and it seems quite likely that they were among correspondence left behind in Cambridge, which became mixed up with William's. For when they were first placed in the Houghton Library they were recorded as from Miss Woolson to William James—whom she had met, so far as we know, only once.

Fenimore's letters belong to the earlier stages of the friendship. Their inordinate length—the four total approximately fifteen thousand words—reveal her propensity from the first to pour herself out to Henry. They contain a strange mixture of adulation and criticism; they exalt him—and they deflate him; they are filled with a kind of mocking and competitive challenge; she plays the woman scorned and the woman pleading; full of self-pity at her footloose state, she at the same time reminds him of her own rooted Americanism. Their tone, above all else, however, is one of despair and of a touching loneliness—a middle-aged woman reaching out to a man younger than herself for a friendliness which she had glimpsed during those long-ago weeks in Florence, and which absence threatened to efface. What he wrote in reply we can only guess; and it is clear that he cautiously measured the intervals of correspondence—for among her complaints is that of his long silences.

She had written an early volume of tales called *Castle Nowhere*; and this itinerant *littératrice*, wandering among the Continental cities to places far removed from the Western Reserve and the American South, felt herself alien and solitary. She was constantly, she wrote, trying to make temporary homes out of impossible rooms at hotels and pensions; she likened herself to an encaged bird trying to build a nest out of two wisps of straw; or a beaver she saw in a zoological garden in Dresden, far from his American haunts, constructing a pathetic little dam out of fragments of old boughs. Fenimore told herself the beaver was as American and as homeless as she was. Did Henry understand this? Surely he knew only beaver hats! he could know nothing of beavers or prairies—he only knew people like Madame de Katkoff, the Russian adventuress in his play version of "Daisy Miller."

The role in which Fenimore cast herself always in these letters was that of a rejected woman—for in the play of "Daisy," as in the story, Winterbourne can never make up his mind; but he does have a European lady in Geneva in whom he is interested. Again and again, in her letters, under the guise of discussing and criticizing Henry's writings, Miss Woolson seems to be saying to him that he is cold, disinterested, does not understand women—does not understand how a woman—say Miss Woolson—feels.

I have been thinking about all this work you have undertaken [she is writing from Venice in May of 1883]; and I have wished that I could send you a message across the ocean—a spoken one. I will write it instead; you will believe, I hope, that it is said with the utmost sincerity, though you may not care for it in itself. —In one of the three novels,—or if that is impossible, in one of the shorter stories—why not give us a woman for whom we can feel a real love? There are such surely in the world. I am certain you have known some, for you bear the traces—among thicker traces of another sort. —I do not plead that she should be happy; or even fortunate; but let her be distinctly loveable; perhaps, let some one love her very much; but, at any rate, let *her* love very much, and let us see that she does; let us care for her, and even greatly. If you will only care for her yourself, as you describe her, the thing is done.

If you will only care for her yourself. And Fenimore ticked off on her fingers the love affairs of Newman and Claire de Cintré, Daisy and Winterbourne, the problems of Isabel Archer. None of these expressed real love. "Take the one further step, and use your perfect art in delineating a real love as it really is. For you will never deny that it exists,—though it may be rare."

This was the deepest argument of her letters. And in long paragraphs, circling again and again to the same question, she would retail all the gossip and all her conversations about Henry with his friends—always in a vein highly flattering to the writer but expressive also of her own affection. She had met Mrs. Bronson in Venice; they had not been interested in each other until the name of James was mentioned. "Mr. James is one of my dearest friends," said Mrs. Bronson. "He is also a friend of mine," said Fenimore. And the Friends of the Friend thereupon "began to smile and be content." Mrs. Bronson told Miss Woolson that it was to her balcony James alluded in his article on Venice, when he spoke of smoking a cigarette at the end of the day and watching the traffic on the Grand Canal. Fenimore has her little spasm of jealousy. She ends the letter: "The lagoons, the Piazzetta, and the little still canals all send their love to you. They wish you were here. And so do I. I could go by in a gondola, you know, and see you on Mrs. B's balcony. That would—be something. Good-bye."

II

There was also a strong competitive jealousy written into her letters. Fenimore was a dedicated writer; and she aspired to some of the greatness of her friend. On the one hand, she proclaimed her inability to do the kind of writing he did; on the other she conveyed to him the helplessness to which this reduced her. She remembered well, she told him, how she had talked to him in Florence, in the Cascine, of her difficulties and the problem of making a clean copy of her stories; and how he had answered, "Oh, I never copy." On a mute gesture from Fenimore he had added: "Do you think, then, that my work has the air of having been copied, and perhaps more than once?" She wrote: "I think I made no direct reply, then. But I will, now. The gesture was despair—despair, that, added to your other perfections, was the gift of writing as you do, at the first draft!"

Again:

I don't think you appreciated, over there, among the chimney pots, the laudation your books received in America as they came out one by one. (We little fish did! We little fish became worn to skeletons owing to the constant admonitions we received to regard the beauty, the grace, the incomparable perfection of all sorts and kinds of the proud salmon of the pond; we ended by hating that salmon.)

And again:

How did you ever dare write a portrait of a lady? Fancy any woman attempting the portrait of a gentleman! Wouldn't there be a storm of ridicule! Every clerk on the Maumee river would know more about it than a George Eliot. For my own part, in my small writings, I never dare put down what men are thinking, but confine myself simply to what they do and say. For, long experience has taught me that whatever I suppose them to be thinking at any especial time, that is sure to be exactly what they are *not* thinking. What they *are* thinking, however, nobody but a ghost could know.

That allusion to the Maumee River by which Fenimore displayed her American geography to Henry had occurred before. "If you had never left the banks of the Maumee," she had written to him, "you would still have been dumbly an 'alienated American' (I suppose you have no idea where the Maumee is!)." Miss Woolson was alluding to one of the rivers important to her in her childhood in the Lake Country. It runs from Fort Wayne northeast to Lake Erie near Toledo.

In one of the letters she suddenly fears she is not being a very literary correspondent, and in the process, gives us a hint of the way in which he wrote to her:

I am writing on in the most inconsequent inartistic way. But you know I never wrote to you half so much for your entertainment as for my own. At present it rests me to write to you. But the letter itself won't be, can't be, good. —If I were clever, I should always bear in mind the fact, that when I have written to you many sheets, I have received a short note in reply, beginning with some such sentence as this: "Dear Miss Woolson. One doesn't answer your letters; one can't. One only reads them and is grateful"; and this followed up by three very small pages (in a very big hand) in which no allusion is made to anything I have said, the "faithfully" of the signature occupying the room of several of my sentences. Then, when I have written you a short note myself, I have received from you a charming letter in reply, eight pages long, and not such a very big hand either, and the "faithfully" even put across the top or side of the first page instead of being relied upon to fill the half of the last! But I am not clever. And then I am always thinking that perhaps you will improve. I hope right in the face of facts. It doesn't do any harm; and it amuses me. My idea is that we shall make a George Washington of you yet.

This is an accurate picture of Henry's epistolary strategy. On the other hand she tells him: "Your letters are better than you are." And then the praise: "The best part of you is your incorruptible and dignified and reasonable modesty and your perfectly balanced common sense. It is such a comfort that you have them." Yet she feels that he does not value her work as much as she would like him to, and she is not certain how much he values her. She knows that he has been rather contemptuous of "literary women." She remarks, "I have recently listened to a rather intimate description of the Miss Howard ('One Summer') of whom you spoke in Rome as the writer-ess who wished to make your acquaintance; I am sure you would not like her. However, I had better be careful; you liked that Miss Fletcher [Constance Fletcher, the author of *Kismet*]. But you do not want to know the little literary women. Only the great ones—like George Eliot. I am barring myself out here, because I do not come in as a literary woman at all, but as a sort of—of admiring aunt. I think that expresses it." (In a tale she had made her heroine say: "You dislike literary women very much." The hero's reply was: "Hardly, I pity them.")

III

If she could not give full expression to her feelings for her correspondent, she could do so freely for his work. When her enthusiasm led her to the man—and she felt that she might overstep the bounds of reticence—she promptly took refuge in praise of his writing, or in recording for him praise spoken by other persons. The affection is thinly masked; the remarks are sufficiently transparent:

You could not possibly have pleased me more than by telling me —as you do in this letter—of your plans for work. I have often thought of the motif you told me about, in Rome; now I shall see it completed. You have undertaken a great deal. But I am very glad you have undertaken it. You will do it all; and superbly. There is no one like you; and pretty much everyone—(who amounts to anything)—knows it now. Turgenev is dying, I hear. You are now our Turgenev. (I don't mean that you are like him; but that you have his importance.)

Then, after describing her rooms in Venice:

There is a very nice sofa here, placed just at the angle that commands the beautiful eastern view. And there is a tea-table, with the same sputtering little kettle you saw in my sky-parlor at Rome. If you could come in now, and rest a while (till time to go to the next dinner-party), I would make you some of the water which you consider "tea." And you would find at least the atmosphere of a very perfect kindness. You say you "fall back" upon my "charity," feeling that it is "infinite." You can safely fall back; for infinite it is. Only charity is not precisely the word. Call it, rather, gratitude. This isn't for you, personally—though of course you have to be included; it is for your books. You may be what you please, so long as you write as you do.

"Your books," she says, "are one of the entertainments of my life and I cannot give up talking about them just to please the author." In another paragraph she speaks of his essay on Venice, "those exquisite pages I love so much myself—whose every word I know, almost by heart." From this, in a sudden burst of emotion, she tells him that "the deepest charm" of his writings is that "they voice for me—as nothing else ever has—my own feelings; those that are so deep—so a part of me, that I cannot express them, and do not try to; never think of trying to." She concludes by telling him—she who had written of Castle Nowhere—that his writings "are my true country, my real home. And nothing else ever is fully —try as I may to think so. Do you think this is quite an assumption,—or presumption?"

This identification of her feelings with his, her home with the very heart of his created work, could not have been lost upon Henry. In the same letter she offers him a gift; certain ancient Greek coins she had had mounted as tie-pins. She remembered that Benvolio had worn a Syracusan coin; and that she had seen Henry wearing "six rings on one hand." Would he accept the gift? She was quite prepared to keep it a secret. "Nobody knows of my coins—the ones destined for you." If he didn't wear tie-pins he would have to wait, she said, recalling the tale of the Emperor's topaz, "until I can dig up an antique intaglio for you on the Campagna." She offers to send the gift to America, or to his London lodgings—"should you ever arrive there during this life." He could choose any one of three—a coin bearing an owl, one with the head of Bacchus and one with the shield of Boeotia. Apparently James chose the Bacchus. At any rate there is a photograph, front-face, of his later years in which the coin-pin is clearly visible in his necktie.

There is only one moment in these long and pleading missives where Fenimore seems to be on the verge of an outburst, some break in her self-control. She had spoken of returning to America. "It is all very well to hold out the prospect of 'talking it over' against an Italian church wall," she writes. "As to a 'church-wall,' there has never been but that one short time (three years ago,— in Florence) when you seemed disposed for that sort of thing." And voicing her complaint about his long absences she remarks, "Don't put in those decorative sentences about 'Italian church' walls."

I V

And so Fenimore took up her residence in England (it would seem) to be near the man whose writings were her "real home." In the letter in which she speaks of having been in England a year she mentions that she has seen only Dover, Canterbury, Salisbury and London itself; and during that year we know that her visit to Dover coincided with Henry's stay there and that from Salisbury they went together to Stonehenge, on September 7, 1884, for she left a record of this excursion. We also know that one evening Henry encountered her in a theatre to which he had escorted Mrs. Kemble; and since he had a better seat he introduced her to Mrs. Kemble and gave her his place.

"The literary one" seems to have been self-effacing, and as might be expected, James rarely alluded to her in letters to other friends; his other friends (save the Bootts) did not know of her existence in his life, or of the intimacy that had grown between them. However there is one distinct allusion in a letter to Howells —since the Howellses, during the previous year, had seen something of Miss Woolson in Florence. Writing from Paris in Feb-

ruary of 1884 to his former editor, James said: "Miss Fenimore
Woolson is spending the winter there [in London]. I see her at
discreet intervals and we talk of you and Mrs. *you*. She is a very
intelligent woman, and understands when she is spoken to; a
peculiarity I prize, as I find it more and more rare." There is
one further remark: "I wish you could send me anything *you*
have in the way of advance-sheets. It is rather hard that as you
are the only English novelist I read (except Miss Woolson), I
should not have more comfort with you."

For the moment he seemed to have arrived at a quiet and
regular *modus vivendi* with Fenimore—a friendship of "discreet
intervals."

THE BESOTTED MANDARINS

I

DURING THE NINE YEARS THAT HAD ELAPSED SINCE HIS VISITS TO
Flaubert's *cénacle*, Henry James had made no attempt to revive
his friendship with Daudet, Zola or the elderly Edmond de Goncourt. He had, however, been reading their works. In mid-winter
of 1884—on February 2—Henry crossed the Channel for a brief
holiday, long promised to himself. It was his first visit to Paris
since his final glimpse of Turgenev; and his Russian friend seemed
achingly absent. Yet there was another purpose in this journey—a
strange, almost intuitive, reaching backward, out of the depths of
his London gloom, for the old bright days of his early European

life, the lost talk and companionship, Turgenev's warmth and Flaubert's shy geniality. One of the first things Henry did after putting up at the fashionable Hôtel de Hollande, in the Rue de la Paix, was to sally forth in search of his French colleagues. He did not try to reach them directly; he seems indeed to have thought that they would not remember him. If he had read them, he was quite certain they had not read him. But they had been young together, and now he—and they—had a certain measure of success; they could be, in middle age, so to speak, famous together! In Gallic fashion, Henry James resorted to an intermediary: his friend Theodore Child was by now a well-established journalist and editor, thoroughly at ease in the Parisian world of letters. He asked him to arrange a meeting.

Child acted promptly. On the third day of Henry's stay he sent a note to Edmond de Goncourt inquiring whether he could bring the American novelist to his home in Auteuil. Goncourt received them the next morning, not yet in the *Grenier*, which he was to establish later in the upper reaches of the house in which he and his brother had lived together for so many years and practiced their esoteric art of self-conscious observation, notation and creation. We know very little of this visit, and our evidence is simply the note written by Child, preserved among the voluminous Goncourt papers, and Henry's statement to various persons that they had had a talk. He offered a single reminiscence, a remark made by the survivor of the fraternal team, that there had been a "great deal of crawling into bed and playing the truant" in the daily life of Flaubert. "*Il faut vous dire,*" he said to James, "*que dans sa journée il y avait énormément de coucheries et d'école buissonnière.*" James quoted this amusedly to Edmund Gosse, and later used it as a footnote in his essay on Flaubert. An inscribed copy of *Germinie Lacerteux*, in James's library, may have dated also from this meeting. The remark about Flaubert suggests, however, that the saturnine Goncourt was sufficiently expansive and anecdotal. A few evenings later, Henry saw him again, this time at Daudet's, where he was once more conducted by the loyal

Child, and where he met not only his host and Zola, but the younger writers Coppée and Loti.

Of this evening we have a much fuller record, in an unusual document publicly printed that spring in the *Atlantic Monthly*, in the "Contributors' Club," but which was sufficiently disguised and anonymous to have escaped attention in all the ensuing years. James was not named in the account, although the French writers were. The document is in the best tradition of Boswell; and there is sufficient evidence in the Goncourt journal to establish—what indeed was obvious—that Theodore Child made the most of the notable occasion.

II

Theodore Child's record of the evening at Daudet's:

One day last February I received a little note, in beautifully formed and almost microscopic characters, signed "Alphonse Daudet," in which the famous novelist expressed a desire that an eminent American novelist, at that time staying in Paris, should be brought to see him. Alphonse Daudet offered a cup of tea, and around the tea-table "a dozen persons,—Goncourt, Zola, Coppée, Loti the sailor; . . . not many people, *mais de la haute gomme littéraire*." The American writer needed but little introduction: when he entered the modest bandbox-like apartment that Daudet occupies on a fourth floor, overlooking the garden of the Luxembourg, Edmond de Goncourt, Zola, and Daudet all remembered to have seen him formerly at Gustave Flaubert's Sunday receptions, where our countryman—whom for the sake of convenience we will call Mr. X—was frequently to be met with, when he was living in Paris, some years ago.

"Why, I have known you a hundred and fifty years!" exclaimed Daudet, with his southern expansiveness and exaggeration. And then began a long talk on literature, Mr. X having expressed to Daudet an immense admiration of his exquisite talent.

"What happiness," said Mr. X, "what joy, you must feel in writing, in composing your works, in all those finds, those *trouvailles*, of phrases and epithets!"

Daudet listened eagerly, nervously twirling the two points of his silky beard, his eye sparkling behind the fixed eyeglass, and with an expression of extreme attention on his worn, fine, delicate features, much drawn and yellowed and ravaged by incessant intellectual work. "My dear sir," replied Daudet, with warmth, "you are mistaken. I work with pain and misery, and I always feel that I have left the best in the inkstand. Beware of the literary fools who are always satisfied; the men who come up to you, rubbing their hands, and saying, 'Ah, my dear fellow, I am happy: I have just written a chapter,—the best thing I have done!' and then go and dine, happy. It is not the idea of a book, it is not the plan, the conception, that troubles me. I observe, I study, I brood over every detail of the proposed work. But when I come to put down my book on paper, then begin the tortures, the torments, of style. I don't know whether it is so in your language or not."

"Yes," replied Mr. X, "I know what you mean. We take less pains with our style than the French writers. We are less observant; our observation is less fine, less rich in shades and refinements and delicacies."

"Really?" said Daudet. "Ah, but if you only knew how unobservant most Frenchmen are! A man will travel with you, or take a walk with you, and afterwards, when you begin to talk with him about what you have seen, you will suddenly find him looking at you with a smile that betrays him: he has seen nothing! He thinks that you are a humbug. The other day an old acquaintance of mine returned from Australia, after five years' sojourn there. I asked him to tell me all about what he had seen: how people lived there; what the country was like, and the trees, and the towns, and the houses. All I could get out of him was this: 'Guess how much a pound of potatoes costs!' The poor devil had seen absolutely nothing, and the only thing that had struck him was the extreme dearness of potatoes."

"I understand; quite so," said Mr. X. "I have frequently remarked that in the English, who are constantly travelling and running about, and who rarely see anything in the course of their travels, and can talk about nothing but comparative hotel accommodation. Nevertheless, it seems to me that the average Frenchman is infinitely sharper in his observation than the average Englishman or American: he takes in more details; he is more appreciative of *nuances* and shades; he is finer, more delicate; and, for me, the proof lies in the wonderful richness of the French language in epithets expressive of the greatest variety and minuteness of variation."

Daudet, then returning to the theme of the pain and torture that his writing cost him, dwelt particularly on the condition of his material, namely, language. "The material is so worn out," he remarked: "everything has been said again and again; every theme has been exploited. There are quantities of subjects and situations and psychological states that we can no longer touch upon: we can no longer touch upon love and sentiment enveloped in nature; we can no longer talk about the influence of flowers, of landscape, of sea and sky. The public finds that kind of thing worn out, threadbare, done for. 'We dare not sing more of roses,' Sully-Prudhomme has said, in one of his poems; and I assure you the poet's cry is one that has profoundly touched us. Then when we have found something new, some fresh combination, we arrive at the expression of it with infinite torment and suffering, and always with that horrible consciousness of having left the best part unwritten. And that combination having been treated, we can never return to it again. The public may forget, but the artist cannot repeat himself, and hash up the same thing again. It is the same with epithets. In a previous page we may have found the right epithet, the word that calls up the precise image; and then when we wish to reproduce a similar effect we cannot employ the same method, we cannot repeat ourselves, and in order to avoid rehashing we use, to our sorrow, some other phrase, less good and less appropriate. Every sentence in our books is wrought with pain and torment. There is no happiness, no joy, in it. The torture of style kills all that. Is it not so, Zola?" he asked, turning to the author of the *Assommoir*, who was sitting with his wife and Madame Daudet, and talking about the less absorbing topic of embroidery and silk.

"Yes," replied Zola. "It is a sad trade,—*C'est un triste métier.* The only happiness is when you are beginning, when you are planning. But when you have attained your object, when success comes, there is an end of happiness. Torture and misery all the time!"

Elsewhere in the article Child also recorded:

"Ah," exclaimed Daudet, the other night, "how I used to envy the calm serenity of Turgenev, working in a field and in a language the white snow of which had so few footprints! He had only to walk ahead; every step left a footprint that you could see! With us, it is like walking over a shingle strand: we have to move bowlders and rocks and cliffs in order to leave our mark."

So much for Child's account of the talk during that evening. Later James quoted Daudet as saying French writers were "perishing" in the flood of books—"they are suffocating us, they are killing us." "*Nous périssons par des livres, ils nous débordent, ils nous étouffent, ils nous tuent.*" It was as if they were back at Flaubert's; something of the old magic seems to have been recovered by James that night and they had discussed indeed Flaubert's favorite subject—the "torment of style," the search for the *mot juste,* the attempt to use prose as a plastic medium.

III

On the next day, February 13, Henry James wrote an account of the evening he had passed with the French writers in a letter to T. B. Aldrich, editor of the *Atlantic Monthly.* This was the letter in which he agreed to do a serial for him during the following year, and in which he three times wrote "1865" instead of "1885." *
The slip of the pen denoted how far in the past his deepest self was probably submerged at this time. He was indeed moving in Paris along the boundary lines of his youth and his middle age. Having promised his novel, Henry gave Aldrich his bit of literary gossip. "Paris is charming, bright, mild and a little dull, and

- - - - - - - - - - -

* I have discussed the significance of this slip of the pen in *The Untried Years,* in the chapter "Heroine of the Scene."

'naturalism' is in possession *sur toute la ligne*." What he went on
to say, however, showed that he found the French capital far
from dull.

I spent last evening at Alphonse Daudet's, and was much impressed
with the intense seriousness of that little group—himself, Zola,
Goncourt, etc. About Daudet's intensity of effort there is something tragical and his wasted, worn, extraordinarily beautiful and
refined little face expresses it in a way which almost brings tears
to my eyes. The torment of style, the high standard of it, the effort
to say something perfectly in a language in which everything has
been said, and re-said—so that there are certain things, certain
cases, which can never again be attempted—all this seems to me
to be wearing them all out, so that they have the look of galley-
slaves tied to a ball and chain, rather than of happy producers.
Daudet tells me that the act of production, and execution, for
him is nothing but effort and suffering—the only joy (and that he
admits is great) is that of conception, of planning and arranging.
This all proves, what one always feels, that (in their narrow circle)
terrible are the subtleties they attempt. Daudet spoke of his envy
and admiration of the "serenity of production" of Turgenev—
working in a field and a language where the white snow had as yet
so few footprints. In French, he said, it is all one trampled slosh—
one has to look, forever, to see where one can put down his step.
And he wished to know how it was in English.

Henry's evening of talk at Daudet's had profoundly impressed
him. We gain a very clear picture of his impressions in a long
passage by Child which follows the account of the conversation;
this contains the comments of "Mr. X" after the two walked away
from Daudet's flat. The novelist felt that the French were without
equal in achieving "an absolute accordance of the expression with
the idea"; and it was this which gave to their prose "a sensation
of harmony, of secret beauty." They were engaged in a search for
the "soul of words," and they were all-too-acutely aware of how
late in time and literature they had come. It seemed, indeed, as
if all the books had been written. In the Anglo-Saxon world, the

public made no distinction between writers who were artists and writers who were competent hacks. The French writers, by their very devotion to their task, were artists.

Nevertheless Henry held that the French writers were extremely narrow in their vision of the world. "They see very little beyond their art; their observation, delicate and complete as it is in a sense, is not very wide, and by no means coextensive with modern French life." To illustrate this, Henry expressed the belief that they neglected provincial life, and focused on the corrupt and ignoble aspects of life in Paris. He admitted that this was an extreme way of putting it. He explained the phenomenon as follows: Zola and Daudet were of humble origin. They had come to Paris to make their way by sheer force of talent. They had led a café-bohemian life, or were students in the Latin Quarter. In neither case had they been in contact with a society that offered them social refinement and a polishing influence. Even though they had attained fame, French society itself did not welcome them. To be sure, there were literary salons, where they were appreciated, but their bohemianism deprived them of "the polish and tact necessary to secure [them] an agreeable position in society." These writers felt ill at ease in talking to society women. They ended, through embarrassment, by ignoring society and so excluded themselves, and were excluded from, a large field of observation. Henry made exception for Edmond de Goncourt, who was an aristocrat before he became a novelist. Zola lived like a hermit, a slave to his great ambition, "sulky, lumpy, and uncommunicative," and when he came to Paris he visited none but his literary friends. Daudet was never encountered save in "purely literary gatherings." And in the few houses he frequented—Pailleron's, Dr. Charcot's, Madame Adam's, his publisher, Charpentier's—he saw only authors and artists.

Henry expatiated upon this. In effect, he told Child, there was a "Chinese quality" to the existence of his French contemporaries. It was "mandarin." They lived in an enclosed world, and studied "warts rather than the beauties of man" and his creations. "French novelists are not getting hold of that larger humanity which is alone eternally interesting." To be sure, they achieved certain incomparable things—"but incomparable in a very narrow way."

That these remarks, set down by Child, belong to Henry James —that this passage is virtually a monologue by the novelist pronounced after the evening at Daudet's—we know from their reiteration in Henry's letters. The favorable side is expressed in a letter to Howells, written from Paris during this visit:

I have been seeing something of Daudet, Goncourt and Zola; and there is nothing more interesting to me now than the effort and experiment of this little group, with its truly infernal intelligence of art, form, manner—its intense artistic life. They do the only kind of work, today, that I respect; and in spite of their ferocious pessimism and their handling of unclean things, they are at least serious and honest. The floods of tepid soap and water which under the name of novels are being vomited forth in England, seem to me, by contrast, to do little honour to our race. . . . Read Zola's last thing: *La Joie de Vivre*. This title of course has a desperate irony: but the work is admirably solid and serious.

The essence of his impression was set down by Henry in a letter to his brother five years later, after another visit to Paris, in which he listened to his French friends and their talk. "Chinese, Chinese, Chinese!" he exclaimed. "They are finished, besotted mandarins and Paris is their celestial Empire."

There was a postscript to this evening. Child's article, though anonymous, was read by Daudet; probably Child himself sent it to him. And it was, understandably, resented.

The article [wrote Edmond de Goncourt in his journal for June 19, 1884] while rendering justice to Daudet's talent, represents him as working in a study the size of a band-box, and makes out the French novelists, with the exception of myself, to be people with no sense of custom, no education, unable to carry on a conversation with a woman, etc., etc. And he [Daudet] sees this article as inspired by the enmity of [Giuseppe de] Nittis. And this supposition, while it is probably ill-founded, exasperates, irritates and makes him nervous.

The intrigue-suspecting Daudet seems never to have regarded the comments as coming from Henry James.

IV

"They are the children of decadence, I think," Henry wrote to Grace Norton, "a brilliant one—unlike ours: that is the English; and they are strangely corrupt and prodigiously ignorant. In spite of all this they represent a great deal of truth." While in Paris he read widely in their works. Nevertheless he could not swallow "naturalism" whole. The Goncourts had been addicts of note-taking and documentation; Zola had introduced the element of reportage—the actual seeking out of scenes, local color, and the "doing" of a given scene in "scientific" fashion. They had extended Balzac's realism to a minute painting of environment; and with this, Zola had adopted also the popularized ideas of Darwin with a pseudo-scientific glibness gathered from his readings in Claude Bernard's works on scientific method. By nature, Henry found Daudet more sympathetic; and they became warm friends. For Zola he acquired an ever-increasing respect. In his final prefaces the name of Zola is constantly mentioned along with Scott, Thackeray, Trollope, Dumas and Balzac—"even the coarse, comprehensive, prodigious Zola." Henry was to write to a friend in 1896: "Zola is awfully *sound*—I have a tenderness for Zola. Not a pennyworth of distinction, but a shopful of *stuff*. What he says is good for you—put on blinders—and jog on the straight road." To his friend Perry, Henry wrote: "Zola's naturalism is ugly and dirty, but he seems to me to be *doing something*—which surely (in the imaginative line) no one in England or the United States is, and no one else here." And again: "Zola has his faults and his merits, and it doesn't seem to me important to talk of the faults. The merits are rare, valuable, extremely solid." In 1903, when Zola was dead, Henry James, in a long analytic essay, took the fullest measure of the man whom he had begun by criticizing and ended by admiring. He likened the Rougon-Macquart series to the packing of the cargo of a ship. Zola's personality in the end pervaded and prevailed—and the ship had set sail and weathered its hazardous voyage. James agreed with Zola that the temperament of a novelist shines through and dominates his art.

"The distance from Paris to London," he told Mrs. Humphry Ward as his visit neared its end, "is surely not hundreds, but hundreds of thousands of miles." To William he said that "Seeing these people does me a world of good, and this intellectual vivacity and *raffinement* makes the English mind seem like a sort of glue-pot."

"I regard you as the great American naturalist," he told Howells. "I don't think you go far enough, and you are haunted with romantic phantoms and a tendency to factitious glosses; but you are in the right path." As for himself: "It isn't for me to reproach you with that, however, the said gloss being a constant defect of *my* characters; they have too much of it—too damnably much. But I am a failure—comparatively."

He always considered himself a failure when he was writing to Howells, who enjoyed so much prosperity in America. But his mind was now working on the lessons of the Naturalists even as he had long ago studied the lesson of Balzac. He was abandoning the "international" theme. His new novels would "do" Boston and London as Zola had done his Paris, and was to do the coal mines—by descending into the very heart of his subject. Henry's fortnight in Paris—extended into a month—had proved much richer than he had anticipated. It had brought him back to the fundamentals of his career, after the long American interval and the unsettled London return. The ferment set up in him continued all that summer, when he began to write *The Bostonians*, and in the autumn it was to emerge in a single splendid manifesto,

his one great leap into the arena of controversy and debate on
the art which he practiced. He was ready to write his essay on
"The Art of Fiction."

AN INSOLENCE OF TALENT

THERE WAS ANOTHER SIDE TO HENRY'S VISIT TO PARIS. HE MADE THE
round of a series of drawing rooms from which he had long been
absent. He called on the Princess Ourousov and had an intimate talk with her about Turgenev's last days. He visited Mrs.
Charles Strong, "flitting with weary eagerness from one exhausted
little Paris pastime to another." He saw the Auguste Laugels, who
were friends also of Henrietta Reubell. Laugel had been reading
him. He told him he was a "moralist," and that such a man de-
served well of his country. "*Vous êtes un moraliste,*" were his
words, "*des hommes tels que vous font du bien à leur pays.*"
Above all Henry spent more time than ever before in Miss Reubell's ornate little salon at No. 42 Avenue Gabriel, and saw much
of her friend, Mrs. Boit, who was now living in Paris. He had
known Henrietta Reubell for a decade; she remained the same
genial, shrewd spinster, a striking figure with her bright red hair
crowning (as one artist saw her) "an expressive but unbeautiful
face." There was a touch of Queen Elizabeth in her physiognomy;
something bird-like in it and in her voice. Henry liked her high
laugh, her lorgnette, her original mind. In street attire, he saw her
as "a young lady with great plumes, great heels, great festoons, a

great parasol and a great air"—small wonder that he addressed her as *La Grande Mademoiselle* and talked of her as "the tall Etta, who has so much *cachet*." She moved in a world of writers, painters, pictures, studios. She numbered Whistler and Oscar Wilde among her friends, and was loyal to both; but of all the celebrities who came to her famous Sunday afternoons, it was left to one who knew her a decade later to describe her with marked accuracy. This was the then young Will Rothenstein, who remembered the turquoise stones loaded on her fingers and her "adventurous conversation." She permitted, in her drawing room, "anything but dullness and ill-manners." She delighted in wit and paradox.

A different portrait of her, somewhat dissimulated, is in *The Ambassadors* where, as Miss Barrace, the American expatriate, Henrietta figures as brightly conversational, with quick darting movements, like a high-feathered free-pecking bird standing "before life as before some full shop-window." Henry had many sentimental memories of her little parlor, and often alluded to a particular alcove, where on a particular sofa, under a golden canopy, he and Miss Reubell would have their intimate gossipy *tête-à-têtes* in a perpetual cloud of smoke: like Mrs. Bronson she was addicted to cigarettes in an age when tobacco was reserved for men. Later Henry nostalgically spoke of the "dear little *lambris dorés*," and the "delightful breakfasts, dinners, evenings, talks." There always seemed to linger in this alcove "the fragrance of all the cigarettes that have been smoked out in discussion of the pleasant things of Paris." As he was about to leave the French capital he scribbled a farewell note to her: "For me you are much of Paris—and to take leave of Paris is, as it were, to take leave in person of you, the graceful incarnation. *Au revoir* Mademoiselle. Continue to shine on Sundays and weekdays, not with a cold light. Look after *votre petit monde*, and, in alternation with Mrs. Boit, be the shepherdess of the studios. I think that you and she, in this capacity, ought to mount little ribboned crooks. Farewell again, dear lady, and may your happiness never be less than your hospitality. The latter has added much to that of yours very faithfully"—and Henry signed his name with his characteristic large flourish.

I

It was in the entourage of this "shepherdess" and of her friend Mrs. Boit that Henry finally met the young American prodigy of painting, John Singer Sargent. He already knew his work and had stood in admiration before the striking picture of the young Boit daughters, which Sargent had done a year before, and certain other precocities, painted when he was barely in his twenties. He was now a mere twenty-seven. The American art world had been waiting for a master, and he seemed to have arrived; Whistler was famous but too idiosyncratic; Duveneck had shown a powerful but not very productive talent. Sargent stepped into the full light of prominence and controversy from the start. Henry encountered a tall, athletic, ruddy-complexioned, dark-haired and dark-bearded man with vivid gray-blue eyes. Quiet, even sedate, cultivated, he formed a marked contrast to the rough-and-tumble bohemians of art, or the dilettantes. The novelist was promptly and powerfully attracted to him. Had Sargent been a little less self-contained, a little less poised and less centered on his painting, Henry probably would have found him as appealing as he had found the amateur Zhukovsky, with whom he had been so taken eight years before. "I like him so much that (a rare thing for me) I don't attempt too much to judge him," he wrote to Lizzie Boott. "I have seen several times the gifted Sargent, whose work I admire exceedingly, and who is a remarkably artistic nature and charming fellow," he wrote to William when he was still in Paris. And to Grace Norton: "The only Franco-American product of importance here strikes me as young John Sargent the painter, who has high talent, a charming nature, artistic and personal, and is civilized to his finger-tips. He is perhaps spoilable—though I don't think he is spoiled. But I hope not, for I like him extremely; and the best of his work seems to me to have in it something exquisite."

They had so much in common that they must have seemed to

each other, in certain respects, mirror-images. Continentalized from their earliest years—Sargent even more than James—innate aristocrats with a penchant for society and the *beau monde* (and taking many of their subjects from it), possessing a dignity and distinction that commanded respect wherever they went, dedicated to their art, capable of extraordinary assiduity, they were almost counterparts in their different mediums. If James had a more subtle mind, and Sargent a greater naïveté, this resided in the differences often to be found between a writer and a painter. A musician also, Sargent at the pianoforte had the subtlety in his finger-tips which James had in his psychology. James was much more strongly intellectual than Sargent; and both had in them the vestigial stiffness of the American Puritan. James's New England conscience was to relax and change much more than Sargent's, however. It was no accident that the author of *The Portrait of a Lady* and this painter of portraits of great ladies should have found common bonds between them. Both were fascinated by the human face and what it expressed.

Sargent took Henry to his studio at No. 41 Boulevard Berthier and showed him his large painting of "Madame X . . ." Henry described it to Lizzie Boott, "a full length of a so-called French beauty (*femme du monde*), half-stripped and covered with paint —blue, green, white, black." This was the portrait of Madame Gautreau which was to have a *succès de scandale* in the Paris Salon a few weeks later. Henry only "half-liked it." But he was struck by the talent that had produced it. And he was worried by this excess of skill in one so young. Success was coming easily to Sargent. Henry, who had won his with much greater difficulty, knew the dangers of too great a facility and too dazzling a virtuosity. "His talent is brilliant," he wrote to Lizzie, "but there is a certain incompleteness in it, in his extremely attaching, interesting nature a certain want of seriousness." He was to say this many times: the same reservations are expressed in his essay on Sargent of three years later. He wondered whether it was an advantage to an artist "to obtain early in life such possession of his means that the struggle with them, discipline, *tâtonnement*, cease to exist for him." Was there not a danger of a certain "larkiness," a skill that, for all its brilliance, would be lifeless? "He knows so much about the art of painting that he perhaps does not fear emergencies quite enough," Henry said. "Observers encumbered with a nervous temperament may at any moment have been anxious about his future," and he added that "his future is the most valuable thing he has to show." Henry was to see that future, and it was to be for him "a knock-down insolence of talent and truth of characterization, a wonderful rendering of life, of manners, of aspects, of types, of textures, of everything. It is the old story; he expresses himself as no one else scarce begins to do in the language of the art he practices."

II

Within a month after he had said good-bye to Sargent in Paris, Henry welcomed him to London. Sargent's reputation at that time was almost wholly French and Henry argued the time had come for him to cross the Channel permanently—as he himself had done. "I want him to come here and live and work—there being such a field in London for a *real* painter of women, and such magnificent subjects of both sexes." Since Sargent was a stranger to London, he gave him "a push to the best of my ability." It was a strenuous push indeed, but both men were up to it. Thus, on Saturday, March 28, 1884, Henry took him to an exhibition of the works of Sir Joshua Reynolds and then to the National Gallery; in the evening they dined together and went to the theatre. On the next day, Sunday, Sargent came to lunch at 1:30 and during the afternoon Henry conducted him through ten artists' studios to see pictures just going into the spring exhibitions; and at eight that evening he entertained him at dinner at the Reform Club to which he invited half a dozen friends including Edward Burne-Jones.

Among the studios visited were those of Sir John Everett Millais and Sir Frederic Leighton, president of the Royal Academy. To the old guard of the Pre-Raphaelite movement and to the flossy erudite Leighton, Henry was introducing a young man who styled himself an "impressionist." Henry was immensely struck by the wealth and power of Millais and Leighton, "the gorgeous effect of worldly prosperity and success" they revealed. "I suppose," he said to Grace Norton, "it is the demon of envy— but I can't help contrasting the great rewards of a successful painter, here, and his glory and honour generally, with the so much more modest emoluments of the men of letters. And the painters who wallow in gold are—some of them!—so shockingly bad! Leighton in particular overwhelms me—his sumptuosity, his personal beauty, his cleverness, his gorgeous house, his universal attainments, his portraits of duchesses, his universal parties, his perfect French and Italian—and German—his general air of being above all human dangers and difficulties!" Burne-Jones invited James and Sargent to see his new painting of "King Cophetua and the Beggar Maid," a characteristic—and since famous— "literary" piece of art, then about to be shown at the Grosvenor. "Burne-Jones was adorable," Henry reported to his friends, and "we had a charming hour." Sargent enjoyed and appreciated the work of the older man, "but I am afraid poor dear, lovely, but slightly narrow B.J. suffers from a constitutional incapacity to enjoy Sargent's—finding in them 'such a want of finish.'"

The English art critics at first felt Sargent to be crude and too startling in some of his effects. Henry admitted that there was "a certain *excess* of cleverness: too much *chic* and not enough naïveté." It was Sargent's character which he felt was "charmingly naïf, but not his talent." Within a year the American painter had settled in England, in Whistler's old house, in Tite Street, Chelsea —as it proved, for life.

MATRONS AND DISCIPLES

THE SPRING AND SUMMER OF 1884 WERE FILLED WITH "INTERRUPTIONS
and distractions," easy sociabilities and the "season," as well as
the pressure of Henry's heavy writing commitments. He seems to
have worked steadily from March until August, but the record of
his other activities during this time may best be suggested by the
fact that nearly all his American friends seemed to be in London;
and a cholera epidemic along the Mediterranean brought Continental friends as well. The result was that if Henry declined invitations right and left, he was himself an almost constant host.
At one moment during that summer his publisher, J. R. Osgood,
and his friends Charles Eliot Norton, John Hay, and Clarence
King were all in London. At another he had Mrs. Strong from
Paris, Mrs. Gardner, freshly arrived from a world tour, and Mrs.
Mason—all demanding his company.

Mrs. Jack heralded her arrival from far away. She wrote to
Henry asking for an introduction to Mrs. Bronson in Venice.
This seemed to Henry almost a joke: he sent the note, but told
Mrs. Jack to throw it overboard; Mrs. Bronson was "so absurdly
easy to know" on her Venetian balcony. In the note he introduced Mrs. Gardner as "a forlorn, bereft, emaciated lady just returned from the Indies." Later that summer he reported to Grace
Norton: "Mrs. Jack Gardner has just passed through London,
at the close of her universal tour and on me *her* hand too was
laid: but very discreetly. She is worn and tired by her travels, but
full of strange reminiscences, and in despair at going back to
Boston, where she has neither friends, nor lovers, nor entertainment, nor resources of any kind left. She was exceedingly *nice*,
while here, and I pity her. Mrs. Mason, Mrs. Strong and she
consorted much together, and the group, as a representative
American-woman one, was sufficiently edifying." Henry added:
"Please burn this odious sheet."

I

Henry formed two new friendships during these weeks with members of the younger literary generation of France and England—two writers who promptly dedicated their books to him. To his rooms in July, Sargent brought a rather flabby-looking Frenchman, with a pronounced myopia, an unstable glass in one eye, and a shy manner. His name was Paul Bourget. Henry remembered having read a book of his a few months earlier, *Essais de psychologie contemporaine*, which he had judged "almost brilliant." Bourget was thirty-two but he looked twenty-eight, not a little (according to his biographer) like an average student whose visage expresses all the cares of a precocious wisdom. A small, rather sturdy man, for all his softness, he wore drooping, trimmed mustaches and parted his hair imperfectly on one side. He had long tapering hands, and searching eyes. He was on obviously good terms with his tailor. He conveyed a mixture of careless elegance and deep melancholy; but he had a tone and style in conversation which gave Henry pause. "I have an interesting—that is, rather—little Frenchman on my hands," Henry in due course reported to his Cambridge friend, "bequeathed to me by Sargent, one Paul Bourget, literary, clever, a gentleman and an Anglomane, but rather affected. I take him next week to spend a day or two at Ferdinand de Rothschild's." Bourget was to write *Cruelle Énigme* that summer. It made him famous in France; and he attached himself to Henry as a disciple. If Henry had been influenced by the French, he was to have now an influence on one of their writers, and one who would very speedily be elected to the Academy. But it is doubtful whether Henry, if he was aware of his influence, would have taken pleasure in it, for he cared little for what Bourget wrote, and some of his most interesting letters to his trans-Channel friends are those criticizing Bourget's novels. It was in Bourget the conversationalist that he was interested above all; and he was to be his adviser in his later journey to the United States which resulted in Bourget's *Outre-Mer*, a brilliant book of travel about America. Henry dined Bourget at the Reform, introduced him to

Gosse, made him his guest at the Athenaeum. Bourget was enormously attracted to Henry and later that summer journeyed to Dover to be with him. In future years the French writer was to co-ordinate his travels with those of his American confrère, so that their paths would cross—often in Italy. Henry judged him, as he came to know him, as "too much of a dilettante," but found him a sympathetic and attractive being with a "brilliant little intelligence," and "one of the most charming and ingenious talkers I ever met." As Bourget in later life became more and more reactionary (he ended by being a bitter anti-Dreyfusard), Henry lost interest in him; he found his aristocratic and monarchical ideas intolerable. Perhaps it was the sense of having in a Frenchman a certain kind of camp-follower that prompted Henry to save all of Bourget's letters to him. These letters contain certain interesting glimpses of literary life in Paris and their preservation in the hands of one who did not spare most of his other papers underlines a deep irony: Bourget shared James's hostility to the leaving of fugitive writings to posterity; yet he, on his side, saved James's letters to him. This is one of the rare instances (another being that of James's exchanges with George du Maurier), in which both sides of the correspondence survive.

"*Bourget est tragique,*" Henry was to write to a mutual friend, "*mais est-il sérieux?*" The question was well put. For what they had in common, in addition to the fact that they were both admirable talkers, was their interest in human motives, in a certain kind of psychological morality. James, however, regarded Bourget's plots as factitious and felt his "psychology" to be increasingly superficial. *Cruelle Énigme* bore a rather flowery dedicatory epistle to Henry, which suggests what their friendship that first summer meant to the French writer. It was inscribed to the "memory of the time when I was beginning to write it and which was also the time when we became acquainted. In our conversations in England last summer, protracted sometimes at one of the tables in the hospitable Athenaeum Club, sometimes beneath the shade of the trees in some vast park, sometimes on the Dover Esplanade while it echoed to the tumult of the waves, we often discussed the art of novel-writing, an art which is the most modern of all because it is the most flexible, and the most capable of adaptation to the varied requirements of every temperament. We agreed that the laws imposed upon novelists by aesthetics resolve themselves into this: to give a personal impression of life."

Henry it appears had talked to Bourget out of his already-written, but not yet published, paper on "The Art of Fiction."

II

The second friendship, less intimate and personal than that which developed with Bourget, was with Violet Paget, a young Englishwoman of twenty-seven, who had lived most of her life in Italy and who had lately published, under the name of Vernon Lee, volumes entitled *Euphorion* and *Belcaro*. They met in various London homes and Henry described her as "a most astounding young female." *Euphorion* was "most fascinating and suggestive, as well as monstrous clever. She has a prodigious cerebration." Tall, angular, with slightly protruding teeth and peering nearsightedly through her glasses, she seemed the traditional man-like bluestocking. Perhaps it was on this account that Edith Wharton, meeting her later in life, made a point of saying that while she had been "fortunate in knowing intimately some great talkers among men," she had met only three women who had that gift. One of them was Vernon Lee. The young woman, then better known as Miss Paget, had lived largely in Florence, and had known Sargent since her childhood.

From Miss Paget's privately printed letters to her mother and half-brother we can recover the impression made on the young woman by Henry James. As was the case with women he found interesting, he paid her marked attention, and as usual he tended to be oblivious of the effect he was having on her.

[24 June 1884] to the Wards' *soirée*, where, despite the presence of Matthew Arnold and Mr Forster I found no one to amuse me except Henry James.

[26 June 1884] Then Henry James came, who is most devotedly civil to me. [They go on to a party where] I talked half the time with Henry James.

[4 July 1884. At a party for Sargent.] Pater limping with gout and Henry James wrinkling his forehead as usual for tight boots, and a lot of artists buzzing about.

[11 July 1884. Watts charming] but Henry James was even nicer: he takes the most paternal interest in me as a novelist, says that *Miss Brown* is a very good title, and that he will do all in his power to push it.

[25 July 1885] He came to see me again yesterday afternoon. He says his plan through life has been never to lose an opportunity of seeing anything of any kind; he urges me to do the same. He says that chance may enable me to see more of English life, if I keep my wits about me. He is really very kind and wise, I think.

Henry James was indeed helpful, curious, encouraging. He offered brave generalities on the art of fiction, little realizing how closely Miss Paget listened and to what extent he was involving the young writer in the emotions of a friendship that was on his side wholly "objective." The first warning sign came when Miss Paget decided that she would dedicate her novel to him. He could hardly refuse. He made a gallant flourish of acceptance. But he became cautious. On reading her works Henry must have had some second thoughts. There was something too sharp, too penetrating, in this inexhaustible young woman's mind. He wrote to her with delicate irony, saying it frightened him to have "the honour of an invocation however casual" and proposed that perhaps "dedication should come *to* you not *from* you." He added: "Please hint that you offer me *Miss Brown* only to encourage me!" Miss Paget missed the subtle hint. Her inscription was literal: "To Henry James I dedicate, for good luck, my first attempt at a novel."

Even before he received the book, Henry had written to his friend, T. S. Perry, expressing the belief her novel would be inferior to what she had written critically; in her criticism he had found a certain amount of "tangled talk." When the novel reached him, Henry realized the danger of a too ardent admiration on the part of the advancing generation. He felt it was hardly the sort of book that should have his name on the dedicatory page; it was raw and violent. There were too many recognizable persons in it. This embarrassed him. He postponed thanking Vernon Lee; and the pressure of writing his serial, plus other pressures, resulted in his putting off acknowledgment from the autumn until the following May. When he finally sat down to write a letter, he was abjectly apologetic, feeling he had returned a gentle courtesy— the dedication—with extreme discourtesy. What he wrote was such a statement as might be given to all young novelists, reflecting as it did something of his own detachment and distance from experience:

You have proposed to yourself too little to make a firm, compact work—and you have been too much in a moral passion! That has put certain exaggerations, overstatements, *grossissements*, insistences wanting in tact, into your head. Cool first—write afterwards. Morality is hot—but art is icy! Excuse my dogmatic and dictatorial tone, and believe it is only an extreme indication of interest and sympathy in what you do.

Speaking of her characters, Henry told her that there was a want of proportion and perspective; she was "too savage" with her poets and painters and dilettanti, "*life* is less criminal, less obnoxious, less objectionable, less crude, more *bon enfant*, more mixed and casual, and even in its most offensive manifestations, more *pardonnable*, than the unholy circle with which you have surrounded your heroine. And then you have impregnated all those people too much with the sexual, the basely erotic preoccupation: your hand was over-violent, the touch of life is lighter."

Miss Paget seems to have paid attention to James's criticisms, and to have recognized their value and authority. She shrewdly saw the difference between James the serious artist and James the social animal addicted to an excess of flourish: this she characterized with complete accuracy to her mother, as his "absolute social and personal insincerity and extreme intellectual justice and plain-spokenness." Thus closed the first incident in one of the more curious friendships of James's life.

Already there was foreshadowed, however, in the friends James was forming during 1884, the future "Master"—the idol of younger writers of the *fin de siècle* and the new century, the giver of counsel and of doctrine. Henry James was to be until late in life on the side of youth and of experiment in art. He had during this year met three of the younger generation—Sargent, Bourget and Vernon Lee. A still more important friendship was to be formed during the coming months under circumstances he would not have predicted during the crowded weeks after his return from Paris.

ATMOSPHERE OF THE MIND

AUGUST CAME AND HENRY WAS STILL IN LONDON—HOT, TIRED, restless, uneasy. "Infinitely oppressed and depressed," he wrote in his notebook on August 6, 1884, "by the sense of being behind-hand with the novel—that is, with the *start* of it, that I have engaged, through Osgood, to write for the *Century*." He had two social engagements, he noted, one at Waddesdon, where he was going with Bourget. He would get these out of the way. "Then I shall possess my soul, my faculties, my imagination again, then I shall feel that life is worth living, and shall (I trust) be tolerably calm and happy. A *mighty will*, there is nothing but that! The integrity of one's will, purpose, faith. To wait, when one *must* wait, and act when one can act!" He had not yet found a name for his novel. It was known for the moment only as *Verena*. Osgood was to pay a flat fee of $5,000 for the book rights, for a specified period; Henry knew what his own earnings would be if he himself serialized and then controlled the book rights; he had driven a good bargain. Moreover he had come to terms with the *Atlantic* for a second novel, for 1885-86. He had asked $500 an instalment, but had settled on $15 a page, or about $350 a month.

I

He had remained in London that summer to write two tales for the New York *Sunday Sun* and its syndicate and had received for these, he told his correspondents, "thousands," but did not name the amount. "It is a case of gold pure and simply," he told T. S. Perry, and he explained that he had no objection to appearing in a newspaper—it would actually give him a wider public. The first of these tales was "Georgina's Reasons," a strange unmotivated sensational little story, written in some misguided belief that this was what newspaper readers wanted. He based it on an anecdote Mrs. Kemble had told him—of some woman in society who married a naval officer in secret, and when she was to have a child gave birth secretly, as if it were illegitimate, and disposed of it to foster parents. James's heroine goes abroad and has her baby in Italy; then she returns to New York, and remarries. When her husband, back from a long voyage, discovers this, he is faced with the dilemma of either denouncing her, or accepting the possibility of bigamy for himself, as she had done. He does neither, however, and feels his freedom has been restricted by the bizarre conduct of his wife. The naval officer, during his travels, had become interested in two young women, sisters, in Naples, whose names are Kate and Mildred Theory. Mildred is dying of consumption—and here, in an early form, are the figures who will return to James's imagination later—Kate and Milly and the naval

man, here named Benyon, later named Densher, to enact the
drama of *The Wings of the Dove*. That "Georgina's Reasons" was
regarded as sufficiently sensational may be judged from the fact
that one of the Western journals which printed it chose to give it
headlines:

GEORGINA'S REASONS!
Henry James's Latest Story
A woman who commits bigamy and enforces silence on
her husband! Two other lives made miserable by her
heartless action!

The second tale written for the *Sun* was in Henry's usual
international vein. Told with great charm through the eyes of a
literal-minded but not insensitive young German diplomat bound
for his country's embassy in America, the tale, "Pandora," drew
on Henry's Washington visits of the previous two years. The diplomat first meets Pandora Day on board ship. He has been reading
"Daisy Miller," and he wonders whether she is the flirtatious type
depicted by the author of that tale. Presently he discovers that
she dominates her parents; that she has a fiancé; and under the
roof of a splendid Washington home very much like that of the
Henry Adamses, he learns that Pandora is really what is known as
the "self-made" American girl. Her parents have totally abdi-
cated to her, and she has taken all the reins into her own hands.
The climax occurs when the President of the United States, attending a party at the home of the Adams characters—they are named
here Bonnycastle—has a chat with Pandora and she obtains from
him a post in the diplomatic service for her fiancé. The amazed
German diplomat feels he now has full documentation on the
resilience and daring of American young women. Henry by now
possessed a fluent mastery of this type of story—the arrival in
New York, the Washington interiors, the social rise of Pandora
and every step seen through the Germanism of Count Vogel-
stein are told in a light vein of ironic comedy. Adroit though James
was, however, he could never deceive his readers, who still regarded

the Teutonic-eye view of the American girl as really Henry's. The tale was as critical of American families and American institutions as James's other international stories; what many of James's readers could not appreciate was his technique and his boundless good humor, which they experienced as depreciatory.

When these tales were sent off and his visits were paid, Henry settled himself in Dover, on the Marine Parade. The port was not crowded; he had almost an entire lodging house to himself. The Channel twinkled under his windows and he felt that he was hanging over the French coast, so near did it seem on the horizon. "I have gone in for privacy, *recueillement* and literary labour," he told Miss Reubell. He had never allowed himself so slim a margin before starting a serial. He was true to his notebook admonition—to "act when one can act." By October 1 he had sent Richard Watson Gilder the first instalment of *The Bostonians* for the *Century*. Bourget came from London, and they sat on Henry's little balcony smoking cigarettes and looking across the Channel. Henry spent six or seven productive weeks here, put himself back into tune with his work, and returned to Bolton Street in late September with his novel well launched.

11

Before leaving London Henry had written a comparatively short, but substantial essay, to which he gave the title "The Art of Fiction" and sent it off to *Longman's Magazine*. He had come upon a pamphlet containing a lecture delivered the previous April at the Royal Institution by Walter Besant, a busy Victorian, who boasted that he had written eighteen novels in eighteen years. Besant's subject had been "Fiction as One of the Fine Arts." The burden of his argument was that novel-writing should be classed with the arts of poetry, painting and music, and taught as the laws of harmony are taught in music, or perspective in painting. Besant also asked that the practitioners of the fictional art be given honors and prizes such as were reserved for the other arts. With much of this Henry had no argument. But when Besant undertook to say what the novel should be, and how it should be taught, Henry demurred. He could not accept Besant's dictum that a novel should possess "a conscious moral purpose." Nor could he agree with his remark that a lady novelist who lived in a quiet village might not write fiction about garrison life. She had only to be an observant damsel, Henry replied, to be able to write on any subject of her choice. By the same token, Henry found it "rather chilling" that Besant should have advised young novelists from the lower classes to refrain from launching their characters in high society. The truly imaginative novelist, he said, knew how to guess the unseen from the seen, "to trace the implication of things, to judge the whole piece by the pattern."

For the rest, Henry's main argument was that the novel, far from being "make-believe," actually competes with life, since it records the stuff of history. Comparing fiction to painting, he said that "as the picture is reality, so the novel is history." He criticized the factitious novel with its spurious happy ending, the "distribution at the last of prizes, pensions, husbands, wives, babies, millions, appended paragraphs, and cheerful remarks." The core of his essay contained a defense of the novel as a free and elastic form, which made it difficult to prescribe "what sort of an affair the good novel will be." The novel would always be a personal impression of life; and its value would be greater or less "according to the intensity of the impression." Humanity was immense and "reality has a myriad forms." It was very well for Besant to say one should write from "experience"—

What kind of experience is intended, and where does it begin and end? Experience is never limited and it is never complete; it is an immense sensibility, a kind of huge spider-web of the finest silken threads, suspended in the chamber of consciousness, and catching every air-borne particle in its tissue. It is the very atmosphere of the mind; and when the mind is imaginative—much more when it happens to be that of a man of genius—it takes to itself the faintest hints of life, it converts the very pulses of the air into revelations.

The best help to give to the fictional novice was not to lecture him on novel of character and novel of incident, but to say to him simply: "Try to be one of the people on whom nothing is lost."

The rest of James's paper was devoted to his argument that the novel was a living organism and that "in each of the parts there is something of each of the other parts."

What is character but the determination of incident? What is incident but the illustration of character? What is either a picture or a novel that is *not* of character? . . . It is an incident for a woman to stand up with her hand resting on a table and look out at you in a certain way; or if it be not an incident I think it will be hard to say what it is. At the same time it is an expression of character.

James denied a *conscious* moral purpose to the novel. The province of art was "all life, all feeling, all observation, all vision," and the critic should not prescribe which subjects were valid and which were not. The critic's concern was solely with what the novelist did with his material. What was wrong with the English novel, Henry argued, was that there existed a conspiracy, "a traditional difference between that which people know and that which they agree to admit that they know." Far from having a purpose, moral or otherwise, the English novel had a "diffidence." Recalling his talks with his French confrères, Henry reached the conclusion that a novel invariably conveyed "the quality of the mind of the producer" and that "no good novel will ever proceed from a superficial mind." This was the essence of his argument. "The Art of Fiction" remains a brilliant statement; it has the character of an individual manifesto, written with Henry's elegance and grace, and with the finger-tip finesse of Matthew Arnold, that of standing his ground firmly and stating his truths with high seriousness. Many novelists had discussed one or another of Henry's points before: but never had the case for realism in fiction, and for the novel as social history, been put in the English world with such force, nor "experience" defined with such psychological understanding.

III

One remark in this essay caught the eye of an invalid at Bournemouth, a novelist who had been having severe lung hemorrhages and who did most of his writing in bed. Discussing reality in fiction, James had alluded to *Treasure Island* and compared it with Edmond de Goncourt's *Chérie*. He pronounced the Goncourt novel a failure and Stevenson's novel a success, remarking: "I have been a child in fact, but I have been on a quest for a buried treasure only in supposition." Robert Louis Stevenson promptly wrote still another essay on the subject, titled it "A Humble Remonstrance," and sent it also to *Longman's* where it appeared two months after James's paper. To the particular remark about *Treasure Island*, Stevenson rejoined that if James had "never been on a quest for buried treasure, it can be demonstrated that he has never been a child." The burden of his argument was that the novel, contrary to Henry, could not compete with life. It had to be "make-believe." Fiction, Stevenson said, simplified some "side or point of life," and stood or fell by its "significant simplicity." He reasoned that life was "monstrous, infinite, illogical, abrupt, and poignant," whereas a work of art was, in comparison, "neat, finite, self-contained, rational, flowing, and emasculate. Life imposes by brute energy, like inarticulate thunder; art catches the ear, among the far louder noises of experience like an air artificially made by a discreet musician."

Thus had been stated in public, during this year, three distinct views of the novel; Besant's had been that of the efficient and good-natured hack, the "maker" of popular fiction; James had argued for the novel as a work of art which re-creates reality; and Stevenson, from his own formula, spoke for make-believe. James had met Stevenson long before, during the "Daisy Miller" period. On September 14, 1879 he had written to T. S. Perry: "I have seen R. L. Stevenson but once—met him at lunch (and Edmund

Gosse) with Lang. He is a pleasant fellow, but a shirt-collarless Bohemian and a great deal (in an inoffensive way) of a *poseur*. But his little *Inland Voyage* was, I thought, charming."

They had never had occasion to develop this acquaintance, Stevenson being much out of England. But when his article appeared, Henry wrote him of his enjoyment "of everything you write. It's a luxury, in this immoral age, to encounter some one who *does* write—who is really acquainted with that lovely art." He thanked him for many of the things he had said—"the current of your admirable style floats pearls and diamonds." His own pages in *Longman's*, Henry said, had been mainly a plea for liberty for the novelist: they represented only half of what he had to say. "Some day I shall try and express the remainder. . . . The native *gaiety* of all that you write is delightful to me," and all the more so, he added, since he was aware how ill Stevenson was.

Stevenson replied that his own efforts were modest indeed beside James's and he spoke of "the despair with which a writer like myself considers (say) the park scene in 'Lady Barberina.' Every touch surprises me by its instantaneous precision." As for their differences, "Each man among us prefers his own aim, and I prefer mine; but when we come to speak of performance, I recognise myself, compared with you, to be a lout and slouch of the first water." He remarked that being sick, he liked visitors; and he invited James to come to Bournemouth where he would put him up and offer him "a fair bottle of claret." These were but the overtures to what was to become—other circumstances intervening—a strong and intense friendship.

THE TWO INVALIDS

WHEN HENRY RETURNED TO LONDON FROM DOVER, HE KNEW THAT his sister would be joining him shortly. The correspondence announcing her plans does not appear to have survived; however a letter from Henry to William of October 5, 1884 mentions that "Alice's advent here is by this time (in prospect) a familiar idea, though I feel naturally a good deal of solicitude about it. It is certainly a good thing for me to do; and if she can adjust herself to a long rhythm, as it were, of improvement, instead of a short one, I have no doubt, solid results will come to her. But she ought to be prepared to spend *three* years. I don't know what she will do, and don't exactly see how I can (when she is alone) be either with her or without her—that is, away from her. But this will doubtless settle itself; and if she learns to become more sociable with the world at large (as I think she will have to, in self-preservation), the problem will be solved."

Her sailing date had not yet been set. What we do know is that Alice James, with both her parents dead and with Katherine Loring available only at certain times, had been leading a rather lonely life in Mount Vernon Street. Miss Loring had a sister Louisa who had weak lungs; she could not therefore give undivided attention to Alice. But she was bringing Louisa abroad, and Alice, rather than remain alone in Cambridge, had decided to journey with her friends.

The ill health and consequent dependency of his sister posed many serious problems for Henry, although he had not yet taken full measure of them. In his customary fashion, as he had said, he felt that time itself would provide the answers. They had talked of some sort of joint domestic arrangement; but with her invalidism this seemed out of the question. He was her one bachelor brother; they had been close to one another during their earlier years; and he considered the responsibility should be his. He had implied this from the moment he had turned over to her the income from his inheritance. Grace Norton, as an old friend of the Jameses, was free to write to Henry, warning him of the dangers he was incurring. Her letter has not been preserved, but Henry's reply sufficiently suggests its contents: "I have quite escaped, as yet, being alarmed by Alice's now impending advent. I *may* be wrong, and it *may* wreck and blight my existence, but it will have to exert itself tremendously to do so." She was not even coming to visit him, he said; she was simply coming to Europe, and "there is no question of her living with me. She is unspeakably un-dependent and independent, she *clings* no more than a bowsprit, has her own plans, purposes, preferences, practices, pursuits, more than anyone I know, has also amply sufficient means, etc. and, in short, even putting her possible failure to improve in health at the worst, will be very unlikely to tinge or modify my existence in any uncomfortable way." It was quite true that Alice did not "cling." Nevertheless her illness, by its very nature, had its clinging side.

I

On the evening of November 10, 1884, Henry journeyed to Liverpool and the next morning at 7:30 he was able to board the *Pavonia* out in the stream, before the ship docked. He found Alice in a deplorable state. The voyage had not been rough, but his sister was in one of her fits of nervous prostration, so that she had to be carried off the ship on a stretcher. Miss Loring had nursed her faithfully across the ocean. Louisa, Katherine's sister, seemed in much better health than Alice, who was "more infirm than I expected," Henry told his Aunt Kate. He had however "perfect belief that she will not seem so after she has been on shore a week. But for the present I must rather give myself up to her."

What Henry discovered after some observation was that his sister was markedly jealous of Louisa. She wanted Miss Loring to herself. And Henry, who had already noticed the attachment between the two—and who was now writing a novel about such an attachment—began to see the extent to which Miss Loring domi-

nated his sister's existence. After Alice had been debarked at
Liverpool, Henry had left her in the hands of a maid he had
brought with him for her. Katherine Loring was taking Louisa to
Bournemouth on the very next day. Henry had first thought Alice
would be taken there as well, but Miss Loring's sister was, on her
side, in a high state of nerves. Miss Loring tactfully suggested that
Alice's arrival at the health resort be postponed. After the better
part of a week, which they spent in Liverpool, Henry took Alice
therefore to London and installed her with her maid at No. 40
Clarges Street near his own lodgings. Later he moved her to No.
7 Bolton Row.

By this time the drama of Katherine Loring and her two invalids was sufficiently clear. Louisa Loring and Alice James were
engaged in a fierce subterranean competition for the nursing and
attention of the stalwart Katherine. Alice probably would have
been the last to admit that she was in a jealous rage whenever
Katherine had to be with Louisa. The consequences, nevertheless,
were that she sooner or later developed alarming symptoms.
Henry would send an anxious telegram, and when Miss Loring
dashed to the rescue, Alice's symptoms would subside. At the same
time Henry observed another queer element in the situation. This
was that even when the crisis was over, Alice insisted on remaining
in bed so long as Miss Loring was available to care for her. "I
may be wrong in the matter," he wrote to William, "but it rather
strikes me as an effect that Katherine Loring has upon her—that
as soon as they get together, Alice takes to her bed. This was the
case as soon as Katherine came to London to see her (she had
been up before) and she has now been recumbent (as a consequence of her little four-hour journey) ever since she reached
Bournemouth." Henry had finally taken her to that seaside resort
when it became clear that Louisa was acquiring a considerable interest in English life and was on her way to recovery. The British
doctors had given Alice a thorough examination: their verdict coincided with that of their American colleagues. They could find

nothing organically wrong, and they ended by treating her as neurasthenic.

The move to Bournemouth was made in January 1885. His sister would have brighter and larger quarters than those available in Mayfair, and Henry commuted at fixed intervals to see her. So long as Miss Loring was with her, she had no particular need for Henry. But he promised her he would spend the spring in Bournemouth: it would be a good place to work and to avoid the London "season." Thus it came about that he took rooms there late in April, when the greater part of *The Bostonians* was written. By that time he had called on still another Bournemouth invalid, Robert Louis Stevenson.

11

Before leaving London, however, Henry James had occasion to perform certain rites of friendship and loyalty for James Russell Lowell. Ever since his return to England, Henry had felt a certain solicitude for his old friend: he knew that his term as Minister to the Court of St. James's would sooner or later end, and when it became clear that Cleveland would be the next American President, the novelist began to conjure up painful images. To Mrs. Godkin, Henry wrote: "He has been living in social and material clover, the pet of countesses, the habitué of palaces, the intimate of dukes; and he will have to give it all up, in order to live again in the suburb of a suburb, look after his furnace, and see that his plank walk is laid down! I regard him as the sport of fortune, his situation preoccupies me much, and I lie awake at night thinking of it." With all the reservations he had about Lowell's rusticity, his inability to be a "real man of the world," Henry dearly loved him; and when, in February of 1885, Mrs. Lowell died suddenly, Henry felt his friend to be the sport of fortune indeed. For some days he remained with him, consoled him, gave him the companionship he needed. "He is very quiet and simple—but I am very, *very* sorry for him," Henry wrote to Lizzie Boott. "The death of his wife leaves him much better conditions for remaining here, but there is no prospect whatever of his being left, and the idea of his returning, after these European years, to live alone in Cambridge, is too horrible." Henry was to a certain extent reading his own ancient horror of Cambridge into Lowell's state. Nevertheless Lowell, too, had now before him the vision of a lonely life in Elmwood, even though his relations with his wife had been rather perfunctory during the last few years, and he had been very much in the company of Mrs. Smalley, wife of the *Tribune's* London correspondent.

In due course Lowell was recalled and left for America. The letter which Henry wrote to him, as he stepped down from the post he had brilliantly filled, was a kind of apotheosis to a whole phase of Henry's London life; and it reflected the deep affection that had existed between them since they had become friends long ago in Paris:

As I look back upon the years of your mission my heart swells and almost breaks again (as it did when I heard you were superseded) at the thought that anything so perfect should be gratuitously destroyed. But there is a part of your function which can go on again, indefinitely, whenever you take it up—and that, I repeat, I hope you will do soon rather than late. I think with the tenderest pleasure of the many fireside talks I have had with you, from the first—and with a pleasure dimmed with sadness of so many of our more recent ones. You are tied to London now by innumerable cords and fibres, and I should be glad to think that you ever felt me, ever so lightly, pulling at one of them. . . . Don't forget that you have produced a relation between England and the United States which is really a gain to civilization and that you must come back to look after your work. You can't look after it there: that is the function of an Englishman—and if *you* do it there they will call you one. The only way you can be a good American is to return to our dear old stupid, satisfactory London, and to yours ever affectionately and faithfully, HENRY JAMES

III

Henry moved to Bournemouth in late April of 1885, when Miss Loring went to London with her sister. *The Bostonians* was all but finished. He was clearing the ground for the writing of *The Princess Casamassima*. It seemed to him that he could profit by his stay—minister to his sister's social needs, enjoy the sea air, and quietly pursue his novel. He took rooms on the ocean side, three minutes' walk from where Alice was staying. He did not much care for his lodgings, but they were adequate. Bournemouth he found wholly uninteresting, "of an almost American newness and ugliness." He enjoyed the view, however, especially of the Isle of Wight, which looked to him like a pretty marble toy on an ultramarine horizon. Alice had a nurse and a maid; and once or twice a day he would drop in for a twenty-minute visit. He did not stay longer because Alice tired easily. In the afternoon, and sometimes in the evening, he became a regular caller at Skerryvore, where his favorite armchair was reserved for him and where he spent hours in happy talk with the euphoric Stevenson.

"An old acquaintance of mine is ripening into a new friend," he told Miss Norton. This friendship had in it probably more intensities of feeling than his friendship with Sargent. Stevenson was thirty-five, seven years younger than Henry; he had all the activity and make-believe of a boy in constant search of adventure. Certain of his letters to Henry, and the quality of his humor, greatly resemble the alertness and the liveliness of William James in his youth. Henry, on his side, seems to have embodied some image of benign authority for the ailing Scot. For one disabled physically, as Stevenson was, he was extraordinarily prolific. He suffered, however, little pain, and he seemed to have a rare capacity of pulling himself back, again and again, from the brink of death. Stevenson wrote verses to Henry, and received him with boundless affection and much ceremonial. Mrs. Stevenson, who was American and older than her husband, treated her fellow-countryman with a certain awe and respect: the two transformed what might have been for Henry a lugubrious stay in Bourne-

mouth into a pleasant literary and social way of life. So long as
Alice had no crises, Henry fell into a happy routine of writing and
visits to the two invalids.

The Stevensons lived in a house on the brink of the Alum
Chine or gulley, a two-story structure of yellow brick with a blue
slate roof, overgrown with ivy. Its front faced away from the road
to a garden sloping almost to the bottom of the Chine. They had
renamed the place Skerryvore, for the great lighthouse built by
the novelist's ancestor. Here, in the blue room, where hung a
Venetian mirror which James had given to the Stevensons, they
often received him and gave him a meal. Stevenson would sit at
the end of the table rolling his cigarettes in his long fingers. He
had wide-set eyes, a straight nose, and long blond mustaches over
his thin lips. He wore bohemian velvet jackets; sometimes, when
it was cold, he would drape himself in a maroon-colored shawl,
like a Mexican poncho. A passionate energy possessed his slight
frame.

Stevenson's verses dedicated to Henry amused him. But when
his friend published them he felt, with embarrassment, that privacy had been violated. The two best known both lead, in their
moment of climax, to the entry of Henry James into Skerryvore—
suggesting perhaps how much his daily coming was awaited. In a
Shakespearean sonnet, in which Stevenson enumerated certain of
Henry's female characters,

> Lo, how these fair immaculate women walk
> Behind their jocund maker;

(Madame de Mauves, Daisy, Lady Barb, Olive Chancellor), he
ended with

> But he, attended by these shining names,
> Comes (best of all) himself—our welcome James.

The choice of characters was perhaps not too carefully pondered.
No reader of *The Bostonians*, then or now, would regard Olive
Chancellor as a "fair immaculate woman." The verses however

were spontaneous and occasional, and must not be scrutinized too critically. The second poem celebrated the gift of the mirror, and its last verse equally foreshadows an entrance. The mirror is speaking:

> Now with an outlandish grace,
> To the sparkling fire I face
> In the blue room at Skerryvore;
> Where I wait until the door
> Open, and the Prince of Men
> Henry James, shall come again.

They had in common their devotion to style, their love of words and wit, their ranging imaginations. Stevenson appreciated to the full the deliberate artistry of Henry; Henry enjoyed Stevenson's flair for vivid storytelling. In the first of the three essays he devoted to him, Henry speaks of his "jauntiness"; he observes that heroines are wholly absent from his works and that "the idea of making believe appeals to him much more than the idea of making love." He characterized his work as "the romance of boyhood"—which Stevenson had given to the world as other novelists deal with the peerage, or the police, or the medical profession. "Though he takes such an interest in childish life, he takes no interest in the fireside," Henry wrote. "To his view the normal child is the child who absents himself from the family-circle." This sense of the eternal boyishness of his friend endeared him above all to James.

"My only social resource," Henry wrote to Howells, "is Robert Louis Stevenson, who is more or less dying here and who (in case that event should take place) gave me the other day a message of a friendly—very friendly—character to give to you when I should next see you. I shall wait till then—it is too long for a short letter. He is an interesting, charming creature, but I fear at the end of his tether; though indeed less apparently near death than he has been at other times." Perhaps it was the fact that Stevenson seemed to consort on such amiable terms with the constant pres-

ence of death, that gave an additional measure of intensity to this
friendship. These were to be the days when they knew each
other best. Stevenson was to live for another decade; and when he
departed for the South Seas, their correspondence took on the
charm and spontaneity of their personal meetings. The letters can
be read in the volume edited by Janet Adam Smith; the tone of
communication on both sides continued to be one of deep affection, of unending friendship. They sent each other their books.
They read each other with obvious enjoyment. It was at Skerryvore in 1886 that Stevenson gave Henry a copy of *Kidnapped*,
inscribing it, "And I wish I had a better work to give as good a
man." The copy, which was preserved in James's library, is
scrawled with Henry's notes made during his reading.

IV

Henry's closeness to Alice during these weeks gave him a clearer
picture of certain of her problems. Whatever her physical ail-
ments, if any, which medicine could not then diagnose, it was
clear that she was involved in an inextricable human relationship
which Henry could describe for himself. Early in May there was
"a cataclysm." The companion-nurse he had engaged for his sister
was something of a martinet and insisted on treating her as if she
were "a morbid and hysterical patient." The companion "proved
a very high-tempered, decided, bridling little body," Henry told
Aunt Kate. But she was merely a small part of the episode. The
point was that Miss Loring's presence was required "and Louisa is
turning out so much better, that she could easily come." An ordinary trained nurse was substituted for the spirited companion:
and Katherine announced that she would, in a month or two, return to Alice, and release Henry. Louisa's weak lungs seemed
cured, and, said Henry, "Katherine comes back to Alice for a
permanency. Her being with her may be interrupted by absences,
but evidently it is the beginning of a living-together, for the rest
of such time as Alice's life may last. I think that a conviction on
K's part *at bottom*, beneath her superficial optimism, that it *may*

not last long, has something to do with these arrangements—for evidently it is a kind of definite understanding between them."

Henry felt that there was no alternative but to accept gratefully Miss Loring's willingness and generosity. He was not convinced that the relationship was a good one. There was something profoundly symbiotic in it. Alice was too dependent on Miss Loring, and took too much joy in being cared for by her friend. But there was nothing anyone else could do. "There is about as much possibility of Alice's giving Katherine up," he told his aunt, "as of her giving her legs to be sawed off. She said to me a few days ago that she believed if she could have Katherine *quietly* and *uninterruptedly*, for a year, 'to relieve her of all responsibility,' she would get well. Amen! She will get well, or she won't, but, either way, it lies between themselves. I shall devote my best energies to taking the whole situation less hard in the future than I have hitherto."

In a second letter to his aunt, a few days later, Henry directly attributed Alice's decline to her having had to share Miss Loring with Louisa. "If Katherine is able to stay with A. with some *continuity*, which is her evident intention, allowing for short interruptions, Alice may go on, I don't say to recovery, but to no more certain or rapid decline, as she would if she were separated from her and constantly yearning and telegraphing for her." And Henry went on to say that whenever Miss Loring would return, "I shall assent with a good grace, for the simple reason that it is the only thing I can do unless I take Alice completely on my own shoulders—which is obviously impossible, from every point of view. And if you were here you wouldn't make that any easier. Alice, too, would then have *five* people under contribution, really, to take care of her, and she has quite enough now."

A *modus vivendi* had been found for a deeply complicated situation. Lousia Loring did make a complete recovery and her elder sister increasingly confined herself to Alice. Henry was thus liberated to pursue his work. But he was to continue to have Alice on his mind, and he frequently hesitated to take trips away from

England on her account. She held him by her invalidism in a delicate moral bondage; but he too, at a later stage, derived an enormous gratification from seeing her frequently and bringing to her bedside the wide world in which he moved. Alice rarely left her bed after her arrival in England. She refused to risk a return voyage to America and during the seven years that remained to her she lived largely in London and in Leamington. In her journal she recorded her gratitude to Henry's devotion, one day in March of 1890:

Henry came on the 10th to spend the day; Henry the Patient, I should call him. Five years ago in November I crossed the water, and suspended myself like an old woman of the sea around his neck, where to all appearances I shall remain for all time. I have given him endless care and anxiety but notwithstanding this and the fantastic nature of my troubles I have never seen an impatient look upon his face or heard an unsympathetic or misunderstanding sound cross his lips. He comes at my slightest sign and 'hangs on' to whatever organ may be in eruption, and gives me balm and solace by assuring me that my nerves are his nerves and my stomach his stomach—this last pitch of brotherly devotion never before approached by the race. He has never remotely hinted that he expected me to be well at any given moment, that burden which fond friend and relative so inevitably impose upon the cherished invalid.

She likened Henry's personal "susceptibility" to their father's. The elder Henry James had spent many hours beside her bed long ago. To the end, Alice wrested from the hovering Miss Loring and the loyal Henry a full amount of attention and love which, in some large way, she felt had been denied to her during an earlier period of her existence.

A VERY AMERICAN TALE

IN "THE BOSTONIANS," HENRY JAMES WROTE THE MOST CONSIDERABLE American novel of its decade. For all its oppressive detail, there is no other novel of such value and distinction to place on the bookshelf of the late nineteenth century. *Huckleberry Finn* might form an incongruous companion, but it belongs to a wholly different genre—as Mark Twain doubtless would have insisted, for he said he would rather be damned in John Bunyan's Heaven than read *The Bostonians*. Most Americans of the time shared Mark Twain's feeling about the Jamesian work; and the editors of the *Century*, where the ill-fated book ran through thirteen months, said they had never published a serial which had encountered such an awesome silence.

The first notation for the book was made on April 8, 1883 when James was in Boston, and in setting it down he spoke of it in the past tense—as if the novel were already written. "I wished to write a very *American* tale, a tale very characteristic of our social conditions, and I asked myself what was the most salient and peculiar point in our social life. The answer was: the situation of women, the decline of the sentiment of sex, the agitation on their behalf." Another notation, however, also exists. It is a single word, scrawled across the flyleaf of the *Correspondence of Thomas Carlyle and Ralph Waldo Emerson*, which James read and reviewed just after his father's and Emerson's death. The word is "Reformers," and the page number attached to it refers us to a passage marked in a letter of Emerson's: "We are all a little wild here with numberless projects of social reform." The novel which he finally began more than a year later brought together the two subjects—Boston reformers and the "situation of women."

Later, as his book took shape, he was to discover that the subject was "less interesting and repaying than I had assumed it to

be." Perhaps he knew Boston too well; the theme was clearly uncongenial. A kind of nagging hand seemed to tug at his pen; the
fluid stylist of the international tales brooded too much and lingered in odd corners. Each scene was described with an exhaus-
tive minuteness. If he was playing the French "naturalist," he was
doing it with a vengeance; he seemed almost hypnotized by his
material. The first evening of the novel is spread through nine
chapters; the next day occupies three more. Almost one-fourth of
the book is used to describe the opening hours of the tale—to be
sure with a great deal of earlier history and retrospective analysis
thrown in. We meet the hero in these chapters, and then he dis-
appears until the middle of the book; the novel thus sprawls in a
manner wholly alien to the author of *Washington Square* or *The
Portrait of a Lady*. It has many fine pages, and much fine writing; and yet a kind of uncontrollable prolixity is everywhere. He
had intended to tell his story as a six-part serial, of the length of
Washington Square. And he was not paid for the seven additional
instalments which he wrote. Having sold the novel outright for a
given period to Osgood, he had nothing to gain by more than
doubling its length save the dubious satisfaction of bringing into
being a weighty 950-page manuscript.

The Bostonians is a strange instance of a writer of power so
possessed by his material that he loses his mastery of it. What
happened may be likened to a lecturer who cannot bring himself
to stop at the end of his allotted time; or to a talker who must rehearse more facts than his listeners wish to hear. Something in the
very nature of the story, its people, the deep animus James felt for
certain aspects of Boston life, took hold. In the end James recognized this. He excluded the novel from his New York Edition.
He admitted that it was "too diffuse and insistent—far too describing and explaining and expatiating." He confessed to William, "I should have been more rapid and had a lighter hand."
His readers of that time would have agreed heartily. The modern
reader may also squirm over some of the *longueurs:* yet today the
book's social documentation has an historical interest, and the

writing is never without its charm. It is a novel which contains memorable scenes and memorable characters; however it must be accounted a failure by comparison with James's best work—even though its place in American literature is significant.

I

The drama of *The Bostonians* centers in a struggle for possession. Olive Chancellor, a wealthy, chill, unyielding Boston intellectual, simmering in a kind of chronic anger over the subservience of women to men, is an intense suffragette. She is capable indeed of no other passion. The usual things of life fill her with "silent rage." Encountering a young and rather inexperienced girl named Verena Tarrant, who possesses a strange histrionic oratorical gift, she recognizes in her the instrument she lacks. Verena's wondrous gift of speech is carefully documented: her "conditioning" began as a baby—in the era before baby-sitters—when she was taken by her parents to the inspirational lectures common in early New England; Verena is a product of the Puritan preacher and the Chautauqua, of primitive American grandiloquence. As a child in modern times may babble the "commercials" heard on television, Verena develops into a finished Boston parrot, with all the orotundities and inflections of the old-time speech-makers in her voice. Her father, by a kind of laying on of hands, turns on this flood of "built-in" verbiage. And Verena, although she does not have an idea in her rather pretty little head, can assemble fragments and phrases of remembered sentences into a meaningless semblance of unity. It occurs to Olive that she should adopt this girl; she would impart noble thoughts and noble aims to her; make her the sounding box of the American feminist movement. Verena's parents readily accept; it seems natural to them that their girl prodigy acquire a patroness. And many pages of *The Bostonians* are devoted to the cosy evenings spent by the two women at Olive's fireside, reading great authors and planning a major assault on the citadels of masculinity.

James intended the story to be "a study of one of those friend-

ships between women which are so common in New England."
Modern critics have tended accordingly to regard the novel as
portraying a "lesbian" attachment; and doubtless Olive's masculinity, her hatred of men and her passion for Verena bespeaks
what would today be called a "latent homosexuality." But in the
terms of James's time, and Boston morality, it is more accurate to
see the relationship in its overt nature: had Olive obtained
physical possession of Verena, her need of her as instrument of
power would have diminished considerably. The focus of the
story is on Olive's fierce possessiveness; and the drama is one in
which she struggles to keep Verena from marrying Basil Ransom,
a rather weak, easy-going but also powerfully possessive Southerner, a remote relative of hers. An "outsider" in Boston and
New York, and all but recently an "enemy" in the Confederate
army, he has come north as a struggling lawyer because his father's plantations were ruined by the war. Ransom has pretensions
to high social ideas; but an editor to whom he submits an article
informs him his "doctrines were about three hundred years behind
the age; doubtless some magazine of the sixteenth century would
have been very happy to print them." While Ransom is sometimes
a vehicle for Jamesian opinions—particularly his fear of the femi-
nization of American life—he is in general presented as a shallow
and egotistical individual. James himself told John Hay he was
made up "of wandering airs and chance impressions" and was
"rather vague and artificial, quite *fait de chic.*" Hay told James that
Lucius Q. C. Lamar, the popular Senator from Mississippi, whom
James had met in Washington, seemed to recognize something of
himself in the character. James confessed that he was "in it a little,
for I met him once or twice in Washington, and he is one of the
very few Mississippians with whom I have had the pleasure of con-
versing."

The struggle between Olive, all rectitude and feminine politics,
and Ransom, determined to place Verena in the kitchen and the
nursery, has in it elements of good drama and even high comedy.
James, however, became so interested in the clashing egos that he

did little with Verena herself. The reader seldom feels that the girl's conflict is serious: at best she will be a kind of oratorical actress; and the alternative is that of becoming a submissive wife. And while James invests the situation with many interesting developments, the tug-of-war is too protracted; moreover the subsidiary characters, which illuminate his study of American life, do not sufficiently advance the action. Had *The Bostonians* been written with James's usual economy and the same wit as *The Europeans*, he would have created something close to "the great American novel" of which he had dreamed in his youth. What he created instead was a series of vignettes; and certain pages valuably critical of American institutions—the invasion of privacy by the press, the meddlesome character of Boston reformers, the general tawdriness and banality of certain aspects of the American life of the time on which he had dwelt in his other tales.

The reader is made to believe to some degree that in the struggle between Olive and Ransom he is watching a struggle between good and evil; James had represented an analogous struggle in *The Portrait of a Lady* between Isabel and Osmond. But again he offers a struggle in reality between mirror-images. Ransom and Olive are both profound egotists. Neither loves Verena for herself; she is something to be acquired and possessed and used as an instrument of a personal idea; Ransom is almost as much interested in defeating Olive as in marrying Verena. And Olive is too morbid and hysterical and jealous to make us believe she has Verena's good at heart. Here again those who have read the novel as "lesbian" tend to see Ransom in a better light than James represents him—for they read him in the belief that he is rescuing Verena from Olive's depravity. The truth is that James has little respect for either. It is their struggle for power which he finds fascinating: they are ruthless, self-seeking, blind to the feelings of others and aware only of their own needs. Olive wants to make Verena a projection of herself; Ransom is sufficiently of the post-bellum South still to believe that some persons should be enslaved by others. A cardboard Southerner, he is never less

convincing than when he is trying to woo Verena. The ending of
the novel splendidly defies the great tradition of romantic fiction
that characters, after struggle, live happily ever afterwards. As
Ransom leads Verena from the large hall in which she was to have
made her most brilliant speech, he discovers she is in tears. "It is
to be feared," says the unreconciled author, "that with the union,
so far from brilliant, into which she was about to enter, these were
not the last she was destined to shed."

II

The print in the *Century* was hardly dry on the early chapters of
this novel when Henry James received word from his Aunt Kate,
from James Russell Lowell and from his brother William that he
had lampooned a much-respected Boston reformer, Miss Elizabeth Peabody, the elderly sister-in-law of Hawthorne, whose good
works and crusading zeal were famous. "It is a pretty bad business," William wrote, and Henry showed some perturbation over
this remark. He pleaded not guilty. At best he had thought of Miss
Peabody's spectacles on the bridge of her nose when he had described his character, Miss Birdseye—"the whole moral history of
Boston was reflected in her displaced spectacles." Doubtless certain passages in the three full pages devoted to her could fit all
reformers. "She belonged to the Short-Skirts League, as a matter
of course; for she belonged to any and every league that had been
founded for almost any purpose whatever." The next sentence
was an example of the way in which Henry tended to editorialize
and judge as well as describe, in this novel. "This did not prevent
her being a confused, entangled, inconsequent, discursive old
woman, whose charity began at home and ended nowhere, whose
credulity kept pace with it, and who knew less about her fellow-
creatures, if possible, after fifty years of humanitary zeal than on
the day she had gone into the field to testify against the iniquity
of most arrangements." This sounds almost as if he were scolding.
When she shakes hands with the hero it is to give him "a delicate,
dirty, democratic little hand."

Henry replied to William that he had not seen Miss Peabody for twenty-five years, and that he had always had the most casual observation of her. "Miss Birdseye," he said, "was evolved entirely from my moral consciousness like every person I have ever drawn." He had wanted to describe "an old, weary, battered and simple-minded woman," so as not to be left open to the charge of treating all the reformers "in a contemptuous manner." In subsequent instalments he enlarged Miss Peabody's heroism; her death scene at the end of the novel, on Cape Cod, is one of the most charmingly-narrated parts of the book. William, when he read the volume entire, withdrew his criticisms and praised it, but felt also that it was overdone. Neither he nor anyone at the time noticed the close relationship between the names of the real-life character and the fictional lady. A "bird's eye" is indeed a "pea-body." Henry James had perhaps imitated life more than he himself allowed.

III

A few weeks before he had begun the writing of this novel, James had composed a short story, published in the spring of 1884 in the *English Illustrated Magazine.* "The Author of Beltraffio" is generally listed among his tales of the literary life. The tale is not concerned so much with literature as with a difficult marital situation, and a Medea-like denouement. It had its origin in James's hearing from Edmund Gosse that the wife of J. A. Symonds intensely disliked his writings. This was all he needed to create his subtle and poisonous little narrative of Mark Ambient's struggle with his wife for possession—body and soul—of their exquisite little boy Dolcino. The mother's morbid fear that Dolcino will be contaminated by what she sees as evil in his father's art causes her to perform the act of Medea. She fails to summon medical help when the child falls ill, and Dolcino dies. The horror of the story is mitigated by James through the "distance" he gives it: it is told through the eyes of an American spectator, an admirer of Ambient's, and the calm suavity of the narrative, as well as the color of the prose, give the tale a benign aloofness. It is complex, subtle, unpleasant, throwing a delicate veil over the mother's ferocity and Ambient's helplessness. For all this Mrs. Ambient is the same baleful female to be found in many of James's writings, capable of doing away with husband or child, whether we meet her in her insouciance, as in "The Pupil," in her calculated perversity, as in *The Other House*, or in her courageous anxiety, as in "The Turn of the Screw." In these tales the bright piping voice of innocence is smothered, the men are symbolically castrated.

This tale of a struggle for possession had heralded the struggle in *The Bostonians*. On a personal level, it seemed as if Henry were back in some dim passage of childhood or youth in which he had felt himself identified with his powerful mother, whose dark side is so often represented in the stories, and at the same time involved with his maimed father. For the rest, the overall picture of the American female in this novel is that of her assertiveness, her pushing, ruling, dominating mastery of men and children, and her threat to American life. The disappearance of the home in Quincy Street, the now permanent absence of a Cambridge hearth, is probably the single deepest emotion out of which *The Bostonians* sprang. There are moments in Ransom's plea for the *status quo*, against *all* change, when he seems to be only a degree less hysterical than Olive. The paradox of *The Bostonians* was that while Henry intellectually was holding up a satirical mirror to the city of his youth, another and younger self within him seemed to plead almost tearfully that nothing be altered, that he could not face the severing of the cable of his old anchorage. In the final scene, in which Ransom insists that at this crucial moment Verena must make her choice, there is an urgency and a shrillness that may bespeak the author's own shrill anxiety. *The Bostonians* was the novel in which James wrote out the hidden emotional anguish of the collapse of his old American ties, and he coupled this with a kind of vibrating anger that Boston should be so unfriendly as to let him go. It incorporated as well Miss Loring's serene and full possession of Alice. The personal venom in *The Bostonians*, and its underlying feelings, indicate the turn taken by Henry's imagination after his departure from America. In accommodating himself to his new London life, he was in some deep underworld of emotion reliving ancient and morbid states. This, we might speculate, lay at the bottom of his inability to discipline the material of his novel, and his tendency to drag it out far beyond its prescribed length. His next novel was to be about reformers as well, and was to contain within it also a struggle for power and possession. But in writing it he could look away from the struggle itself and focus upon its victim. What he had left out of the character of Verena, the orator, in *The Bostonians*, he was able to put into the character of Hyacinth, the bookbinder, in *The Princess Casamassima*.

While the last chapters of *The Bostonians* were appearing, there occurred a serious financial crisis in Henry's affairs. His American publisher, James R. Osgood, went bankrupt. Osgood had published James from the first; he was a man of integrity, but he had apparently managed his business rather poorly. He had five of Henry's books on his list, two early works, two volumes of tales and the impending Boston novel. Henry had not received a penny of the $5,000 promised him for the American, British and serial rights of that work, although Osgood had by now been paid for the *Century* serialization. The novelist acted immediately to recover his various copyrights. Ticknor and Company, which superseded Osgood, at first offered to pay James $4,000 and restore to him the English rights in the novel. These he promptly sold to Macmillan to whom he also sold both English and American rights of his next novel. However, at the last moment, the new firm withdrew its offer and Macmillan took over *The Bostonians* for American issue as well. Not only had Henry not received a penny for the serial, but his advance against royalties from Macmillan did not approximate the substantial sum due him. In a word he had little to show for his year's work.

This financial flurry lasted throughout the spring of 1885 and produced a great deal of uneasiness and insecurity in Henry. He could, however, expect a substantial sum from the solvent *Atlantic Monthly* for his next work. He would have liked, on the strength of this, to proceed to the Continent. He wrote to Lizzie Boott of his yearning to surrender his Bolton Street rooms and to wander for a couple of years in foreign parts. But he was for the moment tied to England by the silver cord—and the common humanity—that bound him to his sister.

BOOK THREE

A London Life
1885=1887

THE NATURALIST

ONE MORNING IN EARLY DECEMBER OF 1884 THE AUTHOR OF "THE Art of Fiction" might have been seen standing in the damp and cold outside a dark and gloomy building with towers, on the edge of the Thames, well-known to Victorians as Millbank Prison. London no longer knows it. A more congenial climate reigns in that neighborhood, for some of the sprawling acres of Millbank today support the Tate Gallery. The prison's walls were bare and brown; the building had ugly pinnacles; its aspect was sad, stern, impersonal. Millbank had been erected in the last year of the eighteenth century, from designs by Jeremy Bentham. Its outer walls formed an irregular octagon; and within these walls it had housed—in its accommodation for 1,120 prisoners—almost a century of human misery. The entire place seemed blighted, and the Thames at this point seemed poisonous: dreariness on this bank and dreariness across the way—long-necked chimneys, deposits of rubbish, unsightly gasometers.

Henry, standing before the forbidding entrance, pulled hard at the bell; somewhere within he seemed to hear a remote stiff ring. Then the gates slowly opened, and he was allowed to go into a kind of dimness, while behind him he heard the rattle of the keys and the slamming of the bolts. After that, looking about him, fixing everything with his eyes, he was conducted through a stony court in which female figures dressed in brown misfitting uniforms and hoods marched in a circle. He squeezed up steep staircases, past circular shafts of cells, where he could see captives through grated peepholes. He edged past prisoners in the corridors, silent women, with staring eyes.

Henry had never felt himself so walled in—walls within walls, galleries on galleries. The daylight had lost its color; and he lost the sense of time.

He was carefully conducted through the establishment in accordance with the arrangements he had previously made. He asked questions. But largely he looked—attentively, reflectively—scanning dark corners and ceilings. The very stones on which he walked seemed sinister. "Millbank Prison," he was to write, "is a worse act of violence than any it was erected to punish." He asked to be shown the infirmary. The chambers behind the grates seemed naked, with small stiff beds occupied by white-faced women in tight, sordid caps. He looked, as if to memorize every detail.

Then he was outside again, in the common London day. The bolts and keys made a scraping noise behind him once more. It was almost as if he were being released from prison, from all the sordid misery within its walls. He regained Bolton Street, the sight of familiar things, the usual movements and sounds of Piccadilly. In his rooms he wrote a letter to Thomas Sergeant Perry: "I have been all the morning at Millbank Prison (horrible place) collecting notes for a fiction scene. You see," he added, "I am quite the Naturalist. Look out for the same—a year hence."

THE PEACOCK AND THE BUTTERFLY

IT WAS A QUEER LITTLE EPISODE IN HENRY'S LIFE; QUEER ENOUGH for him to have kept a small relic of it—and queerer still as we look at it from this long after-time. He had sent off the first chapters of *The Princess Casamassima* from Bournemouth in June of 1885; and then had come up to London early in July to find a house for his sister and Katherine Loring. They had agreed that Bournemouth finally could be abandoned. While in London, Henry received a letter from Sargent, in Paris:

Dear James, I remember that you once said that an occasional Frenchman was not an unpleasant diversion to you in London, and I have been so bold as to give a card of introduction to you to two friends of mine. One is Dr. S[amuel] Pozzi, the man in the red gown (not always), a very brilliant creature, and the other is the unique extra-human Montesquiou of whom you may have heard Bourget speak with bitterness, but who was to Bourget to a certain extent what Whistler is to Oscar Wilde. (Take warning and do not bring them together.) They are going to spend a week in London and I fancy Montesquiou will be anxious to see as much of Rossetti's and Burne Jones's work as he can. I have given him a card to B. J., to the Comyns Carrs and to Tadema. What impression did Stevenson make on you at Bournemouth? I was very much impressed by him; he seemed to me the most intense creature I had ever met. Write me about him and Montesquiou if you have a spare moment.

This letter remained among James's papers although all the other Sargent letters were destroyed, and we can only surmise that it was perhaps James's way of reminding himself of his encounter with Dr. Pozzi, Count Robert de Montesquiou and a third whom Sargent added to his group, Prince Edmond de Polignac. James had found, after a week's search, a cottage on Hampstead Heath which he took for Alice for two months. He was about to return to Bournemouth when the "three Frenchmen," as he wrote to Miss Reubell, "bearing introductions from Sargent and yearning to see London aestheticism," arrived. Henry was perhaps not the best guide to the aesthetes, to Wilde or Whistler. But to do Sargent's introduction proper honor, he put off his departure and devoted Thursday and Friday [July 2 and 3, 1885] to entertaining them.

Our information of what happened is sparse. There was no Theodore Child present to set down a Boswellian record. Robert de Montesquiou was, by this time, well known in Paris for the eccentric and dandy who had in some measure furnished Huysmans his character of Des Esseintes in À Rebours, a novel which, in turn, was to have its effect on Oscar Wilde. A tall thin man, who described himself as looking like a greyhound in a greatcoat, he had upward-pointed and waxed mustaches, used make-up, dressed, as one who knew him said, with such perfection that the art of the tailor became invisible. "A rare flower bloomed in his buttonhole, and also in his conversation." The "Prince of Decadence" cultivated exotic perfumes and exotic colors to match the music he listened to; he called himself the "sovereign of transitory things," and his conversation and anecdotes were as artfully contrived as his manner of life. He was allied, as he claimed, to "the greater part of the European aristocracy" and endowed with sufficient wealth to take care of such an alliance. Proust was to say that he "makes a work of art of his own absurdity" and to add that he had "stylized it marvellously." Léon Daudet, whose bourgeois royalism could not understand that a deeply-dyed aristocrat should seek fame in letters, saw him as "drunk with loneliness and garrulity." The Count was some twelve years younger than Henry; and the only impression James recorded of him—for his reply to Sargent did not survive in the destruction of the painter's papers—was his remark to Miss Reubell that "Montesquiou is curious, but slight." This was accurate enough, so far as it went. Aesthetes never appealed particularly to Henry; and his Gabriel Nash of *The Tragic Muse* had in him a

vein of seriousness which Montesquiou would never have cultivated
—save in the seriousness of his self-contemplation. Dr. Pozzi,
whom James characterized as "charming," and whom he saw
later in Paris, had been an early subject for Sargent, in his red
gown; he was a society doctor, a book collector, and a generally
cultivated conversationalist. He was three years younger than
Henry. The third of the visitors, a man in his sixties, Edmond de
Polignac, was an amateur musician and a man of some personal
charm, who later made an international marriage, of the kind of
which Henry was fictional historian.

On the second of the two days which James consecrated to his
visitors, out of deference to Sargent—and probably because he was
amused—he was host at a dinner to which came James McNeill
Whistler, the Prince and the Count. Whistler and Montesquiou,
adepts at self-contemplation, beautifully charmed one another;
indeed Montesquiou was to find in Whistler mannerisms and ges-
tures which he could imitate. The Butterfly of art fluttered inevitably before such adulation. Sargent had been accurate in the
equation he had drawn of Montesquiou-Bourget and Whistler-
Wilde. The dinner ultimately resolved itself into an unspeakable
desire on the part of Montesquiou to see Whistler's celebrated
"Peacock Room" in the mansion of the shipping magnate, F. R.
Leyland. With Montesquiou it was the case of a dandy fascinated
not only by Whistler but by his choice of the very bird that expressed his dandyism; one might risk the remark that Whistler, his
painted peacocks and Montesquiou were all birds of a feather.
Indeed Montesquiou wrote a poem "The Dying Peacock," which
Proust was to quote with profound admiration in the youthful
and flattering essay he consecrated to the verse-making nobleman:

> His eyes are quenched, but not those of his plumes,
> Living, he shone, and in his death he shines.*

. . . .

* *Il rayonnait vivant, il rayonne défunt,*
  Il enseigne à mourir d'une façon sereine.

Whistler's peacock murals had an extraordinary history which may be read in the biographies of the artist. Some years before he had boldly redecorated the dining room of Leyland's elaborate house, during the owner's absence from London. Its walls had been covered with old Spanish leather brought to England long ago by Catherine of Aragon, and displaying her coat of arms— Whistler found its surface irresistible—and upon it he painted his extravagant birds in a blaze of gold and intensities of blue. Leyland had bowed before this *fait accompli*, which deprived him of his historic and ancient leather, and substituted the flights of Whistler's extravagant imagination; he had even paid Whistler for this self-indulgence.

It fell to James to make the arrangements for the visit to the room, since Whistler was occupied the next day; but the painter, on the other hand, undertook to lunch James's guests on the Sunday and to conduct them personally to the scene of his handiwork. Whistler told James where to write, and late that Friday evening James sent off his "complicated tale" to the family of the American artist George H. Boughton. In conformity with Whistler's instructions he invited Mrs. Boughton and Miss Boughton to lunch on Sunday at Whistler's. "It seems odd that *I* should be inviting Mrs. Boughton and you," he wrote to the younger of the two, "to lunch with Whistler!—especially as I shall not be there myself, as I return to the country tomorrow." And he added: "But on the whole nothing that relates to Whistler is queerer than anything else." He apologized for this "strange, irregular roundabout communication." The gist of the matter was that Whistler "has taken my Frenchmen on his back for a part of Sunday, that they hunger and thirst to behold the mystic apartment, that he begs you and Mrs. Boughton to help him to show it to them (he speaks as if you had all the facilities for it!) and also, if possible to lunch with him—and that I, to further the matter, have undertaken, to save time, to write to you. I hope I don't bewilder or bother you too much."

We have no further documentation on this episode. All we can mention, as a kind of postscript, is that Henry probably would have considered it queerer even than Whistler, if he could have been told what lay in the future—beyond his lifetime. He had spent two days with three of Proust's characters. Montesquiou, as is well known, was destined to become the Baron de Charlus in *À la recherche du temps perdu*. And Proust's biographer tells us that elements of Polignac went into the fashioning of Bergotte, and Pozzi became Cottard. It was a case of a great novelist consorting unknowingly with the real-life material of a novelist of the future.

PICTURE AND TEXT

ONCE ALICE WAS INSTALLED WITH KATHERINE LORING AT HAMPSTEAD, during the summer of 1885, Henry left London for Dover. Here he found the same breezy balconied rooms he had occupied during the previous summer at the quieter end of the Esplanade, and the same iridescence of sea and sky, with the friendly coast of France on the horizon. Dover looked pretty, with its old castle, its silver-white cliffs, the sea, cool and green, covered with vessels whose sails shimmered in the light. Henry had fallen behindhand with his long novel. He worked so industriously that by mid-August he was able to complete the third instalment. "*The Princess*," he wrote in his notebooks, "will give me hard, continuous work for many months to come; but she will also give me joys too sacred to write about."

I

In the autumn of 1885 Henry paid the first of what was to be a series of annual visits to the village of Broadway, in Worcestershire, then still relatively "undiscovered." The old sleepy village, with a name that for Henry spoke of the city of his boyhood rather than of rural England, had become the haunt of two American illustrators, Frank Millet, who had now taken up painting in oils, and Edwin A. Abbey. They shared the large Farnham House (and later the Russell House), on the single meandering mile-long village street. Alfred Parsons, an English landscapist and friend of Abbey, joined them, and on other occasions the illustrator of Dickens, Frederick Barnard. Presently Sargent had arrived, and put up at the seventeenth century inn, the Lygon Arms, halfway up the road, in the widest place, where the coaches used to turn; it was a great gabled mansion, once a stately home and now a rambling hostelry. In November of 1885 James joined the group. He was to come back the following autumn, when the weather was better; and the year after. In a later time he was to have two warm friends in Broadway, Mary Anderson, the American actress, and her husband A. F. de Navarro.

Behind Farnham House was a building called "The Priory," which the resourceful Millet had converted into a studio. Sargent had begun work, during this summer, on a picture which haunted him, children at twilight in a garden, with Chinese lanterns, to which he gave the musical title "Carnation Lily, Lily Rose." When Henry arrived, he found his "brothers of the brush" highly industrious in spite of the lateness of the season. They were painting portraits of each other's wives. They went on long hikes. They had become a tight little artistic "colony." Broadway was for Henry "the perfection of the old English rural tradition." He developed an enormous affection for the wide, long, grass-bordered vista of brownish-gray which was "thatched, latticed, mottled, mended, ivied, immemorial."

Everything seemed a "subject"—open doorways, brown interiors, old-fashioned flowers, "bushes in figures, the geese on the green, the patches, the jumbles, the glimpses, the color, the surface, the general complexion of things." Henry felt himself at a particular advantage; he could enjoy without feeling the impulse to draw, and he took excursions into the Cotswolds in a dog-cart, visiting dozens of picturesque hamlets. He liked particularly to walk to Chipping Campden, "a place of rapture especially when its wide, long, wandering, grassy yet wonderfully architectural high street is seen at the twilight hour." He liked Frank Millet and his "Yankee energy," and he became particularly fond of Ned Abbey and his wife, considering him "pure genius, with the biggest kind of Philadelphian twang and an inspired vision of all old-time English aspects and figures."

Edmund Gosse has left us a picture of Henry's second visit, in September of 1886. Although the novelist spent only four days, he dropped into the little summer colony as if he had always belonged there. Gosse's account suffers somewhat from the tone adopted by all the late reminiscence-writers, who converted the middle-aged Henry into the figure they knew best in his old age. But it evokes a sense of the particular time and the charming rustic idyll Henry was able to enjoy in these interludes away from his London life. Gosse's description of Henry conforms to the small delicate pencil drawing which Sargent did one day at Broadway, in little less than an hour, which was published originally in one of the issues of the *Yellow Book*. He described Henry's beard of "vague darkish brown matching his hair, which had not yet withdrawn from his temples, and these bushy ornaments had the effect of making him in a sense shadowy." Gosse and James did their writing upstairs in the medieval ruin, while the painters and landscapists were within shouting distance. "Not much serious work was done," Gosse said. They were all in towering high spirits; "everything was food for laughter," and there were perpetual games of tennis. He pictured Henry as "benign, indulgent, but grave, and not often unbending beyond a genial chuckle." He said that "we all treated him with some involuntary respect, though he asked for none." This strikes the modern reader as decidedly subjective; for James's correspondence with these men, all a little younger than himself, suggests a highly informal, "unbent" relationship. One suspects that the "involuntary respect" was the literary Gosse's rather than that of the painters. The rest of the picture might be noted:

His talk, which flowed best with one of us alone, was enchanting; with me largely it concerned the craft of letters. I remember little definitely, but recall how most of us, with the ladies, spent one long rollicking day in rowing down the winding Avon from Evesham to Pershore. There was much "singing in the English boat," as Marvell says, and Edwin Abbey "obliged" profusely on the banjo. Henry James I can still see sitting like a beneficent deity, a sort of bearded Buddha, at the prow, manifestly a little afraid that some of us would tumble into the river.

This comes closer to being a picture of James in 1910 than in 1886.

II

Two or three years later Henry was to do a series of prose sketches of the various Broadway artists and their works, for *Harper's New Monthly Magazine* and *Harper's Weekly*, and to embody them in a little book called *Picture and Text*. These were impressionistic biographical-critical notes on Sargent, Abbey, Millet, Parsons, Reinhart and others. With these he also set down a charming picture of Broadway itself. He greatly admired the work of the illustrators, but he was not altogether happy at having his own prose illustrated. As the picture magazines began to appear increasingly, he resented having his stories kept back in order to give the artists time to do their work. "Ah, your illustrations— your illustrations," he exclaimed to an editor of the *Century*

Magazine; "how, as a writer, one hates 'em; and how their being as good as they are makes one hate 'em more! What one writes suffers essentially, as literature, from going with them, and the two things ought to stand alone."

Illustration of prose fiction was a challenge to good prose and to style: but the illustrators could be excellent companions. The series of sketches in *Picture and Text* contained Henry's ironic assertion that in writing about the artists he had "illustrated the illustration." The book is a subtle and delicate piece of appreciation and criticism, a study of the use of the writer's eye and the artist's. The best essays in the book are those devoted to Sargent and to Daumier: and they in turn demonstrated once again Henry's ability to assert the power of language in appreciation of painters, paintings and landscape. Henry's word-pictures of Broadway are perhaps more vivid today than any of the old-fashioned sketches of its little corners left behind by the illustrators.

34 DE VERE GARDENS

HENRY HAD COMPLETED THE FOURTH INSTALMENT OF "THE PRINCESS *Casamassima* at Dover. He had then crossed to Paris, where he spent the autumn of 1885. He went to his old lodging at No. 29 in the Rue Cambon, the now renamed Rue de Luxembourg. The city was filled with a golden haze, and there was endless sunshine. Another instalment got itself written here, in the midst of continuing sociabilities. He saw most of his friends, save Daudet

who was away and ill, *atteint de la moelle épinière* (softening of
the spine), as Bourget told him. He lunched with Dr. Pozzi;
went to the theatre with Mrs. Strong; visited Etta Reubell in her
smoke-filled salon; called on Mrs. Boit and passed several pleasant
evenings with Bourget, including one when they dined at Voisin's
and then adjourned to Bourget's apartment in the Rue Monsieur. Here James met Jules Amédée Barbey d'Aurevilly, the
Norman novelist, who had once known Beau Brummel and was
a curious Cotentin provincial, turned Parisian romantic. Henry
also sat at the bedside of Mrs. Edward Lee Childe, who had been
a loyal friend during his early Parisian days. The elegant chate-
laine of Montargis was dying of tuberculosis, and Henry was impressed by her stoicism, and the dignity with which she continued
to hold her social "court," her "strange, patient, irreducible vitality." Describing her to Grace Norton, he predicted she would be
"agreeable, graceful, intelligent to the last."

October turned wet, muddy, rather prosaic for Paris, but it was
enlivened by the Bootts who arrived for their annual pilgrimage
to the capital before going to Italy. Early in November, Alice had
one of her recurrent crises and Henry was summoned by telegraph. He rushed back, very much as Miss Loring always did, only
to find his sister comparatively recovered. The episode tightened
the silver cord; it alerted Henry to the fragile—and peremptory—
character of Alice's neurasthenia. He knew he would have to continue to be "available."

I

He spent, after this, thirteen consecutive months in London, interrupted only by occasional country visits. For one thing, he
wished to see Alice regularly; he visited her daily to bring the London world into her sickroom. For another, his serial was exacting,
and he had left himself small margin—he was never more than two
or three instalments ahead of the magazine. There was however
still another reason, almost as compelling. Early in December of
1885 he had announced to his friends that he had signed a lease

for an apartment in Kensington—a twenty-one-year lease. Nothing could have sounded more "permanent." His choice of Kensington rather than St. John's Wood was a measure of the perspective he had gained in the two further years he had spent in Bolton Street. He had gravitated to St. John's Wood in 1883 out of childhood memories. Now he moved into the neighborhood consecrated by Thackeray with a sense of its fulfilling immediate needs, its agreeable "suburban" qualities and its proximity to the center of London life. A few decades before it had been distinctly a suburb, with a daily coach to Piccadilly. Henry was to characterize it in his essay on London of a year later as "the once-delightful, the Thackerayan, with its literary vestiges, its quiet pompous red palace, its square of Queen Anne, its house of Lady Castlewood, its Greyhound Tavern, where Henry Esmond lodged." Now it had many splendid houses: and for a walker of Henry's propensities the distance across Kensington Gardens, through Hyde Park to Piccadilly offered salutary exercise after his hours at his desk.

His rooms in Bolton Street had been dark and small; now he had light, space and air in his fourth floor flat in De Vere Mansions, a substantial Victorian building. A long row of western windows flooded the place with light. An enormous window, with the immensity of London spread below it, provided a place for his desk. There was a sitting room, in addition to his study, and a "grand salon" which served also as a library; there was a comfortable bedroom, a guest room, servants' quarters. All his windows offered a great deal of sky; some looked down upon gardens. The place had a lift, very much like a Parisian apartment. The house was located at the end of a wide street named for England's historic De Veres. No. 13 De Vere Mansions, or 34, De Vere Gardens, became Henry's address. He gave his publisher as his reference to a landlord who appeared never to have heard of Mr. Henry James. And he had the enjoyable experience for the first time in his life of wandering in shops, looking for old pieces of furniture and decorating his rooms to his taste. There would be no Chippendale, he assured his friends, and no treasures and spoils: he wanted large fat bourgeois sofas, solid tables and chairs: nothing original, "expectedness everywhere." For his sitting room he chose Whistlerian blues and yellows, and in his salon the "richest crimson." Although the lease was signed in December he did not move until March 6, 1886; and since he was in no hurry, some of the rooms remained empty until the furniture could be assembled. He spoke of "my chaste and secluded Kensington *quatrième*," and "my new-and-airy conducive-to-quiet-and-work apartment." A month after his installation he told William the place was "perfection." Presently he engaged a man and his wife—their name was Smith—on board-wages, for $50 a month. In the mornings Mrs. Smith, wooden-faced and always with the same shy frightened manner, would interview Henry, wearing her large clean white apron, to get her "orders of the day." Presently also he was able to have a long-wanted dog—a dachshund—upon which he bestowed the name of Tosca. She was the first of several to whom he gave a wealth of affection and who in return offered him their disinterested devotion during his working solitude.

Thus was Henry James definitely domesticated in London. He no longer needed to dine out. He could receive his friends and reciprocate hospitality. And he was sufficiently removed from the hubbub of Piccadilly to relish the great tranquillity of his neighborhood. As Henry James emerged from De Vere Mansions and turned left, he had a pleasant view of the green of Kensington Gardens at the end of the street—as he had had the view of the Green Park in Bolton Street. Near by, in all the redundant dignity of its baroque, was the Albert Memorial. And if De Vere Gardens received an eminent novelist, it was to harbor presently a famous poet as well. In the year following James's installation, Robert Browning acquired the house at No. 22, a few doors down, on the opposite side of the street. For the remainder of Browning's years, Henry had as neighbor an author who had once deeply influenced him, and whom he now regarded with a mixture of respect for his genius and surprise at his "worldliness."

During the early months of his residence in De Vere Gardens, Henry James testified to his permanent establishment in the heart of Britain by writing an essay on London, as he had written essays on Rome and Florence and Venice long before. It is perhaps the best of the series, certainly the most saturated with the "sense of place." He wrote of the city of his adoption as a frank "London-lover," and one who had walked it now for years, along Piccadilly or in Camden Town, in Kilburn, or in Lambeth. The city had for him "the most romantic town-vistas in the world," and when he stood on the bridge over the Serpentine, he found that the towers of Westminster, seen from the shining stretch of Hyde Park water, were no less impressive than those of Notre Dame rising from their island in the Seine. He expressed his affection for "dirty Bloomsbury on one side and dirtier Soho on the other," and his profound feeling for the metropolis whose grandeur he knew and whose poverty and suffering had come to be "a part of the general vibration." The essay is written in a vein of autobiography—his memories of his first visits, his perception of London at its different seasons, his knowledge of its clubs and the life of Mayfair and Belgravia. It is felt as only an outsider can feel London; and he was to cherish a dream of writing some day a large, impressionistic book about the city, but only scattered notes for this survive. As he had written his essay on "Venice" when he had emotionally taken possession of it, so his "London" followed *The Princess Casamassima* and his establishment in his own apartment. It was his way of saying that he had at last taken root in the particular spot which, for him at least, communicated "the greatest sense of life."

II

Alice, living in Bolton Row, was having the best and most animated winter of her residence in England. She had moved into small furnished lodgings with Katherine after vacating the house on the Heath. And when her companion left her for a while, she seemed quite reconciled to have Henry serve as a substitute. She

had also at all times a nurse-companion. Her guests were not
numerous. Sometimes Mr. Lowell, when he was in London;
Fenimore appears to have been welcomed; Mrs. Kemble, with the
infirmities of her age, came when she could, and sent flowers
when she couldn't; Mrs. Humphry Ward, Emma Wilkinson
Pertz, Mrs. Mason, Mrs. John Richard Green, widow of the historian Alice had once admired, were among the others. We have
few comments on her callers from Alice, save a remark in one letter to a friend that the "crude and unadulterated American product, Mrs. Mason, comes in very often. She is a very curious study
with much that is generous and fine in the midst of her undisci-
plined crudity." Mrs. Mason belonged to an older and perhaps
more plain-spoken generation. She always succeeded in irritating
Mr. Hoppin at the Legation. But Alice's sharpness was characteristic: and people and events were scrutinized mercilessly from the
world of her sickroom. "My sister is doing exceedingly well and
keeping an American salon," Henry told Godkin. "That is, she lies
on her sofa, and the earnest and the frivolous alike crowd to converse with her. She is much better, and if she should get better yet,
and remain here, she would become a great social success, beating
the British female all round." Alice startled Henry, he said, "by the
breadth of her *aperçus* and her intimate knowledge of English
public affairs." She was absorbed above all in the Irish question;
it provided a generous outlet for her bile and diminished somewhat her excessive invalidical self-absorption; it enabled her also
to express the essential Irishness of her nature and her chronic
hostility toward the English.

By spring Alice had decided she would spend the summer in
Leamington, where an excellent lodging was available; it would be
less expensive than London and she would see how she could
manage with regular visits from Miss Loring. In the autumn she
would return to the city. The move was made at the end of May;
and although Alice suffered her usual fatigue and shock from the
journey, she recuperated rapidly. Miss Loring escorted her to her
new quarters and spent a month with her. Alice seemed quite

content, and urged Henry not to take the long trip to pay visits to her—he was indeed to pay her only one visit during that summer. In early July he dispatched his last instalment of *The Princess*: the novel had again spilled over into additional chapters. Henry offered them to the *Atlantic* without pay, since the miscalculation was his; but Aldrich insisted on giving him the usual rate.

With Alice away and "the interminable work" done, Henry was free to take a holiday. He decided however to remain in London. Since he was setting up house, "for once in a lifetime," he had incurred a great many expenses. "The furnishing and arranging of my place has partly amused and partly exasperated and altogether beggared me," he wrote to Grace Norton. It was economical to remain in town. There was plenty of "high air" for the hot days, and as his rooms gradually acquired their furnishings he was pleased to enjoy the quiet and the luxury of being in his own home. By way of a holiday after his two years of work on *The Bostonians* and *The Princess*, he paid a number of country visits, including one to Osterley Park, the home of Lord and Lady Jersey, which was an hour's drive from Piccadilly. This he found extremely pleasant. Lowell, who had returned to England for the summer, was a fellow-guest. He renewed his old impression of him. "His whole relation to life and the world appears to me infantine—and infantine his judgement, his kind of observation." He thus described him to Grace Norton. "However, he is extremely pleasant (when he doesn't publicly correct people's grammar, pronunciation, pretensions to lineage—as compared with his own—and many other things!) and very contented and happy, apparently, as well as infinitely invited and caressed, as before." Lowell seemed to have all the social advantages of his former position and none of its responsibilities. In midsummer, old Oliver Wendell Holmes arrived and London lionized him. He struck Henry, who encountered him everywhere, as "rather superannuated and extinct (though he flickers up at moments) and is moreover dazed and bewildered" by all the fuss made over him.

Henry's London summer was sufficiently strenuous. "I rush off to Bournemouth for 36 hours to see a poor sick friend—and probably go also to spend a day with Alice at Leamington," he writes to Grace Norton. "All this while I am supposed to be looking after Mrs. Jack Gardner, Mrs. Bronson, the Daniel Curtises and about 30 other Americans now in London, who all are holding by my coat-tails; to say nothing of polishing my periods for the purchase of my contemporaries and the admiration of posterity. So you see I am pretty well engaged."

His Venetian friends had gathered in London at this moment because of an outbreak of cholera in their water-city. Mrs. Bronson, indeed, had installed herself in Hans Place with her big brown gondoliers and her other servants and was living just as if life opposite the Salute had not been interrupted. Henry was a far from unwilling caller during that autumn of 1886. He went often to see her and her daughter, and almost a decade later he could write to his hostess, "I look at your little corner of Hans Place—where the house has vanished—and recall sentimentally those good months you spent there in the quiet summer time with your Venetian suite and your Italian dinners. How I used to eat them!"

The trans-Atlantic visitors settled, for him, the question of whether he was losing anything in his knowledge of Americans by living abroad. "I lose nothing at all," he wrote, "for London is fast becoming an American city—and our national character is vivid and familiar there, in every sort of example and in higher relief and saliency than it is at home. It is quite as good as the English, and more amusing."

He complained to William that his two major novels of the past two years had exhausted him. But to Francis Boott he was complaining at the same time that his visitors kept him from his work. After six weeks of this kind of life—during which he read proof of the book form of *The Princess Casamassima*—he told his brother he felt quite refreshed. "Now I am not tired of work, but of no work, and am again taking up my pen." He planned to write a number of critical articles as well as short stories. And he felt that by early winter he might, if all went well with Alice, go to Italy. Expensive though his furnishings were, he received that autumn from Macmillan a £550 advance for the English and American book rights to *The Princess*, and this meant that with serialization, the work yielded him more than $7,000. With the writing he was committed to do, he would be able to take his longed-for holiday without difficulty. His newest problem was what to do with his flat during his absence; and how to keep his domestics from becoming utterly demoralized by idleness. He was to discover a solution for this also, in due time.

CLOVER

DURING CHRISTMAS WEEK OF 1885, HENRY HAD LEARNED THAT HIS "Voltaire in petticoats" was dead—the sharp-tongued and witty Marian Hooper Adams, whom he had known for so long, and in so many places: in Newport, or at Shady Hill, in Rome, in Paris, during the Adamses' winter in Birdcage Walk in London, and finally in Washington. He imparted the news to Fenimore, who was living in Leamington and working on a novel. The nature of Clover's death was to be a long and well-kept secret. She had been depressed ever since her father's death less than a year before; and she had swallowed some of the chemicals she used in her photography, knowing full well how speedily they would do their work. Henry Adams was absent from the house for a brief walk. When he returned all was over. Clover's acute and morbid animus toward much of life had in the end been turned against herself.

"I suppose you have heard the sad rumours (which appear founded) as to poor Clover Adams's self-destruction," Henry wrote to Lizzie Boott, who had known Clover almost as long as Henry. "I'm afraid the event had everything that could make it bitter to poor Henry [Adams]. She succumbed to hereditary melancholia. What an end to that intensely lively Washington *salon.*"

Clover Adams had at last silenced herself. She was linked with many of the novelist's old associations: his long-dead cousin, Minny Temple; the springtime in Rome, when he had dined at the Adamses' with Elena Lowe; and not least with the life in Washington which Henry had so much relished and depicted with eyes of amusement in "Pandora." If the novelist wrote at this moment to the stricken Adams, his letter has not survived; and for good reason—for the historian destroyed all the papers of this time, including apparently all of Henry James's letters to Clover. Thus we do not possess the moving tribute of the sort the novelist invariably wrote, making his condolences into a muted epistolary elegy. We can obtain a sense of what it might have been, however, from a few remarks in a letter to Godkin some weeks later:

"I thought of you," wrote Henry, "and how you would be touched with the sad story, when poor Mrs. Adams found, the other day, the solution of the knottiness of existence. I am more sorry for poor Henry than I can say—too sorry, almost, to think of him."

Adams was to live under the shadow of this moment for the rest of his life. He never remarried, and he endured into a strange, creative and cynical old age. Clover was buried in Rock Creek Cemetery, then a quiet churchyard in Washington, and Adams placed over her grave a granite figure by Augustus Saint-Gaudens, chaste and draped, as of perpetual sorrow. No language was added to the monument: and here, in the fullness of time, he himself joined the long-absent Clover. In a little tale, "The Modern Warning," written a year after her death, Henry James may have incorporated the suicide scene as he re-imagined it—his heroine taking poison while her husband and brother, to whom she is as attached as Clover was to her father—are out of the house. The lady in the story, however, is not modelled on Clover. She is milder, gentler, less incisive. But the tale itself, with its sharp words between Americans and English—its dialogue between the civilizations of the Old and New World—contains echoes of talk of Henry James with Mrs. Adams.

POLITICS AND THE BOUDOIR

I

"WE ARE UP TO OUR NECKS IN THE IRISH QUESTION," HENRY WROTE to Grace Norton. "The air is positively putrid with politics." And he might have added, although he would have found more elegant words, that it reeked also of the boudoir and of sex. There were three changes of government while *The Princess Casamassima* was being serialized. Parnell was at the height of his fame, exercising his balance of power in the House of Commons with great adroitness. Gladstone had become for Henry a "dreary incubus" mouthing platitudes; and in the midst of this—with a seeming irrelevancy—Sir Charles Dilke, that monument of respectability, who had ardently wooed the middle class and been spoken of as a possible successor to Gladstone, was accused in a divorce case of having committed adultery. Mrs. Donald Crawford, a rather infantile and reckless society belle, had pointed to him as "the man who ruined me."

"England is interesting at present—because it is heaving so, and cracking and fermenting. But the fissures are mainly political and the exhalations often foul," Henry told Miss Norton. After Dilke there was to be the story of Parnell's relationship with Kitty O'Shea, and still later another imbroglio, the case of Oscar Wilde —who happened also to be Irish—and his friend Lord Alfred Douglas. (Henry was to follow the Parnell case with intense interest and he was to attend the trial, in 1889, and to use words such as "thrilling" and "throbbing" to describe it.) Before the 1880's were over there had been also Lady Colin Campbell's divorce suit with the naming of "half a dozen" co-respondents. If the political mores of the Victorians fascinated Henry, he responded even more to the unmasking of the sexual mores: it gave him a little more freedom in his tales. He could say now more casually that Victorian ladies were not always virtuous, and that Victorian gentlemen sometimes behaved like cads.

Dilke had befriended Henry during his early days in London. His account of the scandal to Grace Norton throws a peripheral light on the mysterious case which seemed to be a mixture of flagrant indiscretions by the respected Dilke and perhaps, as his latest biographer believes, a conspiracy to ruin him politically. James told Miss Norton that the scandal was "no very edifying chapter of social history" but that it had a certain "low interest" for him since he had the "sorry privilege" of being acquainted with most of the people who were nearly and remotely involved. After reporting the allegations made by Donald Crawford, he described how Mrs. Mark Pattison (as if to place the cachet of respectability on Dilke) had announced to the press while travelling in India that she was engaged to him and was rushing home to marry him.

Meanwhile another London lady whom I won't name, with whom for years his relations have been concomitant with his relations with Mrs. Pattison, and whose husband died, has had every expectation that he was on the point of marrying *her*. This is a very brief sketch of the situation, which is queer and dramatic and disagreeable. Dilke's private life won't (I imagine) bear looking into, and the vengeful Crawford will do his best to lay it bare. He will probably not succeed, and Dilke's political reputation, with the great "middle class," will weather the storm. But he will have been frightened almost to death. For a man who has had such a passion for keeping up appearances and appealing to the said middle class, he has, in reality, been strangely, incredibly reckless. His long, double liaison with Mrs. Pattison and the other lady, of a nature to make it a duty of honour to marry *both* (!!) when they should become free, and the death of each husband at the same time—with the public watching to see *which* he *would* marry—and he meanwhile "going on" with poor little Mrs. Crawford, who is a kind of infant—the whole thing is a theme for the novelist—or at least for *a* novelist.

The lady James did not name to Grace Norton was named soon enough when the case came to court. She was Henry's old friend Christina Rogerson, daughter of Mrs. Duncan Stewart, at whose home he had had many pleasant lunches and dinners and met certain members of London society. Henry was wrong in his predictions. Dilke was crushed by the case and never recovered from it. There was a distinct doubt whether his liaison with Mrs. Crawford had occurred; but he had certainly, for a man in public life, left himself sufficiently exposed: and it is questionable whether, given his capacity for making public errors, he would ever have been a truly important leader. Henry had long ago characterized him as more fortunate in birth and position than in talent. "Not a grain of genius or inspiration" had been his verdict a decade earlier.

II

When it came to the Irish question, Henry did not share Alice's belligerency on behalf of her ancestors. He found politics tricky and brutal, and the "oceans of talk that are required, more and more for the smallest work of government, make one long at moments for some fine dumb despot." He disliked the turn taken by the Gladstonian liberals. The Tories were simply "stupid." As for Ireland, it was a country "revelling in odious forms of irresponsibility and license." When Miss Norton wrote to say she thought the Irish a "great people," Henry retorted: "I see no greatness, nor any kind of superiority in them, and they seem to me an inferior and third rate race, whose virtues are of the cheapest and commonest and shallowest order, while their vices are peculiarly cowardly and ferocious. They have been abominably treated in the past—but their wrongs appear to me, in our time, to have occupied the conscience of England only too much to the exclusion of other things. Don't think me brutal, dear Grace, or anglicized, which is the same thing." Earlier, however, he had written to his friend Perry: "If I had nothing else to do I think I should run over to Ireland: which may seem strange to you on the part of one satiated in his youth with the Celtic genius. The reason is that I should like to see a country in a state of revolution."

The closest he had come to seeing a revolutionary setting had been that day, long ago, in Paris when he visited the barricades and relics of the Commune. But one day in February of 1886 —before he had moved to De Vere Gardens—he returned in the evening from Bournemouth, where he had gone to pay a visit to Stevenson, and found Piccadilly littered with broken glass and the mansions at the corner of Bolton Street boarded up. He was made acutely aware of the truths he had been writing about in his novel. It had been a day of noisy rioting in the heart of London by the very unemployed for whom he was speaking in *The Princess*. This was not revolution; it was however still another great fissure in the decorous life of the English. Henry wrote to William that he deeply regretted his absence: "I should have seen it from my balcony." Windows had been smashed just three doors away. But Fenimore, then in London, had been abroad in the streets, and could supply an eyewitness account. Armed with her

American innocence, and her deafness, she had wandered into Piccadilly from lodgings in Seymour Street, passing along Clarges Street: she heard distant noises and saw a mob hurry along the edge of the Green Park in the direction of Hyde Park Corner. There were always processions of one kind or another in London, she thought. As she turned into Piccadilly there were still groups of men, eight or ten in a group, clearly of the laboring class, moving about in a certain mood of "larkiness." Then it began to dawn on her that she was the only woman in sight and that traffic was at a standstill. Further along she encountered broken glass and smashed shop fronts. Entering a picture-framing establishment liberally sprinkled with broken glass she politely inquired what had happened. "A mob, madame, a mob," the proprietor said. Fenimore cautiously picked up a lonely cab in a side street and had the driver take her home by a circuitous route. She had been relatively lucky. She learned later that ladies in carriages had been kissed or slapped and roughly handled. Some had their purses snatched. During the next couple of days a dark fog settled over the city, as if to blot out the general aspect of destruction. Describing the scenes to William, Henry told him there was "immense destitution" everywhere. "Everyone here is growing poorer—from causes which I fear will continue." Nevertheless he felt that the usually orderly British populace had shot its bolt and would not riot again in the near future. The episode had sufficiently illustrated, nevertheless, the "topical" character of his new novel.

A LION IN THE PATH

DURING THE PREVIOUS SUMMER HENRY'S FRENCH VISITORS HAD IN-
cluded the aesthetic Montesquiou. This summer, during August,
when London was empty and Henry was enjoying a sense of relief
after the completion of his novel, there appeared on his horizon
the formidable figure of Guy de Maupassant. He was to speak of
him as "a lion in the path" and to say in a memorable passage
that "those who have really taken the measure of the animal"
would not make light of him. Henry took the personal measure
of Maupassant during their few encounters that summer—it was
Maupassant's only visit to England—and wrote one of his most
brilliant essays on him little more than a year later.

I

He had been taking his literary measure ever since Maupassant
had begun to publish his tales. He remembered Flaubert's young
disciple, present always at the Sundays in the Faubourg St. Ho-
noré: a sturdy young man of middle height, with a low forehead,
bushy brown hair combed back, a big brown mustache and much
talk of boating, swimming, Sundays on the Seine—and the conquest of women. Henry's interest in Maupassant was such that he
possessed himself of his books with great promptness. Henry's copy
of *Une Vie* is signed and dated in his hand "Boston, June 19,
1883"; *Contes de la Bécasse* is similarly inscribed "Boston, August
1883." There are other volumes—*Miss Harriet, La Vie errante,
Bel-Ami, Yvette*—all showing signs of having been carefully read.
One or two descriptive passages are marked.

Maupassant, when he had left Paris, was apparently not certain
that James remembered him; he came armed with a letter of introduction from Paul Bourget. "I have told him," Bourget wrote,
"that you were the only man in London with whom it is possible
to talk as with the Gallo-Romans." But it is doubtful whether the

younger man, ten years after Flaubert's Sundays, and at the height
of his fame, was as interested in literary talk as Bourget. He
wanted to be shown English things: he wanted above all to meet
English women. Henry was hardly the best guide for the kind of
encounters Maupassant was seeking. There is an anecdote, attributed to Oscar Wilde, which, even if embellished, must contain
a certain grain of truth. Maupassant, dining in a restaurant with
James, pointed to a woman sitting at a table and asked Henry
to "go over and get her for me." Henry carefully explained that
in England there was the matter of being properly introduced.
Maupassant tried again. Pointing to another woman he said:
"Surely you know her at least? Ah, if I only spoke English!" When
James had refused, with full explanation, for about the fifth time,
Maupassant was said to have remarked irritably: "Really, you
don't seem to know anyone in London."

The anecdote was characteristic. Maupassant's letters to Count
Joseph Primoli—who was his companion on this trip—suggest that
the lion was a relentless woman-stalker. "Monday we will have
several agreeable ladies, it would seem—plus Henry James," he remarks in one missive. And in another from Waddesdon, where he
was visiting Ferdinand de Rothschild, Maupassant writes: "What
a pleasure, my dear friend, to know you are in London, where I
will be on Tuesday. I hope you'll be there on the 11th. I would
like to present you that evening to a charming woman, at whose
home you will find Bret Harte, the American writer, and also, I
think, Henry James."

The woman was probably Blanche Roosevelt. Indeed it might
be said that three figures converged on Henry James during this
episode: Maupassant, Primoli and Blanche. A handsome woman,
with blue eyes and masses of red-gold hair, she had been a hunter
of literary lions from the days when, at seventeen, she had been
told by Victor Hugo that she expressed "the beauty and genius
of the new world." In America she had visited Longfellow and
made copy out of it for the magazines; in France she had visited
Maupassant and made discreet copy out of her indiscretions with

him. And now in London she would have liked apparently to
annex Henry James. He might indeed have invented her; she was
a less conformist and more literary Mrs. Headway, prepared to
besiege any handsome male—if he were a writer—and James met
both requirements. Born in Sandusky, Ohio, raised at La Crosse,
Wisconsin, she had come to Europe to cultivate her voice—it was
to her voice, probably, that Hugo had applied the word "genius."
After studying with Pauline Viardot, she had made her debut at
Covent Garden. Her vocal power was judged insufficient however for grand opera. She had sung Violetta in *La Traviata*, a role
more suited to her personality than to her voice—save for its
renunciatory aspect. Her full name now was Blanche Roosevelt
Tucker Macchetta, Marchesa d'Alligri. We find Henry writing to
Francis Boott, during Maupassant's stay in London: "I have but
just escaped from the jaws of Blanche Roosevelt, who used to
sing in opera—didn't she?—and who is now here married to a
Milanese, trying to be literary and assaulting me (with compliments) on my productions."

Primoli was hardly another Montesquiou. In comparison with
the latter's affiliation with old European aristocracy, he was distinctly *parvenu*. The most that Count Joseph could boast was a
direct descent from two of Napoleon's brothers: his grandparents
had been cousins, the children of King Joseph Bonaparte of Spain
and Lucien Bonaparte, who bore the Papal title of Prince of
Canino. His great-aunt was the Princess Mathilde, whose salon
figures prominently in the Goncourt journals and the correspondence of Flaubert. If Primoli did not move among high French
nobility he had status in the highest French literary circles. "An
odd little member of the Bonaparte family," Henry called him.
He was to meet him on sundry occasions in Paris and Rome and
to visit him in his palace by the Tiber.

11

Whatever Maupassant's wishes in the matter of women, Henry
felt distinctly that the proper literary honors should be paid to a

distinguished master of the short story, and after exchanging a series of notes, the French writer agreed to dine with the American novelist on August 12. Normally Henry would have entertained him at the Reform or the Athenaeum; but the clubs were closed at midsummer. He remembered however that a sufficiently good meal could be obtained at Greenwich, and this was always a charming relief in the monotony of a London August. He invited George du Maurier and Edmund Gosse, and Maupassant brought Primoli. The party convened at 5:15 at Westminster Bridge and boarded one of the small grimy six-penny steamers that plied the Thames. Maupassant was thus given a view of the great English river; for so enthusiastic a river-man this provided a certain picture —gave him a sense of the different civilization on this side of the Channel. The scenery was hardly that of the Seine countryside; there were largely the backs and fronts of the expressionless warehouses, black barges, far-stretching docks and basins and a dark wilderness of masts. But once they came into sight of the Observatory, with its two modest little brick towers, they got a sense of the general English charm of the place.

It is not recorded where they dined. James had described the endless forms of fish available in the Greenwich restaurants and hotels in one of his London sketches, and had recommended a stroll first in the park, on the summit of which the famous Observatory is located, "to get up an appetite." Again, no Theodore Child was present to record the talk. But a letter written by James to Gosse twenty-eight years later throws a brief backward light. "Have you any recollection of once going down the River to dine with me at Greenwich long years ago?—in company with Maupassant, du Maurier, and one or two others. One of those others was Primoli, who had come over from Paris with Maupassant; and on whom you made, you see, the ineffaceable impression. He wrote to me the other day to ask your address—it has lasted all these years—and you meanwhile—*infidèle*—! I have seen him since then from time to time; he is a very amiable and rather singular person. He made on dear du Maurier, I remember, an impres-

sion that remained—though not on your sterner nature! He is a
Bonaparte (exceedingly so in looks); that is his mother was a
Bonaparte Princess."

We are left with the impression that Primoli charmed du
Maurier, and Gosse charmed Primoli. James in all probability
concentrated on his principal guest. And his verdict on the man
—seen through his work—published in the *Fortnightly Review* in
1888, remains the classic essay in English on Maupassant. It
shows the extent to which James was fascinated by the variety of
Maupassant's subjects and the extreme brevity with which he
was able to relate them. Henry wished very much to emulate this
aspect of him. As for the substance of his stories, his admiration
was qualified by their excessive adherence to the life of the senses
—including their eroticism—and their failure to take into account
sufficiently the reflective nature of man. Maupassant went in his
tales to the strongest ingredients and to these alone. He was an
active and independent observer of the human scene, quite un-
ashamed of any of his faculties; but his emphasis on sex, James
argued, was exaggerated, or as he put it, " the impression of the
human spectacle for him who takes it as it comes has less analogy
with that of the monkeys' cage than this admirable writer's account of it."

James wrote plainly as a psychologist: he seized upon a remark by Maupassant that "psychology should be hidden in a
book, as it is hidden in reality under the facts of existence." And
with unerring accuracy James replied that the very facts constituted the revelation. From whom were they hidden? he asked.

From some people, no doubt, but very much less from others; and
all depends upon the observer, the nature of one's observations,
and one's curiosity. For some people motives, reasons, relations,
explanations, are a part of the very surface of the drama, with the
footlights beating full upon them. For me an act, an incident, an
attitude, may be a sharp, detached, isolated thing, of which I give
a full account in saying that in such and such a way it came off.
For you it may be hung about with implications, with relations and

conditions as necessary to help you to recognize it as the clothes of your friends are to help you know them in the street. You feel that they would seem strange to you without petticoats and trousers.

James concluded that "the carnal side of man appears the most characteristic if you look at it a great deal; and you look at it a great deal if you do not look at the other, at the side by which he reacts against his weaknesses, his defeats."

For all this, Henry argued that a healthy art had "an indefeasible mistrust of rigid prohibitions." And the lesson of Maupassant for him was one which was not so much influence as example. There are passages in Henry's notebooks which testify to this. On occasions when he wishes to tell a tale in a small compass, with a few bold strokes, we find him exclaiming to himself "Oh spirit of Maupassant, come to my aid," "À la Maupassant must be my constant motto"; or he will say, "Something as admirably compact and selected as Maupassant," or "practicable on the rigid Maupassant system." This was what Maupassant left with him beyond his shrewd notation of life. When James entertained Maupassant in London, the French writer had already shown certain signs of the effects of the syphilis which killed him seven years later. "The Frenchmen are passing away—Maupassant dying of locomotor paralysis, the fruit of fabulous habits, I am told," Henry wrote to Stevenson in 1893. "*Je n'en sais rien;* but I shall miss him." And when a friend wrote him of Maupassant's end, he thanked him for "the touching two words you had the friendly thought of sending me when the indignity that life had heaped upon poor Maupassant found itself stayed." He added: "My tears had already been wept; even though the image of that history had been too *hard* for such droppings."

In the Maupassant essay Henry introduced a parenthetical remark. He had been speaking of the "unpleasant" side of Maupassant's tales and his "pessimism" and pointed to the tendency of much of English fiction to gloss over reality. "Does not Mr. Rider Haggard make even his African carnage pleasant?" Henry remarked. The allusion belonged to the time of Maupassant's visit to London. That week Henry had been reading Haggard's best-selling tales with a sense of horror and had indited a letter to Stevenson on the subject. He had finished *King Solomon's Mines* and read half of *She*. The fact that *She* was in its fortieth thousand moved him "to holy indignation." He felt that "it isn't nice that anything so vulgarly brutal should be the thing that succeeds most with the English of today." He was struck with the "beastly *bloodiness*" of Haggard's books.

Such perpetual killing and such perpetual ugliness! It is worth while to write a tale of fantastic adventure, with a funny man etc. and pitched all in the slangiest key, to kill 20,000 men, as in *Solomon*, in order to help your heroes on! In *She* the Narrator himself shoots through the back (I think) his faithful servant Mohammed, to prevent his being boiled alive, and describes how he leaped into the air "like a buck," on receiving the shot. They seem to me works in which our race and our age make a very vile figure—and they have unexpectedly depressed me.

Thus in his Maupassant essay James spoke with great clarity of both sex and violence in fiction—not as one who wished to close his eyes upon them, but as one who felt that in the civilization in which the artist worked, it was possible to penetrate deeply into human experience without necessarily stressing the physical or carnal (as in Maupassant) or glorifying the fantastic-violent (as in Haggard). For Maupassant the artist, Henry kept always a tender place in his memory.

THE DIVIDED SELF

IN "THE PRINCESS CASAMASSIMA," WHICH WAS PUBLISHED IN BOOK form on October 22, 1886, Henry James wrote a large and humane work, melting certain of his characteristic themes into a subject unique in the canon of his writings—a "naturalist" subject —the plight of the London working class and its nascent revolutionary impulse. The image of the depressed side of London had been with him ever since his childhood reading of Dickens. There were, however, more recent and actual memories: an old woman "lying prone in a puddle of whiskey," for instance. His theme had been implicit, moreover, in his long-ago remark that the English upper classes were too refined and the lower classes too miserable. His view of English poverty was largely from the "outside"; nonetheless it was the view of a profoundly sentient being and an artist. James subtly meets the possible criticism that he was writing of conditions "observed" outside his immediate experience. His hero is "conscious that the people were miserable—more conscious, it often seemed to him, than they themselves were." James knew that poverty could brutalize the suffering into an insensibility to their lot.

I

The novel was conceived in spacious terms and it ran to fourteen instalments. Within it James drew his pictures of the miseries and splendors of London, the fruit of long nocturnal walks in the city's streets, and of hours spent in pubs and probably at workers' meetings, in the manner of Zola. He had remembered how Zola had described at Flaubert's his notation of verbal obscenities written down in the Paris slums. Henry James had followed his example—the "rich principle of the Note"—and we find him recording "Phrases of the People." They seem well-worn now, although they doubtless were novel then: "That takes the gilt off, you know," he noted, or the remark of a worker talking about his boss, "he cuts it very fine"; or " ''ere today, somewhere else tomorrow,' that's 'is motto." When he wrote the novel, he left out such words as "bloody" and edited "hell" to "h—." The language of the later revised edition could be a little easier. He re-inserted the words he had censored in the Victorian period. Saturated with "high life," thoroughly documented in his observation and recording of the "low," he achieved in *The Princess* what he had failed to do in *The Bostonians*—a mastery over his materials and a dense and rich texture of impression. That the work should have had no appeal to its contemporary audience is understandable, although this baffled James at the time. He believed he had found an original theme, and one that was decidedly "topical." He had fancied that its novelty and its treatment would impress the critics and the public. The work conveyed, however, all too successfully the uneasiness above and below the surface of Victorian London; it came uncomfortably close to the recent riots, the bombs, the dynamiters. And the Victorians tended to look to fiction for comfort and amusement, not for the anxieties of their daily lives. In America the novel fared somewhat better. Nevertheless it was too marked a departure from the tales of international marriages and the adventures of American girls abroad. And then James had committed the grievous error of thinking that an English version of the novels being written on the Continental side of the Channel —with due allowance for the Anglo-Saxon attitude towards sex— would be acceptable. *The Princess Casamassima* was a remote counterpart to *Germinal*, a work about the "class war" published in 1885—before the working class itself understood what the nature of such a war might be.

Most of *The Princess* takes place on Sundays, or in the evenings. Some English reviewers expressed bewilderment at this; it did not occur to them that Henry was describing the impoverished Londoners during their abbreviated hours of leisure rather than at their daily tasks. The settings are dark and drab, save for those Sunday hours which are spent in the parks and the streets, and

the pages of contrast when the working-class hero is invited to the
country house of the Princess. There is an artful chiaroscuro in
the book, a large impressionism. Yet reality is never blurred. As
long ago as in his first year of residence in the British capital
Henry had described in one of his articles the funeral of an English radical agitator and the crowd that followed the hearse: "It
was the London rabble, the metropolitan mob, men and women,
boys and girls, the decent poor and the indecent, who had scram-
bled into the ranks as they gathered them up on their passage."
Henry saw them from the front of a hansom, in which he was
comfortably riding. As he looked from the soft side of existence,
he "seemed to be having a sort of panoramic view of the under
side, the wrong side, of the London world." The "wrong" side—
and also the "wronged" side. There were "strange, pale, mouldy
paupers, who blinked and stumbled in the Piccadilly sunshine";
the beggars' opera scene had remained with him, merging into
other observed scenes of London's grimy, sooty, gin-soaked under-
privileged life.

This was the world James chose to deal with in *The Princess
Casamassima* and to link with themes of the life of ease about
which he had written in his earlier romantic works. At his elbow
stood Balzac, Dickens, Turgenev, Zola—he drew upon them all,
as writers of imagination draw upon their predecessors and upon
the traditions of their form; more important, he drew upon his
constituted imagination. Many years later, when he wished to
describe the origin of this novel, he presented it in terms of his
experience of London. He had conceived of a hero, he said,
"watching the same innumerable appearances I had watched,"
and "watching very much as I had watched." The little bookbinder, Hyacinth Robinson, possesses Henry's visual sense—it
colors his whole mind. London doors had swung hospitably open
for Henry James; for Hyacinth, these doors—save in one instance
—remain tightly closed. Hyacinth has a conflict between "the
world of his work-a-day life and the world of his divination and
envy." In a word, he is an "outsider" and an "observant stranger";

but he looks on from the slums, not from the comparative comfort of Bolton Street.

I I

James made him a craftsman, a bookbinder with an urge to be a writer. He is handicapped by his origins and his poverty. He has read much, felt much; he is "a youth on whom nothing was lost," James wrote, echoing his prescription for young novelists from "The Art of Fiction." He is what someone like Henry James might have been, had he grown up without the novelist's advantages of education and travel, and the opportunity to exercise his talent. James tells us that Hyacinth has the soul of "a genuine artist." He is, in effect, another version of the artist *manqué* James had depicted ten years before in the pages of the *Atlantic*, the ill-formed young sculptor from Northampton, Massachusetts, Roderick Hudson. And the link with this early novel is established directly by the Princess Casamassima. Omnipresent and as alluring as ever, for all her world-weariness, she is the once mysterious and once unfathomable—and still capricious—Christina Light, some ten years after the death of Roderick. As she had crossed the path of the sculptor in the late 1860's in Rome, so now in the early 1880's in London she pulls the little bookbinder into her flashing orbit. Christina has shed her mystery; she is now a characteristic Jamesian beauty, a woman of the world with a "Queen complex," bent on exercising her power over her environment and over men particularly. Hyacinth's mistake (it was also Roderick's) is to care too much for her; she is interested more in men who show indifference to her—they are a greater challenge to her need for conquest.

Hyacinth and Roderick were evolved from the same imaginative sources and their conflicts are similar. Hyacinth, for all his upbringing in the slums, has as much of a New England sense of duty as his predecessor. Roderick had been unable to reconcile his devotion to his art and his passion for Christina. Hyacinth feels an overriding responsibility to his class. But he aspires also to the world of ease, in which he has met the beautiful Princess. Like Roderick, he cannot bring together his two worlds. Their common ancestor is the volatile Benvolio, of Henry's New York scribbling days. Benvolio had his Countess on the one hand and a puritan maiden Scholastica on the other, and swung constantly from the grandeur of one to the sobriety of the other. Roderick and Hyacinth are similarly divided. The flame of passion in each consumes the flame of duty.

Hyacinth, however, unlike Roderick, is endowed with an elaborate and overpowering heredity, after the manner of Zola. He is the illegitimate son of an English peer and a French seamstress who had turned on her seducer and murdered him. "There was no peace for him between the two currents that flowed in his nature, the blood of his passionate, plebeian mother and that of his long-descended, supercivilized sire." He impulsively allies himself with revolutionary elements; he also finds himself "adopted" by the fine world of the Princess Christina, who is using revolution as a retreat from ennui. In her country house the little bookbinder from the slums indulges in all the luxuries of feeling James himself well knew from his visits to the great houses of England. The hyacinthine youth however has committed himself to the extremes of revolution: he has promised to obey the shadowy but powerful Diedrich Hoffendahl, master-mind of terrorism. And the moment comes when he receives a pistol and is ordered to assassinate a Duke.

Between the time of his impulsive adherence to his cause, and the arrival of the weapon, he has discovered that he has no sympathy with the revolutionaries. The metamorphosis had occurred when he inherited a little hoard of savings from the dressmaker who had brought him up. He had used this money to visit Paris and wander in its great squares and boulevards with the recollection that his mother's father had died on Parisian barricades. What he experienced, however, was not the triumph of revolution

but the *gloire* of history. Later he had an equally profound experience in Venice. In these cities of struggle and bloodshed,
Hyacinth the aristocrat rejects Hyacinth the revolutionary.

"What was supreme in his mind today was not the idea of how
the society that surrounded him should be destroyed; it was, much
more, the sense of the wonderful, precious things it had produced,
of the brilliant, impressive fabric it had raised." * These had been
Henry's reflections long ago in the Campagna. From Venice
Hyacinth can only write to the Princess that he has been struck
by "the splendid accumulations of the happier few, to which,
doubtless, the miserable many have also in their degree contributed." The Shakespearean—and Stendhalian—phrase, "the happy
few," is apropos. It is used once again near the end of the book,
in the passage in which Hyacinth thinks how a sentient individual
feels the sufferings of the oppressed more than the oppressed
themselves. "In these hours the poverty and ignorance of the
multitude seemed so vast and preponderant, and so much the
law of life, that those who had managed to escape from the black
gulf were only the happy few, people of resource as well as children of luck: they inspired in some degree the interest and sympathy that one should feel for survivors and victors, those who have
come safely out of a shipwreck or a battle." Hyacinth comes to see
life as "less impracticable and more tolerable" † thanks to "the
monuments and treasures of art, the great palaces and properties,
the conquests of learning and taste, the general fabric of civilization
as we know it, based, if you will, upon all the despotisms, the cruelties, the exclusions, the monopolies and the rapacities of the past."
The conclusion of this eloquent letter could have been an answer
to William Morris, whose socialist beliefs finally led him to exclaim: "What business have we with art at all, unless all can share
it." Hyacinth knows how the revolutionist to whom he has pledged

. . . .

* In his late revision of this novel James made this read "the fabric of beauty
and power it had raised."
† Later revised to "less of a 'bloody sell' and more of a lark."

himself would share it. He "wouldn't have the least feeling for this incomparable, abominable old Venice. He would cut up the ceilings of the Veronese in strips, so that every one might have a little piece." And he adds: "I don't want every one to have a little piece of anything and I have a great horror of that kind of invidious jealousy which is at the bottom of the idea of a redistribution."

Had Hyacinth been a hard-headed opportunist, he would have backed away, pushed open some door of escape, gone to America. He is however as ruthless with himself as his revolutionary mentors are with society at large, and with one another. To kill the Duke would in effect be like killing his father and re-enacting the crime of his mother. Roderick in a frenzy had wandered into an Alpine storm and missed his footing at the edge of a cliff. Hyacinth circles London in his loneliness and desperation. He feels himself helpless and unwanted. He can find no footing in his conflict. In the end he comes closer to the *crime passionnel* of his mother, rather than a political crime. He turns the pistol on himself—upon that organ which in his sensitive and romantic young body has suffered most—his heart.

III

Readers—and critics—coming upon *The Princess Casamassima* have tended generally to depreciate it: knowing James to be a chronicler of the upper middle class and of Americans abroad they have assumed that his attempt to treat a "social" subject must be factitious, or as artificial as *Romola*, a product of libraries and "influences," and of a scant knowledge of working-class life and politics. One critic has found James politically "naïve"; another, going to the opposite extreme, has made him out to be more documented in anarchism than he was; and a third has accused him of making his radicals more conspiratorial than they were at that time. This last is true. James did follow the newspapers, who saw an "organized" conspiracy in sporadic acts of violence by malcontents and fanatics. For the rest, James's

achievement in this novel must be seen in his belief in the
novelist's capacity to deduce the unknown from the known. He
had known radicals from childhood; his father was himself a religious radical, who consorted with Fourierists and utopians; and
Henry had known the dreams of a changed and new society peculiar to New England with its Brook Farm and its Fruitlands.
Abroad he had met, in Turgenev's entourage, Nihilists and émi-
gré revolutionaries and had participated in their feast days. He
had been an honored guest at the Nikolai Turgenevs on the an-
niversary of the freeing of the serfs. Long before, he had been
in Paris during the aftermath of the Commune, and had spoken
of the lingering smell of gunpowder and of blood. And we have
seen that where he had no knowledge, he sought it: his visit to
Millbank Prison was a case in point.

The rest was his artist's imagination, melting these materials
together, feeling deeply the predicament of his characters, and
evoking his pictures of the as yet unformulated class struggle. He
may have met Prince Kropotkin, the theorist of anarchism, at
Turgenev's bedside in 1880; he was to know him later—after he
had written *The Princess*—in London. We may best judge the
accuracy of the novel as observed and "felt life" if we note that
Kropotkin, arriving in London in 1881, complained that there
was "no atmosphere to breathe in." He found the workers torpid,
unorganized, inarticulate. The action of *The Princess Casamassima*
is set in the year 1881. Kropotkin said that during this visit to
England there had been "no sign of that animated socialist movement which I found so largely developed on my return in 1886."
This was the year in which *The Princess* appeared as a book. The
two dates mentioned by Kropotkin fit perfectly the fictional and
actual boundaries of James's novel, and help us define the true
character of its "revolutionary" contents. The politics of the novel
are naïve—for the book reflects the naïveté of the workers at that
time; it is a novel which records the primitive beginnings of
British Marxism, and it shows the general muddle which then
existed. This is why James's workers seem so helpless and so con-

fused. The Independent Labour Party and the Fabian Society were being founded during the period of the writing of *The Princess*. And it had barely been published, when the Haymarket bombing occurred in Chicago and the Piccadilly riots in London.

James had been "topical" indeed; more, he had been prescient. And the book would have had the fate of all such "topical" novels, but for one thing: if James was not grounded in political science and the writings of Marx and Engels (Bernard Shaw was then just beginning to read Marx), he understood better than the early Marxists the dynamics of power, the relationship between idealism and the manipulation of people; and he characterized with complete accuracy the predicament of nineteenth century liberalism which hated the violence of revolution, wanted the lot of the workers changed, and feared the self-seeking of men like Henry M. Hyndman and his Democratic Federation. This was the very essence of Fabianism and the very essence of Hyacinth's plight. The case of Hyacinth was to have its parallels in our century, in the young man who burns his finger-tips playing with revolution and spends his middle age writing his *apologia pro vita sua*.

In the émigrés James pictured, he embodied, with great affection and charm, the men whom he had known: their idealism, their sense of having outlived history, their chronic pain of exile. In the figure of Paul Muniment, the young worker, Henry foresaw the future union organizer and labor politician, in his coolness, self-centeredness, apathy to feeling, capacity for opportunism. He is the cautious "practical" revolutionary: "Ah no; no smashing, no smashing of valuable property. There are no wrong places—there are only wrong uses for them." Muniment lives with his sister Rosy who, like Alice James, is bed-ridden (and we may judge that her asperities and hostilities portray not a little of that side of Alice for which Henry had the greatest antipathy). Hyacinth and Paul become bosom friends; but the affection is really on Hyacinth's side. Paul can be quite ruthless. The portrait of the two duplicates the earlier glimpses we have had of the relationship of William and Henry: it is the characteristic Jamesian picture of the younger man who feels he is misunderstood by the older to whom he is nevertheless deeply attached.

In this group, the Princess too must be considered as a kind of "radical"; she belongs to the ranks of the exalted—those who have all the good things of life and make of their association with the cause of reform a kind of perpetual picnic or parlor game. With his usual subtle playfulness, Henry creates an opposing character to the Princess. If her name was Christina Light, her opposite is named Aurora. Christina Light has forgotten her own shabby beginnings, and is ostentatiously slumming. Lady Aurora belongs to the English aristocracy and like Miss Birdseye in *The Bostonians* is a humanitarian; she has the gift of true kindness. The two women offer a contrast once again between the self-interested social reformer and the dedicated and generous spirit.

I V

James confessed in his notebook after starting *The Princess* that he had never found himself "engaged in a novel, in which, after I had begun to write and send off my manuscript, the details had remained so vague." This vagueness is not, however, to be found in the completed work. He was too careful and adroit an artist ever to let slip the thread of his narrative and what he did not know he told "from the outside." He had long before learned the rules of fictional verisimilitude: and when he could not paint a detailed picture he had always the resources of atmosphere and impression. There is often, in this book, a subdued eloquence when James is describing the downtrodden and the unemployed. Notable are the scenes of the workers who come to the tavern, the "Sun and Moon," during the hard winter of 1880-81, articulate only to the point of such utterances (in his revised version) as "And what the plague am I to do with seventeen bob—with seventeen bloody bob? What am I to do with them—will ye tell me that?" The language James heard was probably more violent.

Or such asseverations as: "Them was my words in the month of February last, and what I say I stick to—what I say I stick to." Articulate only to the point of general ejaculation, without leadership, the workers of the time could be rendered simply in their state of helpless despair:

They came oftener, this second winter, for the season was terribly hard; and as in that lower world one walked with one's ear nearer the ground the deep perpetual groan of London misery seemed to swell and swell and form the whole undertone of life. The filthy air came into the place in the damp coats of silent men, and hung there till it was brewed to a nauseous warmth, and ugly, serious faces squared themselves through it, and strong-smelling pipes contributed their element in a fierce, dogged manner which appeared to say that it now had to stand for everything—for bread and meat and beer, for shoes and blankets and the poor things at the pawnbroker's and the smokeless chimney at home. Hyacinth's colleagues seemed to him wiser then, and more permeated with intentions boding ill to the satisfied classes; and though the note of popularity was still most effectively struck by the man who could demand oftenest, unpractically, "What the plague* am I to do with seventeen shillings?" it was brought home to our hero on more than one occasion that revolution was ripe at last.

And the following speech, with a change of a word or two here and there, might have been a part of any revolutionary pamphlet of the time; Bernard Shaw was to endow certain of his socialist characters with this kind of eloquence on the stage:

People go and come, and buy and sell, and drink and dance, and make money and make love, and seem to know nothing and suspect nothing and think of nothing; and iniquities flourish, and the misery of half the world is prated about as a "necessary evil," and generations rot away and starve in the midst of it, and day follows day, and everything is for the best in the best of possible worlds.

. . . .

* Later changed to "What the hell am I to do with half a quid?"

All that is one half of it; the other half is that everything is doomed! In silence, in darkness, but under the feet of each one of us, the revolution lives and works. It is a wonderful immeasurable trap, on the lid of which society performs its antics.

Not the least of his successes was Henry's creation of the character of Millicent Henning, Hyacinth's childhood friend in the slums. She is as cockney as Shaw's Eliza, and rings true in everything she does and says. George du Maurier, whose observation of London was even more deeply rooted, wrote to Henry that she was "the best character in the book." She was "truly loveable, and her friendship for Hyacinth, with its admirable background of foggy streets and gaslighted shops, has attracted and delighted me almost more than anything else—her freedom, her readiness for a row, her potentiality for barricades or triumphal processions (in spite of her hands and feet)—and the background of London is ever there, treated, I venture to think, as it has not been treated before."

It is doubtful whether Millicent had a potential for barricades: but du Maurier describes her essential qualities. She is in many ways a cockney cousin of Daisy Miller, with a great deal more vitality.

v

The personal statement in this novel, in the light of James's "orphaned" state on returning from America, lies this time near the surface. His identification with Hyacinth seems to have been considerable. He felt himself an aristocrat by birth, who had also to labor for his bread; he could move among princesses and lords yet at a given hour each day he was pledged to his task in Bolton Street and later De Vere Gardens—never more so than during the two years in which, month after month, he delivered instalments of The Bostonians and then of The Princess Casamassima. Feeling himself alone in the world after the death of his parents, he seemed truly disinherited, clinging to art and civilization amid the unrest in British society. He expressed this with great clarity to Charles Eliot Norton at the time of the publication of *The Princess*:

The subject of the moment, as I came away [he was writing from Italy], was the hideous Colin Campbell divorce case, which will besmirch exceedingly the already very damaged prestige of the English upper class. The condition of that body seems to me to be in many ways very much the same rotten and *collapsible* one as that of the French aristocracy before the revolution—minus cleverness and conversation. Or perhaps it's more like the heavy, congested and depraved Roman world upon which the barbarians came down. In England the Huns and Vandals will have to come *up*—from the black depths of the (in the people) enormous misery, though I don't think the Attila is quite yet found—in the person of Mr. Hyndman.

The sense of being bereft of his parents is emphasized by the number of fathers and mothers Henry allots to Hyacinth. There had been his original parents, Lord Frederick Purvis, murdered by his French mother, Florentine Vivier, whom he had seen but once, in the Millbank infirmary. There is Mr. Vetch, the old violinist, and the dressmaker, Miss Pynsent, who brought up Hyacinth: both constitute a parental pair, advising, admonishing, helping. Miss Pynsent's savings, when she dies, enlarged by a gift from Mr. Vetch, enable Hyacinth to make his trip to Paris and to Venice. And then he has acquired still another, a disciplined and resolute father, in the person of the anarchist Diedrich Hoffendahl, seen in a nocturnal interview, to whom the bookbinder had pledged absolute obedience. Hoffendahl in James's imagination belongs with the crippled elder Henry James—for Henry endows the anarchist with a maimed arm.

Hyacinth's parents and parent-figures demand a great deal; to obey the rule of the stern "father" Hoffendahl, he must kill the Duke and thereby re-enact his mother's murder. He is divided between an exigent, though maimed father, upon whose behalf he is called to risk his own life, and the memory of a powerful Clytemnestra mother. His immediate parent-surrogates, Miss Pynsent and Mr. Vetch, want him to cut loose from his revolutionary commitment. His "parents" have put him in an impossible position. His big brother—in the shape of still another revolutionary, Paul Muniment—is of no help to him.

Thus in *The Princess Casamassima*, a novel which seemed farthest removed from himself, Henry wrote out the personal emotions of this period: the acute melancholy experienced in the years following the death of his parents. He seems to have disposed of a primitive helplessness and rage in *The Bostonians*; and in his novel of London and the anarchists he re-imagined his subterranean world of feeling in terms of his hero's revolt, loneliness, despair and the need for action. He siphoned off into his work a lugubrious state of mind, leaving himself freer and more possessed of his mature self. One solution had been his finding a new and more permanent home. And when the last chapters, written in De Vere Gardens, were done, his thoughts turned to Italy. He had been away for six years. It was time to go back.

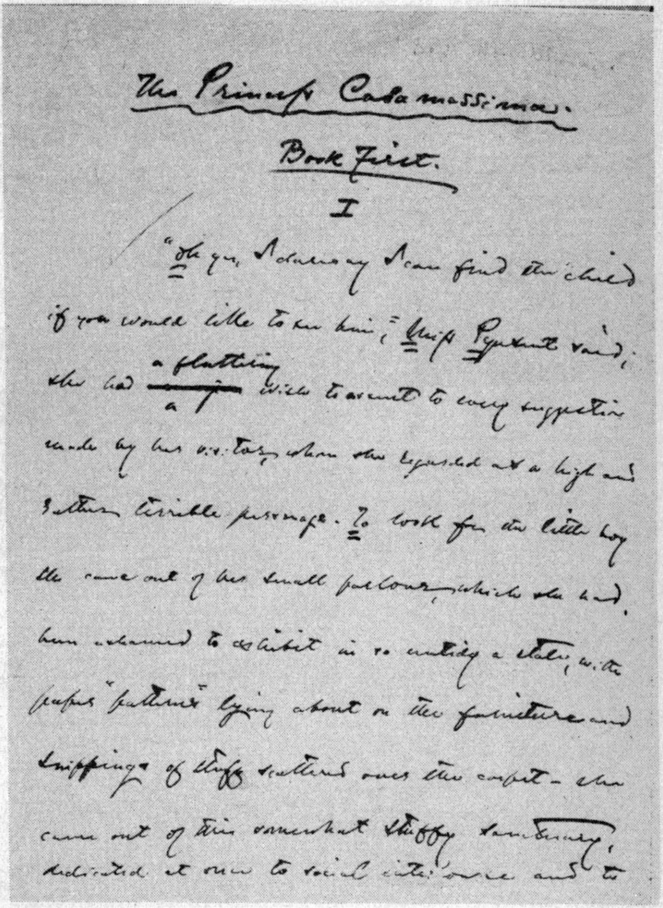

THE PRINCESS CASAMASSIMA
First page of the manuscript

ELIZABETH AND FRANCIS BOOTT AND FRANK DUVENECK
At the Villa Castellani, with Lizzie's nurse, Mary Ann Shenstone.
From a photograph

BOOK FOUR

Bellosguardo
1887

THE LONELY FRIENDS

ON THAT FEBRUARY DAY OF THE RIOTS IN 1886 WHEN FENIMORE walked innocently through London's cluttered streets, she had been on her way to the Strand to purchase a trunk. She was going to Italy. She had been living for three years in England writing her novel, *East Angels*. "I grow less and less of a traveller each year," she had written to a friend. But now she craved the south, a warm sun, Italy. We have very little knowledge of her movements in England between 1884 and 1886. We know that in London she occasionally went to the theatre with Henry James; that they had paid a visit together to Stonehenge; that they met in various places. For a while we lose sight of her completely. In September of 1885 she was at Leamington, a year before Alice James spent her summer there. She had been working quietly and making excursions—to Stratford, Coventry, Kenilworth, Oxford. She had fallen "desperately in love" with Oxford. She was enchanted by Warwickshire; she took solitary walks, inspecting

sleepy villages, with their half-timbered houses and thatched roofs;
and small ancient churches with gray Norman towers. She liked
to walk on the red battlements of Kenilworth in the sunset light
and in the gardens of Warwick Castle; or among the oaks and the
elms of Stoneleigh Abbey, near Leamington. Her love of Warwickshire and of Oxford "makes a balance-weight for my love of
Italy so I shall not grow one-sided," she wrote to her friend.

In December of 1885 we come upon another Leamington letter, this one to her friend John Hay. She has just heard from
Henry James about the death of Clover Adams. "I should like to
die without warning myself," she remarks. "But for those who are
left it is very terrible." She tells Hay she has three friends watching her work-table: three photographs. "Mr. Howells smiles and
smiles; you look poetic; and Henry James cynical." And she an-
nounces to Hay her plan to go to Italy in January.

In February of 1886, as we have seen, she was still in lodgings
in Seymour Street. She had accumulated a great many belongings;
hence the new trunk. In March she finally left, shortly after Henry
James moved from Piccadilly to Kensington. When she reached
Venice, late one evening, and her gondola shot out into the
moonlit Grand Canal, she experienced a throb of joy. It was
April; the air was as warm as an American July. "I think I felt
compensated for all my years of toil, just in that half hour." Her
subsequent destination was Florence. She put up at the pension
on the Arno: Henry James had come calling there six years before.

I

"I wonder, my dear Francis, whether you will do me rather a
favour," Henry James wrote to his friend Boott, on May 25, 1886.
"My excellent friend Constance Fenimore Woolson is in Florence
and I want to pay her your compliment and administer to her
some social comfort. The finest satisfaction I can confer upon her
will be to ask you to go and see her, at Casa Molin, the old Pension Barbensi, on the Lung'Arno, which you will know. She appears to know few people there (i.e. in Florence), and though she

has not made any sort of request of me touching this proposal (by which I don't mean that I want you to 'propose' to her, either for me or for yourself), I am sure the sight of you would give her joy. She is a deaf and *méticuleuse* old maid—but she is also an excellent and sympathetic being. If Lizzie could take a look at her and attract her to the villa I should be very glad."

Boott called on Miss Woolson with some promptness, and she was made welcome at the Villa Castellani, where in due course she rented some rooms in one of its wings. Her grand-uncle, James Fenimore Cooper, had once lived on Bellosguardo, as had Hawthorne. The Castellani had figured in *Roderick Hudson* and *The Portrait of a Lady*, so that Miss Woolson enjoyed a sense of communion with Bellosguardo's Jamesian past—and with the friends of her friend. Before she left Italy that summer to spend the hot months in Switzerland, she had signed a year's lease for the adjoining fourteen-room Villa Brichieri-Colombi. In a letter to Lizzie Boott, Henry wrote, "tell your father I thank him for the kindness which she [Miss Woolson] tells me he has shown her in profusion." Fenimore had a great liking for Boott, and the sentimental songs which he composed. Boott on his side had become fond of Fenimore—indeed it is only in Henry's letters to Boott and his daughter that she is referred to as "Fenimore." Elsewhere she figures either with her full three names or simply as "Miss Woolson." By the end of that summer, Henry was writing to Boott: "I have promised to go and see her after she is settled at Bellosguardo."

II

A great change had occurred on Bellosguardo that year, shortly before Fenimore's arrival. Lizzie Boott, after almost six years of indecision and courtship, had married Frank Duveneck. The union between this descendant of the New England Bootts and Lymans with the son of a German-American immigrant had been opposed by many of Lizzie's friends; how Francis viewed it we cannot say. To judge from Henry's comments, he seems to have acquiesced in all his daughter's wishes. Nevertheless he was seventy-three, and for forty years he had had Lizzie's undivided company. Now a third figure had moved into the Castellani, a stoutish, provincial-mannered, inarticulate and polite painter from Cincinnati. In congratulating Lizzie on her engagement, Henry remarked that if Francis did not like the marriage "he must come over and live with me—I have a room for him." To Francis he wrote: "I hasten to express my sympathy in all you must feel on the subject of her engagement—the apprehensions (as to becoming No. 3) as well as the satisfaction that she is to take a step that has in it so little of precipitation." He cautioned his old friend: "Take care lest between two easels you fall to the ground, you can so easily trip over the legs." Later, when he saw the three together, he distinctly felt that for the time at least Boott had been "shunted," but was making the best of it. He was to recognize that in a sense Duveneck also could feel "shunted," for the ties binding father and daughter were strong indeed. An observer might have said that in reality nothing had changed on Bellosguardo: father and daughter had lived there for decades, and the daughter's painting master, who had also been there for a goodly time, had now simply been added to the household. A striking snapshot of the period reveals all the ambiguities of this triangle: Lizzie stands erect in the foreground, beside her seated father; the husband is in the background, on the steps leading to the Castellani terrace; he seems rather large and ungainly in his ill-fitting clothes and bulky beside the elderly, trim Mary Ann Shenstone, who had been Lizzie's nurse when she was born and who had lived with the Bootts ever since. Boott might feel that his daughter had left him; but she was still at his side. And Duveneck must have continued to feel that he was still in the background.

Henry had followed Duveneck's career from the first with some fascination: the painter seemed so ill matched with the "admirably produced" Lizzie whose education Henry had described in *The Portrait of a Lady*. When Duveneck had arrived from Munich he was like a big child suddenly transferred from the bucolic life of a farm into that of a palace. He had not been formed for the drawing room. He had bought himself new clothes and tried his best to fit himself into Florence's international "society" in which Lizzie moved. Now he had married the heiress (Boott's income was derived from certain profitable New England textile mills). He lived in a grand villa; he had to say goodbye to cherished evenings of idle drinking in low *trattorias* and wine-cellars. Henry wrote to Lizzie that although he congratulated her, he congratulated Duveneck even more. They should become, he said, "the *Brownings* (more or less—in a sort of way) of pictorial art." He urged her to "make *him* work—make him do himself justice."

To Henrietta Reubell he described the father-daughter-husband triangle on Bellosguardo in candid terms: "I am much interested, and very sympathetic, in *your* interest in Lizzie Boott's new departure. She is judging for herself, with a vengeance; but she is forty years old, and she has the right. Duveneck won't beat her, nor *la rudoyer*, nor perhaps even neglect her, and will be completely under her influence and control; but he is illiterate, ignorant, and not a gentleman (though an excellent fellow, kindly, simple, etc.) and she gives away to him her independence and freedom. His talent is great, though without delicacy, but I fear his indolence is greater still. Lizzie, however, will urge him forward and be an immense help to him. For him it is all gain—for her it is very brave."

Was it all gain for Duveneck? He could take a place in "society," show his works to great advantage, receive commissions for portraits. He had married not only his pupil but his patroness. He was a painter of great vigor; there was something of Hals or Rubens in his brush; he had an affinity with that side of the Dutch and Flemish schools in which ruddy faces, hearty eating and lusty life were depicted. The question was whether such a native talent, a figure as unbuttoned and as primitive as Duveneck, but with a distinct touch of mastery in his palette, could fit the tight clothes Lizzie wished him to wear; whether he could adapt himself to the manners of the American gentry abroad and over-come his easy-going nature.

Henry saw, and was to see, a psychological situation on Bellos-guardo which he would re-imagine and re-create years later in *The Golden Bowl*, although with quite different characters—that of a father and daughter so attached to one another that the husband of the daughter feels himself superfluous. He was also, in that novel, to deal with the problems encountered by the father as a consequence of his daughter's secession from their close life together. In the real-life situation, Henry's greatest sympathy was with the elderly Boott; and during this period we find him writing to Francis more frequently than hitherto. When summer came, the father went north in search of cooler weather; this year, for the first time, Lizzie was not with him. He made his lonely journey through Switzerland, a country he never much cared for. Henry wrote and asked him how he was facing "the terrible prob-lems" of having to be with only "the inspiration of your *own bien être*, a stimulus never, in the past, sufficient for you." He also re-marked: "Perhaps you are not alone—I hope not—perhaps even you have met our friend Fenimore somewhere." Henry had last heard from her, he said, from Geneva, where she had described herself as hanging over the balcony of the Hotel National, looking upon the placid waters of the Lake. If he had sent Boott to Feni-more in Florence, hoping to soften some of her hours of loneli-ness, he seemed now to be thinking of the loneliness she might soften for Boott in his old age. This too he would, in the fullness of time, subtly incorporate into his late novel.

THE TWO VILLAS

AFTER THE PUBLICATION OF "THE PRINCESS CASAMASSIMA" IN 1886 Henry decided he would break his long sojourn in London by a month's trip to Italy, to keep his promise to Fenimore and to see Francis and the Boott-Duvenecks. Alice had spent the summer in Leamington. All had gone well, save at the very end when there was an unexpected crisis, a parochial comedy. Two young clergymen, rooming in the same house, attempted to enter Alice's apartment late one evening. At first Henry's letters made this sound as if they had designs on his invalid sister. He said they "pretended" they had been discussing theology; what they had discussed "was of course whiskey." Alice, at any rate, developed palpitations and hysterical prostration. The clergymen were contrite and offered formal apologies. Miss Loring wrote a stiff letter to their ecclesiastical superiors. The moral of the matter, Henry told a friend, was that "there are apparently strange little cads and brutes in the great Church of England." The evidence suggests that the clergymen, if they were a trifle buoyant and tipsy at the end of their amiable evening, had simply tried the wrong door. Alice, however, could be easily upset, and what would have been, to some other lady, a credible mistake, became for her, in her cloistered state, a sinister episode.

It blew over, however. In due course she was able to come to London, where Henry found some rather small rooms in Gloucester Road, Palace Gate, around the corner from De Vere Gardens. By November she seemed sufficiently settled and comfortable for Henry to write to Lizzie that he would leave on December 1. He looked forward to seeing his friend in her newly-married state, and to "many a delightful and long-deferred talk." And "our good Fenimore must also be worked in—but I shall be equal even to this. I am very glad you are nice to her, as she is a very good woman, with an immense power of devotion (to H.J.!)." He asked the Boots and Fenimore to keep his arrival a secret; he did not wish to be drawn into the complications of Florentine society. Before he came away it was settled that he would sublet the Brichieri villa from Fenimore during December, since she had her rooms at the Castellani until the new year. He would this time realize a very old dream: he would actually reside on Bellosguardo—and under circumstances that seemed to him very agreeable. The Boots expressed concern lest he find the Villa Brichieri cold. "It is very good of you to offer to put in *wood,* but I have an idea that Fenimore, whose devotion—like my appreciation of it —is *sans bornes*—has stacked me up a pile with her own hands. She is a gallant friend, but I am afraid she has bored you with me. Never mind, you will have your revenge; she will bore *me* with *you.*"

If his arrival was generally a secret, he nevertheless informed Vernon Lee of it two days before leaving London. "I shall come and see you very quickly," he wrote, "though I mean to lodge, for sweet seclusion's sake, out of town—in one of your grand old villas. The thought of going to Italy again, after a long and loathsome divorce, is absolutely rapturous to me."

He left on December 3, 1886, promising Alice he would return within a month. He bypassed Paris and travelled via the St. Gotthard. On the 5th he was in Milan "drinking in the delicious sun"; on the 7th he was in Pisa; the next day he reached Bellosguardo. By this time he knew that he and Fenimore would be alone on their hilltop. The Boots were in Florence proper. Lizzie was momentarily expecting a child.

I

The two ancient villas on Bellosguardo, the one in which Fenimore was living temporarily and the one which was to be her home at the beginning of the new year, stand near one another. The Villa Brichieri-Colombi is a substantial rambling two-story building, the blank rear of which rises high from the wall on the winding road leading to the brow of Bellosguardo. It is situated near the summit, and a small gate, as one approaches, permits a sideways glimpse; but the high wall shuts it in and only the upper story is visible, so that one gets no sense of its large terrace, offering a sweeping view of Florence on one side and the Arno valley on the other. Cypresses tower on either side; and an umbrella pine stands off a little, establishing a neat balance in a warmly human landscape. As one climbs for another two or three minutes on the steep road, following the wall, one comes to the small piazza where today a commemorative plaque lists, among others, the three famous Americans who lived on Bellosguardo —Hawthorne, Cooper and Henry James. Fenimore is not remembered, although she could have a certain claim, since the other names range from Galileo to Ouida, the Brownings to Robert Lytton. Dominating the square is the yellow façade of the massive Villa Castellani, which rises directly from the roadway, offering, through a heavy grille, a glimpse of its thick walls and its noble *quattrocento* court. The Bootts lived in the north wing. The Castellani, however, had some fifty rooms, and here American Greenoughs and Huntingtons from the early part of the century, and others, such as Browning's friend Isa Blagden, had occupied apartments. Miss Blagden had also lived earlier in the Brichieri. Fenimore, standing in the Boott garden and looking across a patch of mountain terrain, could command a splendid view of the eminently practical and solid Brichieri, with its faded yellowish walls and its strong tile roof.

James had never been in the Brichieri, though he knew its long history and Mrs. Browning's "Aurora Leigh" which celebrated it: *I found a house at Florence on the hill of Bellosguardo.* When he entered, he discovered that it gave him such a view as he had never had from the Castellani. To the north he saw a panorama of Florentine domes and towers, with Fiesole and the Apennines beyond, range upon range. On the other, the Arno side, he looked upon a soft valley in its winter dress, with sleepy white towns and the gleam of the river—old castles, towers, campaniles; and across the western end, the abrupt Carrara hills in the December sky.

When there was sun he felt well out of London. But the season was on the whole wet and cold. Fenimore had indeed laid in a large store of firewood and Henry built himself roaring fires. He occupied a drawing room and a bedroom on the ground floor, a section of the villa which had been built before the discovery of America. Fenimore made available to him her cook Angelo who acted also as his valet.

The two writers seem to have fallen very quickly into a regular way of life. Both were industrious; their working hours were sacred. A letter from Henry preserved among the papers of John Hay shows the novelist—otherwise consummately discreet—unbending sufficiently to mention his neighbor. Describing the view from his windows, he wrote that "they are not my windows —but those of our amiable and distinguished friend Miss Woolson, and I will leave her to deal with them. She has taken this roomy and rambling old villa, furnished, on a lease, and [she] being still in possession of another and not able to enter it till the first day of January, has very obligingly sublet it to me for a month with the services of a queer old melancholy male-cook, whom she had put in to take care of it. She dwells at five minutes' distance, and I see her every day or two—indeed often dine with her. She has done a brave thing in settling herself here (for two or three years) in a somewhat mouldy Tuscan mansion—but I think it clear that she will get much enjoyment and profit from it *à la longue*. She will get quiet, sunny, spacious hours for work (a prospect, on her part, in which I take an interest, in view of the great merit and progress of her last book), and have Florence in the hollow of her hand."

II

We know very little more about the life these two writers led on their Florentine hill-top. In the absence of documents there are only mute witnesses. Certain books which Henry gave to Fenimore have survived; nearly all of them bear the dates of this time. To commemorate his tenancy, he inscribed a copy of the three-

volume *Bostonians*, "To his *padrona* Constance Fenimore Woolson, her faithful tenant and friend, Henry James, Bellosguardo,
December 1886." An edition of Shelley, selected and arranged by
Stopford Brooke, on large paper, limited to five hundred copies,
was inscribed: "Constance Fenimore Woolson, from her friend
and confrère Henry James, 1887." There is also George Eliot's
Romola in a two-volume edition; this again has her name written
out in full and the copy is signed and dated "Florence January
1887." Perhaps the most significant document is the one that
was most public: an article Henry consecrated to the work of Fenimore, which he published in *Harper's Weekly* on February 12,
1887. Its appearance at that date suggests that it was probably
written shortly after Henry moved into the Villa Brichieri.

During the previous year he had contributed an article on
Howells to the same weekly. Thus in writing the essay on Miss
Woolson, Henry—who had hitherto confined himself to major
Continental novelists—was turning his attention to an American
contemporary whom he esteemed and whom he ranked as worthy
of attention with Howells. He had told Howells as much some
years before. The occasion for the essay was the recent appearance of *East Angels*, Fenimore's most ambitious novel. Henry's
tribute was the expression of a sincere admiration for the person
as much as for the writer. And yet a reader of the article in the
files of *Harper's*, or in its revised book appearance in *Partial Portraits*, cannot but be puzzled: that Henry should have bestowed
upon work as regional and as "magazineish" as hers the discriminating literary taste which he had hitherto reserved for the leading European writers of fiction, or upon figures such as Hawthorne or even Howells, strikes one today as curious. For Miss
Woolson was on the whole rather prosy and banal, a journey-
woman of letters. Without style, and with an extreme literalness,
she lacked ease and the richer verbal imagination. Her work is
minute—and cluttered; she is an ardent devotee of "local color."
That Henry should have thrown his very considerable weight into
the enhancement of her reputation is singular on the ground of

literary criticism, although understandable on the ground of loyalty and friendship. His essay is graceful; and yet somewhat la-
bored. He tried very hard to say right and honorable things, and
it required effort and ingenuity. The final impression can only be
that he is honoring Fenimore's dedication to letters less than her
devotion to himself. Again and again what he seizes upon in her
novels is her capacity for loyalty; her heroines immolate themselves for others; she has a belief in "personal renunciation, in its
frequency as well as its beauty"; she is fond of "irretrievable personal failures, of people who have had to give up even the memory of happiness, who love and suffer in silence, and minister in
secret to the happiness of those who look over their heads." In
his discussion of *East Angels* he speaks of her heroines as trying to
"provide for the happiness of others (when they adore them)
even to their own injury." This remark recalls Henry's words to
Lizzie about Fenimore's "immense power of devotion (to H.J.!)."

Apparently he was reciprocating this devotion. The essay in
Harper's Weekly contained a biographical passage of considerable
critical liveliness, in which James pretended to have gained his
facts from her work. "It would not be hidden from a reader of
Anne and *East Angels* that the author is a native of New England, who may have been transplanted to a part of the country
open in some degree to the imputation of being 'out west,'" he
wrote. And he goes on to speak "so far as my knowledge goes," of
her education in New York and her life in the South. He is not
above describing "her earnest, lingering manner" in *Anne*, or
her prolixity. In criticizing her for having dwelt so little on
her picture of a snowbound military post at Mackinaw, he observes this is "the only case that I can remember, by the way, in
which she has abandoned an opportunity without having con-
scientiously pressed it out." The net effect, however, is laudatory,
as when he speaks of her liking for Florida reflected in *East
Angels*—"a high appreciation of orange gardens and white
beaches, pine barrens and rivers smothered in jungles, and a peculiar affection for that city of the past, so rapidly becoming a

city of the future, St. Augustine." The sketch concludes with Henry's wondering whether she intends to make use of her "personal familiarity with Rome, Florence, Venice and other irrepressible cities." Has she, he asks (not without a touch of coyness), "a story about Europe in reserve or does she propose to maintain her distinguished independence?"

This rather strange and fulsome biographical excursion was deleted by Henry when he transferred the essay into his book. In its place he inserted a further passage of criticism, pointing out "two defects" in *East Angels*. One defect was that Miss Woolson described in this novel a group too detached and isolated, a group which seemed thus to be on a desert island. Its members went to and fro, to New York and to Europe, but "they have a certain shipwrecked air, as of extreme dependence on each other, though surrounded with every convenience." The other fault, which he deemed more significant, was their total preoccupation with the famous "tender sentiment"—the complications of the plot were all complications of love. "Our impression is of sky and sand— the sky of azure, the sand of silver—and between them, conspicuous, immense, against the low horizon, the question of engagement and marriage." Henry's criticism generalized into his finding that women writers tended to give too much place to "love" in a novel, and to forget that in life there were other things. Indeed, "in men's novels, even of the simplest strain, there are still other references and other explanations; in women's, when they are of the category to which I allude, there are none but that one."

In the essay Henry dealt, one by one, with Miss Woolson's various books: he praised her for giving a voice to the inarticulate South so early after the Civil War; he professed to not having read her Lake Country sketches in *Castle Nowhere*, but in *Rodman the Keeper* he found much "interesting artistic work." Miss Woolson had perceived that "no social revolution of equal magnitude" to that in the South "had ever reflected itself so little in literature, remained so unrecorded, so unpainted and unsung." Nevertheless her pictures ended by conveying "dreariness." Of her popular novel *Anne*, he complained that it was her weakest work because the strong element of devotion and renunciation in her other novels was largely absent from it. The reader, he said, builds up great hopes in a character named Tita, but "Tita vanishes into the vague" after an infant marriage. Miss Woolson, Henry complains, "likes the unmarried, but she likes marriages even better, and also sometimes hurries them forward in advance of the reader's exaction." Her short novel, *For the Major*, the story of a woman's effort to wear a constant mask of youth in spite of her being older than her husband, Henry found "fantastic" but "eminently definite." The heroine is aided by her husband's ill health "so that she is able to keep on the mask till his death, when she pulls it off with a passionate cry of relief—ventures at last, gives herself the luxury, to be old." It was the first time, Henry observed, that a woman was represented as painting her face, dyeing her hair and "dressing young" not out of vanity but out of tenderness for another—"the effort usually has its source in tenderness for herself." Miss Woolson had done nothing neater "than this fanciful figure of the little ringleted, white-frocked, falsely juvenile lady, who has the toilet-table of an actress and the conscience of a Puritan."

That Henry liked Miss Woolson for having a "fruitful instinct" in seeing novels as pictures of the "evolution of personal relations" is understandable. And yet it is difficult, in the large scale of literary values, to read Miss Woolson's work and to see why she was included in *Partial Portraits*. The volume consisted of several new essays, written during that year, some on Bellosguardo, and others of a slightly earlier time: there was the magisterial essay on Maupassant, and the memorial to Turgenev; he included his now celebrated essay on Emerson, two articles on George Eliot, his obituary study of Trollope and his essays on Daudet and Stevenson. The character of this volume differed markedly from *French Poets and Novelists*. The title of *Partial Portraits* contains within it a quiet pun: the earlier volume was historical; it dealt with writers Henry had never known personally. *Partial*

Portraits deals entirely with writers whom he had met and liked. The "portraits" can be said to be "partial" also because they are not complete: and they are hardly impartial. On this ground, Miss Woolson does belong in the volume: but to modern eyes she cuts a strange figure. To be sure she is propped up by Robert Louis Stevenson on one side and Alphonse Daudet on the other. The question still can be asked: why did Henry put her there at all? The things he chose to say about her, he could say sincerely enough. And the article may be a form of "criticism by omission." A few years later, when a friend asked him how he had come to write an article about the novels of Mrs. Humphry Ward, his reply was, "I have written no article on Mrs. Ward—only a civil perfunctory *payé* (with words between the lines) to escape the gracelessness of refusing when asked." Nevertheless, he reprinted this article in his *Essays in London.*

No greater pen was to commemorate the work of Miss Woolson. Posterity was to assign her a footnote in the regional fiction of America. In the life of Henry James, she occupied a larger place.

A POLYGLOT SOCIETY

TWO WEEKS AFTER HENRY HAD SETTLED BESIDE HIS WOOD FIRES IN the Villa Brichieri, word was sent up from Florence that Lizzie Duveneck had given birth to a robust male child. To a household which already had a Frank Boott and a Frank Duveneck, there was now added a Frank Duveneck Jr. Henry wrote to William that the child was born "very quickly and quietly." He described it to his Aunt Kate as "a little red worm." Lizzie was blooming and evidently happy. "She is much in love with her husband— who will never do much, I think, but who is all the same a fine, pleasant, polite (though perfectly illiterate) man, whom it is impossible not to like." The baby would "apparently live and thrive —but Lizzie will plainly be much more of a wife than a mother." To William he described Duveneck as "a good frank fellow, without any small or nasty qualities"; however, it was impossible to converse with him for more than two minutes. He would be a weight for Lizzie to carry for the rest of her life—"I mean socially, and in the world. He is only half-civilized—though he is very 'civil.'" Henry thought Boott's acceptance of him at every hour of the day to be "pathetic and heroic." He also remarked that the new grandfather seemed "old and shrivelled and laughs much less than in the old days." Francis Boott's dilemma struck Henry as "the subject of a little tale by Turgenev."

I

On January 1, 1887, Fenimore moved into her villa as planned and Henry descended into Florence where, he wrote to Grace Norton, "I am told I went 'out' a great deal. Why I don't know —as it was very exactly what I had left London not to do. I am also told I was 'lionized'—and the wherefore of this I know still less. On reflection, in fact, I greatly doubt it. But I did see a great many people; too many, for what they were." Henry moved into the Hôtel du Sud on the Arno; and although the dusty *tramontana* and the cold were uncomfortable, he relished the bright winter sunshine. Florence, he told Miss Norton, "had never seemed to me, naturally and artistically, more delightful. And the views from the villas on the hills (I was at a good many) are as beautiful—really—as your memory must tell you."

His winter now took an unexpected turn. He had left London for one month. In due course, Alice wrote complaining that her lodgings were too small. A new crisis seemed to be impending. At this moment Henry had the sudden inspiration to do for his sister what Fenimore had done for him. He offered her his flat, complete with domestics. Alice accepted the idea with joy; it was like installing herself in "home" instead of lodgings. Henry assured her that she was conferring a favor on him, for she gave his servants something to do. If all went well, he would now be able to postpone his return and spend the entire spring in Italy. "Foreign lands offer me better conditions of work," he explained to his brother, "quieter, fresher mornings, less pestered by the postman —than London does in these months, especially the forthcoming ones." He also wrote to him: "I have been driving the pen steadily."

Whenever he drove the pen, he turned to society for relaxation. How often Henry saw his erstwhile "landlady" we do not know. What we do know is that suddenly he was dining out, paying calls, attending tea parties. "I won't tell you their names, or more than that they were members of the queer, promiscuous, polyglot (most polyglot in the world) Florentine society." Thus to Grace Norton, in a letter in which he then devotes many pages to telling the names of all his hostesses and describing them. There was Madame de Tchiatchev, an Englishwoman married to a rich retired Russian diplomat; there was the Marchesa Incontri, a Russian once married to Prince Galitzin, and subsequently to a Florentine, and now widowed. Madame de Tchiatchev was "remarkably pleasant and sympathetic" and the Marchesa Incontri was "singularly clever and easy." Madame de T. was "very good and yet not dull"; the Marchesa was probably "*bad*—though not dull either." She went in for the arts. She had a salon, in her splendid villa outside of the Porta San Gallo, in which she received literary people—like Henry—and also very "smart" folk. She even wrote novels, under false names, rather poor things, and in English, which she spoke perfectly. Henry thought her on the whole "rather dangerous."

Near Fiesole, there was the Baroness Zunch, "a very kindly person," who was Anglo-Italian and who had Henry to dinner. He called on the Countess Peruzzi for old time's sake: she was the former Edith Story, whom he had known at the Barberini. "She has grown plain, and is motherly and snobbish—and yet I liked her for she is genial and kindly and more to my taste than in her high-flying maidenhood." He became friendly with Dr. W. W. Baldwin, an American with a wide medical practice in Florence. In particular, he liked the sculptor, Adolph Hildebrand, who lived at the foot of Bellosguardo, in the former convent of San Francesco di Paolo. He had the "feeling of the Greeks and that of the early Tuscans too, by a strange combination." Janet Ross, the former Janet Duff-Gordon, invited him to her picturesque villa of Castagnolo. A vigorous and active Scotswoman, who had been married to a man much older than herself (his name was Henry James Ross), she was a friend of Meredith and of Symonds, and had been painted by Watts and Leighton. She had lived as a young woman in Alexandria, with her husband, and later they had settled near Florence where she interested herself in agriculture. "She wants me to stay with her—but I like you better!—and fear you less," Henry wrote to Mrs. Bronson. He overcame his fear sufficiently to spend three days at Castagnolo. Mrs. Ross played her guitar, sang Italian songs and talked a great deal. "I am not so sure of Mrs Ross's mind as of her eyes, her guitar and her desire to sell you bric-à-brac!" he told Mrs. Wister. "She is awfully handsome, in a utilitarian kind of way—an odd mixture of the British female and the dangerous woman—a Bohemian with rules and accounts."

A long letter of February 5, 1887 to Mrs. Bronson in Venice throws more light on the extent to which James was lionized by polyglot Florence. He was just leaving, he wrote, to visit Mrs. Ross for the day. He would dine with the Marchesa Incontri the next day. The following Monday he was to dine with a kinswoman of Mrs. Bronson's; on Tuesday with Vernon Lee to meet an Italian critic, "[Enrico] Nencioni, who has translated me." The previous evening he had dined with the Huntingtons at the Castellani, and the night before that with some Americans named Lofton "in extraordinary and overdone splendor"; the night before that at the Cantagallis', in company "with that extraordinary and most amusing woman the Countess Gamba," and the night before that with Edith Peruzzi, in company with Corsinis, Farinolas and Antinoris. He had met the McClellans, the widow and daughter of the Civil War general, at their Torrigiani cousin's, "where I went by the latter's invitation, to see the pretended Raphael Madonna—which is no more a Raphael than Daisy Miller is Shakespeare."

To John Hay, Fenimore wrote: "I have never seen anyone to be so run-after as he was while in Florence."

Vernon Lee's salon, while also polyglot, offered Henry a much more substantial milieu. There was Vernon Lee herself, "the most intelligent person in the place," Henry said. He went quite often to No. 5 Via Garibaldi, where Miss Lee received daily from four to seven and as often in the evening as people would come. He described her as "exceedingly ugly, disputatious, contradictious and perverse." He liked her clever half-brother, Eugene Lee-Hamilton, formerly attached to the British Embassy in Paris but now bedridden—or rather sofa-ridden—by paralysis. There was also a "grotesque, deformed, invalidical, posing mother, and a father in the highest degree unpleasant, mysterious and sinister" who had not sat down at table with his family for twenty years. In spite of such drawbacks, Vernon Lee attracted to the Via Garibaldi "all the world," discussed "all things in any language, and understands some, drives her pen, glares through her spectacles and keeps up her courage." She was "a really superior talker," he told Gosse. "She has a mind—almost the only one in Florence"; it was almost worthy to be French. It made Henry "a little less ashamed of the stupid English race."

Florentine society, on the whole, was "very thin and flimsy" and "a vain agitation of particles." After ten wintry weeks, he packed his bags and "escaped from the whirlpool of idiotic card-leaving of which Florentine existence is mainly composed."

II

Henry proceeded to Venice, where he arrived on February 22, 1887, to find it altogether strange in its dampness and cold, with watery sunshine and the *gondolieri* beckoning as if it were midsummer. He had long promised Mrs. Bronson he would be her guest. Casa Alvisi, opposite the great baroque Salute, was a kind of social *porto di mare*, at the mouth of the Grand Canal. Mrs. Bronson used an apartment in a Giustiniani palace attached to the rear of Ca'Alvisi for her guests. Browning had often stayed there, for weeks at a time; and Henry, hugging a big plastered stove in which a fire cracked and roared, at first found it adequate, if a bit gloomy. His hostess provided a gondolier who served as cook, so that Henry had total privacy; after Florence he felt he could enjoy some quiet, and possess his soul. He had been chased from Florence, he wrote to Howells, "by the amiable effort that was manifested to retain me."

The novelist spent what he later described as "seven unsuccessful weeks" in Venice. The "glutinous malodorous damp" in the *calles* and campos bothered him. He developed a series of splitting headaches shortly after his arrival; and his state of mind was not helped by a heavy snowfall in mid-March. "Yesterday there were sinister carts in the Piazza and men who looked like Irishmen shovelling away snow. One was almost sorry to have left Boston," he wrote Boott. He confined himself largely to the company of Mrs. Bronson, her daughter Edith, and to the Daniel Curtises, whom he had met long before but whom he now saw for the first time in their splendid palace, the Barbaro, on the Grand Canal not far from the Accadémia. He was to become accustomed to Curtis's anecdotes ("doing his best to make the Grand Canal seem like Beacon Street"), and to become fond of his wife, Ariana Curtis, daughter of an English admiral. His social life was cut short, however, by an acute attack of jaundice. He took to his bed and ran a slight temperature for sixteen days. "This made it," he wrote William, "the *longest* illness I have had since I was laid up with typhoid fever so many years before, at Boulogne." He had good medical attention and his gondolier was a faithful nurse. He blamed his illness on his "insalubrious" rooms. "The apartment is not *simpatico*," he said. Fenimore wrote offering him his rooms in the Villa Brichieri again, since she was occupying only the upper apartment. She made arrangements for a cab to meet Henry at the station in Florence, and for his transportation to the hill-top. Mrs. Bronson's gondolier all but wept at the Venice station when he saw Henry off; and his old Roman acquaintance of the *Roderick Hudson* period, Eugene Benson, the painter, whom Henry had seen in the Palazzo Capello in the Rio Marin (the palace which the novelist would use in "The Aspern Papers"), turned up to say good-bye. In Florence, Dr. Baldwin, having heard of Henry's illness, met the Venice train, when it arrived on a Saturday evening in April, and insisted on escorting him personally to the Brichieri. The "breezy Tuscan hilltop suits me better," the novelist wrote to his Venetian hostess. "I have the most majestic, and at the same time the most *allegro* quarters here—and the place is more beautiful than ever."

THE ASPERN PAPERS

HENRY'S LETTERS FROM HIS HILL-TOP, DURING APRIL AND MAY OF 1887, breathe an air of calm and release—a sense of enchantment —rarely to be found in his correspondence. After his illness, the gloom of his uncomfortable quarters in Venice, and the sense of mouldiness and decay in the water-city's winter atmosphere, he lived on Bellosguardo among his devoted friends canopied by blue sky and cradled in soft light, with domes and campaniles, mountains and valleys, and a large expanse of cultivated nature as a constant refreshment to the eye. He could sit on the wide terrace of the Villa Brichieri or read and write in its pleasant rose garden. His "vast and vaulted" rooms offered him coolness and a sense of space. Sometimes he had his meal out-of-doors, in the twilight, probably in the company of Fenimore, with the tinkling of the little bell in a church near by sounding its notes in the golden sunset. At night there would be the mournful but characteristic cry of the little Tuscan owl, and the repertoire of the nightingales amid the pines and cypresses. His illness was forgotten: he had privacy or sociability as he wished. He had discovered, for a time, an Italian paradise.

In letter after letter he speaks of having "the most beautiful view in the world." To a friend in London he wrote: "I am completely restored and have taken, till the first of June, part of a delightful villa on this enchanting hilltop just out of the gates of Florence, where the most beautiful view in the world—as beautiful, and somehow as *personal*—and as talkative!—as a lovely woman—hangs before me as often as I lift my head. As soon as I can stop making love to it I shall go back to England—somewhat ruefully, for I feel myself again somewhat tainted with the taste for living abroad." To Gosse he wrote that "at this divine moment" Italy was perfectly irresistible. In England his villa would be "suburban," but here it was "supercelestial." To William he wrote, after describing his view, "I am working very well again."

He was indeed working well again; he entered upon one of the great productive periods of his career—that interval between *The Princess Casamassima* and *The Tragic Muse* which might be called his "Italian phase"—during which he wrote some eight or ten of his most celebrated tales and a short novel. His pen seemed to take strength and power from the beauty around him and from his mode of life. He avoided, this time, the pitfalls of Florentine society, but descended into the city with curiosity to take part in one or two of the fetes arranged that spring in celebration of the unveiling of the new façade of Santa Maria del Fiore, the Duomo. It had been under construction for some years. Henry and Fenimore could well remember the tremendous scaffolding which covered the front of the church when they were sightseeing in Florence together in 1880. The King and Queen attended some of the observances and Henry fell sufficiently into the holiday spirit to don a crimson *lucco* and black velvet headgear and attend the historical ball at the Palazzo Vecchio in the great Sala dei Cinquecento. "I wish you could have seen me," he wrote Mrs. Kemble. "I was lovely." Here, under Vasari's frescoes, Henry witnessed the royal ceremonial and costumes reflecting three centuries of Florentine life. There was however a want of warmth, in spite of the profusion of color; he found this instead in the great historical procession in Florence's streets. Here descendants of the Strozzis, Guicciardinis, Rucellais, Gherardescas, and others, mounted on magnificent horses and wearing "admirable dresses with the childlike gallantry and glee with which only Italians can wear them," rode through the brown old streets followed by an immense train of citizens, all in fifteenth-century garb. It made a "noble picture"; it testified to the "latent love of splendour which is still in those dear people."

I

Henry and Fenimore were living for the first time under the same roof. For this reason, no doubt, there was no allusion to her in any of his letters, although in December he had spoken of her to his friends as his *padrona*, clearly underlining the fact that she was in another villa. He had then made it clear also—to Grace Norton and to William—that in January he had moved out of the Brichieri, when Fenimore took possession of it. Now, however, he had quietly moved back in again, and merely remarked casually to his friends that he had splendid rooms in a fine old

place on Bellosguardo, with a superb view. As for the Boott-
Duvenecks next door in the Castellani—for they had reoccupied
their apartment—they would see no special significance in his
tenancy. The usually cautious Henry, always supremely careful to
avoid any "involvement" with a woman, seems in this instance
to have accepted blandly Fenimore's offer to let him have the
rooms; apparently he felt there was no danger of any public notice being taken of their joint residence. To his more intimate
friends, James simply suggested that Fenimore was a "neighbor."
Thus in a letter to Mrs. Bronson, he speaks of meeting a Florentine kinswoman of hers who "appeared here yesterday punctually
to call on my neighbour Miss Woolson, on whom I was also calling."

We know of one visitor who came to the Brichieri and spent
an evening with Henry and Fenimore. This was the novelist
Rhoda Broughton, whom he had encountered in London drawing rooms and who was to be a good friend of his later years. He
described her to Mrs. Kemble as coming up to his standard of appreciation of Florence; he liked her, he said, "in spite of her rough-
ness." Percy Lubbock, who knew Miss Broughton when she was
sixty, has testified to the "clean lash" of her words, her "crisp
habit," her "uncompromising Britishry," her way of "slashing"
into an argument. She possessed, in other words, the temperament of Henry's elderly London ladies. She was Miss Woolson's
age and she possessed a fund of human wisdom and wit, and an
ease and liberality in her Victorianism—her novels had been considered uncommonly "bold"—which made her interesting to the
American novelist. From James's allusion to this evening in a letter
to Miss Broughton long after, it would seem that she met Miss
Woolson merely as an old and valued friend of Henry's who happened to be on Bellosguardo.

Discreet as they were, we may speculate that they saw each
other with some frequency, even while spending their days in solitary pursuit of their individual work. Fenimore's cook Angelo

served them both; they may indeed have taken certain of their meals together. It is equally likely that even though they were under the same roof, they lived very much as they would have lived had they been housed apart. That Henry, in other circumstances, continued to be cautious we know, for in the following year, when he kept a special rendezvous with Fenimore in Geneva, he mentioned it only to Francis Boott: and to him Henry carefully explained that they were staying in hotels a mile apart. Given Henry's reticences, and the fact that he seems to have attached at this time no particular significance to Fenimore's devotion to him (save that it called for kindness on his part); given Fenimore's personal shyness, for all her epistolary bravado and candor—the evidence would seem to point to a continuing "virtuous" attachment, in which Henry accepted with pleasure all the attention and admiration Fenimore gave him and offered a kind of disinterested and aloof affection in return. There was not a little, in this, of Henry's powerful egotism: why shouldn't Fenimore like him? and if she did, why shouldn't he make himself agreeable to her? That this pleasant and *méticuleuse* old maid may have nourished fantasies of a closer tie does not seem to have occurred to him at this time. If it had, we might assume he would have speedily put distance between himself and her. There was a kind of truce of affection between them. And perhaps the best evidence of this is to be found once more—in the absence of correspondence—in a public document. This was "The Aspern Papers," the most brilliant of all of Henry's tales, which he began and all but completed at the Villa Brichieri.

II

The idea for the tale was in his notebook when he came to stay with Fenimore. He had set it down as far back as January during his stay at the Hôtel du Sud. He had just paid a call on Vernon Lee and her brother and while there had met the Countess Gamba, whom he described as "clever, natural, exuberant." The Countess was the daughter of a Tuscan poet and had married a nephew of Byron's last attachment, Teresa Guiccioli. The Gambas, she told Henry, had a great many of Byron's letters to Teresa; she declared them quite shocking and unprintable. "She took upon herself to burn one of them up!" Henry exclaimed in a letter to Grace Norton; he reiterated this in his notebook—that Eugene Lee-Hamilton elicited from the Countess "that she had *burned* one of them!" This spontaneous indignation from a novelist who built one of the biggest bonfires in Anglo-American literary history to destroy his private papers may seem rather strange. Henry, however, held that it was a writer's duty to clear away the approaches to his privacy. If documents did survive, it was questionable whether others could take it upon themselves to destroy them. Miss Lee's brother told Henry that the Gambas were rather "illiberal and dangerous" guardians of their literary heritage, and refused to show or publish the letters. The Countess Gamba indeed had been angry with Lee-Hamilton when he suggested to her that it was her duty—especially to the English public—to let Byron's letters be seen. "*Elle se fiche bien* of the English public," Henry wrote in his notebook.

On this afternoon, after the Countess Gamba left, Lee-Hamilton told Henry an anecdote prompted by the visit of the Countess and the talk of Byron. There had lived in Florence, to a ripe old age, Mary Jane Clairmont, or "Claire Clairmont" as she called herself, Byron's mistress and mother of Allegra. She had a house in the Via Romana. For some time before her death there lived in it a lodger, a Boston sea captain, named Silsbee. Hardly a Trelawny, Silsbee was nevertheless a typical American skipper with a fund of anecdote. His passion in life was Shelley, and Vernon Lee related that he would come and sit gloomily in an armchair, "looking like some deep-sea monster on a Bernini fountain, staring at the carpet and quoting his favorite author with a trumpet-like twang quite without relevance to the conversation." Silsbee had long known that Claire Clairmont had in her possession certain Shelley and Byron papers. He made every possible effort to acquire these, and had finally obtained domicile in the very house in which they were kept. There were stories that he never ventured far from home lest Miss Clairmont should die while he was away. In one version of the anecdote, he did, however, have to go to America and it was then—in 1879—that she died. Living with her was a Clairmont niece of about fifty, and Silsbee rushed back to see whether he could obtain from her the papers Miss Clairmont had hidden from the world. The niece had long nourished an admiration for the rugged Captain and she said to him, "I will give you all the letters if you will marry me." Lee-Hamilton said that Silsbee was still running.

Henry entered the bare anecdote in his notebook on January 12, 1887. What fascinated him was the thought of Miss Clairmont's having lived on into his time; and that he himself had often passed her door. Sargent remembered her as a handsome old lady, whom he had seen once when he was young at his dancing class when she had replaced an absent pianist. He recalled that she was dressed in black and had a certain faded elegance.

"Certainly there is a little subject there," Henry wrote in his notebook, "the picture of the two faded, queer, poor and discredited old English women—living on into a strange generation, in their musty corner of a foreign town—with these illustrious letters their most precious possession. Then the plot of the Shelley fanatic—his watchings and waitings—the way he *couvers* the treasure. The denouement needn't be the one related of poor Silsbee; and at any rate the general situation is in itself a subject and a picture. It strikes me much," Henry wrote. The interest would be in some price that the man would have to pay—a price the old woman, the survivor, would set upon the papers. The drama of the story would be his hesitations and his struggles, "for he really would give almost anything."

III

"The Aspern Papers" was an attempt by Henry to recapture "the visitable past"—that past which in any generation is still within the reach of its memory—and to convey "the poetry of the thing outlived and lost and gone." This is what he achieved in his extraordinary tale of an old woman living beyond her time in a decaying Venetian palace—for he transferred the scene from Florence—and clinging to the precious letters written to her by a great American poet. The cat-and-mouse game which he devised between his Silsbee character and this lady provides the mounting tension: and in the tale Henry used his characteristic technique, that of having his hero be his own historian—writing his story with such candor and ingenuousness that he reveals his own duplicity, his easy rationalizations and his failure to grasp the fact that, in his zeal for literary history, he is an invader of private lives. In this sense the tale is a moral fable for all historians and biographers. It has set down, once and for all, their anomalous role: and it makes clear, as James's notes did not, on which side the novelist placed himself. He might have been shocked at the Countess Gamba's having burned a Byron letter; but in the tale all of the Aspern papers are burned—a little sadistically, we might say—"one by one." The strange tension of the story resides in the fact that James provided two climaxes; so that when Sir Michael Redgrave converted the tale into a play he had that rare thing among modern dramas, both a second-act "curtain" and a genuine third-act denouement. There are two dramas in this story. The first is that eerie moment when Juliana discovers the narrator trying to gain access to her desk and turns her blazing eyes upon him—those eyes which hitherto had been covered by a green shade—the eyes that had once looked into those of Jeffrey Aspern:

. . . her hands were raised, she had lifted the everlasting curtain that covered half her face, and for the first, the last, the only time I beheld her extraordinary eyes. They glared at me [they were like the sudden drench, for a caught burglar, of a flood of gaslight],* they made me horribly ashamed. I never shall forget her

. . . .
* Inserted in later revision.

strange little bent white tottering figure, with its lifted head, her attitude, her expression; neither shall I forget the tone in which as I turned, looking at her, she hissed out passionately, furiously:

"Ah, you publishing scoundrel!"

This is the *coup de théâtre* of the story: the narrator has been caught red-handed; the hero-worshipper, the lover of poetry, the gallant gentleman, is nothing but a common thief in his compulsive need to acquire a memento of the man he worships. But the splendid theatricality of this scene is surpassed by the denouement in the "third act," in which the middle-aged niece, after the death of Juliana, suggests to the narrator that the Aspern papers could be his if he only became a member of the family. "If you were not a stranger . . . Anything that is mine would be yours." The pathos of this scene has dramatic grandeur; and it is too much for the narrator. He had been ready to steal; he had even said playfully he would be willing to make love to the younger Miss Bordereau. Now all he can stammer is "Ah, Miss Tita—ah, Miss Tita— It wouldn't do, it wouldn't do!" He flees the palace, and surrenders all hope of getting the Aspern papers.

The passage which follows is perhaps the most exquisite in this masterpiece. The narrator's thoughts and feelings are described as he is rowed through the canals by his gondolier. The vision of the bright decaying city melts into his personal disaster. "I could not accept. I could not, for a bundle of tattered papers, marry a ridiculous, pathetic, provincial old woman." He may have trifled with her affections; he now understands this; yet he is not sufficiently without principle to achieve his ends at any cost. Late in the afternoon he finds himself standing before the church of Saints John and Paul looking up at the great equestrian statue of Bartolommeo Colleoni, the old buccaneer, who had grabbed at life with his two fists. Seldom had James fused scene and subject more artfully than at this moment when the literary narrator searches the "small square-jawed face" of the statue and thinks of the career of "the terrible *condottiere* who sits so sturdily astride of his huge bronze horse, on the high pedestal on which Venetian gratitude maintains him."

I only found myself staring at the triumphant captain as if he had an oracle on his lips. The western light shines into all his grimness at that hour and makes it wonderfully personal. But he continued to look far over my head, at the red immersion of another day—he had seen so many go down into the lagoon through the centuries—and if he were thinking of battles and stratagems they were of a different quality from any I had to tell him of.

This is all but the end of the narrator's stratagems. So tense a drama, unfolded step by step and with an inexorable logic—an old palace, two solitary ladies, and a bundle of papers as the principal properties and all Venice for a backdrop—would have been nothing without the measured tread of the narrative. There is no faltering footstep in it, from the opening scene in which James introduces the all-knowing Mrs. Prest (a re-creation of the benevolent Mrs. Bronson), to the last scene in the old palace when the narrator learns of the fate of the papers. Once the situation had been established there had ensued a long period in which the narrator simply lived in his rooms, cultivated the garden, "bombarded" the ladies with flowers, and found every door closed in his face. James must make the reader feel the passage of several weeks from spring to hot summer, and he does this in half a dozen pages with the beautiful assurance of one who can make the clock take the rhythm of his tracing pen. We walk the palace with the restless storyteller in his cat-and-mouse game, watching always for some move, some bit of action from the ladies who are his prey. "Their motionless shutters became as expressive as eyes consciously closed, and I took comfort in thinking that at all events though invisible themselves they saw me between the lashes." This brief section (it is the fourth of the nine equal parts into which the narrative falls) ends with the narrator's account of Jeffrey Aspern, the American Romantic poet he idolizes: and in Aspern James evokes himself as he was, and as he would

have liked to be—a kind of Hawthorne figure liberated from the
parochial and from all Puritan constriction—"that at a period
when our native land was nude and crude and provincial, when
the famous 'atmosphere' it is supposed to lack was not even
missed, when literature was lonely there and art and form almost
impossible, he had found means to live and write like one of the
first; to be free and general and not at all afraid; to feel, understand and express everything."

Such was James's flight of fancy on the hill of Bellosguardo, his
vision of past and present, of a dying city, a crumbling palace, and
a dying old lady who had once known a great passion for a great
poet. What had begun as "a final scene of the rich dim Shelley
drama played out in the very theatre of our own 'modernity,'"
ended in a beautifully-wrought tale which was, above all, a defense of privacy and an exposure of the unfeeling egotist who exploits others' feelings for his own ends. Nor is the old Juliana,
with her green eyeshade, exempt from this predatory character;
she knows her position of advantage, and on the brink of the
grave, clings to life with all the greed and rapacity and cunning,
as well as the vitality, of that other strange expatriate Venetian,
Volpone. She knows how to bargain for the narrator's dollars or
pounds—one wants to say ducats—and use her advantage to the
full. If Venice in literature had been gilded by the poetry of Shakespeare, the satire of Jonson, the aesthetic of Ruskin, it was now
immortally touched by the pen of fiction, by Henry James, as it
would be by Proust and Mann after him. "The Aspern Papers"
is a pathetic comedy raised to the level of an extraordinary time-
vision, a superb play of the historic sense.

IV

Henry James had transferred the scene of the Silsbee anecdote
from Florence to Venice: and in the writing of it he transferred
—also from Florence to Venice—certain circumstances of his immediate life. On Bellosguardo he was occupying an apartment in

an old Italian villa, next to a garden, even as the narrator of the tale moves into a suite of rooms in the old Venetian palace and is given the privilege of the garden. In both the actual villa and the imaginary palace there was living a middle-aged niece—a grand-niece, to be exact in each case—of James Fenimore Cooper in the real-life circumstances and of Juliana Bordereau in the fiction. Fenimore too reached back to a "visitable past" of American literature and to the very period in which Jeffrey Aspern flourished. Aspern would have been contemporary both of Cooper and of Byron and—in the re-created and re-imagined past—was on the Continent at the same time as these writers. His name, moreover, may have been selected for those further ironic overtones which James often invoked in baptizing his characters. Aspern, in Austria, was the scene of a great encounter: here Napoleon met his first crushing defeat. James distinctly identified himself with Aspern: we have seen how he endowed him with the same free energetic qualities he possessed or wished to possess; and he furthermore said, in his late preface, that he had "*thought* New York as I projected him," thereby conferring on him the city of his own birth (and also the state with which Fenimore Cooper was identified).

There are other such links between life and James's imagined tale. Not only is it specified that Tita,* who is referred to throughout as a "niece," is actually a "grand-niece." Her name, common enough in Venice, is an uncommon one to find in one of Miss Woolson's own novels—that of Tita Douglas in her most popular work, *Anne*. We might, if we wished to pursue such will-o'-the-wisps of suggestion, note also that the name Tito Melema, the young Greek, figures in the pages of *Romola*, George Eliot's novel given by James as a gift to Fenimore while he was staying on Bellosguardo.

These are but fugitive hints and perhaps matters of coincidence. Much closer and more significant is the nature of the rela-

. . . .
* In his late revision of the tale, James altered the name to Tina.

tionship between the narrator and Tita and the way in which
he woos her sympathies, takes her sightseeing in the gondola,
re-enacts those gallantries James had bestowed upon Fenimore
during the first weeks of their acquaintance. The course of this
relationship in the story suggests markedly that James was—perhaps at this moment intuitively—beginning to feel uneasy about
the familiar life into which he had been led with the deaf Miss
Woolson. The relationship may have been propriety itself; but
had he not perhaps gone too far? Of Fenimore's feelings Henry
could never have been wholly in doubt; her letters to him, written
when he was in America, had carried an unverbalized refrain demanding attention, affection, proximity: she had written to him
long ago, from the very scene of "The Aspern Papers"—"the
lagoons, the Piazzetta, and the little still canals all send their love
to you. They wish you were here. And so do I." And in that
very letter she had told James he was unable to portray women
in love. "If you will only care for her yourself," she had written,
urging him to pay attention to his heroines. Miss Woolson
would hardly suggest to Henry that they should find some more
intimate ground of communion, or urge upon him as directly as
Tita had urged the narrator, with the Aspern papers in her hands,
the need for an alliance. Nevertheless she had been saying as
much indirectly ever since their Florentine meeting. Her letters
and her acts attest to her desire to be near him, not least her
choice of an uncongenial climate in which she had lived for three
years, we may suppose, to have the occasional privilege of Henry's
company. All evidence points, otherwise, to her having had a very
lonely life in England. The narrator in "The Aspern Papers," fleeing Tita and the old palace, tells himself at the last that he had
"unwittingly but none the less deplorably trifled." He repeats to
himself, "I had not given her cause—distinctly I had not." He had
been "as kind as possible, because I really liked her," and he asks
himself, "since when had that become a crime where a woman of
such an age and such an appearance was concerned?" This seems
to have been Henry's logic as well. He treated Miss Woolson as

a friendly and charming old maid for whom he had a feeling of kindness because she was devoted to him. And now, through the wall of his ego, he was beginning to feel that perhaps she, on her side, nourished more affectionate thoughts than he suspected. The tale suggests that Henry had begun to wonder whether Fenimore was not expecting more of him than mere displays of kindness—the presentation and inscription of books and the attentions of a discreet *galantuomo*. "At any rate, whether I had given cause or not it went without saying," the admirer of Jeffrey Aspern tells himself, "that I could not pay the price."

The narrator may have told himself "I had not given her cause" —but the reader knows that he had. He had enlisted Tita on his side from the first by cajoling and flattery; he had invited this cloistered middle-aged woman, to whom the very sight of a man was a novelty, to play his particular game and even to betray her great-aunt: even as Henry had allowed his own needs for friendship, companionship, understanding, to blind him to what he might stand for in his relationship with Fenimore, and what he might be doing to her affections. He had treated her as if she were as old as Mrs. Procter or Mrs. Kemble. In the tale, the unfeeling cruelty of the narrator is softened somewhat by his dedicated artistic nature, his sense of the past, his love for the great poet. Nevertheless his behavior has in it a quality of selfishness, a kind of easy innocence that belongs to that of a cad—an aesthetic cad, perhaps, but certainly not a sentient gentleman. In life, Henry seems to have gained a glimmer of insight, or sensed the danger of incurring the same charge, or a charge even more serious—that of being so blinded by egotism that he might be held guilty of a total failure in awareness—he the novelist who of all writers could know, and feel and understand.

We may carry this speculation one step further. He had probably had an opportunity to see that Fenimore, with her innumerable trunks and possessions, was unable to throw anything away. And for all their promise to each other that they would destroy their correspondence, the thought may have occurred to him that somewhere among her accumulations were impulsive, scribbled pages he had dashed off to her, at various times, filled with his spontaneities of affection and irresponsibilities of feeling. "The Aspern Papers" may have been a screen for deeper thoughts, nourished by the novelist, that somewhere, in the Brichieri, there might lurk some Henry James papers.

PALAZZO BARBARO

I

HENRY LEFT BELLOSGUARDO ON MAY 25, 1887 TO SPEND TEN DAYS with the Curtises at the Palazzo Barbaro. He spoke of returning to Florence for another three weeks or a month "though not to Bellosguardo," but he lingered in Venice and his ten days became a visit of five weeks, the longest private visit he had ever paid. He had never lived in so princely a style: he was fond of the sedate palace, with its marble and frescoes, and its portraits of the doges; he particularly liked his quiet cool rooms at the back, which looked into the shade of a court, through Gothic windows set at quite arbitrary levels. He worked in a room with a pompous Tiepolo ceiling and walls of ancient pale-green damask, slightly shredded and patched. The Curtises proved congenial hosts once Henry became accustomed to Mr. Curtis's puns and anecdotes, and Mrs. Curtis's high tone and social fastidiousness. Henry found them "intelligent, clever and hospitable." They had left Boston some years before in the wake of an episode of social comedy, in which Mr. Curtis, in a moment of anger, had tweaked the nose

of a fellow-aristocrat and been jailed briefly for assault and bat-
tery. This had quite soured his love for America and they had
purchased the Barbaro in 1885 and settled down to being permanent Venetian-Bostonians. "They can't keep their hands off their
native land," Henry observed; this tended, he said, to fan his own
patriotism to a fever. With their great ménage—servants, gondoliers, visiting friends, daily excursions to the Lido—they provided
Henry with large access to a sociable world, from which he could
withdraw to complete privacy in his apartment.

Venetian society proved less strenuous than Florentine, and
more indigenous. It was casual and "exoteric." Henry described it
as "a thing of heterogeneous vivid patches, but with a fine old native basis." One of the most remarkable of its members was the
Countess Pisani, a lady who made Henry believe in the romantic
heroines of Disraeli and Bulwer. She was partly English; and she
too had a link with Byron. Her father was the doctor who bled
the English poet to death at Missolonghi. Her mother had been a
French odalisque out of the harem of the Grand Turk. The late
Count Pisani, "a descendant of all the Doges," had married her
for her beauty thirty-five years before. Now, at fifty-five or sixty,
"widowed, palaced, villaed, pictured, jewelled, and modified by
Venetian society," she impressed Henry as the sort of woman one
might have found in the early years of the century "receiving on a
balcony at two o'clock on a June morning."

Staying with the Countess Pisani was May Marcy McClellan,
daughter of the Civil War general, whom Henry had met in
Florence. He found himself observing a character out of his own
novels. That Miss McClellan should be favored with the hospitality of the Countess struck Henry as an anomaly. She had created
a stir the previous winter in Venetian circles by writing a gossipy
letter to an American newspaper about the very society which had
entertained her. The letter had been "as long, as confidential, as
'chatty,' as full of headlong history and lingering legend, of aberra-
tion and confusion, as she might have indited to the most trusted
of friends." It had appeared in the full light of day in the col-

umns of a New York newspaper. This kind of public chatter had always shocked Henry; he had himself been a victim of it on sundry occasions—had found that charming females, who dined with him in London, later turned out to have pens in their handbags and some kind of ink in their veins.

The American habit of the public chronicling of private life had already been satirized by the novelist in Henrietta Stackpole and in the unprepossessing newspaperman, Matthias Pardon, of *The Bostonians*. Henry was to say later that "no power on earth would induce me to designate . . . the recording, slobbering sheet" in which Miss McClellan's effusion appeared; it is however identified in his notebooks, and a search in the files of the New York *World* reveals the offending letter in all its dull prolixity in the issue of November 14, 1886. By modern standards it is sufficiently mild: in its own day it must have been a scandalous repayment of various kindnesses. Miss McClellan had visited Varese, near the Swiss border, and had stayed in the Hotel Excelsior, formerly a villa belonging to the Morosonis of Venice, who had sold it, she proclaimed, for "pecuniary reasons." Everyone she met there "rejoiced in some sort of a handle to his or her name." The women's jewels—and she named the women—were "something gorgeous." Thus the daughter of Prince Pia dei Lavvia wore sapphires as "big as pigeon's eggs" and diamond solitaires "which any New York millionairess might envy." She described the "lurching walk and excessively British garments of these Italian dudes." The men were handsomer than the women and "one countess who is considered something quite lovely would not attract attention in a New York ballroom." Such had been her aimless gossip; nevertheless the Countess Pisani "has that foolish virgin staying with her." Henry described her as "a rather flippant, spoiled girl." He had had some talk with the McClellans, mother and daughter, in Florence that winter and had described them in full to his friend Mrs. Bronson, who as an American-Venetian was profoundly shocked by the girl's betrayal of her well-meaning friends. Miss McClellan "spoke to me of the matter with less humility—with

a certain resentment, as if she herself had been wronged," the
novelist told Mrs. Bronson. The mother was more contrite and
referred to her "daughter's lamentable *faux pas*." Both were concerned, however, not so much with the girl's thoughtless act, as
with their fear that if they returned to Venice they might find
"every back turned to them." Henry added: "Good heavens, what
a superfluous product is the smart, forward, over-encouraged,
thinking-she-can-write-and-that-her-writing-has-any-business-to-exist
American girl! Basta!" He also wrote: "She is Americanissimo—in
the sense of being launched as a young person before the Lord,
and no wonder the poor dear old Venetian mind can't understand
such incongruities. I should like to write a story about the business,
as a pendant to Daisy Miller, but I won't, to deepen the complica-
tion."

That autumn in London, however, he changed his mind. He
may have felt that if Miss McClellan could presume to write about
others and invade their privacy, he could do the same to her,
providing he used sufficient art to give the entire matter a different setting. In his notebook he spoke of the girl's "inconceivable
letter" and "the strange *typicality* of the whole thing." He remembered that the girl was amazed that her aimless gossip should
have been resented. "One sketches one's age but imperfectly if one
doesn't touch on that particular matter: the invasion, the impu-
dence, the shamelessness of the newspaper and the interviewer, the
devouring *publicity* of life, the extinction of all sense between
public and private." Out of this Venetian episode Henry derived
The Reverberator, a short novel published in 1888. The story
dealt with another facet of the activities of "publishing scoun-
drels"; it was a journalistic pendant to the literary "Aspern Papers."

II

In mid-June Paul Bourget turned up in Venice and during their
many talks offered Henry still another theme. He told him of the
suicide of a young friend, who had jumped out of her hotel win-

dow in Milan. Bourget had an hypothesis: the girl had discovered that her mother had lovers, and this had weighed upon her. He also believed that she had tried to escape into a marriage—that is, she had suggested to an attentive young man that he might indicate what his intentions were. The young man had been acutely embarrassed; his interest had been friendly but not marital. The girl had felt ashamed; all doors seemed to be closing around her and she had taken her life. It later developed that much of this was Bourget's fancy. Henry responded however to this new version of a woman proposing marriage to a man; and in his hands the material was turned into an Anglo-American picture—a story of an adulterous international marriage in London in which a puritanical young girl, horrified by her sister's immorality and seeking escape, proposes marriage to a young American. Before he left Venice, Henry was at work on this tale, to which he gave the title "A London Life"—and for the first time in his quarter of a century of writing found himself taking an indulgent, though not altogether approving, view of the laxity of the married American woman and a critical view of the inflexible morality of her sister.

III

At the beginning of July, Henry reluctantly quitted Venice and brought his long Italian stay to an end. He had a final dinner with Mrs. Bronson and her daughter, in their gondola, on the glassy lagoon, "in the pink sunset, with the Chioggia boats floating by like familiar little phantom ships, red and yellow and green—the impression of that enchanting hour has never left me—and I have only to close my eyes to see you and Edith sitting there on the other side of the narrow but abundant board and the unoccupied Domenico hemmed in behind you, squatting philosophically on his haunches." Of such memories were his Italian hours composed, and they filled out romantically the hours of his other Italian years. The "season" would be over in London by the time he reached it: and he always enjoyed being in the British capital at midsummer. Alice had vacated De Vere Gardens and returned to Leamington. It was time to leave. He had had his fill of Italian impressions—and Italian experience. He thought again that he might take some little apartment in Venice, create a permanent Italian *pied à terre* for himself, so enamored had he become this time with the life of the place. However, he decided not to force the issue; he would let time decide whether this would be an advantage or not. There remained only one further promise to redeem. When on the Continent in the summer he always paid his respects to Mrs. Kemble. Henry journeyed from Venice without haste to Vicenza, Mantua, Cremona, Brescia, and Bergamo. Mantua was dreary and pestilential; the fleas drove him away. But he enjoyed the beefsteaks of Brescia and the beautiful bronze Victory in the museum, "second only" to the Venus de Milo. "And she has wings—and such beauties—which Venus hasn't," he wrote to Mrs. Curtis.

On July 6 he joined Mrs. Kemble at Stresa and spent several interesting days with her. He found her an "extinct volcano," a shadow of her former self. "Given the temperature, the shadow is better—and we manage to discuss a little," he told Mrs. Curtis. There were few tourists; the hotels were empty; it was very hot and Henry lingered briefly. Then he crossed into Switzerland, over the Simplon, on foot, as he had done in the days of his youth, "a rapture of wild flowers and mountain streams—but it was over in a flash." After that he went straight to London. On July 22 he was back at De Vere Gardens, his Italian holiday—with the great release of creative energy it had given him—at an end.

It had given him much more: he had never had such a sense of personal freedom. Describing his call on Mrs. Kemble to Grace Norton, he commented on the way in which she moved, as in one mass, "and if she does so little as to button her glove, it is the whole of her 'personality' that does it." He had the feeling however that it was rather "a melancholy mistake, in this uncertain life of ours, to have founded oneself on so many rigidities and rules—so many siftings and sortings." And then, in this letter to

Miss Norton, he suddenly exclaimed—as if he were addressing his correspondent, and himself, and perhaps all of New England: "Let us be flexible, dear Grace; let us be flexible! And even if we don't reach the sun we shall at least have been up in a balloon."

BOOK FIVE

Art and the Marketplace 1888–1889

A MASSING OF MASTERPIECES

HE HAD, IT WOULD SEEM, BEEN UP IN A BALLOON IN THE IMMENSITIES of the Italian sky and above the beauties of Bellosguardo. He had undergone the last stages of an almost imperceptible evolution begun years before—a process which had converted this hardworking, pleasure-loving, duty-haunted sentient American, with his large and generous gifts, from an old Calvinistic inheritance of codes and rules and rigidities into a more relaxed (though still laborious) Americano-European. From his new altitude he had discovered new meanings in the word *flexible*. The little tragicomedies and comediettas of man engaged in his civilized round which had absorbed him seemed now less "final" than he had ever before believed. Had it been worth while for Roderick Hudson to tear his passion to tatters and fall over a Swiss cliff, all because of an unfathomable woman? Might not his creator have offered him certain alternatives? Was passion necessarily inimical to art? If hearts were broken, they seemed sometimes to mend. If man sinned, sins sometimes seemed to be forgiven. If man erred, he seemed somehow to have a capacity for growing scar tissue over his errors. Even "fallen women," as he himself knew, could sometimes make their way in society. Society actually found them a source of entertainment. He had pictured in his art the inflexible character of society—accurately enough—but he had also written as if everything were irreversible. He had frustrated his American, and doomed Daisy Miller, and adhered to the *status quo*, when life seemed constantly to be built on shifting sands. Italy alone seemed to remain (so he wrote to his Philadelphia-Roman friend Mrs. Wister), after other things collapsed—"the support given by religion, the domestic affections, the loss of fame, the hope of glory, the desire of fortune and various other squeezed oranges." But to the irony and cynicism of this he might have added that a squeezed orange was not a disaster. The fruit of this earth was abundant.

These were hardly Henry's reflections after his eight months in Italy: but they are the reflections we catch in the bright mirrors of the tales he had written during this period and which he continued to write in London during the next year. In these tales it seemed as if, in the fullness of time, Henry had come to recognize that people could, on occasion, defy fate—and society—and survive. He had from the first—it was his heritage from his father's old religious crisis—had an uncanny sense of evil, not as mere wickedness or transgression, but as an eerie extra-human force, baleful and terrifying, an actuality existing beyond man's control yet capable of destroying him. This had been the meaning of the Emperor's topaz, or the unearthed Juno—disinterred relics of history which belonged to old barbarisms and cruelties and which had, quickly, to be covered up again, lest new and terrible harm be done. Henry had not altogether overcome this panic sense of evil. His essay on Emerson of this period, however, shows a new and benevolent view of man's earthly weaknesses and a feeling that Emerson represented American innocence and naïveté only half-understanding that the tree in Eden had offered not only knowledge of evil but access to the world's wisdom. Henry had left London with the newspapers screaming about Lady Colin Campbell's divorce suit, and he had predicted that the case would "besmirch exceedingly the already very damaged prestige of the English upper class." He returned to find that nothing had been besmirched. The perishable newspapers had had their little day, and the upper classes were as indestructible—and as unbesmirched —as ever. Moreover they seemed to make their own rules, in the most arbitrary fashion imaginable.

Henry had finally abandoned his American innocence. He could still portray it as subtly as of old; but he himself now understood it as never before. He was aware that what he had visioned as "corrupt old Europe" represented a splendid façade of civilization, formed over the centuries, behind which existed all manner of things Americans might judge harshly, and regard as evil—but that this façade also concealed a life of liberty; and that it offered a veil of public decency, codes and standards of judgments, with which to protect "the private life." To have a private life was to have freedom; and a loss of freedom, he said, was "the greatest form of suffering." To be impervious to others' judgments and others' meddlings was to have freedom: and this is what Henry had been discovering ever since he left Quincy Street in 1875.

I

The moral substance of his work now underwent a change. The evil in "The Aspern Papers" lay not in Juliana's ancient indiscretions or Jeffrey Aspern's "love-life." It lay in the invasion of privacy, the failure to enter into human feeling. The narrator had been not only a "publishing scoundrel," but a hopeless meddler as well. In "A London Life" Henry set out to describe the sense of shock experienced by his American innocent over her sister Selina's adulteries. But what he depicted was the panic state of a girl too rigid and meddlesome to recognize that in this world adulteries do occur, marriages do break up; that people may act irresponsibly

—but that this is their affair, and no one else's. Moreover the world does not thereby come to an end. All the personages in "A London Life" try to explain this to Laura. Old Lady Davenant, the charming and witty reincarnation of Mrs. Duncan Stewart, says to her candidly that she has no patience "with the highstrung way you take things"—and she speaks out of fondness for her. Laura, however, "bristling with righteousness," pursues her sister into Belgium, after Selina has run off with Captain Crispin, as if her missionary zeal could bring her sister back. "She exaggerates the badness of it," says Lady Davenant. "Good heavens, at that rate where should some of us be?" And while James the moralist does not necessarily approve of society's flaunted immoralities, he demonstrates the futility of Laura's self-righteous "morality." Evil is still terrifying to certain of James's characters —as terrifying as to Mrs. Ambient, for whom a dead child was better than an "exposed" living child. Laura, in her sense of her own goodness and rightness, foreshadows the anxious and panic-stricken governess of "The Turn of the Screw."

The Reverberator was a light comedy based on the story of Miss McClellan's adventure in Venetian society, and in it James returned to the Paris of *The American*. His portrait of the two Boston sisters and their father, in the Hôtel de l'Univers et de Cheltenham, has all the perfection of his "Daisy Miller" period and much greater maturity. The significant figure in this tight little Franco-American drama is Mr. George Flack, the Paris correspondent of the American society newspaper, the name of which provides the resounding title to this short novel.

Mr. Flack is the embodiment of the new journalism: and he will have many counterparts during the twentieth century in his native land. "You can't keep out the light of the press," he says. His conception of this light is the ferreting out of society gossip —often with the help of society: "The society news of every quarter of the globe, furnished by the prominent members themselves (oh, *they* can be fixed—you'll see!) from day to day and from hour to hour and served up at every breakfast-table in the

United States—that's what the American people want and that's what the American people are going to have." He was right. For in Flack, Henry James demonstrated that America would develop its own peculiar corruptions. And when the journalist writes his scandalmongering letter and endangers Francie Dosson's marriage into French society, her father expresses surprise at all the fuss. He wants to know whether the French were not aware "of the charges brought every day against the most prominent men in Boston" by the newspapers. Libel, in other words, was routine in America. Francie, however, begins to wonder whether the lively and chatty letters she had herself relished in the papers had not really meant "a violation of sanctities, a convulsion of homes, a burning of smitten faces, a rupture of girls' engagements." The sanctimonious side of Mr. Dosson's national character emerges when he reflects "that if these people had done bad things they ought to be ashamed of themselves and he couldn't pity them, and if they hadn't done them there was no need of making such a rumpus about other people knowing." Henry James had seen the handwriting on the wall: he had forecast the evolution of a press which would, under the guise of "names make news," make capital of people's privacy, increasingly weaken the laws of libel, and increasingly turn themselves into journals of gossip rather than of political and national intelligence, which had been their original and primary function. For the Americans in this novel the corruption has already occurred, "the newspapers and all they contained were a part of the general fatality of things, of the recurrent freshness of the universe, coming out like the sun in the morning or the stars at night."

"The Lesson of the Master," which Henry wrote when he had returned to De Vere Gardens, reflected the moral change in the area closest to him. The Master in the tale, the great novelist, reads a lecture to the young would-be writer: marriage, dressing one's wife, educating one's children, taking one's place in the world, are costly matters. The artist must choose. He can either marry and cheapen his art—and be a success—or choose a celibate course, and produce the masterpieces which the world will not understand and which alone justify his dedication and self-denial. Success in itself, he suggests, is a cheapening process. But the Master does not follow his own counsel. One wonders at the end of the tale what this ironic "lesson" really is. Admirable though James's statement may be, on behalf of the sanctity of art and the danger of worldliness, the reader—and the young idealist —feel rather "sold."

In thus re-examining his old high standards and their relation to the facts of existence, Henry James was now pondering the extent to which an artist must be prepared to make his compromises with the marketplace; and whether life itself wasn't a "sell." If people could sin and get away with it in society, an artist could be a "success"—or even a humbug—and get away with it in art. The question was now formulating itself in Henry's consciousness in some such fashion and it would be written out in a long novel for which he already had the title: *The Tragic Muse.* The words seemed to be there, seen through his high west window in De Vere Gardens as he looked out upon teeming London, and surveyed the long road he had travelled since "Daisy Miller."

II

Henry was ceasing to believe that Americans were composed of finer moral fibre than the Europeans. He still believed that their innocence had great charm; nevertheless he now discerned in this innocence a claustrophobic ignorance. Worse still, a need to impose it upon others. He had set out to proclaim the forthrightness of the Christopher Newmans of his race and their noble gift of friendliness and egalitarianism. He had discovered that "the first thing a society does after it has left the aristocratic out, is to put it in again." He had also come to see that perhaps the faults and virtues of the Americans and the English were "simply different chapters of the same general subject." We find him writing to his brother William a long and reflective letter late in 1888, when he had fully assimilated his experience of the previous year. After reaching a certain age, he said, and living in a country not his own, and applying to it his ironical and cynical disposition, certain truths became apparent. One was that he was "deadly weary of the whole 'international' state of mind." He positively *ached*, he said, "with fatigue at the way it is constantly forced upon one as a sort of virtue or obligation." He continued:

I can't look at the English and American world, or feel about them, any more, save as a big Anglo-Saxon total, destined to such an amount of melting together that an insistence on their differences becomes more and more idle and pedantic and that that melting together will come the faster the more one takes it for granted and treats the life of the two countries as continuous or more or less convertible.

From this he went on to a statement justly famous, certainly one of the most enlightened artistic statements of his time:

I have not the least hesitation in saying that I aspire to write in such a way that it would be impossible to an outsider to say whether I am, at a given moment, an American writing about England or an Englishman writing about America (dealing as I do with both countries), and so far from being ashamed of such an ambiguity I should be exceedingly proud of it, for it would be highly civilized.

Henry not only said this privately to his brother; he published a charming dialogue in *Scribner's*, in March of 1889 ("An Animated Conversation"), which is an early appeal for a merging of Anglo-American cultures. He makes the claim that this is inevitable: "What other nations are continually meeting to talk over the reasons why they shouldn't meet? What others are so sociably separate—so intertwinedly cohesively alien?" He foresees that England and America can cultivate with talent "a common destiny," united in the arts of peace "by which I mean of course in the arts of life."

In his letter to William, Henry alluded to his inability to do much reading since "I produce a great deal." This was a matter on which William often touched, tied as he was to the university and his academic work. Henry observed that he had chosen early in his London life to take aboard "an amount of human and social information" (in preference to the information contained in books) and that he would do the same if he were living his life over. "One can read when one is middle-aged or old; but one can mingle in the world with fresh perceptions only when one is young." He added, "the great thing is to be *saturated* with something—that is, in one way or another, with life; and I chose the form of my saturation."

This saturation had been in reality with forms of civilization, with the study of national traits and character, and in particular with the forms of Anglo-American life to which he was exposed. The "Italian phase" had given him his perspective. New choices, new decisions, would have to be made.

III

Energetic "producer" though he always was, Henry had never been as productive as during his eight months in Italy and immediately after in London. In sequence, he had written "The Aspern Papers," "A London Life," and *The Reverberator*, all in less than a year—and in the midst of other writings as well. The tales were held back by the editors for a number of reasons, and they appeared simultaneously, so that for the better part of the following year Henry James dominated the magazines as never before. Howells likened Henry's literary "show" to an art exhibition. What had occurred was that the magazines were now using illustrations on a large scale; and certain of Henry's stories, sent to *Harper's New Monthly Magazine*, the revived *Scribner's* and the *Century*, had to wait their turn on illustrators' drawing-tables. Moreover, Henry had dispatched "The Aspern Papers" to the *Atlantic* without prior consultation with the editor; and its three instalments could be fitted with difficulty into the already pre-empted space of the current issues. Henry, accustomed to prompt publication, complained at the beginning of 1888 to Howells that he remained "irremediably unpublished." He wondered whether the failure of *The Bos-tonians* and *The Princess* had ruined his reputation. Editors kept his manuscripts back "for months and years, as if they were ashamed of them"; he felt he was being "condemned apparently to eternal silence." The passage has often been quoted by critics but wholly out of context: for if the editors were keeping back his manuscripts, it was not because they had rejected them, but be-cause they wished all the more advantageously to publish them. James's remark, made in this letter, that "very likely too some day all my buried prose will kick off its various tombstones at once" has been quoted as a prophecy of his posthumous "revival." He was not looking that far ahead. Nor was his prose deeply buried. Presently it blossomed forth. "Louisa Pallant" came out in Febru-ary 1888 in *Harper's*; *The Reverberator* ran in *Macmillan's* from February through April, although written after "The Aspern Pa-pers," which emerged in the *Atlantic* from March through May; "The Liar" was in the *Century* in May and June, "The Modern Warning" in *Harper's* in June, and "A London Life" ran in *Scrib-ner's* from June through September. In the meantime "The Lesson of the Master" was appearing during July and August in the *Uni-versal Review* and "The Patagonia" overlapped during August and into September in the *English Illustrated*.

This was not all. His essay on Maupassant was in the *Fort-nightly Review* in March, that on Pierre Loti in April, and a long review of the Goncourt journals came out in October. His ap-preciation of Stevenson appeared in the *Century* in April (held up almost a year while an artist was doing a portrait of Henry's friend); and his since-celebrated essay on "London," with illustra-tions by Pennell, was in the *Century* in December. Altogether 1888 was a successful and prosperous year, and James's mournful complaint to Howells was that of an impatient rather than of an unpublished and unpopular author.

Howells said as much in commenting on this sudden eruption of his friend's work in the journals. "One turned," he wrote in his column in *Harper's*, "from one masterpiece to another, making his comparisons and delighted to find that the stories helped rather than hurt one another, and that their accidental massing enhanced his pleasure in them." He went on:

It will certainly amaze a future day that such things as his [James's] could be done in ours and meet only a feeble and conditional acceptance from the "best" criticism, with something little short of ribald insult from the common cry of literary paragraphers. But happily the critics do not form an author's only readers; they are not even his judges. These are the editors of the magazines, which are now the real avenues to the public; and their recent unanimity in presenting simultaneously some of the best work of Mr. James's life in the way of short stories indicates the existence of an interest in all he does, which is doubtless the true measure of his popularity.

The new batch of tales constituted a series of "masterpieces," Howells said, because "the language does not hold their betters for a high perfection of literary execution at all points." And analyzing this quality he spoke of Henry's "light, firm touch," the "depths under depths" of his characterizations and the "clutch upon the unconscious motives" revealed by the writer. This was a measure of discernment rare in James's day, and even in the ensuing decades, during which this group of tales merged with the entire stream of James's productions and the full richness of this period was never adequately recognized.

Howells had thus seen that James had entered a new phase. And indeed his entire output between *The Princess Casamassima* and *The Tragic Muse* shows him narrating his stories—even when trifles—at the top of his form; they possess an extraordinary *allégresse*. The stories coincided with the series of essays and "portraits" also set down with the richness of a charged and vigorous critical imagination. The tales have an excess of charm and of high amusement; and this is far from a defect, for no tale is more enjoyable than one which the teller himself enjoys.

ELIZABETH DUVENECK

I

ON MARCH 31, 1888, HENRY WENT TO PAY A VISIT TO THE CYRIL
Flowers, at Aston Clinton in Tring Park. He came to this Easter
week-end party with a heavy heart. Sitting at a table in a room in
which guests were coming and going, he wrote a letter to Henrietta
Reubell. His handwriting, usually forceful and well controlled,
is in this letter disorganized and shaky. "I am writing in a room
full of people talking—and they make me write erratically," he
told Miss Reubell. But this was hardly the cause. It was that he
could not conceal the depths of his emotion. Lizzie Boott was
dead. She had died that week in Paris where she had been spending the winter with her husband and child, in a house in the Rue
de Tilsit. Only a short while before she had written Henry a letter
filled with her busy life and news of her baby: she had taken up
water-colors, she said—they could be combined more easily than
oils with the duties of maternity. Henry had replied: he had spoken
of Fenimore's illness at Bellosguardo in the autumn. But Fenimore was better and was writing again. Francis Boott had been
to America but was now in Paris. Then suddenly Lizzie had
pneumonia. On March 22 she died, leaving her aged father, her
husband, her fifteen-month-old child.

Boott had written Henry the barest details. Henry had responded by saying he was prepared to come at once to Paris, if he
could be of help. He had received no reply; and he turned now,
in the midst of the gay chatter and laughter in the big house at
Aston Clinton, to appeal to his old Parisian friend, Etta Reubell,
for news:

"Lizzie's sudden death was an unspeakable shock to me—and
I scarcely *see* it, scarcely believe in it yet. It was the last thing I
ever thought of as possible—I mean before Boott's own surrender
of his earthly burden." When would she see Boott? would she tell
Henry what impression he made on her? what did he intend to

do? what was the relation between him and Duveneck? Had Etta seen Lizzie before her death? "What a strange fate—to have lived long enough simply to tie those two men with nothing in common, together by that miserable infant and then vanish into space, leaving them face to face!"

Lizzie Boott—Pansy Osmond—the friend of Minny Temple in their youth, and his own friend for twenty-three years, was gone. It was the first important loss he had experienced since Minny and Wilky in the ranks of his own generation, for Lizzie was but three years his junior. "I shall miss her greatly," he wrote. "I had a great affection for her. She was a dear little quiet, gentle, intelligent laborious lady." He was to echo this from letter to letter. And then he inquired whether Miss Reubell had seen any of Duveneck's work that winter. Duveneck had just painted a portrait of Lizzie. "Is it good or interesting?"

I I

It was just a year since he had been with the Bootts and with Fenimore at Bellosguardo; he had wandered with Lizzie in the deep grass of the beautiful terrace and they had looked at the view over the old parapet. Henry would see her there always, he told Boott. He knew how deep an attachment this had been and how much the Bootts and their Florentine villa had become a part of his life—even when years passed and he was not in Italy. "The quiet, gentle, loveable, cultivated, laborious lady!" he echoed himself, writing to Mrs. Curtis. "Poor Boott—poor Boott—is all I can say!" When he returned to De Vere Gardens from his week-end he found a letter from Francis, and replied to it with deep tenderness. Boott had apparently written to Henry that Lizzie had undertaken an effort beyond her strength. In this Henry acquiesced. "She staggered under it and was broken down by it," he wrote to Lizzie's father. "I was conscious of this as long ago as during those months in Florence when superficially she seemed so happy and hopeful. The infirmity was visible beneath the optimism—the whole thing seemed to me without an issue. This particular issue is the most violent—but perhaps after all it is not the most cruel—the most painful to witness—for perpetual struggle and disappointment would have been her portion. I mean on account of the terrible *specific gravity* of the mass she had proposed to herself to float and carry.—It is no fault of *his*—but simply the stuff he is made of."

There was for Henry something pathetic in all the "little heroisms of her plans, her faiths, her view of the future—quenched forever—but quenched in a void—that is a soundless rest—far sweeter than anything the hard ache of life has to give." And he added: "I pity you, my dear Francis, almost more than anything else, for some of the canting consolations that must be offered you. I am more glad than I can say that your vision of her situation happens to be the one which makes sorrow the least absolute. Don't answer this—I shall write soon again."

"What *clumsy* situations does fate bring about, and with what an absence of style does the world appear to be ruled!" Henry exclaimed to Mrs. Curtis. He was thinking of Boott and Duveneck now back at the Villa Castellani, strange companions, held together by the child. Twice in Boott's long life had such a cruel situation come about: Lizzie had been left to him when Mrs. Boott died, a year after the death of their infant son; now Lizzie was gone, leaving her child on his hands, for Duveneck promptly recognized that he—with his artist-bohemian way of life—was hardly one to rear the boy. "My imagination can scarcely take in Duveneck's *afloat* condition again—after his having embraced the faith that he was, for life, safe from all winds and waters," Henry wrote to Boott. "I kiss the child and shake hands with Duveneck. For you, my dear Francis, I can only repeat that I bear you constantly in the participation of my thoughts."

III

Francis Boott and Frank Duveneck brought Lizzie back to Italy. There, toward the end of April, she was committed to the Florentine earth, in a grave in the Allori Cemetery, beyond the Roman

gate, beneath a row of tall cypresses. Great masses of flowers were
heaped on it; and her Florentine friends, among them Fenimore,
gathered in large numbers to say farewell. It was probably Fenimore who described the scene for Henry: Boott calm and Duveneck sobbing. Duveneck's "demeanour has won all hearts here,"
Henry's friend wrote to him. For a while the two remained in the
villa, the old man and the young, and in time Francis Boott re-
versed the journey he had made almost half a century before. He
took Frank Duveneck Jr. to Boston, to rear him there among Ly-
man relatives, and there to pass the rest of his days. He was to
live for many more years, in Cambridge, a short grizzled man,
who would of an evening walk into William James's house in
Irving Street while the family were eating, refuse to join them at
their board, but sit and chat of many things. He had lived through
three generations and seen so much—his memories went back to
the days of Garibaldi, and to Papal Rome, and he had had the long
sweep of the Bellosguardo years.

For Duveneck the artist, it was the end of the second phase of
his life. The first had been his carefree days in Munich. The third
would be a long anti-climax in America. Duveneck had been
almost pathetically attached to his wife: she was a grand lady,
whom he had had the good fortune to marry. He had painted her
portrait that winter in Paris dressed for the street—wearing her
hat back on her head, so that her dark tightly pulled down and
parted hair is revealed; her lips are closed in a gentle smile, and
her large candid eyes look affectionately out of the canvas. She is
holding her muff; her arms are relaxed; and if his view of her
was as a *grande dame* in this painting, he visioned her also as a
knight's lady in death—and so he posed her, recumbent with her
hands folded on her breast, amid flowing drapery, on the tomb
he designed and sculpted himself. It was cast in shining bronze
and when Henry first saw it, after it was placed, he confided to
friends that it seemed to him too glaring and in bad taste. Time,
however, would coat it and soften it, so that today it is gray-

green and ghostly, and Lizzie lies in her eternal sleep, her eyes closed to the Italian skies; brown, dry pine needles sift at certain seasons gently into the folds of the drapery.

Duveneck eventually returned to Cincinnati. It had beer gardens and certain vague echoes of Munich. He taught at the Academy of Fine Arts for many years. Sargent had spoken of him as "the greatest talent of the brush of this generation." He had indeed given the impression, during his earliest phase, that he would develop into a master; but he remained a talent, eventually in decline, as Henry had predicted. He was unable to rise above his early achievement. And it is doubtful whether art historians will ever settle whether Lizzie, in taming him, tamed his talent as well.

This was the end of the Bellosguardo chapters in Henry's life. More than a year after Lizzie's death, Alice James wrote in her journal, "Henry says he misses Lizzie Duveneck more and more." This was true. She had been a certain kind of American girl—the quiet gentle Europeanized *jeune fille*, not the daisy but the pansy, and he had had much feeling for her. She was to remain enshrined in materials as durable as Duveneck's bronze, in the delicate beauty of Pansy Osmond.

A MEETING IN GENEVA

I

IN MARCH OF 1888, SHORTLY BEFORE HE RECEIVED THE NEWS OF Lizzie's death, Henry agreed to write a serial for the *Atlantic Monthly* to run through 1889. He was to receive the same rate of pay as for *The Princess*—$15 a page. He announced his title would be *The Tragic Muse*—"she is an actress. But there will be much other richness, and the scene will be in London, like the *Princess*—though in a very different MONDE: considerably the 'Aesthetic.' There you are. It won't be improper, strange to say, considering the elements."

That year there tumbled from the presses *Partial Portraits* in May, *The Reverberator* in June and two volumes containing "The Aspern Papers" with two other tales ("Louisa Pallant" and "The Modern Warning") in September. "How you can keep up such productivity and live, I don't see," his brother William wrote to him. "All your time is your own, however, barring dinner parties, and that makes a great difference. Most of my time seems to disappear in college duties, not to speak of domestic interruptions." William said he had "quite squealed" through his reading of *The Reverberator*. "It shows the technical ease you have attained, that you can handle so delicate and difficult a fancy so lightly. It is simply delicious."

By September Henry had dispatched his first two instalments of *The Muse* to Aldrich. Early in October he crossed to the Continent, bypassed Paris and went straight to Geneva. He took rooms in the old Hôtel de l'Écu, those which had been occupied by his parents during the family's stay in Geneva in 1859-60. "I am sitting in our old family *salon* in this place," he wrote to his brother on October 29, "and have sat here much of the time for the last fortnight, in sociable converse with family ghosts—father and mother and Aunt Kate and our juvenile selves. I became conscious, suddenly, about October 10th, that I wanted very much to get away from the stale, dingy London, which I had not quitted, to speak of, for fifteen months, and notably not all summer—a detestable summer in England, of wet and cold. Alice, whom I went to see, on arriving at this conclusion, assured me she could perfectly dispense for a few weeks with my presence on English soil; so I came straight here."

On occasion Henry felt that he had to explain his movements

to William; even at forty-five this feeling had not wholly left him. It was not however a matter of being away from Alice—from whom he had been away much longer the previous year. Henry felt some need for justifying his presence in Geneva at this moment for quite another reason, one that he did not mention to his brother. His choice of the city of Calvin was prompted not by family sentiment or a desire to recover a boyhood past. He was keeping a scheduled rendezvous with Fenimore. She had, as usual, passed her summer in Switzerland. Not wishing to go to Italy that winter (because of the serial), he was meeting her in Geneva to pay her a promised visit before she travelled south.

In his tale of "Louisa Pallant," written during his Italian phase, Henry had described how the elderly narrator and the love-smitten youth, on their way to Baveno on the Italian lakes to see the heroine, found it more decorous to stop at Stresa "at about a mile distance." They would not inhabit the same hotel as their friends, and "nothing would be easier than to go and come between the two points." The only record of the Geneva rendezvous is in a letter from Henry to Francis Boott. "You have been a daily theme of conversation with me for the past ten days, with Fenimore," Henry wrote to his old friend. "That excellent and obliging woman is plying her pen hard on the other side of the lake and I am doing the same on this one. Our hotels are a mile apart, but we meet in the evening, and when we meet she tells me, even at the risk of repetition to which I am far from objecting, the story of your last months, weeks, days, hours, etc. at Bellosguardo. We often talk of Lizzie and it is a great pleasure to me to do so with one who had entered so much into her life in so short a time."

II

Henry's letters written at this time—to William, to Henrietta Reubell, to Mrs. Curtis—create the picture of a writer who has fled society and is enjoying a solitary three weeks, contemplating Mont Blanc, and taking quiet walks to observe the "admirable

blue gush of the Rhône," as he had done in his sixteenth year
when he was attending Monsieur Rochette's preparatory school
in Geneva. The weather was beautiful and full of autumn color;
the mountains seemed to hang, day after day, over the blue lake.
Geneva seemed both duller and smarter than in 1859. The
Academy had now become the University (he was to interpolate
this fact into his revision of "Daisy Miller"), and was housed in a
large, winged building in the old public garden. All the old
smells and tastes were present. But what his relatives and friends
were not told—save Boott—was that his stay was less solitary
than might have been thought.

Of Fenimore there is only one more mention. It is again in a
letter to Boott, written three months later, on January 18, 1889:
"On leaving Geneva I parted with Fenimore—she went back to
Bellosguardo and I went (through the Mont Cénis) to Genoa
and the Riviera. I spent two or three weeks at the delicious Monte
Carlo and the month of December in Paris." He then reiterated
that Fenimore's mind and talk were full of her last year or two
on Bellosguardo. "She cherishes the mystical survival there of
dear Lizzie." He added that Fenimore's sister was staying with her
at the Brichieri. There is also one silent witness. Miss Woolson's
copy of the two-volume edition of "The Aspern Papers" is inscribed with her name and "from the author, Geneva October
16th, 1888."

Of this entire Continental trip we know very little. It is perhaps the least documented of Henry's journeys. There survive
some fragmentary pages of notes which show that he planned
later to write a comedy with Monte Carlo as a setting; but nothing came of it. He stayed at the Hôtel des Anglais there; and before that, was briefly at Turin as well as Genoa—"such a little
whiff, or sniff, of Italy." The sun was dazzling in Monaco: and
there were mosquitoes at night. Our only clues to Henry's visit
to Paris are three *pneumatiques* from Paul Bourget to the Grand
Hôtel. On December 18 Henry seems to have been at the salon
of Madame Straus (Geneviève Halévy), thus most certainly en-

countering, if not the young Proust himself, some of his future characters. One of the messages from Bourget expresses regret that he was not able to accompany him on this occasion, to do him the honors (as he had been scheduled to do), but that he was certain this "adorable and exquisite" woman would receive Henry well. There is also an allusion to the Parisian visit, in a letter the following spring to Charles Eliot Norton. Paris had struck Henry, "after a long intermission of habit there, as bright, charming, civilized, even interesting."

In addition to Bourget he saw Miss Reubell, as always, in the Avenue Gabriel. And his notebooks record that he visited the Théâtre Français backstage and had a chat with the comedienne, Julia Bartet, in her *loge*, an experience re-created in some detail in *The Tragic Muse*. He was back in London in time for Christmas.

THE EXPENSE OF FREEDOM

I

HE HAD CAPTURED IN ITALY IN 1887 THE TRUE SENSE OF FREEDOM— that freedom which the artist seeks, and in a pressing, interfering, demanding world seldom can attain. Now it seemed to him that the time had come to embody the conflict of "art and 'the world'" in a novel which he had begun to plan as far back as the winter of 1886 when he was preparing to move into De Vere Gardens. The novel seemed to him later to be framed by the wide west window in his flat, where he sat writing day after day during fog-filtered Kensington mornings or in the short winter afternoons with near and far London sunsets, "a half-grey, half-flushed expanse of London life." He had first thought of it as a short work, a study of the nature of an actress, her egotism, her perseverance, her image as a creature for whom reality was illusion and illusion reality. He had long ago discussed this with Mrs. Humphry Ward, whose novel, based on the success of Mary Anderson in London, he had carefully read. In the summer of 1887 he had told Grace Norton he was beginning *The Tragic Muse*, that it would be half as long as *The Princess* "thank God!" and that it would not be serialized. But by early 1888 the design had grown much more complicated and he had committed it to the *Atlantic* where—in spite of his "thank God!"—it became his longest serial, running to seventeen instalments, from January 1889 to May 1890.

What had happened to enlarge the work was his desire to present an antithetical case to that of the actress, enslaved by her art and the conditions of the theatre. This may very well have offered itself to him in the spectacle of the Cyril Flowers, in whose home he had been a visitor, and where he found an intensely political environment. Flower, an amateur of the arts, a man who moved among poets, painters, musicians, had married a Rothschild wife whose memoirs reveal how much she cherished political rather than artistic power; and Flower—who had even made friends across the Atlantic with Walt Whitman—found himself a Member of Parliament, and later (after *The Tragic Muse* was published) a member of the House of Lords. We may speculate that this "case" interested James; and the coincidence that within the domain of the Flowers was a village named Sheringham, in which they at one time contemplated living, may have given him the name of the diplomat-theatre lover, Peter Sherringham. It was at the home of the Flowers—Cyril Flower, later Lord Battersea—that Henry encountered the later Gladstone and the political *ambiance* upon which he drew for his novel; although we must recognize that his various visits to Lord Rosebery and *his* Roth schild wife also furnished him with ample materials for the creation of Mr. Carteret, the wily politician of *The Tragic Muse*.

These instances may be mentioned if only to illustrate that James—who could hardly be said to have an intimate knowledge of English politics—nevertheless found in his path sufficient examples to yield him his "political case" which he could use as a parallel to his "theatrical case." Of the theatre he had had ample observation during his entire European career: he knew intimately the playhouses of England and France and to some extent of Italy. At the time that he was sketching out *The Muse* he had renewed his acquaintance with Coquelin in London, who came to lunch at De Vere Gardens. Henry delighted in his art and found "a rare magnificence" in it; his personality he considered "insupportable," though he was "an admirable talker (on his own subjects)." Struck again, as he had been many times, by the self-centeredness and "self-exhibitionistic" character of stage folk, Henry felt he had all the materials at hand for his novel and he began it with an excitement and interest which he carried with him to the Continent when he went to his Geneva meeting with Fenimore.

The book is a large cheerful mural of English life and art; it is filled with witty talk; and parts of it read as if Henry were writing one of his critical papers rather than a piece of fiction. It has a hard dry essay-like quality. The novel incorporates a picture of the English stage, the Parisian theatre, the life of a comedienne attached to the Théâtre Français, the high bohemia of London on the very edge of the 'nineties, and offers also in the anomalous character of Gabriel Nash, a glimpse of Montesquiou-Whistler-Wilde aestheticism. With this we are given a picture of solid English upper-class Philistinism in the struggle of a young man to resist being pushed into Parliament by his family and the woman he loves. He would much rather be a painter.

Henry James had never undertaken a work so crowded with characters and so split in themes. He was, in reality, trying to put together two novels in one, and sometimes the seam shows. But it is a novel rich in portraits of people and pictures of contemporary life. In it James at last wrote out, on a large scale, that duality which existed within himself and which he had long ago depicted in "Benvolio."

I I

There are four central characters and they serve to illustrate the problem which is at the heart of *The Tragic Muse*. First there is Miriam Rooth, the half-Jewish, half-English girl, who wants to be an actress and who dedicates herself to this goal with all the ferocity of her egotism and the discipline of her art. The divine spark is not evident when we meet her, but she possesses a ruthless ambition which carries her to achievement. Nowhere in all his work has James given us a more carefully documented picture of the evolution of a certain type of artist, and of an artist-nature, and of its implacable selfishness and self-assurance. The "theatrical case" fascinated him, for he had been fascinated by the stage from his youth. And Miriam's history was learned in many forms, during long evenings with Mrs. Kemble—she the archetypal actress who believed in her art and abhorred the stage; during evenings at the Théâtre Français, whenever he was in Paris; and at his meetings in certain London homes with Henry Irving, Ellen Terry and other of the stage folk who dominated the late Victorian era.

His political case is drawn with a less firm hand: but the ingredients of it are familiar—Nick Dormer's powerful mother, his deathbed promise to his father to keep the family name in Parliament (he is again a second son who must assume the responsibilities of the first-born, in this case a titled brother whose sole interests are hunting and shooting). The family fortunes of the Dormers are negligible and Nick is expected to make an excellent marriage with Julia Dallow, who aspires to Downing Street, and to inherit a fine fortune from his father's old friend, Mr. Charles Carteret, an elderly fox of a politician. The situation is admirably painted: everyone sees Nicholas Dormer not as he is, but as what they want him to be: he is totally rejected for himself—the quiet thoughtful artistic young man—and is offered a public self he does not want. Only his sister understands him.

The opposite of Nick Dormer is Peter Sherringham, one of the most important characters in the novel, for it is he who expresses the dilemma at the heart of the book—and of its author. Sherringham is Julia Dallow's brother and a successful diplomat. His passion is the theatre; and it is a true passion save that it will not be permitted to interfere with his career. He "discovers" Miriam Rooth, and helps her take her first steps toward the stage. What he does not allow for is that he should fall in love with her. Nevertheless an actress will not fit as an ambassadress, and, as Basil Ransom does with Verena in *The Bostonians*, Sherringham asks Miriam to marry him and give up her career. Miriam and Nick Dormer face the same predicament. Nick is asked to be a politician rather than a painter: Miriam is asked to be a diplomat's wife, rather than a stage personality. Sherringham believes in "a passion exercised on the easiest terms," and he will keep the drama as a "private infatuation." In other words, what he is saying is that one can trifle with one's passion, whereas his friend Dormer holds this is impossible. What Sherringham discovers before the novel is over is that there is no halfway road to art: if one is committed to it, it must be faced, as Dormer does, when he throws over the chance to marry Julia, rejects Mr. Carteret's money and the solicitations of his electorate, and resigns from Parliament. Miriam puts the case with considerable force to Sherringham. She tells him that the stage has "a deep fascination for you, and yet you're not strong enough to make the concession of taking up with it publicly, in my person." And again: "You consider that we do awfully valuable work, and yet you wouldn't for the world let people suppose that you really take our side." Miriam does not marry the diplomat; she marries an actor, and at the end of the book is well on her way to becoming a significant figure in the theatre.

Nick Dormer's decision is more difficult than Miriam's. His choice, James makes amply clear, is not only that of throwing over wealth, public office, status, society; it is that of finding himself face to face with the trials and joys of his art—it is his acceptance of loneliness, with faith in his creativity as his companion. This is the expense of freedom, the price the artist must pay. The actress, by the very circumstances of the interpretative art, is involved in a gregarious existence. The painter—or the writer—is alone with his canvas—or his blank sheets of paper. It is for this statement, above all else (the reader feels), that James wrote *The Tragic Muse:* his picture of Nick, in his studio, closing the door as Miriam leaves, and taking up his palette to rub it with a dirty cloth—

. . . the little room in which his own battle was practically to be fought looked woefully cold and gray and mean. It was lonely, and yet peopled with unfriendly shadows (so thick he saw them gathering in winter twilights to come), the duller conditions, the longer patiences, the less immediate and less personal joys. His late beginning was there, and his wasted youth, the mistakes that would still bring forth children after their image, the sedentary solitude, the clumsy obscurity, the poor explanations, the foolishness that he foresaw in having to ask people to wait, and wait longer, and wait again, for a fruition which, to their sense at least, would be an anti-climax.

Going to the great galleries, and seeing historic paintings, he is made to feel that the artist works according to his lights, unknown, misunderstood, a fool in the public eye who casts away the gains of the marketplace for some cherished ideal that is his own and no one else's, some creative urge that he cannot explain to anyone else. Before great portraits in the National Gallery he has a vision of a posthumous triumph which for him may well be the only triumph—

As he stood before them sometimes the perfection of their survival struck him as the supreme eloquence, the reason that included all others, thanks to the language of art, the richest and most universal. Empires and systems and conquests had rolled over the globe and every kind of greatness had risen and passed away; but the beauty of the great pictures had known nothing of death or change, and the ages had only sweetened their freshness. The same faces, the same figures looked out at different centuries, knowing a deal the century didn't,* and when they joined hands they made the indestructible thread on which the pearls of history were strung.

This is Nick's vision and Henry James was to cling to it during the coming years as he created the enduring masterpieces of his art which in his own time were misunderstood or ignored.

III

In this sprawling and uneven novel, into which James put so much skill, the figure of Gabriel Nash has understandably attracted the attention of many readers. He is a "Gabriel"—hardly angelic, but much addicted to trumpeting. And he is an aesthete whose performances tend to be those of word rather than act. In certain ways he is a distraction: for James intended some of his trumpetings to sound loudly his own beliefs. He describes, with Jamesian wit, the predicament of the dramatist who is asked to place the "exquisite" on the stage of a theatre between dinner and the suburban trains. He speaks with all the Jamesian warmth for sentience and high ideals: "Where there's anything to feel I try to be there," he remarks; the reader senses however that this makes him too ubiquitous. His business is "the spectacle of the world." To this extent he "talks" Henry James; and in appearance, he even resembles his creator. But he is far from being the novelist. He belongs rather with those characters in James's fiction whose sole existence depends on their having an audience. Nick Dormer discovers this when Nash comes to sit for his portrait. He finds that Gabriel is increasingly uncomfortable in this role. Nick

. . . .
* In the revised version James made this read "knowing so many secrets the particular world didn't."

finally catches a glimmer of what this discomfort means. It was "simply the reversal, in such a combination, of his usual terms of intercourse. He was so accustomed to living upon irony and the interpretation of things that it was strange to him to be himself interpreted, and (as a gentleman who sits for his portrait is always liable to be) interpreted ironically." James hammers this home: "From being outside the universe he was suddenly brought into it, and from the position of a free commentator and critic, a sort of amateurish editor of the whole affair, reduced to that of humble ingredient and contributor." That such an individual's portrait should start to fade and become ghostly, after the manner of portraits in some of Hawthorne's tales, is understandable. It is the fate of most aesthetes who talk, but never *do*; who spin their theories, but never adhere to them. Nick says to Nash that he wishes "very much you had more to show"—but all Nash can show are his trumpetings. He is much more the Count de Montesquiou than Oscar Wilde or Whistler—the latter had much to offer, where the French imitator of Whistler's manner could toss off certain valuable ideas but without a grain of seriousness.

We know the actual model for Nash; in him James kept a promise to himself of his first Venetian days in 1881 and incorporated the image of Herbert Pratt, who had talked so well and been so beautifully anecdotal during Henry's long stay in the water-city. "He was a most singular, most interesting type, and I shall certainly put him into a novel. I shall even make the portrait close and he won't mind." It is probably not as "close" as he had originally intended; rather is it, like most of James's fictional portraits, a composite drawn from the novelist's saturated experience.

IV

Re-reading the novel many years later, James felt that he had not succeeded with his young politician-artist Nick Dormer. The better part of him was "locked away from us." This is true. And it is strange. For it is Nick who carries the burden of what James most deeply felt: it was he who enunciated the message of the artist, his loneliness and the solitary refuge of his art. It was he, also, who made clear that the true artist must be prepared to sacrifice everything to his commitment; that one cannot be half artist and half something else; that he must strip himself of all worldliness, or accept the easy compromises society exacts. The "lesson of the Master" is here stated with much less cynicism and therefore much greater force. But the reason for Nick's elusiveness did not reside altogether in James's view of English political life from the "outside"—it was his paradoxical failure to identify himself with this character. He is much more identified with Peter Sherringham, Nick's double, who doesn't want to make the supreme sacrifice for his art. Henry's own worldliness stands between him and Nick. And Sherringham, at certain moments, is our old friend Benvolio: even the words of the old tale recur in a slightly modified way—"there were two men in him, quite separate, whose leading features had little in common and each of whom insisted on having an independent turn at life." The personal statement in this novel is that of the James who on the one hand was strongly pleasure-loving, who without his vaulting ambition and genius might have been an easy-going Herbert Pratt and an aesthetic dilettante to boot. At this moment in his life he had not yet reconciled himself to the loneliness of which he wrote: he wished, like Sherringham, to eat his cake and to have it also. Sherringham did not succeed, and James knew he couldn't, but he himself was still willing to try. He knew that he had an enormous facility and that he could, like so many other excellent writers, simply have continued to spin some of his more thin-blown tales in the magazines, as he had done with his minor "international" stories and his exploitation of his inter-continental Daisy Millers. He had, however, always been artist enough to over-ride this temptation, even after yielding to it for a while. And yet there he was—established in De Vere Gardens, with the look of "success," and prosperity, and still condemned to scribble away his time in order that he might capture occasional vagrant moods in Paris or in Venice. But the plan which was materializing, and which he publicly debated in *The Tragic Muse*, now took firm hold. There was a possible solution in this middle-aged choice which he found himself forced to make—for he was thus constituted—a choice of quite a different order from the one of his youth, when he had turned to Europe to find the freedom of his first phase. What he needed now was a double freedom: that of "the great good place" of Art and that of the marketplace, and these two places "trumped" each other, in a kind of grim, ironic game of cards. The paradox of success was that it cheapened everything, while offering him the expensive solution. It put money in his pocket, and somehow created a clinking dissonant sound beside the rhythm of prose and the sonorities of "style." There was, however, one possible issue (he told himself), and he would seriously test it. He could descend into the marketplace and try to be a playwright—an honorable and income-producing career for a man of letters—while at the same time preserving his art of fiction from all violation by the money-changers, preserving it for his sacred creative hours. Henry the playwright would "bail out" Henry the novelist. It was not the same as his taking a job, or being a secretary of legation as Lowell had wished to make him a decade before. If he succeeded as playwright he might very well incorporate the stage—if not the "sordid" life of the theatre—into his distinguished literary career. There had been a time when the greatest poetry had been associated with the actor, and England's finest genius had been wholly wedded to the apron-stage and to the groundlings. Times had changed. Victorian England had produced no dramatists to speak of, and its poets—Browning, Tennyson—had foundered when they approached the theatre. Wasn't this precisely, then, the moment for someone like himself to seek an entrance? Perhaps he would fare better. He knew, from far back, that he could launch a scene and create a drama; his artist's sense told him that in his pen there was a great ability to dramatize. What had *Washington Square* been but a series of dramatic episodes, relating themselves? And in the very novel in which he discussed the stage he had boldly put together his story by scenic alternation, not by telling the reader everything, but by letting the scenes explain themselves, as in a play. He had even perpetrated an anomaly in fiction—been an omniscient author who boasted of his lack of omniscience. This occurs in the very middle of *The Tragic Muse*, when James pauses to explain to the reader that his method of telling his story prevents him from imparting certain facts. The passage must be noted:

As to whether Miriam had the same bright, still sense of cooperation to a definite end, the sense of the distinctively technical nature of the answer to every question to which the occasion might give birth, that mystery would be cleared up only if it were open to us to regard this young lady through some other medium than the mind of her friends. We have chosen, as it happens, for some of the advantages it carries with it, the indirect vision; and it fails as yet to tell us . . .

This is the artist calling attention to his own method and by the same token to his own virtuosity. It presents us with the anomaly of a novelist who has chosen "the indirect vision" intruding in the most direct fashion possible to explain his indirection. On the stage, however, James would not be able to intrude. The play would have to explain itself.

A CHASTENING NECESSITY

LONG BEFORE "THE TRAGIC MUSE" WAS COMPLETED HENRY JAMES had made his choice. He felt that he had reached the time of life when he could no longer continue within a vicious circle of constant publication in order to live. The books of other novelists, successful with the public at large, yielded continuing royalties. He, one of the most prolific writers of his time, knew from his publisher's statements that however much magazine editors used him, his work had little sale in book form. The advance he received for a book usually constituted his total earnings; and quite often the sales did not earn out the advance. This had been the case with his two big novels, *The Bostonians* and *The Princess Casamassima*; and he could anticipate that it would be the case with *The Tragic Muse* as well. Indeed, when serialization ended and he assembled the manuscript for Macmillan, he was warned of that publishing house's narrow view of future sales by an offer of an advance of £70 instead of the usual £200 or £250. The letter Henry wrote to Frederick Macmillan is justly famous. He began by saying that "in spite of what you tell me of the poor success of my recent books, I still do desire to get a larger sum, and have determined to take what steps I can in this direction." He went on:

These steps I know will carry me away from you, but it comes over me that that is after all better, even with a due and grateful recognition of the readiness you express to go on with me, unprofitable as I am. I say it is "better" because I had far rather that in those circumstances you should *not* go on with me. I would rather not be published at all than be published and not pay—other people at least. The latter alternative makes me uncomfortable and the former makes me, of the two, feel least like a failure; the failure that, at this time of day, it is too humiliating to consent to be without trying, at least, as they say in America, to "know more about it." Unless I can put the matter on a more remunerative footing all round I shall give up my English "market"—heaven save the market!—and confine myself to my American. But I must experiment a bit first—and to experiment is of course to say farewell to you. Farewell, then, my dear Macmillan, with great regret—but with the sustaining cheer of all the links in the chain that remain still unbroken. Yours ever
HENRY JAMES

The letters in the Macmillan archive do not disclose what the final arrangement was; Macmillan did however publish *The Muse* in England and this suggests that either Henry's terms were met or some compromise was reached. Nevertheless Henry had used the word "experiment" advisedly. When he wrote this letter he had begun the writing of a play.

Almost a year before he dispatched this letter to Macmillan, Henry had faced his problems clearly. Of his reputation as an artist, of his distinction in the literary world, there was now no question. His problem was wholly one of money. He was living on a larger scale than in Bolton Street; he travelled a great deal; he always stayed at good hotels. He was generous to a fault: he took upon himself the giving of various gifts to impecunious relatives, feeling that William, with four children, must not have additional money burdens. His own income from the Syracuse properties was paid, according to his instructions, to Alice. Early in 1889 his beloved Aunt Kate died—his last link with his childhood, and his and Alice's old travelling companion of the 1870's. She remembered him rather meagerly in her will; we do not know how much he received, but we know that the bulk of her estate went to certain relatives of hers and of Henry's mother. Henry continued in any event to live on current income. He felt his books should be yielding him more. His decision was in conformity with the debate he was conducting in the pages of his novel; and it is incorporated in a long entry in his notebook of May 12, 1889. This was prompted by his having received a letter while he was in Paris the previous December (after his rendezvous in Geneva), from Edward Compton, a young English actor who had his own troupe and had for ten years been touring the British Isles playing old classical comedies and costume pieces. Compton's wife, the American actress Virginia Bateman, had read in a theatrical journal an article by some critic suggesting that James's novel *The American* would make a good play. Compton's letter inquired whether James would be willing to do a dramatic version. Christopher Newman struck him as offering a splendid part for himself.

The request, as James's note attests, could not have been made at a more opportune time.

I had practically given up my old, valued, long cherished dream of doing something for the stage, for fame's sake, and art's, and fortune's: overcome by the vulgarity, the brutality, the baseness of the condition of the English-speaking theatre today. But after an interval, a long one, the vision has revived, on a new and a very much humbler basis, and especially under the lash of necessity. Of art, or fame *il est maintenant fort peu question:* I simply *must* try, and try seriously, to produce half a dozen—a dozen, five dozen—plays for the sake of my pocket, my material future. Of how little money the novel makes for me I needn't discourse here. The theatre has sought me out—in the person of the good, the yet unseen, Compton. I have listened and considered and reflected, and the matter is transposed to a minor key.

He would accept the circumstances, he said, "in their extreme humility." The field was wide and free, and he could proceed with caution. If there would be money in it, that would greatly help. What profit he might make would mean

real freedom for one's general artistic life: it all hangs together (time, leisure, independence for 'real literature,' and, in addition, a great deal of experience of *tout un côté de la vie*). Therefore my plan is to try with a settled resolution—that is with a full determination to return repeatedly to the charge, overriding, annihilating, despising the boundless discouragements, disgusts, *écœurements*. One should *use* such things—grind them to powder.

And then, settling down to a review of the story of *The American*, Henry wrote: "Oh, how it [the play] must not be too good and how very bad it must be!" Which may explain why he invoked the masters of the "well-made play" in France—"À moi Scribe, à moi Sardou, à moi Dennery!" These were to be his guide and example. They had written splendid clock-like dramas; Henry had seen their works and seen the money pouring into the box office. There was never, from the first, any doubt in his mind that the theatre would be for him a kind of artistic slumming expedition: it would offer its amusement and its rewards; it would be a great compromise—an exciting gamble.

He explained his plan to bridge art and the marketplace in precise terms to Stevenson, who by now was in the South Seas. On the one hand he announced to him that he would cease to write long novels and would concentrate on shorter fictions, thereby freeing himself for play-writing. On the other he spoke of his plays as a means by which he would free himself to produce fictional masterpieces. On July 31, 1888 he wrote that after *The Tragic Muse* "with God's help, I propose, for a longish period, to do nothing but short lengths. I want to leave a multitude of pictures of my time, projecting my small circular frame upon as many different spots as possible and going in for number as well as quality, so that the number may constitute a total having a certain value as observation and testimony."

A year and a half later, confessing to Stevenson that he had begun experimenting with the theatre, he wrote: "Don't be hard on me—simplifying and chastening necessity has laid its brutal hand on me and I have had to try to make somehow or other the money I don't make by literature. My books don't sell, and it looks as if my plays might. Therefore I am going with a brazen front to write half a dozen." This was to be his hazardous experiment.

THE GALLO-ROMANS

I

IN THE LATE 'EIGHTIES AND EARLY 'NINETIES, AS HENRY STOOD ON
the threshold of his dramatic years, he found himself increasingly
linked with a group of Gallo-Romans—Bourget thus liked to
characterize himself—various Frenchmen, in London and Paris,
who represented all that Henry loved in the Gallic and the Ital-
ianate spirit. In all the years of his association with France he
had never found many close French friends. Bourget was the sole
exception. Henry had become fairly intimate with Daudet, but
the author of *Tartarin* was an invalid, and there could not be
with him that camaraderie Henry had with Bourget when they
met on either side of the Channel or in Italy. Now, however, there
came to London a brilliant young diplomat, Jules Jusserand, Coun-
sellor of the French Embassy; and also a young student from the
French provinces who had written verses and attracted Bourget's attention, Urbain Mengin. With these two men—Jusserand,
alert, swift, active, and Mengin, quiet, modest, studious and poetic
—each moving on a different level of London life, Henry found
new resources of friendship, and he responded warmly to them. "A
remarkably intelligent and pleasant little Frenchman," Henry said
of Jusserand. Thus on September 30, 1888, Henry wrote to Grace
Norton:

I am going in half an hour (this is a decent Sunday afternoon),
to pick up a very nice and accomplished little man of whom I have
lately seen a good deal, Jusserand, the French *chargé d'affaires*,
in order to go with him up to Hampstead. We often do this of a
Sunday afternoon when we are in town, and having scaled the
long hill, which used to be so rural and pretty, and now is all red
brick and cockney prose, we go and see du Maurier and he comes
out and takes a longish walk with us—usually, or sometimes, with
his pretty daughters (one of them is very pretty indeed) and his
two little dogs. Then we go home and dine with him *à la bonne*

braquette and walk back to London at 10 o'clock. Du Maurier is an old and good friend of mine and has a charming Anglo-French mind and temper.

Henry added that Jusserand was "a little prodigy of literary and diplomatic achievement effected at an early age. He is alive to his very small finger-tips, ambitious, capable and charming—and if he were a few inches less diminutive, I should believe that Europe would hear of him as a diplomatic personage. But he is too short! Up to a certain point, or rather down to it, shortness, I think, constitutes a presumption of greatness; but below that point not." Jusserand was to overcome his shortness, quite beyond Henry's prediction, and to be one of the great French ambassadors in Washington during the Presidency of Theodore Roosevelt. In his memoirs, the French diplomat describes the Sunday evenings at du Maurier's and remarks that the James of the late 'eighties "enjoyed and spread merriment and showed a disposition to sarcasm and raillery which did not spare the British, at least as a nation."

Urbain Mengin was destined to have a less spectacular, but distinguished, career in education, and to be an early authority in France on Shelley and the English Romantics. He had turned up one day at De Vere Gardens with a letter of introduction from Bourget. He had a certain delicacy of spirit and a temperament which Henry liked. He was a mere youth, in his early twenties, and he had come to London to teach French and study English. Henry received him with a cordiality and a warmth that Mengin remembered all the days of his long life. "I passed almost an entire Sunday with Henry James. One drinks excellent claret at his table," he wrote to his parents. "I've just left Henry James, after a long walk in Hyde Park," he told them on another occasion, "where bands of Amazons on horseback constantly passed us." In an unpublished memoir, Mengin remembered Henry as wearing "a beard neatly trimmed and still dark, his hair at the temples was just beginning to turn grey, he was bald and his forehead was very fine; his glance expressed kindness and was at the same time distinctly analytical. He spoke French admirably, with a slight hesitation, sometimes repeating twice the same syllable of a word." Bourget, the young French tutor, and James were to form a triangular friendship in which Henry expressed to Mengin the harsh opinion he held of certain of Bourget's novels which he could not say to Bourget himself. When Mengin, who became tutor to a future Duke of Sutherland, wrote Henry that he was reading his novels, the American rejoined: "Don't read me— when you have all English literature before you—for heaven's sake." His letters to Mengin are written in a mixture of English and French. There is a charming one in which Henry urges him to apply himself to his study of the English language: "One's own language is one's mother, but the language one adopts, as a career, as a study, is one's wife, and it is with one's wife that *on se met en ménage*. English is a very faithful and well-conducted person, but she will expect you too not to commit infidelities. On these terms she will keep your house well."

The most notable of his letters to young Mengin is the one he wrote on receiving the French scholar's work, *L'Italie des Romantiques*. Mengin had taken a walking tour, scrupulously visiting all the scenes which had figured in the lives of Shelley, Byron and their circle. The letter is of a later date; it shows admirably the benign yet critical eye Henry kept on his friend. After telling Mengin he had read his book attentively and had found much entertaining matter, well represented, he went on to say he especially liked his pictures of Lamartine, Chateaubriand and Madame de Staël. "How little they all *saw* compared with *nous autres!* And to have had to become *romantique*, and break a thousand window-panes, to see even that little! The only thing one can say is that they saw more—(more beauty) than the President des Brosses. But we could kick their posteriors today for what they *didn't* see—especially that big yellow-satin *derrière* of Madame de Staël." He went on to regret that Mengin had treated a poet of "a vertiginous lyric *essor*" like Shelley's without indicating his quality and splendor.

He is one of the great poets of the world, of the rarest, highest effulgence, the very genius and incarnation of poetry, the poet-type, as it were. But you speak only of the detail of his more or less irrelevant itinerary, and put in scarce a word for what he signifies and represents. I regret it for the reason that French readers have very rarely occasion to hear of him, so that when by chance they do I can't but be sorry that the case isn't stated for him more liberally as *poet*. He was the strangest of human beings, but he was *la poésie même*, the sense of Italy never melted into *anything* (*étranger*) I think, as into his "Lines in the Euganaean Hills" and *d'autres encore*. "Come where the vault of blue Italian sky . . . !" is, for *me*, to *be* there *jusqu' au cou!* And *de même* for Keats, the child of the Gods! Read over again to yourself, but *aloud*, the stanzas of the *Adonais* (or I wish I could read them *to* you!) descriptive of the corner of Rome where they both lie buried, and then weep bitter tears of remorse at having sacrificed them to the terrestial *caquetage* of A. de Musset! Forgive my emphasis.

Jusserand, Mengin and the Anglo-French du Maurier offered Henry that elegance of spirit, delicacy of expression and fertility of mind which he sought periodically in the French capital. And Henry was never more aware of this than on the day in May of 1889 when Jusserand arranged a little luncheon in honor of Taine, and invited Henry to meet his distinguished guest. Henry had never encountered the French critic and historian, whose major work he had reviewed during his Cambridge days. He speaks of finding Taine "remarkably pleasant"; and much more good-natured than his "hard, splendid, intellectual, logical style and manner had led me to expect." He was a charming talker and gave Henry a renewed feeling "of the high superiority of French talk." After describing his "obliquity of vision" and his fine head, his straight strong regular features, "a fine grave masculine type," Henry recorded that Taine rated Turgenev higher in form even than he himself had done. Taine used a very happy expression, Henry noted, when he said that Turgenev "so perfectly cut the umbilical cord that bound the story to himself." Henry recorded in his notebook that Taine's talk about the Russian novelist "has done me a world of good—reviving, refreshing, confirming, consecrating, as it were, the wish and dream that have lately grown stronger than ever in me—the desire that the literary heritage, such as it is, poor thing, that I may leave, shall consist of a large number of perfect *short* things, *nouvelles* and tales, illustrative of ever so many things in life—in the life I see and know and feel—and of all the deep and delicate—and of London, and of art, and of everything: and that they shall be fine, rare, strong, wise—eventually perhaps even recognized."

I I

The summer of 1889, when Henry was working at *The Tragic Muse*, had its usual interruptions. He wanted to go to Paris to see a great many plays, in preparation for his siege of the theatre; but June and early July were devoted to entertaining in De Vere Gardens his old friend E. L. Godkin, who had been so genial a host to him in New York during Henry's last visit to America. Godkin had begun his career by emigrating from Ireland to the United States; and now, as the successful editor of the *Nation* and of the New York *Evening Post*, he gazed upon the Old Country through American eyes. His fresh impressions interested Henry and he was struck by how much Godkin found that was unfavorable to the United States—in spite of his own irreducible Americanism. James enjoyed his visit but felt that it had "punched holes" in his working days. Godkin was barely gone when William arrived to attend a psychological congress and to see Alice. He stayed with Henry briefly in De Vere Gardens and they had a day in Leamington together, where Henry first lunched with his sister, prepared her for William's sudden appearance (they had not told her of his coming so as to avoid creating needless excitement and tension in Alice), and then tied a handkerchief to the balcony of No. 11 Hamilton Terrace as signal that William might safely enter. The episode is humorously recorded in Alice's journal. She writes that Henry had a "queer look on his face" as he said to her, "I must tell you something." Her assumption had been, "You're not going to be married?" He had quickly told her that William was outside, after visiting Warwick Castle, and was awaiting the appointed signal in the Holly Walk. Alice fortified herself with some bromide; Henry affixed the handkerchief.

Later that summer Henry went to Whitby, where Lowell was staying. He found his friend with undiminished powers of "walking, talking, joking, smoking, drinking and playing host and guide—in the kindest, gayest, most fifteen-year-old way." They had a ramble on the wide moors after a rough lunch at a stony upland inn; they made an excursion by rail to see Rievaulx Abbey, a graceful fragment of a ruin. They wandered on the great curving green terrace in Lord Feversham's park overhanging the Abbey and visited a battered bit of castle where they saw young Yorkshire folk playing lawn tennis. They met again for three days in Devonshire at Lord Coleridge's "amid the clustered charms of Ottery," and Henry travelled back with his friend to London. He missed him when he called to say good-bye, before Lowell's return to America, and penned a hasty note wishing him "a winter of fine old wood fires and a speedy return." A day or two later Lowell left. This was his last journey to England.

In September Henry went to Dover planning to proceed to Paris. Katherine Loring was with Alice and he could allow himself a comfortable absence. He found the Channel port so comfortable and quiet, however, that he lingered, walked, worked, enjoyed solitude and exercise and decided he would cross the Channel later. He returned to London, dispatched further chapters of *The Muse*, and after three or four weeks crossed to the French capital on October 24.

By now he had still another task to perform. He had agreed to translate Daudet's new *Tartarin* novel, and was to work on it from the printer's galleys. Between this chore and the writing of the last chapters of *The Muse*, Henry visited the last days of the Exhibition of 1889, spending his mornings and early afternoons in his room at the Hôtel de Hollande. To re-read the final chapters of

his novel, he wrote later, was to remember how the "tone of
the terrible city seemed to deepen about one to an effect strangely
composed at once of the auspicious and the fatal." Paris was "terrible" because it was distracting. Nevertheless he saw his job
through; the last chapters of his longest serial were sent early in
December. He had an evening with Daudet, and they talked
novel and theatre. Daudet, in the Naturalist tradition, was taking
notes on the progress of his disease. In the midst of this, he was
writing his "new, gay, lovely" *Tartarin*. The serial would be profusely illustrated and Henry was to "represent him in English, a
difficult, but with ingenuity a pleasant and amusing task." He saw
much of Bourget and something of François Coppée. He dined
twice in the company of the dramatists Meilhac and Ganderax, the
drama critic Sarcey, Blowitz, Paris correspondent of the London
Times, and Edmond de Goncourt. He distinctly cultivated the
theatrical side of the city. His French confrères were still, however, besotted mandarins, when all was said and done. "Nevertheless I've enjoyed it, and though I am very tired, I shall have been
much refreshed by my stay here," he wrote to William. Early in
December he returned to London.

THE PRIVATE LIFE

I

TWELVE DAYS AFTER HENRY'S RETURN, WORD CAME THAT ROBERT
Browning had died in Venice. The poet had spent a part of the
late autumn with his and Henry's friend, Mrs. Bronson, at La

Mura, her summer home in Asolo. He had dedicated a book to her—his last, *Asolando*—"To whom but you, dear Friend, should I dedicate verses," his epistle began. At the massive Palazzo Rezzonico, on the Grand Canal, where he had gone in November to stay with his son—who was also the son of the beloved and long-departed Elizabeth Barrett Browning—the poet contracted a chill, and bronchitis followed. On December 12, as San Marco's clock chimed its ten bronze hours in the evening, another of the great Victorians was dead.

Little more than a year before, Henry had been in the same carriage with Browning, at the funeral of their ancient friend, Mrs. Procter. He had seen him occasionally, and Browning had lunched with him, chatting as always about mundane things in a mundane way, without the remotest suggestion that this was the same poet James had read and loved in his youth. They had never become friends: they had always been the pleasantest of dinner-table acquaintances.

The novelist went to Westminster Abbey on the last day of 1889. It was a day of deep fog that seemed to make St. Margaret's bell toll even more deeply. Henry saw Browning laid to rest—he, one of the most "modern" of poets—among the ancients in the Poets' Corner. The boy-voices of the choir soared and descended, "angelic under the high roof." The obsequies were in every way national. "His funeral was charming, if I may call it so," Henry wrote in a touching letter to Mrs. Bronson, "crowded and cordial and genuine, and full of the beauty and grandeur of the magnificent old cathedral." And to Francis Boott, who had known the poet in his old Florentine days, when Elizabeth Barrett was still alive, Henry wrote, "The great Abbey grandly entombs him."

As always, Henry's elegiac note was capable of a high flight. "We possess a great man most when we begin to look at him through the glass plate of death," he wrote in a brief memorial article contributed to a London journal which he entitled "Browning in Westminster Abbey." It was a simple truth "that the Abbey never strikes us so benignantly as when we have a valued voice to commit to silence there." He said it would have taken the author of *The Ring and the Book* to render all the "passion and ingenuity, irony and solemnity, the impressive and the unexpected" of the occasion. "A good many oddities and a good many great writers have been entombed in the Abbey; but none of the odd ones have been so great and none of the great ones so odd."

Browning had been a magnificent master of poetic emotion. He took into the Abbey, Henry wrote, a great expression of life and a very genuine modernity "rendered with large liberty and free experiment." He was unmistakably in the great tradition, a wonderful mixture of "the universal and the alembicated." He had never been more powerful than when he had voiced the things best liked by his race—"the fascination of faith, the acceptance of life, the respect for its mysteries, the endurance of its charges, the vitality of the will, the validity of character, the beauty of action, the seriousness, above all, of the great human passion."

11

Years before, when he first met Browning in London, Henry had been struck by his double personality—the poet incarnated in an individual as hearty and conventional and middle-class as any of the numerous privileged with whom he and Henry dined out constantly during the late 'seventies. Again and again in various letters, Henry had expressed his sense of this paradox. Now that his neighbor was gone, Henry allowed his imagination to play over the image of a great poet who could be deadly prosaic. With Henry, to meditate on such a matter was to seek out some opposite case: and the opposite seemed to him to exist in the president of the Royal Academy, Sir Frederic Leighton, who had all the gifts and all the versatilities of his art, could make graceful after-dinner speeches, was charming and inventive so long as he had an audience. He was, so to speak, the poet of diners-out—and Henry imagined that he evaporated into thin air the moment he had no audience.

These reflections became, a year after Browning's death, a little tale to which Henry affixed the title "The Private Life." He called it a "conceit" and it is a pretty flight of fancy—his picture of a playwright staying at a Swiss inn who has promised an actress a play, but who seems quite incapable of writing it for her. The narrator, however, discovers that he has a double, who stays in his room and does his writing for him. The "playwright's opinions were sound and second-rate, and of his perception it was too mystifying to think. I envied him his magnificent health," the narrator observed. On the other hand Lord Mellifont, also staying at the inn, is a man whose personality pervades English life. "He *was* a style." Where the playwright's talk suggests "the reporter contrasted with the bard," Lord Mellifont is "the host, the patron, the moderator, at every board." He put more art into everything than was required.

The tale is largely that of the adventures of the narrator and one friend who discover the strange natures of their fellow-guests at the mountain inn. In their inductions and investigations they resemble the house party at Newmarch which Henry was to describe in his later novel *The Sacred Fount*. But above all, the tale is Henry's picture of Robert Browning as he had known him. The world had seen always the commonplace Browning; the genius was in his books. Browning had been all "private life" and had no life in public, save the usual and the expected. Leighton had been all public, and to Henry's vision had no corresponding private life. Henry remembered that when he had heard Browning read, it had been almost as if he were reading the work of another.

Such was Henry's little fantasy about the poet. It was also a fantasy about himself; it reflected the dichotomy which he envisaged in his own life: his dedication to art, and his willingness, at this moment, to accept the worldliness of the stage.

BOOK SIX

The Dramatic Years
1890-1894

THEATRICALS

THE 1890'S USHERED IN A NEW LIFE FOR HENRY JAMES. HE EMERGED from his study in De Vere Gardens to confront the theatre: and this confrontation induced a state of malaise and often of acute anxiety. By nature he was a retiring writer, whose desk was a private citadel; one never talked about work in progress until the book was ready to be given to the world. Henry negotiated directly with publishers and editors, and had been accustomed, until recently, to prompt publication. The world of the theatre seemed to him the exact opposite of all this: everything was done in a glare of publicity and with interminable delay. If he so much as had a talk with a manager, the theatrical gossip columns immediately knew of it. There seemed to be *Reverberators* everywhere, and an incessant public chatter in which actors and actresses joined. Henry found this irritating in the extreme. He shrank from it; he sought to avoid it. Much as he liked going to the theatre, and cherished the art of illusion behind the proscenium, he hated the stage itself: hated it and was fascinated by it. Moreover, he had a curious story-book conception of it, not a little like a young stage-struck person: this was based on his study of the rigid traditions of the Maison de Molière and his own nights in the Rue de Richelieu, going back to the early 1870's; and upon his long friendship with Mrs. Kemble and her talk of the theatre in her day. He was to speak of the stage as a straitjacket for any self-respecting man of letters. Henry put his jacket on even before he approached the theatre.

During the next five years, from 1890 to the beginning of 1895, the novelist devoted himself largely to the writing of plays. His plan was simple. He told himself that one play could never be a real test of his abilities as a dramatist. He would therefore, as he had recorded in his notebook, write several and submit them to the verdict of the marketplace. Only then would it be possible to know whether he could make the theatre yield him the needed revenues to liberate him for literature. His artist-self enjoyed enormously the planning of plays, the writings of scenarios, the reading of them to actors and actresses, the atmosphere of excitement engendered by matching of real persons to fictitious characters. The very novelty of the experience attracted Henry. Presently he discovered that the theatre was a place where nothing seemed to happen. Actor-managers always took their time—and as few risks as possible. "They talk of years as we talk of months," Henry said. If a play failed, they could always pull some "sure-fire" thing, some classic, to hold the boards while they planned their next venture. They seemed, on the whole, little interested in art or literature, save in the most general way. What interested them was how they would appear on stage, and whether the "vehicle" would keep the theatre filled. These were the realities Henry had to accustom himself to—these and the actual conditions he had described so charmingly through his character Gabriel Nash, the hasty dinners swallowed in restaurants, the lines of cabs at the theatre doors, the race with the clock to release the audience.

Fancy putting the exquisite before such a tribunal as that! There's not even a question of it. The dramatist wouldn't if he could, and in nine cases out of ten he couldn't if he would. He has to make the basest concessions. What can you do with a character, with an idea, with a feeling, between dinner and the suburban trains? You can give a gross rough sketch of them, but how little you touch them, how bald you leave them! What crudity compared with what the novelist does!

A would-be dramatist, approaching the stage with so acute a sense of its shortcomings and material difficulties, was hardly in a frame of mind to attack it with the required defenses—resourcefulness, patience, resilience, and a capacity for facing continual discouragement. Henry James had perhaps intuitively realized that it would be better to begin with a modest company, and discover in the provinces some of the secrets of this "most unholy trade." Edward Compton, after his decade of touring, wanted to establish himself in a theatre in London. He gave Henry a £250 advance to dramatize *The American,* and early in 1890 the novelist—having disposed of *The Tragic Muse* and made arrangements for its appearance as a book—set himself to his task. His correspondence is filled with brief allusions to his mysterious project; he cultivates secrecy; he adjures William to silence. His sister's private journal however mirrors his activities; they seem to have filled her sickroom with a lively sense of personalities and of adventure. Henry had ceased to be merely a man sitting at a writing-desk. He was abroad in the wide world of theatrical action. He had all his life talked of "the art of representation" in the novel. He was now committed to it on the stage. "My zeal in the affair is only matched by my indifference," he wrote to Stevenson. He was certainly far from indifferent. In the same letter he could write: "I find the *form* opens out before me as if it were a kingdom to conquer." Then he remembers that it is, by his standards, a rather paltry kingdom "of ignorant brutes of managers and dense *cabotins* of actors." All the same, he feels as if he has at last found his form, "my real one—that for which pale fiction is an ineffectual substitute." Realizing that this contradicted his expressed belief, he adds: "God grant this unholy truth may not abide with me more than two or three years—time to dig out eight or ten rounded masterpieces and make withal enough money to enable me to retire in peace and plenty for the unmolested business of a *little* supreme writing, as distinct from gouging—which is the Form above-mentioned."

It is no use trying to find any consistency in James's utterances of this time. He apologizes right and left for going into the theatre, feeling that as an artist he is soiling his hands by so much worldliness and so much involvement with the values of the marketplace. He is also enjoying himself enormously. He likes writing scenarios and plays. And he writes very strange plays—this master of the dramatic within the novel form. The simplest explanation lies precisely in the ambiguity of his letters and of his attitude toward the theatre. To come into the open and into the life of practical action—as distinct from the life of imaginative action—was so foreign to Henry's nature that he was doomed to failure. No citadel can be assaulted through mere contempt for the conditions of the assault; no original creativity is possible when it is mixed with so much distaste. The experience was too bitter-sweet for the novelist. Out of ambivalence there could only come—ambivalence.

I

The American was dramatized rapidly. On February 6, 1890 Henry recorded in his notebook that he had sent the second act to Compton; at this moment he was calling the play *The Californian*. He added a single sentence: "Perhaps the best formula for the fabrication of a dramatic piece *telle qu'il nous faut en faire*, in the actual conditions, if we are to do anything at all is: Action which is never dialogue and dialogue which is always action."

"I have written a big (and awfully good) four-act play, by which I hope to make my fortune," Henry confided to Henrietta

Reubell. He felt, he told his sister, that he had met "exactly the immediate, actual, intense British conditions, both subjective and objective," of the theatre. The play would run two and three-quarter
hours. The writing of it had been an education. Superior acting
would of course help. He feared, however, the mediocrity of the
provincial troupe. He was to receive a 10 per cent royalty on gross
receipts. And he had hopes of $400 a week during the provincial
run and $1,500 a month when the play came to London. These
were castles in the air and they were stimulated by a lively young
man, a friend of Howells's, who had come to London from America
to act as agent for a New York publishing house. His name was
Wolcott Balestier, and his energy, his exuberance, his business
ability, his charm, captivated Henry. They became friends almost
immediately. Balestier was twenty-nine. He had a way of living in
a dream of greatness—of large contracts and vast enterprises—
which could easily feed Henry's imagination at this moment of his
career. Balestier did translate some of his dreams into action. Gosse
was to say of him that "he was not merely one of our con-
querors, but the most successful of them all." Balestier had
recognized that the impending international copyright agreement
would end years of piracy in America. With sound business sense,
he had set out to sign contracts and make arrangements with
English writers for legal publication of their works. Small wonder
that his dreams were infectious and that he was greeted by the
writing world in England with open arms. He was the harbinger
of a new era: a bringer of royalties from beyond the sea. He established an office at No. 2 Dean's Yard, overlooked by the towers
of the Abbey and overlooking a portion of Westminster School,
where association football was played in the winter afternoons.
Here amid the chiming of Abbey bells this young American combined the picturesque with the commercial. He had no sense of
difficulty and no awe of greatness. Henry consulted him in all his
theatrical affairs; and had Balestier lived he would have been
James's friendly "agent" in all his business affairs. He was one of
the first of the group of young acolytes that now began to form

around "the Master," the young men of literature and of publishing who could offer him solace and comfort—and affection—during the coming years.

II

Fenimore, lonely on her Florentine hill-top after the death of Lizzie and the departure of Boott and Duveneck, lingered for another year and then gave up the Villa Brichieri. The process was difficult. She had become deeply rooted in the place, almost morbidly, one might say, for in a tale she wrote about Bellosguardo her widowed heroine prefers death to leaving her villa and wastes away for no other visible reason than her grief and her memories. Fenimore was of stronger fibre. She went through her ordeal of getting her belongings together. Henry wrote Boott that it took her "upwards of two months of incessant personal labor, night and day, to get out of a Brichieri bed or two," and "the rupture of our last tie with that consecrated spot has really taken place." Fenimore came first to England and spent a month in the autumn of 1889 at Richmond, where Henry probably saw her. She was joined by her sister and the two left for a winter's tour of the Mediterranean—to Corfu and the Holy Land—which furnished Fenimore copy for some travel articles in *Harper's*. Early the following spring, however, she returned to England and fixed upon Cheltenham as her new abode. She preferred it to London, for she had started work on another novel. Also she would be once again nearer to Henry. In May, however, once his play was in Compton's hands, he decided to leave for Italy. From Venice he wrote to Francis Boott, who was in England that summer, to "see Fenimore without fail—at 4 Promenade Terrace, Cheltenham." Boott went, for Henry learned from his sister, as he wrote to Boott, that "your visit was a great pleasure to her—and I should doubtless have heard in the same sense from Fenimore if I had heard at all. But I have scarcely had news of her since I came abroad." Henry himself paid a visit on his return, for Miss Woolson's copy of *The Tragic Muse* is dated "Cheltenham, September 15, 1890."

That Henry should have gone to Italy that summer was not altogether strange: but it may have seemed so to Fenimore. He was not in the habit of journeying directly into the Italian heat. Nevertheless we find him at Milan in the middle of May, where he writes William about Howells's new novel, *A Hazard of New Fortunes,* finding in it much "life and truth of observation and feeling." "His abundance and facility are my constant wonder and envy—or rather not perhaps, envy, inasmuch as he has purchased them by throwing the whole question of form, style and composition overboard into the deep sea—from which, on my side, I am perpetually trying to fish them up." He could write however a sincere letter to Howells praising this large work of his, telling him "You are *less* big than Zola, but you are ever so much less clumsy and more really various."

Henry travelled to Genoa, Pisa, Siena, Lucca, Florence; he paused to pay two sad visits to Bellosguardo, and went on to Gubbio, Urbino, Ravenna and Rimini. While in Florence he stayed with Dr. Baldwin; then he went on to Venice to stay with the Curtises at the Barbaro. The palace was "cool, melancholy, empty, delicious." The Curtises decided to go to Oberammergau to see the 1890 Passion Play, and persuaded Henry to accompany them in their carriage. He was enchanted by the Dolomites. The play struck him as "primitive" and he disliked the way in which it was commercialized. Returning from this excursion he made a little tour of small Tuscany towns with Dr. Baldwin and stayed at Vallombrosa briefly, near the Countess Peruzzi, enjoying the high mountain coolness. Mrs. Gardner had rented the Barbaro from the Curtises for the rest of the summer and Henry promised her a visit before returning to England. As he was preparing to descend from his Miltonic altitude, an urgent telegram came to him from Alice and he set off for London at once.

He had gone abroad in the comparative security that he could

linger until late summer, since Alice seemed comfortable in
Leamington and Katherine Loring had once again come out from
America to be with her. The sudden summons, however, meant a
new breakdown; and Henry, arriving in London, acted rapidly.
He decided that Alice had been immured too long in the provinces. With Miss Loring's help he had her moved to London, to
the South Kensington Hotel. In due course he found rooms for
her in Argyle Road, Campden Hill, about ten minutes from De
Vere Gardens. Alice's journal records that Dr. Baldwin had come
from Florence and was staying in De Vere Gardens with her
brother. "Can she die?" Henry and Miss Loring had asked Baldwin (whom apparently Alice refused to see—she had developed
hostility toward physicians). Baldwin answered, "They sometimes do." Alice recorded this in her journal with a mixture of self-
pity and a kind of mockery of death that grew more pronounced
as the months passed. For she had learned that she was doomed.
There came a moment when a doctor had to be summoned, and
he found the beginning of a tumor of the breast. Some months
later she allowed Baldwin to examine her when he was again in
England. He diagnosed cancer, and predicted to Henry the form
it would take. Miss Loring from now on remained with Alice. A
kind of grim and as yet remote death-watch had begun, and one
which Alice herself kept—oscillating between moments of fear and
of courage, mingling these with her devotion to Parnell and the
Irish, and the record of Henry's theatrical adventures which she
kept on noting in her journal. Her entries are exclamatory and
rather astringent, shot through again and again with the felicities
of style which she shared with Henry and William.

III

Henry now began to discover in earnest that plays bore no re-
semblance to novels or tales. Editors might complain of length,
but they never presumed, in those days at least, to suggest
alterations. With *The American*, which went into rehearsal
that autumn, he found himself doing a great deal of carpenter

work. A scene did not sound right: it had to be rewritten. Actors objected to certain lines. Speeches needed to be made more colloquial. He submitted grudgingly to the first managerial cuts and kept dashing into the provinces through rain and damp to meet the touring company wherever it might be. After a while he found himself showing the actors how he thought certain "bits" should be played: he called on all his memories of the stage; and on all that he had learned from Mrs. Kemble. Most important of all was the task of teaching the tall and handsome Edward Compton how to talk "American." The typescript sent to the Lord Chamberlain's Office for the licensing of the play was the copy used by Compton; written into it, in James's hand, are the American pronunciations, the guiding principle of which seems to have been to speak everything "a little from the nose." In making his compromises with the stage, Henry was not above caricaturing his American.

Southport, near Liverpool, was selected for the opening of the production. There was a large winter population and a comfortable theatre, the Winter Gardens. Here, on New Year's Day 1891, Henry arrived in a state of feverish excitement for the last rehearsals. Balestier joined him. "My dear Suzerain of the Drama," he had written, "If you will let me 'assist' at the first performance of the first play of our first dramatist this is to intimate that nothing short of legal proceedings to restrain my liberty can prevent my being present." Also to Southport came William Archer, the drama critic, who was helping to launch Ibsen in England and who presently would be collaborating with Shaw in his earliest dramatic efforts. Archer had been urging English novelists to take the theatre seriously; and his arrival at Southport, after writing to Henry for permission to come, indicated that at least one important notice of the production would be written.

The first night took place on January 3, 1891 and Henry spent a nervous day writing letters to all his friends, asking them to pray for him, explaining to Urbain Mengin that it was "the thirst for gold that is pushing me along this dishonorable path," telling

William he was in a state of "abject, lonely fear." But the hour finally came; Henry, watching the play from the right wing, found the audience appreciative and enjoyed its laughter. He enjoyed also, for the first time in his life, being dragged in front of an applauding house, and giving himself up, as he said, to a series of simpering bows while from the "gas-flaring indistinguishable dimness" came the pleasant sounds of acclaim. Compton pressed his hand. So far as Southport was concerned "the stake was won."

In a preface he was to write to Balestier's posthumous tales, Henry alludes to this episode as "a wet winter night in a windy Lancashire town—a formidable 'first night' at a troubled provincial theatre to which he had made a long and loyal pilgrimage for purposes of 'support' at a grotesquely nervous hour—such an occasion comes back to me, vividly, with the very quality of the support afforded, lavish and eager and shrewd; with the pleasantness of the little commemorative inn-supper, half-histrionic and wholly confident, and with the dragged-out drollery of the sequel next day, our sociable, amused participation in a collective theatrical fitting, effected in pottering Sunday trains, besprinkled with refreshment-room impressions and terminating, that night, at an all but inaccessible Birmingham, in independent repose and relaxed criticism."

On the next day Henry left the strolling players to pay a visit, but he told no one where he was going, save Miss Loring. He journeyed from Birmingham to Cheltenham, to spend the day and rehearse his minor provincial triumph with Miss Woolson. A month later he wrote to his brother: "You can form no idea of how a provincial success is confined to the provinces."

EDWARD COMPTON AS THE AMERICAN
From a photograph

HENRY JAMES
*From a pencil sketch
by Sargent*

ALICE JAMES AND KATHERINE LORING IN LEAMINGTON
From a photograph

A LONDON DEBUT

I

HENRY HAD BEEN GIVEN A SHARP TASTE OF WHAT IT MEANT TO BE A strolling player. His sallies into the provinces, his continuing rehearsals and his constant amendment of scenes were providing him with a liberal education in theatricals. "The authorship in any sense worthy of the name of a play," he now explained to William, "only *begins* when it is written, and I see that one's creation of it doesn't terminate till one has gone with it every inch of the way to the rise of the curtain." For him the evening at Southport had not been in reality a rising of the curtain: that would occur only after *The American* was brought to London. In the meantime Compton gave the play on an average once a week in the provinces, as part of his otherwise perpetual repertory of classical comedies. *The American* represented his one venture into the "modern."

Balestier wrote to Howells: "The most delightful feature of the success of the piece is its effect on James. He is like a runner ready to run a race. He has the air of one just setting out—a youngster with an oldster's grip and mastery: surely the most enviable of situations." William sensed Henry's excitement in his letters. "It is an extreme delight to see you in your old and sedate age going in for experiences as keen and uproarious as this, and I do most devoutly hope, now that you've made your plunge, that you'll keep at it and become a Dumas *fils*."

James caught the play at its second performance at the Theatre Royal, Wolverhampton and a few days later at the Memorial Theatre at Stratford-on-Avon, where he was noticed in the audience and took a bow. He saw it once again in Leamington on January 16, where he was still rehearsing some of the scenes. "I show 'em how to do it—and even then they don't know," he wrote to Miss Reubell.

Edward Compton had taken a long lease on the old Opera

Comique Theatre in the Strand where the early Gilbert and Sullivan operas had been performed. He invested a substantial sum in renovation; he installed "the latest sanitary arrangements," and added two new stone staircases. He could not, however, alter the theatre's basic design, including a long subterranean passage to the stalls, which playgoers found rather discouraging.

While he was waiting for his London first night Henry had begun to write his second play, and presently a third. His second was a comedy called *Mrs. Vibert*; later the title was changed to *Tenants*. He had long ago read a tale in the *Revue des Deux Mondes* called "Flavien: Scènes de la vie contemporaine"—a little melodrama which had in it all the ingredients of James's early tales: a general, a ward, the general's mistress, the sons of the general and of the mistress who are really half-brothers, and who fight a duel. He transferred the setting to England and out of these stock situations he now manufactured a trite little comedy, substituting fisticuffs for the duel. Sir John Hare, an enterprising actor-manager, had asked Henry to submit a play and he offered him *Mrs. Vibert*. A search began for possible interpreters. The novelist fixed his attention on Geneviève Ward, who had had a career on the operatic stage in New York and later in the theatre, and W. H. Vernon, who had been her leading man in a number of productions. There were letters and telegrams, flustered arrangements, tea-hour readings of the play, aided and abetted by Henry's friend Mrs. Hugh Bell, herself the author of a number of closet dramas. In his characteristic manner of this time Henry wrote to Mrs. Bell that the third act of his *Mrs. Vibert* was "a pure *movement*, intensely interesting and suspense-producing, lasting forty minutes and subtly calculated to capture the Genevan and Veronese mind." He also said he had abridged his second act "as effectually and bloodily as the most barbarous dramatic butchers could desire." The images of the butcher shop were to increase the longer James aspired to the theatre. He was to exclaim later of one of his efforts: "Oh, the mutilated, brutally simplified, massacred little play!" Mrs. Ward decided against the part and Henry turned to the celebrated tragedienne, Helena Modjeska. She, in turn, told him she could only see Geneviève Ward in the role. Hare speedily lost interest in the comedy and Henry set it aside.

That winter he wrote still another comedy, during six weeks spent in Paris. This was based on a recent tale, "The Solution," which had gone back to the days of his adventures in the saddle and his Roman sightseeing with Mrs. Wister and Mrs. Mason. It was the story of the diplomat who is persuaded that he has compromised a young woman by taking her on an unchaperoned walk. James transferred the scene once more to England. In the hands of Oscar Wilde this could have become an amusing drawing-room farce. Henry's play, however, was a series of unmotivated entries and exits. He thought of the comedy as suitable for Ada Rehan, the Irish-American actress who had made a great hit on the London stage in classical comedy under the management of the New York stage veteran, Augustin Daly. Daly readily took an option on the play on the strength of Henry's literary reputation. For the next year and a half the novelist-playwright waited for his comedy to be produced. What held it up was that Daly was building a theatre in London. Henry was scheduled to be one of the "attractions" in the new house.

This was his situation as a dramatist by the time he had to begin rehearsals for the London production of *The American*.

II

During one of his calls on Geneviève Ward—on January 12, 1891 —Henry encountered a poised young woman of considerable charm, with extraordinary large clear blue eyes, which looked straight into his, and more "personality" than he had found among most of the actresses he was meeting in London. She was indeed an actress, and an American. Her name was Elizabeth Robins. She was twenty-seven, and had been on the stage for almost a decade. Born in Louisville, Kentucky, she had played small parts in New York, worked with James O'Neill, the father of Eugene, and later been attached to the company at the Boston Museum. She had toured up and down the United States with the Booth-Barrett company playing minor Shakespearean roles and then had gone abroad. During a visit to Norway she had heard the name of Ibsen. Now, in London, she was appearing in *A Doll's House* before scandalized Victorian audiences. The battle for Ibsen had begun, and in this young woman he had a vigorous and intelligent interpreter. She had a certain ease and quiet in her relations with people; she knew the value of few words, and the charm of being an attentive listener. This was why she had been able to impress into her service Oscar Wilde and Beerbohm Tree, when she had decided not to return to her trouping in America. What James thought of her on that day we do not know, but Miss Robins's diary leaves no doubt of her impression.

Delightful experience. He tells me about his play *The American*. We talk Ibsen and he is coming to see me in *Doll's House*. I like this man better I think than any *male* American I have met abroad. He is delightfully *grave* and without the Yankee traveller's thin pretence of cosmopolitanism. This meeting is a ray of sunshine in a dark day.

On January 27 at a matinee of the *Doll's House* which he attended with Geneviève Ward, he watched Miss Robins act; it was the first Ibsen play he had seen. Later that spring he saw Miss Robins again as Hedda and was greatly taken with her playing of that role. "Ibsen's *Hedda Gabler* is the talk of the town," he wrote to Miss Reubell, "with the most interesting English-speaking actress (or rather the *only* one), that I have seen for many a day—Elizabeth Robins, an American of course. *Le coeur ne vous en dit-il pas?*" And to Mrs. Gardner he said: "She is slightly uncanny, but distinguished and individual." Henry took Compton to see her perform and it was settled that they would invite her to play Claire de Cintré in *The American*, a role Mrs.

Compton had taken in the provinces but which she was relinquishing in London because she was with child.

What Henry could not have known was that Miss Robins's gift lay precisely in the playing of Heddas and Noras; although she had an adequate bag of tricks, as an experienced actress, she was constitutionally incapable of creating so shrinking a flower as Claire—a woman all renunciation and passivity. The casting may have seemed wise at the time: and doubtless Henry had reason to believe that Miss Robins's gifts were less specialized. Nevertheless the role offered her could not have suited her less and she was to have great difficulty with it. Several other changes were made in the cast. Kate Bateman, Mrs. Compton's older sister, came out of retirement to play the Marquise, and a young and vivacious French actress, Adrienne Dairolles, was given the part of Noémie.

New scenery was built; the furniture was imported from Paris; much attention was paid to the costumes. However, the critics were to be puzzled over the fact that Henry dressed his American in a long chocolate-colored coat with sky-blue trimmings and buttons "as large as cheese-plates." The costume reminded them of a travelling showman; they knew that American millionaires dressed in much better taste. There was a strong element of travesty in Compton's appearance; and in his romantic story James could not—on the stage—draw the line between his comedy and his pathos, between outright farce in the elements of the production, and the high comedy of his original. The London rehearsals proved more strenuous than those in the provinces; and Miss Robins has left us an account of Henry's charm behind scenes and his consideration for the actors. Sandwiches and other delicacies were brought down to rehearsals from De Vere Gardens by his servants. "No other playwright, in my tolerably wide experience," she wrote, "ever thought of feeding his company."

III

In the spring of 1891, when he had virtually completed the new casting of *The American* in collaboration with Compton, Henry had a bout of influenza. It left him weak and dispirited. He had always wanted to pay a longer visit to Ireland, and this seemed to him an opportune time; he would be within easy call of Alice and at the same time would take a respite from his theatrical fever and write some short stories. He went at the end of June to Kingstown, six miles from Dublin, and settled in the Royal Marine Hotel. Here he wrote "The Private Life," and his pleasant little tale of "The Chaperon," another of his stories of how a lady could breach the laws of society and then, with society's own amused consent, be re-accepted. The irony of the tale was that instead of the daughter's being chaperoned by the mother, it is the mother who is chaperoned—after a series of indiscretions—and re-escorted into society by the daughter. The dramatist Arthur Pinero, on reading this tale, pointed out to Henry that it had all the elements of an amusing stage comedy. Henry promptly made notes to that end, but he never completed the play. A fragment of a scenario, dictated by him almost fifteen years later, is all that survives.

In Ireland he found "peace and obscurity and leisure" and he recovered rapidly from his illness. "The sea is sapphire—in this lovely weather—the hotel is good, and Ireland generally seems sympathetic," he told Miss Reubell. In mid-July he wrote a gossipy letter to Francis Boott, mentioning among other things that Fenimore was moving from Cheltenham to Oxford "for a year, a very right and good place for her. She believes she is then—after a year again—going to Italy to spend the rest of her life. But *chi lo sa?* I haven't either seen or heard of her 'Bellosguardo story,' but shall demand of her to send it to me." This was the tale called "Dorothy" which had reflected Fenimore's difficulty in uprooting herself from the Villa Brichieri. The tale contained several allusions to Boott's musical setting of John Hay's poem "Through the long days and years," and its publication created a sudden sale for the song, written long before on Bellosguardo. Thanks to Fenimore, Francis Boott, in his middle seventies, after a lifetime of amateur composition, experienced this brief show of public interest in his work.

On July 20, Henry wrote one of his continuing series of letters to Lowell, who was dying. The letters are all filled with the warmth of an old and sympathetic friendship. Henry described the charming Irish coast, the blueness of sea and greenness of shore, the graceful Wicklow mountains and hills of Howth and Killiney. "The very waves have a brogue as they break—and they broke Bray Head, the fine southernmost limit of the bay, long ago.

But let me not have the air of inflicting upon you that deadliest of all things a scenery-letter, when my foremost wish is to throw myself into *your* environment. I have, somehow, a vision of you which makes my heart ache a good deal—and makes me brush from my eye the tear in which old London pictures—other pictures—are reflected. Your non-arrival—this spring—made me for the first time in my life willing to say that I 'realised' a situation. I seemed to see that you were tied down by pain and weakness, that you were suffering often and suffering much. I don't like to ask for fear of a yes, and I don't like not to ask for fear of your noticing my silence. In point of fact I *have* asked. . . .

And Henry went on to speak nostalgically of his lonely walks in London.

But, my dear Lowell, I don't write to rehearse to you your own incommodities. I have walked across the Park alone this summer and when I have had to go to Paddington I have slackened my step—oh so vainly—in Radnor Place, in the hope that from the little afternoon sittingroom you would call me in.

He went on to say that "these melancholies" had not prevented the season from "roaring and elbowing along" in a manner less and less to his taste.

This was Henry's last letter to his friend. Lowell probably received it and read it a few days before he died, on August 12, 1891. "It is a loss, and a pain, and a dear friend the less," Henry wrote to du Maurier a few days after he had the news (he was now back in De Vere Gardens). "And it seems a brutal negation of all his vitality—juvenility—almost, as it were, his promise." Before the year was out he was to compose his long memorial essay, published in the Atlantic, in which he reviewed Lowell's career and writings and his own fond memories of him. Once again he began it in his high elegiac tone with certain reverberant sentences:

After a man's long work is over and the sound of his voice is still, those in whose regard he has held a high place find his image strangely simplified and summarized. The hand of death, in passing over it, has smoothed the folds, made it more typical and general. The figure retained by the memory is compressed and intensified; accidents have dropped away from it and shades have ceased to count; it stands, sharply, for a few estimated and cherished things, rather than nebulously, for a swarm of possibilities. We cut the silhouette, in a word, out of the confusion of life, we save and fix the outline, and it is with his eye on this profiled distinction that the critic speaks.

The words had about them the sense of solemn obsequies and of the limitations of immortality. This was Henry James's public— and private—funeral oration for his friend.

IV

No part of the production of The American is more touching than the record of it reflected in Alice James's journal which she wrote herself, in her round and warm handwriting, or dictated to Miss Loring—the joy with which, from the four walls of her sickroom, she allowed her imagination to soar to the footlights in the Strand. In his letters to William, Henry came to speak of his play and Alice as his two invalids. For his sister, the episode was "so shot through with the threads of golden comedy that we grew fat with laughter." For her nervous and anxious brother, with the spectacle of Alice slowly wasting away, there were the vicissitudes of his play to preoccupy him when he was not in her sickroom.

Six days before the opening night William James suddenly appeared in London after a rapid autumn crossing. He had come to say good-bye to Alice. He spent as many hours as he could with his sister; and he was at Henry's first night, and the intimate supper which Henry gave afterwards. The guests were the Comptons, Miss Robins, William Heinemann, the publisher, and Wolcott Balestier. Heinemann had recently met James; it was he who had set up a small acting edition of *The American*, just enough copies for the cast and the author, in the hope of publishing the play if it should be a success.

The first night on September 26, 1891 in the refurbished theatre was a dubious artistic success, but distinctly a social one. Robert Lincoln, the American Minister, was in a box, and several of the stage journals spoke of the presence of various "millionaires" from the other side of the Atlantic. The literary world turned out in force; also the painters. Grace Norton was in London, and so— with William—Cambridge, Massachusetts was thoroughly represented. And Fenimore, by this time settled in Oxford, came to London for the occasion. It is possible to see it through her eyes, as she reported on it to a friend:

I put on my best, and we looked well enough, but were nothing to the others! Pink satin, blue satin, jewels of all sorts, splendour on all sides of us. The house was packed to the top, and the applause was great. When the performance was ended, and the actors had been called out, there arose loud cries of "Author, author!" After some delays, Henry James appeared before the curtain and acknowledged the applause. He looked very well— quiet and dignified, yet pleasant; he only stayed a moment. The critics have since then, written acres about the play. It has been warmly praised; attacked; abused; highly commended, etc.

To read the critics today is to see quite clearly what was wrong with *The American*. The writing was obscure at points; the play was more melodramatic than the novel warranted. Miss Robins's playing of Claire tended to be frantic and nervous—as one critic said, it imported into the play "the hysterical manners of

Ibsen's morbid heroines." A comedy Christopher Newman was not altogether liked. Newman's chocolate-colored coat was the subject of much satiric reference, and the anonymous critic of the *Era* put matters bluntly when he remarked: "We are as anxious as the critics of the newest school to hail the advent on our stage of literary men, but it is on condition that they bring their literature with them." Nothing more pointed could have been said. The truth of the matter was that Henry would probably have been more successful if he had tried to remain himself, within the theatric form, instead of becoming the theatrical hack seeking to perpetrate a "well-made play."

The critics who were eager to see novelists working on the stage—men like William Archer—spoke in more muted terms. Yet they too had to acknowledge that Henry had sacrificed too much of the originality of his novel for mere melodrama. A. B. Walkley, admiring the amount of busy action Henry had infused into his drama, exclaimed: "What, Mr. James? All this 'between dinner and the suburban trains'?" It was probably Walkley, one of the most literate of drama critics, who twitted James also in an anonymous review for his "stage American, with the local color laid on with a trowel, and strong accent, a fearful and wonderful coat and a recurrent catch-word." Compton definitely had the accent, and for the rest "a great deal of ugly overcoat."

The production was lagging when the Prince of Wales decided that he wanted to see it. Compton asked Henry to "dress up" a couple of boxes with "smart people." Henry obliged him; he told Alice, "I'd do anything for the good Compton, but it will make me charitable to the end of my days." The visit of royalty had its desired effect; the play's run was prolonged. Henry and Compton decided to give it a further "lift" and resorted to the unusual procedure of inviting the critics to a "second edition" on the fiftieth night—Henry having taken a number of the critical suggestions and revised certain of the scenes. The critics were flattered at being taken so seriously, and did find the play improved. Miss Robins's acting was pronounced less "somnambulistic";

however, Compton had not been persuaded to doff his garment and he still sprinkled his dialogue with the tag-line—"That's what I want t'see." The play eked out seventy nights. Henry felt it was "humiliating" to be beholden to royalty for part of his run; nevertheless that run had now been "honorable," and he took solace in this fact. The royalties had been negligible.

Ten days after the closing of the play Henry was summoned to Dresden where Wolcott Balestier had gone on publishing business. The young American had typhoid and James arrived in time to stand at his graveside, with Balestier's mother and sisters (one of whom was to marry Rudyard Kipling shortly afterwards). "The young Balestier, the effective and the indispensable, is dead!—swept away like a cobweb, of which gossamer substance he seems to have been himself composed; of simply spirit energy, with the slightly fleshly wrappings." This was Alice's comment in her journal—a tribute of the dying to the dead.

A DIVINE CESSATION

ON MARCH 5, 1892 ALICE JAMES DICTATED TO HENRY A CABLE TO send to William and his family. It read: "Tenderest love to all. Farewell. Am going soon. ALICE."

She had then but a few hours to live. And during those hours she dictated to Katherine Loring the ultimate passage in her journal: "I am being ground slowly on the grim grindstone of physical pain and on two nights I had almost asked for Katherine's lethal dose; but one steps hesitatingly along such unaccustomed ways, and endures from second to second. I feel sure that it can't be possible but what the bewildered little hammer that keeps me going will very shortly see the decency of ending his distracted career. However this may be, physical pain, however great, ends in itself and falls away like dry husks from the mind, whilst moral discords and nervous horrors sear the soul." That sentence bothered her; during her last night Alice tried to improve it. "Oh, the wonderful moment when I felt myself floated for the first time, into the deep sea of divine *cessation*," she dictated, "and saw all the dear old mysteries and miracles vanish into vapour." She was probably alluding to the fact that she had fainted away the previous evening, and had felt as if she were dying. She came to just as Henry was being sent for, and afterwards was "perfectly clear and humorous" with him about it. She wanted to talk, but could not, for it provoked spasms of coughing.

On one of her last nights she had a dream which she told Katherine Loring. In her dream she saw a boat in which were Lizzie Boott and their common friend Annie Dixwell, who had died some time before Lizzie. They were putting out into a tumbled sea, seeming to pass from under the shadow of a cloud, and looking back at Alice. This "impressed and agitated her much," Henry wrote to Francis Boott.

The climax of her long years of invalidism came suddenly. She had been merely weaker at the end of February and had been given doses of morphine to assuage her pain. At William's suggestion Dr. Lloyd Tuckey, an eminent psychiatrist, had been called in some months before and had used hypnotism as a further aid. At the beginning of March Alice contracted a cold; her doctors later speculated that a second tumor, perhaps in or near the lung—which Baldwin had predicted—exacerbated her condition. Henry, coming to see her on March 5, was struck by the supreme death-like emaciation that had come over her within forty-eight hours. Hypnotism helped to hold nervousness in arrest; and Katherine Loring was taught by Tuckey how to use it.

It was on this day, a Saturday, that she dictated the farewell cable to William. On the next, Henry himself sent the final word. The "divine cessation" for which she had prayed had come.

On the last page of Alice's journal, in Katherine Loring's hand, is a postscript: "The dictation of March 4th was rushing about in her brain all day, and although she was very weak and it tired her much to dictate, she could not get her head quiet until she had it written. Then she was relieved and I finished Miss Woolson's story of 'Dorothy' to her." Thus the last story Alice listened to was Fenimore's Bellosguardo story—the story of the slow death of a woman who does not want to live.

I

This was the first time that Henry had watched someone through the hours of death—and someone close to him. His mother had died quite suddenly, when he had been away from home; his father had been dead when he arrived after crossing the Atlantic. He looked on now with the helpless hurt and suffering that other great novelists have recorded; and it was both as brother and as novelist that he set down the final scene of his sister's undramatic life, for their Cambridge brother. "Alice died at exactly four o'clock on Sunday afternoon (about the same hour of the same day as mother), and it is now Tuesday morning," he began, and then followed a painful step-by-step account. On Saturday, when Alice had taken on the look of death, the pain diminished, and "left her consciously and oh longingly, close to the end." Katherine and Henry sought to create an intense stillness around her. They hoped that in these circumstances she might sleep. In the late afternoon Henry left her bedside for a while; Tuckey saw her during the evening for the second time that day and came back later still. Henry wanted to stay the night on Campden Hill, but Miss Loring thought this was pointless. There was nothing he could do. Alice said a few barely audible things to him, above all "that she *couldn't*, oh, she COULDN'T and begged it mightn't be exacted of her, live *another* day." Then she sank into a gentle sleep. "From that sleep she never woke—but after an hour or two it changed its character and became a loud, deep breathing —almost stertorous." This was her condition when Henry reached the house again on Sunday morning at nine. From that hour until four Katherine, the nurse and Henry sat beside Alice's bed. Tuckey came in the morning at 11:30 expecting to find her dead; when Katherine described his patient's condition to him he said there was nothing he could further do or suggest, and that he would refrain from seeing her unless it was insisted upon.

Alice wished for death, yet she died reluctantly. Her automatic breathing continued for seven hours with no look of pain in her face, only more and more the look of death.

They were infinitely pathetic and, to me, most unspeakable hours. They would have been intolerable if it had not been so evident that all the hideous burden of suffering consciousness was utterly gone. As it is, they were the most appealing and pitiful thing I ever saw. But I have seen, happily, but little death immediately. Toward the end, for about an hour, the breathing became a constant sort of smothered whistle in the lung. The pulse flickered, came and went, ceased and revived a little again, and then with all perceptible action of the heart, altogether ceased to be sensible for some time before the breathing ceased.

An hour before the end there came a "blessed change." She began to breathe without effort, gently, peacefully and naturally, like a child. This lasted an hour, and then her breathing seemed to become intermittent, about one breath in a minute, and "Her face then seemed in a strange, dim, touching way to become clearer." Henry went to the window to let in a little more of the afternoon light upon Alice's countenance. "It was a bright, kind, soundless Sunday." When he came back to the bed Alice had drawn, he wrote William, "the last breath." Then the novelist crossed out the word "last" and made the sentence read, "she had drawn the breath that was not succeeded by another."

Alice had asked to be cremated with the simplest possible ceremony, thereby following, in the latter respect, the wishes her father expressed when he was dying. Her body lay in her room, in the bed in which she died, from that Sunday evening until Wednesday. During that time Henry spent many hours beside her. "She looks most beautiful and noble—with *all* of the august expression that you can imagine—and with less, than before, of the almost ghastly emaciation of those last days." Her ashes, by her wish, were to be sent to Cambridge and interred beside the graves of her parents.

At 11:45 Wednesday morning, March 9, 1892, Henry, Katherine Loring, Alice's nurse, and an old Cambridge friend who lived in England, Annie Ashburner Richards, took the train to Woking at Waterloo Station. The hearse and the horses had been put on the train in a special car. At Woking they had a couple of miles' drive. There was a short simple service, "read by an inoffensive, sweet-voiced young clergyman." For an hour and a half, Henry and his companions waited in a room next to the chapel, while the cremation was carried out. On his way back from Waterloo, the novelist stopped at the Reform Club and wrote half a dozen sentences to William, describing the scene. "It is the last, the last forever. I shall feel very lonely in England at first. But enough."

II

In the days that followed, Henry answered many letters of condolence. In all his replies he spoke of the release which had come to his sister. He rejoiced that this sudden illness had put an end to her lingering invalidism; and he mourned her as "a rare and remarkable being." One of the first to whom Henry wrote was Francis Boott. To him, however, he spoke of his "great sorrow," because "even with everything that made life an unspeakable weariness to her, she contributed constantly, infinitely to the interest, the consolation, as it were, in disappointment and depression, of my own existence. But it's all over, and peace, for her, had been intensely and pathetically desired."

Henry rejoiced in her cremation: it was "a positive joy to me that we hadn't left her alone, and far off, in the wintry earth."

Alice left an estate valued at $80,000. This she divided among her three brothers and Katherine Loring. Henry, William and Katherine received $20,000 each. Robertson was left a smaller amount and her silver. Her reason was that the younger brother's wife and children had large expectations, whereas William and Henry had none. The balance was distributed in small gifts to nieces and nephews; certain old friends were remembered, and Alice left an annuity for her nurse. Robertson James protested this discrimination, and Henry announced that he was willing to transfer $5,000 from his inheritance, since he felt Katherine Loring could hardly be asked to do so, and that William, with four children, should not be asked to part with any share of what he was receiving. Henry and William both agreed that in this division of her estate Alice had "most justly" placed Miss Loring "on the footing of a brother."

Alice's journal remained in Miss Loring's possession. Some time later, by agreement with William, four copies were printed, for the three brothers and herself. When Henry received his copy he expressed great alarm. The journal was filled with much minor gossip retailed by him to Alice to entertain her; it reflected, for all its fervent Irishness and stout Americanism, the state of mind of an invalid confined within four walls. He feared very much that the journal, disseminated, would have the effect of his fictitious *Reverberator*. All evidence points to the destruction of his own copy. And at his request, Robertson's copy was not given to him, lest it fall into unauthorized hands. William's copy is preserved among his books in the Houghton Library. The manuscript was retained by Miss Loring, who lived to an advanced age, and was given by her to the descendants of Robertson James. They published it, in a corrupt text, during the 1930's. A slender volume, with not much substance, and filled with the minor items of the sickroom, it attracted much attention —for it embodied Alice's spirited will to survival, to have her place in this family of articulate boys in which she had had the misfortune to be the only girl. "I have been immensely impressed with the thing as a revelation of a moral and personal picture," Henry wrote to William on reading the journal. "It is heroic in its individuality, its independence—its face-to-face with the universe for-and-by herself—and the beauty and eloquence with which she often expresses this, let alone the rich irony and humour, constitute a new claim for the family renown. This last element—her style, her power to write—are indeed to me a delight." On this occasion Henry had his profound insight—he wrote that Alice's "tragic health was in a manner the only solution for her of the practical problem of life."

In Dante, William found a passage which both he and Henry agreed could fittingly be inscribed upon her grave. In 1892, when William was in Italy, a marble urn was executed with these words on it:

> *ed essa da martiro*
> *e da essilio venne a questa pace*

III

Three years after Alice's death, Henry found himself riding one evening in London, in a four-wheeler, on his way to dine with Lord Lovelace. As he rattled through the cold clear night there came to him—he was unable to say why or how—the thought of a story he might write about "the existence of a peculiar intense and interesting affection between a brother and sister." As he recorded this in his notebook he spoke of "two lives, two beings, and *one* experience." The story would contain "the idea of some unspeakable intensity of feeling, of tenderness, of sacred compunction, as it were, in relation to the *past*, the parents, the beloved mother, the beloved father—of those who have suffered before them and for them."

On this evening Lord Lovelace showed Henry James the long-suppressed letters of Byron and Augusta Leigh, Byron's half-sister. The novelist later mused on the coincidence: that he should have himself thought of a tale of brotherly and sisterly love, on the very night that he was to be shown this evidence—although his tale would have been without "the nefarious—abnormal—character" of the Byron-Leigh relation. His subject he felt would present "the image of a deep, participating devotion. . . . The brother suffers, has the experience and the effect of the experience, is carried along by fate, etc.; and the sister understands, perceives, shares, with every pulse of her being. He has to tell her nothing—she *knows*: it's identity of sensation, of vibration. It's, for *her*, the Pain of Sympathy: that would be the subject, the formula."

The note contains no mention of Alice and Henry never wrote this story. Perhaps because he had long before, and for many years, lived it.

THE WHEEL OF TIME

I

HENRY ADAMS, SOJOURNING IN LONDON EARLY IN 1892, SAW HENRY as "a figure in the same wallpaper." But then, for Adams, life had taken on a sameness after Clover's death from which he was to escape only by consorting with the Middle Ages. E. S. Nadal, who had looked at Henry in so circumstantial a fashion when he was in Bolton Street, returning now to London after a decade, left his card at De Vere Gardens, and Henry promptly replied, "Welcome back to old England," and invited him to lunch. "I found him in a handsome apartment in Kensington," the former Second Secretary of Legation wrote. "He had a butler of a most respectable appearance, and he had a dachshund bitch with a beautiful countenance. He sat with the dachshund in his lap much of the time."

Somehow they got to the subject of sex and began to compare European and American women. Nadal argued that American women had less "sex" than European women, "that in many American women it was negative, and in European women positive, and that many American girls looked like effeminate boys." In his reminiscences however he does not tell us what Henry thought; unless indeed Henry said nothing. He merely records one rejoinder, by the novelist as he stroked the head of his dog: "She's got sex, if you like, and she's quite intelligent enough to be shocked by this conversation."

Henry candidly told Nadal that his books were not selling. He seemed "tired" of English society. He told him that he would never again enter an English country house for a staying visit. He expressed horror at the American women tourists increasingly invading Europe with their Baedekers. And the Henry who, in the 1870's, had amazed Nadal and Hoppin by his exploits as a diner-out, now astonished his old acquaintance by confessing to him that he dined at home, usually alone in his apartment. "Don't you find that dull?" Nadal asked. "No, I don't mind it," James replied. Nadal thought it a mistake that the novelist should be allowing himself so large a measure of loneliness when he had his clubs. "He didn't seem as happy as he used to be, and I could have wished him back in his old lodgings at No. 3 Bolton Street, 'the half of my old number,' without the very respectable butler, and looked after by the tall, slender, dark, rather pretty 'person' with the sensitive risibilities."

They talked also of *The American*. Nadal told him he had heard that in spite of the critical notices, the play had been liked by the gallery. Henry said he believed this was true. He spoke of play-writing as a difficult art. Nadal observed:

He was not dramatic, certainly not theatrical. His talent was critical and narrative. In this attempt, he was moving in a direction away from, rather than toward, his true gift, the introvertive monologue in which he delighted, such as I used to hear from him in our nocturnal walks about the London streets. But then monologue would not have given him a nice apartment and a combination valet and butler. The nice flat and the butler in a swallow-tail coat were perhaps the result of living in England.

Disregarding some of Nadal's gratuitous reflections, we nevertheless can remark that he had recognized the fundamental question preoccupying the novelist at this time: the relationship of his art to the world. "He liked to have a look of success," Nadal said.

11

William James, on seeing Henry in De Vere Gardens in 1889 after their long separation, had written home to his wife: "Harry is as nice and simple and amiable as he can be. He has covered himself, like some marine crustacean, with all sorts of material growths, rich sea-weeds and rigid barnacles and things, and lives hidden in the midst of his strange heavy alien manners and customs; but these are all but 'protective resemblances,' under which the same dear old, good, innocent and at bottom very powerless-feeling Harry remains, caring for little but his writing, and full of dutifulness and affection for all gentle things."

"Powerless-feeling," to be sure whenever he was in William's presence; and William's picture of his "dear old, good, innocent" Harry is essentially that of the "angel" of long ago. William, on his side, had particular reasons for feeling powerful at this moment. He had just published his *Principles of Psychology*, the work on which his fame was to rest together with his later writings on pragmatism and his *Varieties of Religious Experience*. He was coming into belated success at the very moment when Henry, celebrated and respected in the literary world, was beginning to question the meaning of the fame that had come to him a dozen years before. Henry had never been more ambitious and indeed never more powerful than at this moment. Between the time of William's description and the death of Alice—between 1889 and 1892—he had brought out a long novel and a volume of tales and had written many articles. During the year of Alice's death he published ten tales and four articles. Not a month elapsed without his being in one or another of the leading magazines on either side of the Atlantic. And in the year following Alice's death—1893—he surpassed all his previous records of publication by bringing out five books, three volumes of tales and two of essays. Three of these books appeared in one month, June 1893: *Picture and Text*, his essays on art; *Essays in London*, largely a series of tributes and memorials of his recently dead friends; and *The Private Life and Other Tales*. In addition, there now lay on his desk the scripts of four comedies and that of *The American*.

Henry had a full sense of the power he wielded in literary circles. But he also had a sense of encroaching loneliness as familiar figures in his life continued to drop away: Mrs. Procter and Browning, the young Balestier, the beloved Lowell. In the autumn of 1892 Henry was invited to the Abbey to still another funeral, walking with his fellow men of letters at the interment of the Bard himself, the seemingly indestructible figure of Alfred Lord Tennyson. "It was a lovely day, the Abbey looked beautiful, everyone was there, but something—I don't know what—of real impressiveness—was wanting." There were "too many masters of Balliol, too many Deans and Alfred Austins." Henry sent a copy of the Order of Service to Fenimore in Oxford and told her that "Crossing the Bar" was sung beautifully by the Abbey choir, especially the line "one clear call for me," which sounded like "an angel's voice from on high."

A much more personal loss was recorded by the novelist a month later, when he learned that his loyal friend Theodore Child had died in the East. Child had been the Boswell of his talks with the Naturalists. He had published him in his little Paris newspaper. Henry had known him ever since the summer

of 1876 at Étretat. Now he was gone, "prematurely and lament-
edly," while on a journalistic tour of exploration in Persia. He had
died near Ispahan, and been buried in a lonely grave at Tulfa.

There were not only deaths but unexpected breaks with the
past. For old times' sake Henry had kept up a correspondence with
his Newport friend, Thomas Sergeant Perry, and had regularly
sent him his books. Some impulse, perhaps envy, some sense of
his own failure in the American literary world, where he had
wholly ceased to publish, had prompted Perry to send Henry a
"most offensive and impertinent" letter in which he expressed dis-
approval of his expatriation. "It was too idiotic to notice and it
was almost impertinent enough to return and it set the seal upon
the conviction I have always privately had that he is a singularly
poor creature," Henry told William and he decided to have nothing further to do with this "singular helpless mediocrity." This
explains the large gap which now occurred in the otherwise
voluminous correspondence. The friendship was not resumed
until they met again in late middle age.

III

If these old figures in the crowded life of Henry James now dis-
appeared, Henry became increasingly aware that new ones were
on his horizon—a generation of attractive young men, gifted and
appreciative, only too willing to be acolytes and to hail him as
"Master." They had grown up with his books and they sought
him out. They were young and full of promise; there was something touching in their worship of him, and in the affection his
work seemed to inspire in them. One of Henry's heroes of this
period "observed the young now more than he had ever done;
observed them that is, as the young." Balestier had been one of
the first; others came rapidly. One of the most sentimental of
these attachments was formed with a gifted young man from
New England, William Morton Fullerton, who came to London
to work as a newspaperman. He had a poetic sense and a style
already deeply influenced by Henry's. He was what might be called

un homme de cœur: a romantic journalist full of the world and of its promise, and happy to give Henry his confidences. Henry encouraged him, listened to him, sought his company. A native of Norwich, Connecticut, Fullerton was about twenty-five when he obtained a position on the *Times* in London. He was invited often to De Vere Gardens. Presently the *Times* sent him to Paris to work with Blowitz. There is a note in an unpublished portion of Alice James's journal in which she speaks of "the ascendancy of the American," as emphasized by the fact that a young man "I believe named Fullerton, not more than twenty-five, was sub-editor of the *Times* and now is sent to Paris in process of time to undermine Blowitz, I suppose." Fullerton was to make the rest of his career in the French capital and he replaced Theodore Child in the regular round of Henry's Parisian visits. How pliant Fullerton was may be judged by the fact that he continued to write for the *Times* in "kilometric sentences," after the manner of the later James; and Henry used to tease him at his using Jamesian phrases in his letters. He later Gallicized himself by leaving English journalism and writing for *Le Figaro*. He lived into modern times and became a friend, in the new century, of Edith Wharton. American soldiers, arriving in Paris after its liberation in the Second World War, found him a hardy octogenarian, among his books and papers in the Rue du Mont-Thabor. Henry James's letters to Fullerton testify to a genial camaraderie between journalist and *homme de lettres,* Fullerton being as it were on the border between the two. "With your margin of youth and your close text of Talent," Henry once wrote to him, envying him his years and his immersion in the wide world. He was a kind of boon companion, someone with whom Henry did not need to be formal and to whom he could write with none of the inhibitions of other correspondence. Early in their acquaintance they got into the habit of exchanging confidences. Thus in the autumn of 1890 Henry writes to Fullerton: "Bury in deep and charitable oblivion my rather confused gush on the question theatrical. Excuse my nervously repeating this." And he also tells him: "Have as many adventures and impressions as you can, the next month, to the end that you may promptly thereafter come and relate them to yours affectionately HENRY JAMES."

There was also Jonathan Sturges, a young graduate of Princeton. Sturges, a New Yorker, had been badly crippled in childhood by poliomyelitis; from the waist up he was a good-looking, broad-shouldered young man, with fine distinctive features. He liked best to go riding in Hyde Park in an open hansom, to conceal his infirmities. He inspired in Henry a great tenderness; it was almost as if, having had an invalid sister to care for all these years, he now could have a substitute for her. In later years, at Lamb House, Sturges would pay prolonged visits and provide Henry with much sociable and literary talk. Through Henry, he met Miss Reubell in Paris and frequented her salon; he became a friend of Whistler as well. He wrote a number of stories and he translated a group of Maupassant's tales which were published with a preface by Henry. In London he usually lived at Long's Hotel, where he was much sought after socially during periods of comparative health.

There was another young American, Logan Pearsall Smith, from a Philadelphia Quaker background, who came out to Oxford, with an introduction to Henry James. Although Logan was to become an arch-purveyor of Jamesian anecdote in his late years, his correspondence with Henry shows that he figured as a lesser intimate during the 1890's and never occupied in the life of James the place given to Sturges or Fullerton, or later to such diverse acolytes as Hugh Walpole and Jocelyn Persse. But then James had a way of pigeonholing his friends; and of keeping them apart, each reserved for his own particular role in the novelist's life.

Into Henry's orbit at this time came also Henry Harland, author of certain popular novels written in New York under the pen-name of Sidney Luska, and later the editor of the *Yellow Book*. It was Harland who brought Aubrey Beardsley to the novelist and induced him to publish certain of his tales in that hard-bound journal of the late aestheticism. A still more interesting though passing figure was Henry Bennett Brewster, who attracted Henry by his achieved cosmopolitanism. "Know Brewster? Why I invented Brewster—ten years ago," Henry wrote to an inquiring friend in Rome in 1899. For Brewster was a character out of Henry James. His ancestors had come to the United States on the *Mayflower*; he numbered among them two Yankee clergymen and one minuteman. His father had been a physician; and this handsome bearded figure with clear sharp eyes had grown up in Europe with a mastery of several tongues and several literatures and a penchant for meditative writing. He wrote a book called *The Theory of Anarchy and of Law*, and a work *L'Âme païenne* which had many admirers. He has been much described in the memoirs of Ethel Smyth, whose lover he was, and his sophistication and "Europeanization" led Henry to devote certain sentences to him in his *Notes of a Son and Brother*. In these he recalls that this master of three tongues, who was "scarce American at all" had depreciated *The Marble Faun*. But then "homely superstition had no hold on him," and he viewed Hawthorne only from his Continentalized vision; there would have been small use in Henry's trying to make him see what was "exquisite" in Hawthorne's Roman story. Henry and Brewster were to dine whenever they met, in London or abroad; and Henry was to cherish his memory, after he died at a comparatively early age: "I am haunted by the tragic image of our fine and inscrutable Brewster, who hadn't really half done with the exquisite mystification he somehow made of life—or perhaps received from it!" Henry felt him to have been "such a strange handsome questioning cosmopolite ghost."

They came, these younger men, into Henry's life, and some survived to create the later legend of the Master. We catch their reflection in the tales of the literary life: always, in these tales, whether it is that of "The Death of the Lion" or of "The Figure in the Carpet," there is a young acolyte, a youthful spirit touched by the art of the Great Writer. One of the first of these tales was to be written by Henry during his fiftieth year. He called it

"The Middle Years" and it was the only new tale he published during 1893. In this story, a middle-aged writer has had a serious illness and fears he may die before he has his "second chance," his opportunity for a "later manner." "It had taken too much of life to produce too little of his art. At such a rate a first existence was too short." He finds a young doctor who is prepared to abandon everything to take care of him, so powerfully had he been affected by the novelist's books. And Dencombe, dying, realizes that perhaps the most important thing is not whether there is to be another chance, a second existence. The important thing was to have created a work which could arouse a response, make someone vibrate—"It *is* glory—to have been tested, to have had our little quality and cast our little spell. The thing is to have made somebody care."

These new young men surrounding James cared; they cared deeply. The world might ignore him; but Henry knew that so long as certain readers experienced his work as profoundly as this his personal *gloire* was assured. Thus Henry could end his sad tale with the noble words of the artist: "We work in the dark—we do what we can—we give what we have. Our doubt is our passion and our passion is our task. The rest is the madness of art." He was coming to realize at this moment, midway in his dramatic years, that the greatest art is not that which creates a sensation or a success—as his new friend Rudyard Kipling was doing at that moment—but that which, by some strange and divine process of human relation, inspires in others an interest, a depth of feeling, an attachment. This touching tale, fruit of these troubled months, ends in philosophic resignation. "It's frustration that doesn't count," says the great writer. The wise young acolyte-doctor replies: "Frustration's only life."

IV

There was another tale also written during this period—in 1892. It was called "The Wheel of Time." In it we may discover a passage in which the hero muses on his forty-ninth birthday. He thinks a great deal of his youth.

He regretted it, he missed it, he tried to beckon it back; but the differences in London made him feel that it had gone forever. There might perhaps be some compensation in being fifty, some turn of the dim telescope, some view from the brow of the hill; it was a round gross, stupid number, which probably would make one pompous, make one think one's self venerable. Meanwhile, at any rate, it was odious to be forty-nine.

The author of these lines, writing them at forty-nine, now spins a little tale which is a variation on a story he had written when he was thirty-six, and which he had then called "The Diary of a Man of Fifty." At thirty-six one could imagine oneself fifty, without too much pain; at forty-nine he made his character—forty-nine. It was, as he put it, "odious" enough without adding years. It will be remembered that the hero of "The Diary of a Man of Fifty" tries to persuade a young man to do as he had done—to turn his back on the daughter of the woman about whom he had been so unsure; and the young man does not heed his advice and marries happily. In "The Wheel of Time" the forty-nine-year-old hero Maurice Glanvil is shown to us first in his twenties, when he turns his back on the plain but charming Fanny Knocker, in spite of her great fortune. He goes off to the Continent; contracts a bohemian marriage. His wife dies leaving him a daughter who grows up to be very plain. Then at forty-nine he meets Fanny Knocker again. She is now the widowed Mrs. Tregent and at middle age her early charm has blossomed into beauty. Moreover she has a handsome son—who repeats the history of the hero, by turning his back on Glanvil's plain daughter, in spite of Mrs. Tregent's efforts to bring about the marriage. Her revenge is double, in spite of herself.

There is however a deeper discovery made by Maurice: he discovers that he has really been the one passion in the life of Fanny

Knocker Tregent—and this passage gives us pause. For the date on which the tale was set down in the notebook, May 18, 1892—a month after Henry James became forty-nine—was also a day on which he had paid a visit to Constance Fenimore Woolson at Oxford. Maurice, in the tale, discussing the past with Mrs. Tregent, at one point provokes her to tears, and his discovery makes him feel "humiliated" for an hour, but after that "his pleasure was almost as great as his wonder." And he meditates:

She had striven, she had accepted, she had conformed; but she had thought of him every day of her life. She had taken up duties and performed them, she had banished every weakness and practiced every virtue; but the still hidden flame had never been quenched. His image had interposed, his reality had remained, and she had never denied herself the sweetness of hoping that she would see him again and that she should know him. She had never raised a little finger for it, but fortune had answered her prayer. Women were capable of these mysteries of sentiment, these intensities of fidelity, and there were moments in which Maurice Glanvil's heart beat strangely before a vision really so sublime. He seemed to understand now by what miracle Fanny Knocker had been beautified—the miracle of heroic docilities and accepted pangs and vanquished egotisms. It had never come in a night, but it had come by living for others. She was living for others still; it was impossible for him to see anything else at last than that she was living for him. The time of passion was over, but the time of service was long.

At forty-nine, Henry James, like his wondering heroes, was still trying to fathom the heart of woman; still trying to unravel the mystery—to understand whether all his surenesses of thirty-five about fickle womankind had been a mistake. He had finally come to understand Christina Light. But had he understood himself? The remark about "living for others": he was to say this of his mother in his autobiographies. But he seemed at this moment to be saying it of Constance Fenimore Woolson, as he had said it in his essay describing the self-immolation of her heroines.

v

Had Henry James reached some crisis in his long involvement with Fenimore? We know that he went to see her ten days after Alice's funeral. On the day after his sister's cremation he wrote to Francis Boott: "Our poor Fenimore, at Oxford, which she likes, has had a painful illness—an affection of the head, brought on by trying *false drums* (a new invention) in her ears. But she is better, though her hearing isn't. I go to see her next week." He went to see her on March 17 and was there the entire day. How often he went again we do not know. But there is a further record of his spending a day at Oxford on May 18, 1892, a month after his forty-ninth birthday—the very day he sketched in his notebook the tale of Fanny Knocker.

That Alice's death brought about some kind of change in Fenimore's attitude seems possible, and is indeed suggested in the novel she was writing at this time. In this work, *Horace Chase*, the heroine has an invalid sister who plays a large and even dominating role in her life. Alice had played such a role in Henry's life; and we may speculate that the question which now arose between them was whether Henry—now that Alice was gone—was not free to be more attentive to Fenimore. Fenimore's essential data in the novel are sufficiently eloquent: the heroine, although married to the elderly and wealthy Horace Chase, loves a younger man who is not interested in her: but for whom she is prepared to leave her husband and to take all possible risks. We cannot help thinking of plain Fanny Knocker and elderly plain deaf devoted Constance Fenimore. The speculation might be gratuitous, were it not for a solitary paragraph which spilled out of Fenimore's pen a few months after James published "The Wheel of Time" in the *Cosmopolitan*. This was almost a year after Alice's death. In writing a letter to her nephew, Samuel Mather, Miss Woolson discussed her plan to leave England upon completion of her novel and to return to Italy, as she had done once before. "You will see in all this," she wrote, "I am giving up being near my kind friend Mr. James." She went on:

I don't know what made me tell you and Will that last message of his sister to me, that touched me so much. But I suppose it was simply the relief of having some of my own family to talk to, after being so long gone. I felt that I could say anything to you, without having to think whether it was safe or not, wise or not, prudent or not.—But Mr. James will come to Italy every year. And perhaps we can write that play after all.

"Safe or not, wise or not, prudent or not"—these weighty words offer wide margin for speculation; and while this paragraph gives us no details, it tells us of the importance Fenimore had attached to being near Henry James, indeed it once again explains her presence in England when she preferred Italy; and it suggests that some kind of truce, some *modus vivendi*, has been reached: almost, one might say, like an "arrangement" after a separation or a divorce, the adjustment to circumstance, the annual visit. For the rest—what Alice's message had been, is lost from sight. It might have been praise for the Bellosguardo story; it might have been something more significant, some comment on the relationship between Henry and Fenimore. All we know is that the invalid sister in *Horace Chase* expresses herself with great freedom on the heroine's relations with her husband and the man she really loves. As for the talk of collaboration on a play, it can only leave us wondering. This is the only time in Henry's long career in which the question of collaboration comes up—save that at this very time the word becomes also the title of one of his tales. He was, in all of his writing years, an arch-solitary of literature. He took no guidance; he consulted no one—although he talked freely enough about the problems of the marketplace. He would have regarded collaboration as an abandoning of sovereign ground, the most sacred ground of his life.

We must recognize, however, that the collaboration mentioned was in the writing of a play—and within the medium of the stage, James might have been willing. Given the nature of the relationship, one must also consider the possibility that since Henry could not "collaborate" with Fenimore in the one way in which she would have liked him to, that is in the realm of the affections, he might have suggested a union in this art. Was the play begun? It is doubtful whether we will ever know—the destructive hand of the novelist, the burning of the papers, seems to have been thorough. It may never have gone beyond the stage of conversation.

The tale titled "Collaboration" was in some ways prophetic of the sinister meaning the word would take on during the Second World War. It is one of Henry's trifling and artful anecdotes. A young French poet and a young blond German composer fall in love with each other's work and set out to write an opera together. In doing this the Frenchman rejects his French fiancée, whose father fell in the Franco-Prussian war and whose mother can tolerate no alliance of any kind with a member of the race that invaded France. The brother of the German musician, who has been supporting him, also cannot tolerate collaboration with a member of the former enemy. The two artists are left alone, and the narrator can only proclaim the supremacy of art over nationalism, as Henry had proclaimed it when he wrote William he was tired of the "international" theme. The deeper implication, if we wish to read it, is that of the love of the two men for each other, disguised in the love of each other's work. They take up life together—and the fiancée is spurned. She is spurned, as the woman was spurned in "The Diary of a Man of Fifty," or as Fanny Knocker was spurned, or Maurice's ugly daughter. If the spurning was a mistake—as these various personages wonder or believe—the mistake is made and will be made again. Henry could not conceive of it otherwise. And however much the novelist might appreciate and admire Fenimore's devotion to him, there was nothing he could give in return save a certain tenderness and consideration, and the pledge of a yearly visit. Things would have to go on pretty much as before. Whatever his affections might be, his career, his London life, his complicated relations with the older generation of his friends, and the new young friends, were his way of life. He had never been ready to sacrifice any part of this for Fenimore. And Henry probably was only too glad to think that by his pledge he might incorporate Italy even more than before in the annual round of his life.

IN SIENA

IN THE SPRING OF 1892, WHEN HENRY JAMES HAD ACCUSTOMED HIM-self a little to the absence of Alice, he set out for Italy. His theatrical ventures were at a standstill. Augustin Daly had one of his comedies and he was waiting to hear from him; *The American* was being played in the provinces by the Compton Comedy Company once or twice a week. There was nothing for the moment to retain him in London; and with the season about to begin, this was an ideal moment for flight. His friend Paul Bourget had married during the previous year, and gone to Italy on a prolonged honeymoon. He was now at Siena and he urged James to join him and his wife. On her side, Mrs. Gardner had once again rented the Palazzo Barbaro for the summer from the Curtises; she signalled that she expected him to pay her the visit he had been obliged to cancel the previous summer.

He could leave London at will. There would be no more summoning telegrams, no more continuing letters and conferences with Miss Loring. "Alice's death has only left my life more *regular*—more an affair of little slow contracted literary habits and small decorous London observances," Henry wrote to Grace Norton shortly before leaving. He might have added that it had left him with a wider margin of personal freedom.

Henry reached Siena on June 5, going there straight from London, with none of his usual stop-overs. He put up at the Grand Hôtel de Sienne, where the Bourgets were staying. He found his erstwhile disciple stout, red, robust, *mieux assis* and rather beefy, like Balzac. He was charmed by Bourget's wife, the former Minnie David. She was slim, *petite*, fragile, "a beautiful child," Henry said; he described her as ministering to Bourget "like a little quivering pathetic priestess on a bas-relief." Henry as usual engaged two rooms, a large cool drawing room in which he worked, and a bedroom. Toward noon the writers would have their *déjeuner* together; then they would retire to their rooms. Bourget was finishing a novel; Henry was working hard at a series of tales. At six they would sally forth into the town, dine together, walk in the Lizza, eat ices, hang over the Castello and enjoy the medievalism of the ancient Tuscan town. Henry knew it well, but he had never paid so enjoyable a visit to it and never at this time of the year. There was something enchanting in the way "the Italian summer broke in great verdurous waves at the foot of our far-seeing ramparts"—corn and wheat and mulberries, linked to "cachottes" by vines, which seemed to him "like joyous bathers—girls in the water—dipping up and down while they give each other their hands." On balmy moonlight evenings he found the place a "revel of history vivified." It was a pleasure, moreover, to look at things in the company of the fragile and charming Minnie "and to study the beautiful in her society." As for Bourget, Henry had long ago formed his opinion of him. He thought him one of the most civilized of conversationalists—and he despised his novels. Moreover he sooner or later told him what he thought of them. Bourget possessed a certain delicacy of perception and an admirable prose instrument; his fiction was narrow, deterministic, mechanistic; it was Zolaesque naturalism with a little superficial psychology added. If Bourget had absorbed Henry's theories of fiction, he had neither his largeness of view nor his humane grasp. The two were strangely dissimilar: the younger man, in his progress in life, moved rapidly into a kind of stratification that left him old before his time; whereas Henry became increasingly tolerant of the world and of himself. Their meeting in Siena was a kind of midway point, during which they appeared briefly to move side by side. They were bound, however, in opposite directions. Two or three years earlier, Henry, reading Bourget's *Mensonges*, had expressed to his friends his keen disappointment in the turn his trans-Channel protégé was taking. And to Bourget himself he had said, quite bluntly:

I absolutely don't like this work. It's a pity—such a pity—she's a whore!—your manner of wishing to incarnate yourself each time in a prostitute—and to see men only as little hysterical, angry types who beat women with whom they sleep (and who deceive for them either husbands or lovers), or who try, like your detestable poet, to disfigure them. I speak with no false delicacy or hypocrisy; but your out-and-out eroticism displeases me as well as this exposition of dirty linens and dirty towels. In a word, all this is far from being life as I feel it, as I see it, as I know it, as I wish to know it.

Such candor was only possible between friends; and if Bourget demurred it was because he, on his side, could see life only in this particular way. His book justified itself pragmatically by having a considerable vogue in France. James cared much more for Bourget's travel essays, and felt there were "exquisite" pages in his *Sensations d'Italie*. In the end, when Bourget lost himself in black pessimism, became an anti-Dreyfusard and threw in his lot wholly with reactionary forces, Henry began to avoid him. William James met the Bourgets in America and was unfavorably impressed by the French writer; he was to chide Henry for making friends with so unworthy an individual. On that occasion Henry replied:

Oh yes, you are right in saying that in a manner he has got much more out of me than I out of him—and yet you are wrong. I have got out of him that I know him as if I had made him—his nature, his culture, his race, his type, his *mœurs*, his mixture—whereas he knows (as a consequence of his own attitude) next to nothing about me. An individual so capable as I am of the uncanniest self-effacement in the active exercise of the passion of observation, always exposes himself a little to looking like a dupe—and he doesn't care a hang! And yet I like Bourget and have an affection for him; he has a great deal of individual charm, sensibility, generosity; and the sides by which he displeases are those of his race and the, in so many ways, abominable *milieu* in which his life has mainly been passed.

The impressions on which these conclusions were reached began to be gathered during this visit in Siena. However critical Henry might be of Bourget, they enjoyed each other's talk to a point where differences vanished when they were together. One day in June they drove to San Gemignano, "a long, lovely day of the teeming Tuscan land, a garden of beauty and romance," and Henry saw the little old half-ruined city with its beautiful towers, perched on its hilltop, with sweet old chimes still ringing and "the breath of the middle ages still in its streets." He encountered four American women there, and learned that one of them was a journalist, who discovered later what two prize subjects she had missed. She sent a card after them asking for interviews, to the great amusement of the author of *The Reverberator.* On July 3 they saw the Palio from a balcony of the Marchese Chigi's palace. They also visited the *archivio* in the Palazzo Piccolomini; and Henry studied closely during this stay the Sienese School of painters. Each day had its adventures; and in the middle of their stay there arrived another Gallo-Roman, this one even more a mixture of the two than Bourget. This was Count Primoli, whom Henry had met on that memorable day when he dined Maupassant at Greenwich.

Early in July, when the heat had become intense, the Bourgets left for the mountains and Henry turned toward Venice and the hospitality of Mrs. Jack.

THE TWO QUEENS

I

MRS. GARDNER, IN A PALACE ON THE GRAND CANAL, WAS QUITE AS much at home as in any of the domiciles she had created, on Beacon Street, in Brookline, or indeed ultimately in Boston's Fenway. *C'est mon plaisir* . . . And it was her pleasure, for the second summer in succession, to occupy the Palazzo Barbaro, to create within it the "court" with which she liked to surround herself. Awaiting her in Venice were seven gilded and painted armchairs acquired at the Borghese sale that spring, said to have been presented by the Doge of Venice to Pope Paul V. In London, she had negotiated the purchase of a magnificent ruby, and had acquired a Madonna and Child supposedly by Filippino Lippi, but later attributed by Bernard Berenson to an unidentified pupil of the painter; also a canvas by Rossetti. During this year she purchased the last of her series of strings of pearls. In Paris, en route to Venice, she had acquired her first piece of Gothic carving, a panel representing Joan of Arc; and her first fine tapestry. She had not yet had the idea of creating her composite palace in the Fenway, but the heterogeneous items were being assembled.

When Henry arrived, he found her thoroughly at home in Venice: the Palazzo was filled with guests, and to Henry's delight she placed a bed in the library, where, like his heroine Milly Theale much later, he awoke every day to find himself staring at the medallions and arabesques of the ceiling. Here the servant, Tita, coming in on diffident tiptoe, brought him his hot water in a large coffee urn. He was surrounded by comfortable pink chairs and had a lemon-colored sofa, and the shutters were clean and wrapped in white paper. There was a scorching sirocco in Venice; inside the palace, however, he was cool. Henry revelled in the grandeur and the loveliness of the city—and this game of modern life carried on within the frame of the past. He had always enjoyed it—and as for dreams of power and glory, he had but to walk across marble floors and great spaces to feel almost as if he were a doge himself—conferring in this instance favors on a great lady from Boston.

The great lady—diminutive, tightly corseted, be-jewelled and be-pearled—was "of an energy," he wrote to Miss Reubell, using, as he often did, the French form in English. Henry had informal as well as formal glimpses of the queenly Mrs. Jack, as we may judge from a letter written later that summer. "Dear Donna Isabella, I don't know where this will find you, but I hope it will find you with your hair not quite 'up'—neither up nor down, as it were, in a gauze dressing-gown, on a seagreen (so different from pea-green) chair, beneath a glorious gilded ceiling, receiving the matutinal tea from a Venetian slave." And later in the letter: "Don't tell me that you are *not* seated there in the attitude and costume which it was apparently my sole privilege to admire—I mean only *my* not my *only* privilege." His fellow-guests included a young painter, Joseph Lindon Smith, Alfred Q. Collins, whom Henry described as "robust but not restrained," and sundry others—people were always coming or going. There was much music and much floating in gondolas. "It is the essence of midsummer, but I buy five-franc alpaca jackets and feel so Venetian that you might almost own me," he wrote to Mrs. Curtis. "She showed me yesterday, at Carrer's, her seven glorious chairs (the loveliest I ever saw) but they are not a symbol of her attitude—she never sits down."

The more permanent and more reticent American Queen of the Grand Canal, she of Ca'Alvisi, was at Asolo. Even as Isabella Stewart spoke of her descent from the Stuart kings, so Katherine De Kay Bronson had come to identify herself with a queen whose name was also Katherine—Caterina Cornaro, she who had been Queen of Cyprus, Jerusalem and Armenia, and who in 1489 had taken possession of Asolo, in the mountains behind Venice, and held court there in her ancient stone house, La Mura. Caterina had been art-loving and charitable; and Mrs. Bronson, too, had had her poet, in Robert Browning, and her far-flung charities in Venetia. Of these, Henry had written to her, "Dearest lady, I hope things are comfortable with you and [that] the beggars of Venice haven't yet reduced you to their own condition." In contrast with the rather short, half-shy yet dynamic Isabella Gardner, Queen Kate of Asolo was a soft, benevolent woman, with blue eyes and chestnut brown hair drawn back from a round face. Discreet, and of a mild temperament, she felt no threat to her sovereignty in the Boston queen's advent for a temporary *villeggiatura* on the Canal. Instead there was a kind of noble exchange of salutations reflecting a fine respect for each other's domains and each other's queenship.

The two queens corresponded, as queens might. "Dearest Lady Isabel," wrote Mrs. Bronson to Mrs. Jack at first. Her letters became increasingly affectionate. "Dearest Charmeuse," she called her later. She offered counsel, out of her long residence abroad—and as women might exchange recipes, so Kate gave to Isabella the lore she had gathered from visiting royalty in Venice on the care of pearls; and her own lore on the care of lapdogs.

"I am glad to hear that our dear friend Henry James is with you," came the word from the tower-house in Asolo. "Tell him I wrote to him at Siena the other day and have just despatched a card to the director of the Hotel to forward that valuable missive to the Barbaro. I hope he will be able to come here, and that you will find it agreeable to be here at the same time."

Fond as Henry was of Mrs. Bronson ("you have all the sweet inventions of the heart," he told her), he was not fond of Asolo. Its conditions of life were too primitive. "I believe I am to go to Asolo for a day or two next week," he wrote to Mrs. Curtis, "and I confess that I have a dread of exchanging this marble hall for the top of a stable." This was perhaps a little strong, but James was underlining to Mrs. Curtis the comforts of her *palazzo*; nevertheless he seldom mentioned Asolo without referring to its discomforts. La Mura had originally been a part of the rampart at Asolo, and was set into one of its eighteen towers. Highly ro-

mantic and picturesque, and inspiring to Robert Browning, it
did not correspond to Henry's ideal of Venetian splendor. He
was reluctant to leave his pink chairs, his lemon sofa, and the
lagoons. The expedition however was a success. Donna Isabella
accompanied her famous courtier in a journey which she remembered as "so romantic, so Italian." Henry's recollection was
also nostalgic. He spoke of "the *loggia*, the mountains, the sunsets, the mornings, the evenings, the drives" and he wrote to Mrs.
Bronson that his ride with Mrs. Jack "in the fragrant Italian
eve, is one of the most poetical impressions of my life."

I I

That summer—1892—William James, on sabbatical leave, brought
his family abroad for the first time—four children, two of them
very young, and his wife. His two older boys seemed like younger
versions of himself and his novelist brother—save that Billy,
here, was the second son. Henry had memories only of little
Harry, aged two or three, seen when he was last in America. After
Billy had come Peggy and the baby, Alex. There had been another son, who died of whooping cough. William's family had
thus duplicated that of his father—there would have been four
boys and a girl. The family had gone straight to Switzerland,
where the elder Henry James had taken his children long ago, in
1855 and later in 1859. Now they were at Lausanne. From Venice
Henry announced he would join them. But when the time came
he would have gladly remained in the amusing entourage of
Mrs. Jack, to watch her play her grand game at the Barbaro. The
pleasures of a palatial existence had not yet palled. Early in
August he remarked, "When I haven't a cousin in Venice, I
have a brother in Switzerland," and took train for Lausanne.
Henry had not seen William's wife, Alice, since the time of his
father's death. He put up at the Hôtel Richemont, expecting to
join an intimate family group and to enjoy, for the first time, the
full extent of his unclehood. William, however, had not kept
Henry informed of his plans, and two days after the novelist ar-

rived, the psychologist departed on a walking tour in the Engadine. Henry discovered his young nephews had been parcelled out
in pensions with Swiss pastors, and Alice with the two younger
children was staying in a Vaudois pension, tied down by maternal duties. "Sufficient unto the day are the nephews thereof,"
he wrote to Mrs. Jack. "I have been here since yesterday noon,
intently occupied in realizing that I am an uncle." But he felt
let down. He had quit the shining softness of Venice for the
Swiss mountains out of a sense of duty, and found a scattered
family. It reminded him with sudden sharpness of his own itinerant childhood days in Europe, when he and William had felt so
acutely that they were "hotel children" who had been handed
over to substitute parents—couriers, tutors, governesses—while
the father and mother went sightseeing and lived at a distance in
some hotel. One evening Henry went to Ouchy, to pay a call on
Henrietta Reubell, who was spending the summer there, and his
notebook records that "the conversation had run a little upon
the way Americans drag their children about Europe."

He remained for just ten days. During this time he did what
he could in his avuncular role. He wrote a formal letter to little
Harry James: "Will you please say to M. Ceresole, with all my
compliments, that your uncle and brother, with your mother's
consent, are coming to pay you this little visit—if he doesn't dis-
approve." Then he picked up Billy at his pension and they arrived
by boat, after luncheon, landing at Vevey, where Daisy Miller
had flourished several years earlier. There were a few encounters
of this sort, and Billy, who grew up to be a portrait painter and
his uncle's favorite nephew, was to remember years later the extreme gravity and politeness of the massive uncle. When the time
came to leave, he told his nephews that if they wished to embrace,
and it bothered them to do so in his presence, he would turn his
back. This he promptly did, after adding that his nephews must
not think it unmanly to express their natural affections.

From Lausanne, in mid-August, Henry journeyed to Paris. By
the end of the month he was back in De Vere Gardens.

MRS. KEMBLE

I

"THE YEAR'S END IS A TERRIBLE TIME," WROTE HENRY TO MISS REUbell, on January 1, 1893, "and the year's beginning is a worse." In a bare three and a half months he would be fifty: and how "terrible" a time it was he found out shortly after he had clinked hot punch with London friends to see the year in. His plan was to return to Italy in mid-January. He had made a series of revisions in his comedy for Augustin Daly, and at Daly's request had strengthened Miss Rehan's part. There seemed no likelihood of immediate production, however. "I think I *must* call on you to appreciate the heroic self-control with which I forbear to ask you *when* there is a calculable possibility of the play's being produced." Daly was vague; and Henry could write tales in Italy as easily as in London. But he did not get away as he had planned. First, he caught a cold; and when this seemed to be going away he was reminded, in the most acute fashion possible, of his personal wheel of time. He had his first attack of gout. "It is an atrocious complaint," he told Miss Reubell in mid-January, when he had expected to be on his way south. "I am still very lame and it will be several more days before I can put on a Christian shoe."

On the evening of the day he wrote this, Mrs. Kemble, while being helped to bed by her maid, gave a little sigh and fell dead. And on January 20, still hobbling, and with a shoe slit so that he could put it on, Henry made his way to Kensal Green to say farewell to one of the oldest and most cherished of his London friends. He had known her since their meetings in Rome in the 1870's, when she had appeared in purples and mauves and possessed in her voice the manner, the style and grandeur of the Kembles. The day of the funeral was soft, balmy, and, as he said, "kind." The number of mourners was limited. At eighty-four, Mrs. Kemble had long outlived her time. She was laid in the same earth as her father, under a mountain of flowers. Returning to

De Vere Gardens, Henry wrote one of his elegiac letters to Mrs. Wister, in far-off Philadelphia, to bring home to Fanny Kemble's daughter the scene he had just witnessed. "It was all bright, somehow, and public and slightly pompous." He spoke of the good fortune of Mrs. Kemble's instantaneous death; and he described the aspect of her maid standing by the graveside, "with a very white face and her hands full of flowers." Then Henry wrote: "I am conscious of a strange bareness and a kind of evening chill, as it were, in the air, as of some great object that had filled it for long had left an emptiness—from displacement—to all the senses." Mrs. Kemble had wanted to go, he said, and "she went when she could, at last, without a pang. She was very touching in her infirmity all these last months—and yet with her wonderful air of smouldering embers under ashes, she leaves a great image—a great memory."

II

On the day of the funeral George Bentley, who had published Mrs. Kemble's various books, asked Henry to write a tribute to her in the magazine *Temple Bar*. Henry, who from one moment to another had hoped to get away to Italy, where his brother and his family were fixed in Florence for the winter, decided once again to postpone his departure. "She ought to have rested in some fold of the Alps—which she adored—and which she in a manner resembled! I feel a great responsibility in speaking of her," he wrote to Bentley.

The article, which was published almost immediately, is one of the most vivid of his series of tributes and memorials. Long, leisurely, it sketches his various recollections of Mrs. Kemble. He had seen her when he was a boy, one day in a park in New York, on horseback; later he had heard her read Shakespeare in London, in St. John's Wood; and then he had known her in Rome, in Philadelphia, in London. She could take him back to the 1820's—the time of Jeffrey Aspern and to that of his later novel, *The Sense of the Past*—and to the days when she had written the famous journal of her experiences with slavery on a Georgia plantation. He described her "robust and ironic interest in life" and the far-away past to which she gave continuity. She had sat to Sir Thomas Lawrence for her portrait; and Sir Thomas had been in love with Sir Joshua's "tragic Muse"—Mrs. Kemble's aunt, Mrs. Siddons. She had breakfasted with Sir Walter Scott and sung with Tom Moore; she had seen Edmund Kean and Mademoiselle Mars on the stage. She had "felt, observed, imagined, reflected, reasoned, gathered in her passage the abiding impressions, the sense and suggestion of things."

His reminiscences sought to sketch in "the grand line and mass of her personality," to bring Mrs. Kemble back to a new generation, and he filled them with examples of her talk. When someone had told her that she was a clever woman, she had answered, "How dare you call me anything so commonplace." She used to say, "If my servants can live with me a week they can live with me forever; but the first week sometimes kills them." In Switzerland, the guides used to call her *la dame qui va chantant par les montagnes.*" Her talk had been filled with "the ghosts of a dead society." She never read or allowed newspapers in her home. She had detested the stage, to which she had been dedicated when young; but if she left her profession, she could not get rid of her instincts, "which kept her dramatic long after she ceased to be theatrical." Henry remembered taking her to a comedy and her saying: "Yes, they're funny; but they don't begin to know how funny they might be."

With his tribute to Lowell of the previous year, the memorial to Frances Anne Kemble belongs to James's fine art of painting portraits in prose; and when, later that year, he brought out his *Essays in London,* that volume seemed indeed to be an extended series of obituaries. To the Lowell and Kemble memorials he added the one on Browning. He included also his admirable essay on Flaubert's letters—this too a kind of memorial.

"A prouder nature never affronted the long humiliation of life," Henry wrote of Mrs. Kemble, and if there was a touch of

bitterness in these words, he also said that the death of the actress seemed like the end of some reign, the fall of some empire.
In his own life this was decidedly true. Mrs. Kemble was the last
and the most important of the three old queens of his London
life. She had reigned for many years, given him love and tenderness and the support of her grandiose aggressivity. Now all that
remained to him were her few letters, in her shaky hand, which
he saved, and her travelling clock which she had left him, and
which ticked away the hours on his table—and his crowded memories of old occasions, meetings in Switzerland, the little tour in
France, and above all her London fireside, where she had talked
from an inexhaustible fund of experience and anecdote. From
Mrs. Kemble had come more *données* for novels and tales than
from anyone else, as Henry's notebooks testify. She exemplified
for Henry the various—and the copious—in life. Her photograph,
an aged and wrinkled, worldly-wise female, some ancient matri-
arch, hung ever after in his study.

EPISODE

WHILE HE WAS STILL RECOVERING FROM HIS GOUT, HENRY RECEIVED
a letter from Morton Fullerton in Paris inquiring about a tale by
Vernon Lee just published which was supposed to have satirized
Henry James. The story was "Lady Tal," and it appeared in a volume of what Miss Lee termed "Polite Stories," bearing the gen-
eric title *Vanitas*. Henry replied he had heard that "the said

Vernon has done something to me." He did not know what she had done and was determined not to find out, so that he wouldn't have to bother—"I don't *care* to care," he said.

Henry had indeed been satirized and quite pointedly by his Florentine friend. What seemed to have rankled had been his interest during the writing of *Miss Brown* nine years before, and the coldness with which he had received the book. In her tale she depicted an American writer named Jervase Marion, a "psychological novelist," "an inmate of the world of Henry James and a kind of Henry James." Having thus clearly labelled him, she went on to describe his mannerisms and his speech. Marion encounters in Venice the striking Lady Tal, who is writing a novel. Given to fathoming people, he has difficulty fathoming her, and he interests himself in her work so that he may find out more about her. There were many remarks in the tale which James (if he had read it) would have found cruel and unkind, not least the statement that he was "not at home" in England, and that he had "expatriated himself, leaving brothers, sisters, friends of childhood" and "condemned himself to live in a world of acquaintances."

Henry had originally urged William to call on Vernon Lee in Florence. Now he wrote warning him that he should "draw it mild with her on the question of friendship. She's a tiger-cat!" He said there was a "great second-rate element in her first-rateness." He told William he had not read her story and knew of it only by hearsay. Nevertheless he considered that she had indulged in a piece of "treachery to private relations." She had done this sort of thing to others, and it was "markedly 'saucy'" and a "particularly impudent and blackguardly sort of thing to do to a friend and one who has treated her with such particular consideration as I have."

His warning came too late. William had already dined in the Via Garibaldi. Far from following Henry's advice, to ignore the matter, William wrote to Miss Lee that he had read the story, found the portrait "clever enough," and not exactly malicious. However to use a friend for "copy" implied on her part "such a strangely *objective* way of taking human beings, and such a detachment from the sympathetic considerations which usually govern human intercourse, that you will not be surprised to learn that seeing the book has quite quenched my desire to pay you another visit."

Vernon Lee was penitent. William wrote to her a week later; "A woman in tears is something that I can never stand out against! Your note wipes away the affront as far as I am concerned, only you must never, *never*, NEVER, do such a thing again in any future book! It is too serious a matter." When Henry learned of William's *démarches* on his behalf, he expressed himself as "partly amused and partly disconcerted." He would have preferred indifference. "I don't find her note at all convincing; —she is doubtless sorry to be disapproved of in high quarters." Henry was convinced that what she had done was "absolutely deliberate, and her humility, which is easy and inexpensive, after the fact, doesn't alter her absolutely impertinent nature."

From then on Henry "cut" Vernon Lee. An attempt by a mutual friend to bring the two together again in 1900 proved unsuccessful. Henry said he regretted to have failed "of sight and profit of one of the most intelligent persons it had ever been my fortune to know." The use of the "had ever been" was eloquent, and final. Years after—in 1912—at the home of a friend, they did meet, and "had a good deal of talk." This was, however, an isolated encounter and probably their last. Miss Lee had committed, as far as Henry was concerned, an unpardonable sin: she had taken a portrait from life, one filled with shrewd observation and understanding, and had not exposed it to the process of art. Even his own portrait of Miss Peabody, in *The Bostonians*, which had turned out to be a likeness, had been re-imagined; and it had been done without malice. Miss Lee had sinned twice. She had invaded Henry's privacy; moreover, she had committed an artistic sin. There could be no forgiving on Henry's part. But Henry too had been at fault. He had shown a well-intentioned friendliness and interest in a young woman writing her first novel; yet it had been an egotistical interest and it had not reckoned with the effect it might have. Henry had once again been the victim of his inability (when he dropped his usual aloof manner before certain women) to recognize that his intentions might be misinterpreted.

In the end, however, Miss Lee seems to have accepted Henry's criticism. "I feel every day more and more that I don't know enough of life to write a novel I should care to read." And she added, in a letter to her mother: "Life is too serious to be misrepresented as in *Miss Brown*."

IN THE MARKETPLACE

I

AT THE BEGINNING OF 1893, WHEN HE WAS RECOVERING FROM THE gout, Henry's situation in the theatre was as follows: *The American* had been revised and turned into a comedy; the gloom of the last act had been dissipated by having Valentin de Bellegarde recover instead of die after the duel. The play continued in the provinces. *Tenants*, the play written for Sir John Hare, was for the moment on the shelf. *Mrs. Jasper*, the play for Daly, was scheduled for production at the end of the year. He had sketched out a second play for Ada Rehan, which would later become the tale "Covering End," and ultimately a three-act play. He had three other scenarios either on paper or in his head, for he spoke of them later that summer. He had spent now almost three years trying to launch himself as a dramatist: the best he could say was that he had had an "honorable" run of a single play in London.

He lingered in De Vere Gardens after writing his article on Mrs. Kemble, and went to Paris toward the end of March. He had planned to go to Florence, to be with William and his family; it now looked, however, as if William was coming north. When Henry inquired why he was abandoning the city at the best time of the year, his brother answered: "I don't wonder that it seems strange to you. *Your* view of Italy is that of the tourist; and that is really the only way to *enjoy* any place. Ours is that of the resident in whom the sweet decay breathed in for six months has produced a sort of physiological craving for a change to robuster air." Henry accordingly settled in the Hotel Westminster, to work at another play, and to enjoy the Parisian spring which was uncommonly warm that year. He visited Daudet and found him more of an invalid than ever; they dined together twice and on one of these occasions Henry encountered in his home Maurice Barrès, whom he had met in Florence (sent to him by Bourget) two or three years before. He found the French novelist a *poseur* —"an adventurer whom it isn't really (in spite of his cleverness), important to keep the run of." Daudet's younger son, Lucien, late in life, said he "seemed to remember" seeing also James and the young Proust at table in the Daudet dining room in the Rue de Bellechasse at this time.

A further attack of gout limited Henry's activities for a few days and Morton Fullerton came with some regularity to see him at his hotel. When he recovered he dined and went to art exhibitions with Miss Reubell, had lunch with Jusserand, and encountered some of the "babyish decadents." On one occasion he went to tea with the Whistlers, installed now "in their queer little garden-house of the rue du Bac, where the only furniture is the paint on the walls and the smile on the lady's broad face." He did not know it then, but this garden would be the setting for the climactic scene in the first half of *The Ambassadors*. He remembered the place well: he could look up from Whistler's garden and see his own ghost at one of the windows, where fifteen years before he used to visit old Madame Mohl and look down into this place and the adjoining mission. One afternoon Henry spent in bright sunshine, talking with Henry Harland at a café in the Champs Élysées; he liked him and pitied him, felt that Harland's literary ambition was much greater than his literary faculty.

On May 4 he went to Lucerne and put up at the Hotel National, to be near his brother. William's sabbatical year was running to its end, and he had seen little of him or of his nephews. The family was about five miles away, on the lakeside; Alice was in Munich, but returned during Henry's stay. His relatives were numerous in Europe that summer; he ticked them off to Mrs. Wister— one brother, three sisters-in-law and eight nephews and nieces. His stay at Lucerne was not prolonged. Theatrical affairs were summoning him to London—the opening of Daly's new theatre and the production of *The Second Mrs. Tanqueray*, in which Elizabeth Robins had yielded the main role to the then relatively unknown Mrs. Patrick Campbell. He had been invited to the opening night.

II

Sitting in his hotel room in Lucerne he confided a few eloquent sentences to his notebook:

Among the delays, the disappointments, the *déboires* of the horrid theatric trade nothing is so soothing as to remember that literature sits patient at my door, and that I have only to lift the latch to let in the exquisite little form that is, after all, nearest to my heart and with which I am so far from having done. I let it in and the old brave hours come back; I live them over again—I add another little block to the small literary monument that it has been given to me to erect.

He was destined during this year, however, not to lift the latch. He had published ten tales during 1892; during 1893 "The Middle Years" appeared and that was all. The greater part of his fiftieth year was spent in the theatrical marketplace.

He was back in time to see Mrs. Patrick Campbell win her

great triumph on the first night of *The Second Mrs. Tanqueray* and on the following morning wrote to Arthur Pinero: "I was held, as in a strong hand, by your play." What was more, the production convinced him that George Alexander was a manager for whom a serious drama might be written. Henry sought a meeting with him and told him he was prepared to outline three subjects. This he did on July 2, in a letter written from Ramsgate on the Channel. The first was a romantic costume play about a young man destined for the priesthood, one act of which Henry had completed and sent to Alexander; the second was a sketch of "a three-act comedy, pure and simple," and the third was "a three-act contemporary play, less purely a comedy, but on a subject very beautiful to my sense"—probably his plan to dramatize "The Chaperon."

Alexander liked the play about the young priest. He had a fine pair of legs and was always partial to costume; his matinee audiences were devoted to his fine figure and his handsome features. Henry settled down at Ramsgate to the writing of his drama, first labelled "The Hero" and later called *Guy Domville*. It was based on a note he had set down the previous summer, after his visit to Venice, an anecdote of a member of an old Venetian family who had become a monk, "and who was taken almost forcibly out of his convent and brought back into the world in order to keep the family from becoming extinct." No theme could have been closer to Henry at this moment. The monk forced into the world from his cloister was in the same position as Henry James, forcing himself into the marketplace from the "literature that sits patient at my door." Thus was formed, at this moment, a curious partnership in the theatre—that of the fifty-year-old Henry, exasperated by his unsuccessful efforts to get himself produced on the London stage, and the actor-manager of the St. James's, who had a flourishing theatre and a loyal audience, and who, moreover, was the talk of London because of *Mrs. Tanqueray*.

George Alexander was thirty-five and full of plans and enterprises. Henry Irving had once remarked to him at a rehearsal,

"Now Alexander, not quite so much Piccadilly." The actor-manager *was* Piccadilly to his finger-tips. Decidedly a dandy, his dress was a matter for *Punch* cartoons: he had the best-creased trousers in London in an era when they were worn baggy. He was variously described as a hard-headed businessman and a "tailor's dummy." For his acting, critics had chary praise. "Mr. Alexander," Bernard Shaw wrote of one of his performances, "gave us a finished impersonation of Mr. George Alexander." His contemporaries agreed that he lacked the larger imagination; he compensated for this by a kind of furious efficiency. His theatre was a model of good management. There was an air of "competence" about everything he did. He was all the professional, and all profile and elegant appearance. He had taken the measure of his talents; he was careful to surround himself with good actors—but none that would show him to poor advantage. He was having trouble with the fiery temperament of Mrs. Pat at this time, and their quarrels, on stage and off, are a part of the theatrical history of the 1890's. He boasted that his "fans" could fill his house for a month even if a play were pronounced a failure. And on the whole he chose good plays. It was for him that Oscar Wilde, with his unerring shrewdness in stage matters, wrote *The Importance of Being Earnest*.

From the first, Henry had no doubt that he was dealing with an individual hardly concerned with his own dream of restoring art to the stage. Alexander was a cool businessman. This was clear from the terms the manager offered him. Like Daly, he agreed to pay Henry £5 a night; however he placed a ceiling of £2000 on royalties, with the full rights in the play to go to him after the ceiling was reached. "I should be obliged to you if you can put the case to me more dazzlingly, another way," Henry wrote to him. Whether they reached a compromise, we do not know. Henry brought him the completed play that autumn, knowing that he would have to wait until *Mrs. Tanqueray* had run its full course; and Alexander had to meet at least one other commitment—a play by Henry Arthur Jones.

The novelist visited Whitby in September and stayed in Lowell's old rooms; there were memories of his friend on every side. He was consoled by the company there of George du Maurier. Late in September he returned to London and met Zola, who was in England for a brief visit. They had lunch and talked of Bourget's disappointing novels; they agreed that Bourget had been neglecting his literary reputation in Paris and was travelling too much abroad. He was at this moment on a tour of the United States. Henry observed that the Bourgets, in their "complete and cautious absence from Paris," seemed in reality to be running away from themselves and the problem of settling down. Henry found Zola "very sane and common and inexperienced." To Stevenson he wrote: "Nothing, literally nothing, has ever happened to him but to write the Rougon-Macquart."

REHEARSAL

I

AUGUSTIN DALY HAD LONG BEEN A MANAGER, AND A FAMOUS ONE, IN New York. A "man of the theatre" in the old sense, he had been a drama reviewer in his youth, and later an adapter of plays from French or German into American settings. During his lifetime he fashioned more than ninety such "vehicles." He had now built his theatre in London, and while his reputation rested largely on his staging of comedies of manners, in which Miss Rehan brilliantly played, he had welcomed the opportunity to do a new play by an American novelist of James's eminence. The original script of *Mrs. Jasper* had seemed to him rather weak, and earlier in the year James had made many revisions at his suggestion. Daly was hardly a literary figure, but he knew what he wanted; and what he wanted above all was a strong part for Miss Rehan. Henry, aware of this, had yielded ground on almost every proposal save one: this was that he give Miss Rehan some rhymed couplets at the end of the play in the classical manner. The novelist balked at this. He had never been a writer of verse. Daly did not insist.

The script however must have been rather carelessly read by Daly, and even by Miss Rehan. For when they finally took it in hand it became clear to them that they had a much more amateurish play than they had supposed. Entrances and exits of the characters were handled with an awkwardness that could have created laughter in the theatre. The characters had occasional funny lines; yet they never came to life even as caricatures. The play was mechanical and contrived, as attempts in later years to produce it showed.

With Daly as his producer and with Miss Rehan's gift for artificial comedy, Henry was letting a splendid opportunity to make a name for himself in the theatre slip through his fingers. His tales of the late 1870's had shown that he could write Miss Rehan's kind of comedy; and it was probably this which had given the manager and the actress complete faith in the novelist's script. Henry relied for his humor, however, on "tag" lines, and a certain amount of verbal repetition. Daly, in asking for changes, had said that the play's faults were "fundamental." The principal one was the slenderness of the theme—the young man who believes he has compromised a young lady. James conceded that the lack of action in his original version was "vainly dissimulated by a superabundance of movement." This was especially true of the last act. But he repaired the play half-heartedly.

Daly had publicly announced the work when he opened his new theatre. During August of that year he and Henry had gone over the models of the stage sets; and the Daly account books

record payments made by the manager in preparation for his production. Daly's season, however, ran into difficulties. The manager
discovered that the London audiences were attached to certain
playhouses and had not yet accustomed themselves to the existence of his new establishment; each playhouse had to win its own
audience in those days of actor-managers, matinee idols and permanent companies. In the autumn, Henry believed that with the
losses Daly had suffered, his play would be a distinct feature—and
asset—for the new season. He explained to William that "my play,
inconceivable as it appears, is the only 'novelty' with which he
(Daly) seems to have armed himself for his campaign in his new
and beautiful theatre. If I 'save' him, it will be so much wind in
my sails—and if I don't, the explanation will be, largely, not dishonorable to me. But I long for the reality, the ingenuity and the
combined amusement and disgust of rehearsals."

Late in October Daly re-read the play with more misgivings than
ever, and asked for further cuts and revisions. "I will go over the
copy," Henry replied, "and be as heroic as I can." Six days later
James reported "utter failure." He assured Daly, however, that he
would leave himself quite "open to impressions" during the rehearsals. In November Daly announced the production of Henry's
play for January and promised rehearsals early in December. The
manager was still unhappy over the new title, *Disengaged*. It did
not say enough to the public. He wanted to get Miss Rehan's
role into it. Henry bombarded him with more titles, and *Mrs.
Jasper's Way* was finally selected.

In the production of *The American*, Henry had been a partici-
pant from the first; now, however, he had to wait for signals
from the managerial office. Daly had his own methods of work established by long usage. One or two readings of the play seem to
have taken place privately in Daly's office and the first James
heard of these was in a letter from the manager on December 3
informing him that the comedy still lacked "story." Since James
had conceded this point long ago, it seemed to him late in the
day to have it brought up again. "I am very sorry, not a little

alarmed," he wrote to Daly; and it was agreed that they would hold their first rehearsal on December 6. To Elizabeth Robins the dramatist confided that "they have begun, or are just beginning, I believe, some intensely private preliminaries at Daly's—which make me very uneasy."

II

What happened at the rehearsal we shall never completely know, for we must depend on Henry James's rather colored version. He arrived expecting to be allowed to read the play to the actors and to explain its fine points to them as dramatists did in France, when they had large enough reputations to have plays produced on their terms. No such thing happened on this occasion. "I was not given a simple second's opportunity of having the least contact or word with any member of the company," he complained afterwards. It was all "a ghastly and disgraceful farce." The actors read their parts "stammeringly" (he also called it a "mumbled reading") and vanished at the end of the third act. James described Miss Rehan as looking "white, haggard, ill, almost in anguish." He could not bring himself to speak to her.

The next morning Henry wrote to Daly withdrawing the comedy. He said that his play might not contain "the elements of success" but that at "my stage of relationship to the theatre I am much too nervous a subject not to accept as *determining*, in regard to my own action, any sound of alarm, or of essential skepticism, however abrupt, on the part of a manager." It was clear to him that Daly was no longer interested; at the same time Henry could not for a moment "profess that the scene I witnessed on your stage" had thrown any light on the play. On his side, he had only derived an intenser impression "of the quick brevity of the three acts and their closeness and crispness of texture." Daly replied that he was as disappointed as Henry "at the unexpected results" of the several readings. He had been "from the first attracted (and perhaps blinded) by the literary merits of the piece." The rehearsals, "however crude they may have seemed to you, convinced me that the lack of situation and dramatic climax could not be overcome by the smartest wit however much it might be accentuated by expression or enforced by the actor's art."

Writing to William, the novelist expressed his opinion that Daly had arranged this reading in order to induce him to withdraw the play. "He is an utter cad," he wrote, "and Ada Rehan is the same. They simply kicked me between them (and all in one 'rehearsal') out of the theatre. How can one rehearse with people who are dying to get rid of you?" It was true that Daly wished to get rid of the play. From his point of view he had taken an option on a poor vehicle, with which his actors could do nothing. The correspondence between the manager and Henry, however, does not substantiate the novelist's charge that Daly deliberately sought to provoke withdrawal of *Mrs. Jasper's Way*.

"At the rehearsal you attended," Daly wrote, "there was no pretence on my part, or that of the actors, to give you anything approaching a performance. The players merely gave you a reading of their lines, and an indication of their movements and positions on the scene—from a view of which I had hoped you might have gathered, as I had already, that something was needed (besides accentuation and expression) to make a success of the work." As instance of his own good faith he reminded Henry of scenery under construction and costumes ordered in Paris by Miss Rehan. James's reply was a long and bitter recapitulation of the entire history of the negotiations. He complained that he had never had an opportunity to discuss the role of Mrs. Jasper with Miss Rehan and that Daly had not adequately demonstrated to him the shortcomings of the play. And he took a parting shot at both Daly's unsuccessful season and his actress by expressing "the regret that the actress who had been willing to act the parts I have, for the most part, seen her act this winter, should not have been moved even to *study* that of the heroine of my comedy."

The play, and the possibility of being produced by Daly, loomed much larger in Henry's life than in that of the manager; and there is no doubt that the "rehearsal" would have had much more meaning for the experienced Daly than for the nervous author. The keenness of James's disappointment must have contributed to the network of motivation he wove around a commonplace in the theatre: the loss of interest by a manager in a play. The truth was that faced with an experienced manager and a highly competent company, Henry James had offered it a trivial and inconsequential piece of work. He had counted too much on help from the actors. More important still, he had despised the theatre too much to give it of that best of which he was capable.

BOOK SEVEN

The Altar of the Dead

1894=1895

A VENETIAN CHRISTMAS

I

"MR. JAMES WILL COME TO ITALY EVERY YEAR. AND PERHAPS WE can write that play after all." Fenimore packed her trunks at No. 15 Beaumont Street in Oxford. There were more trunks than ever. She sent the heavy ones by sea to Venice and a heavy box of books. Among the books were the volumes Henry had inscribed and given to her including his latest work, *Essays in London;* the works of Turgenev in French, which she had had bound in dark green; and her own books, some of which she had had rebound in morocco. She had finished the serial of *Horace Chase* and planned that summer to revise it for the book form. It was June when she was ready to leave. In London, she paused for some visits to the dentist. And then early one morning at her hotel she awoke with a high fever. A doctor was sent for at 4 A.M. and she was ill with influenza for some days. When she finally left for the Continent, she felt weak. And she was deeply depressed.

She had had no thought of returning to Florence, much as she

loved that city. There had been too much heartache in leaving
Bellosguardo. But she longed for Venice. She had spent happy
weeks there almost a dozen years before. And now, arriving in
late June, gliding through the canals, it seemed as if she could recover some of her old happiness. She found rooms in the Casa
Biondetti, not far from the Salute, with views up and down the
Grand Canal. She had five windows on the Canal and she
spent hours looking at the water traffic. She had a fair-sized drawing room, a small dining room, two bedrooms and a one-room
penthouse, where there was always the sea breeze and a splendid
view. The woman of the house cooked for her.

Fenimore, however, wanted a furnished apartment rather than
mere lodgings, and began an active search almost immediately. It
was part of her Venetian adventure, to travel by gondola to various palaces and smaller houses, in search of a home. There seemed
to be ample choice and she could not make up her mind. She
met the Curtises—probably through Henry James—and on July
14 (while he was at Ramsgate writing *Guy Domville*), Henry
spoke of her in a letter to Mrs. Curtis: "I am very sorry indeed
Miss Woolson has trouble in finding a house, or a *piano*. But I had
an idea she wanted—I think she does want—to abide for a winter
experimentally, first, in a *quartiere mobigliato*." On September
19 he wrote to the same correspondent: "I shall do my best to
prove to Miss Woolson that Venice is better than Cooperstown.
I am very glad to hear that she has at last a roof of her own.
The having it, I am sure, will do much to anchor her." In October he wrote to Francis Boott and announced he would go to
Italy—to Tuscany—in the spring. "I shall take Venetia by the way
and pay a visit to our excellent friend Fenimore. She has taken,
for the winter, General de Horsey's Casa Semitecolo, near the
Palazzo Dario, and I believe is materially comfortable; especially
as she loves Venice, for which small blame to her! But I figure
her as extremely exhausted (as she always is at such times), with
her writing and re-writing of her last novel—a great success, I
believe, in relation to the particular public (a very wide Ameri-

can one), that she addresses. She is to have, I trust, a winter of bookless peace."

II

Fenimore had not altogether made up her mind to stay permanently in Venice. There were times when she thought, as Henry said, of returning to ancestral Cooperstown in New York; and she used to wonder whether, after a villa in Florence and a palace in Venice, she would not find life a little humdrum in America. She was certain she would find it more expensive. General de Horsey, who never stayed in Venice in the winters, was delighted to have Miss Woolson as his tenant. He had been an enthusiastic reader of James Fenimore Cooper during his youth; and he told Miss Woolson that when he was in America forty years before he had gone especially to Cooperstown to make (what was rare for a military man) a literary pilgrimage. The General offered Fenimore two floors of his Casa, for $40 a month, for a period of eight months; and this suited Miss Woolson admirably. She would know by the end of that time whether she would want more permanent quarters. For this sum she had two drawing rooms, a winter bedroom on the side opposite the Canal looking down into a little *calle*; a summer bedroom on the Canal; a dining room, kitchen and three servants' rooms. The furniture was excellent. She had left certain furnishings in Florence and she now sent for them—the Brichieri chair Mrs. Browning had sat in once, which Boott had acquired and given her; her high desk—she always wrote standing up, sometimes for hours on end—and various linens.

Her deafness had always tended to make her a *solitaire*. She found it easier to decline invitations than to accept them. And while the Americans in Venice were friendly, she spent much time alone. That summer, when she was still in the Casa Biondetti, she rapidly established her routine of work: her maid called her at 4:30 A.M. when the dawn was beginning to shine on the Venetian waters. She would write until 9:30 A.M., when her cook would bring her breakfast. Then, still remaining in her rooms, with the shutters closed to keep out the heat, she would continue to work until about 4 P.M. Her gondola would then take her to the Lido. She liked a late afternoon dip in the warm Adriatic waters; and she would let herself float endlessly on the little waves. Refreshed, she would return for dinner at 7:30. The evenings were always spent on the water, looking at the lights and listening to the music. Mrs. Bronson was kind and hospitable; and Fenimore became very good friends with her daughter Edith, later Contessa Rucellai.

By early winter she was installed in the Semitecolo. There, with her Pomeranian, whom she named Othello and called affectionately Tello, she gave herself over to the lonely life she had always led. She began a series of visits to various islands and lagoons and made copious notes. These have survived; they are a succession of minute details:

September 3rd, six P.M. Warm, still, not at all hot, autumnal. The water of a pearl and dove colour. Dove-coloured clouds gathered in the west. The beautiful line of the Euganean Hills like dark blue velvet. The sun comes out below the clouds behind S. Giorgio in Alga, lighting it up in profile with its trees and meadows. The sun in *rays*. One fishing boat. The two piles inky black. I saw the Dolomites or Venetian Alps for the first time at the time of this sunset, after three months in Venice! In September the islands all begin to look nearer and clearer.

October 10th, six P.M. Sun gone down, and the whole west, salmon colour and gold. Euganean Hills and all the Alps violet velvet. Low tide and men with legs bare searching for things in the seaweed and islands. Vast plains of seaweed. Millet's Angelus. S. Giorgio in Alga like a farm in the plain.

Dec. 3rd. White snow on the mountains; vaguely seen against dove or slate-coloured sky and dove-coloured mist. Like crayon drawing.

She began to do research, and compiled for Mrs. Bronson a
list of islands which during the centuries had been swallowed up
by the sea. She often visited San Niccolò di Lido, once with Mr.
Curtis, where there was a fort and a cemetery with English and
German graves. She had always been a walker in cemeteries, a
habit begun in the American South where she had visited and
written about those of the Civil War, particularly in "Rodman
the Keeper." There were notes also on many islands, visited patiently, day after day, during December. She seemed to be contented with a cataloguing of these scraps of land and what the
play of light and the fishing boats did to them in the way of constantly changing their background. Thus her notes on San Mi-
chele, Cemetery Island:

The old brown gondola rowed by the cemetery
monk
The Mass of the Dead which I saw.
The appearance of the cemetery on All Souls' Day.
Pink walls. Cypresses (?) near the church. Campanile of cemetery
church, pink bricks with white corners.
White marble top story with round topped windows.
White dome with a red circle.

She told herself she would begin a new novel with the new
year. In the spring Henry James would pay his promised visit.

III

Toward Christmas she seemed to have made up her mind that she
might take root in the place, for she began to look at unfurnished
apartments, often with Edith Bronson for company. She liked
Venetian society; it was small and not very demanding; she found
it rather lazy, if sometimes "exclusive." Its members did not trouble themselves to pursue strangers. "I have never been so kindly
received as here; but there are few young people. It is essentially
a society of older persons," wrote this woman of fifty-three. She
had just looked at a magnificent apartment in the Palazzo Pesaro,

on the Grand Canal, below the Rialto—ten or twelve superb high-ceilinged rooms with great balconies on the Canal, all in perfect order, owned by the Duchess of Bevilacqua, available for $400 a year. But how did one heat such a place in winter?—especially with those high ceilings? And where would she find enough furniture?

On Christmas Eve it was so warm in Venice that Fenimore found she had no use for her fur cloak. She could simply wear her jacket. She went to the Lido in her gondola and walked for two hours on the Adriatic beach. Othello chased up and down the sand. For a while she sat on the grassy embankment of the Fort San Niccolò, after asking permission of the military guard. The sea and sky were exquisitely blue and the long line of the Alps was visible with more distinctness than she had ever seen it before. Never one for imaginative imagery, she observed that "the snow peaks looked like pink ice cream." She also remarked that the large tree at San Niccolò was a sycamore; and she wrote down the inscription on one of the graves in the cemetery:

. . . *dopo 45 anni di vita laboriosa ed onesta, affranto dalle sventure, per troppo delicate sentire, finiva di vivere, agosto 1887* . . .

In her notebook, on a somewhat more imaginative plane, she reflected that the pink-flushed peaks were riding through immeasurable space— "they are the outer edge of our star, they cut the air as they fly. They are the rim of the world." And then a strange note of melancholy: "I should like to turn into a peak when I die; to be a beautiful purple mountain, which would please the tired, sad eyes of thousands of human beings for ages."

That same day she wrote to an old friend, and the melancholy note recurred: "I have taught myself to be calm and philosophic, and I feel perfectly sure that the next existence will make clear all the mysteries and riddles of this. In the meantime, one

KATHERINE DE KAY BRONSON
From a water color by Ellen Montalba

CASA ALVISI
From a painting

CONSTANCE FENIMORE WOOLSON
From a photograph taken in Venice

HENRY JAMES IN CORNWALL
With Mrs. Leslie Stephen and her son Adrian.
From a snapshot, 1894

can do one's duty or try to do it. But if at any time you should hear that I have gone, I want you to know beforehand that my end was peace, and even joy at the release. . . . Now I am going out again for another walk through the beautiful Piazza."

IV

In London, in De Vere Gardens, Henry James spent a lonely Christmas, rejoicing in his solitude. A few evenings earlier, calling on Elizabeth Robins, he stayed past midnight, and apparently talked at length of his difficulties in the theatre. Miss Robins wrote to her and Henry's friend, Mrs. Bell: "James stayed till after one in the morning and I'm dead beat." She added: "H. J. was ghastly depressing." The episode with Daly had shaken him severely; however he persevered in the hope that he would fare better with Alexander. Just before Christmas he made certain cuts and revisions in the *Guy Domville* script at the manager's request. "Alexander's preparations of my other play are going on sedulously as to which situation and circumstances are all essentially different" —different from those surrounding his Daly play, he explained to William.

On the day after Christmas, sitting by his fire, in a still empty London, he gave himself over to reverie; and to dream thus was to pick up his pen. "Vague, dim forms of imperfect conceptions seem to brush across one's face with a blur of suggestion, a flutter of impalpable wings," he wrote. And he began to sketch a new play. Calm though London was, and peaceful the season, Henry's consciousness seemed filled with violence. He drew up an outline for a play of Ibsenian intensity in which he devised a climax more terrible than he had ever thought of before. There would be a dying woman, who would exact a pledge from her husband that he should never remarry so long as their child was alive; and this would be an open invitation, as it were, to another woman to do away with this human obstacle.

The wife dies. The "Bad Heroine" is "fearfully in love with my Hero." There is also a "Good Heroine," whom he loves.

Then, somehow, *this* is what I saw half an hour ago, as I sat in the flickering firelight of the winter dusk. The women have a talk—I won't answer, nor *attempt* to, now, here, of course, for links and liaisons—the women have a talk in which the good girl learns with *dismay* that it is the life of the child that keeps her from her lover. The effect of this revelation upon her is not, to the bad girl's sense, what she expected from it. She rebels, she protests, she is far from willing to give him up. Then my young lady takes a decision—she determines to poison the child—on the calculation that suspicion will fall on her rival. She does so—and on the theory of *motive*—suspicion does fall on the wretched girl.

This was an amalgam of a thriller and Ibsen: and probably James was already seeing Miss Robins in the role of the Hedda Gabler-like "Bad Heroine." Later he would amend his form of violence; in *The Other House* the child is drowned rather than poisoned. This was a strange and unusual fantasy for a man in whose novels little violence occurs, save the death of the little boy through the mother's agency, in "The Author of Beltraffio," and the death of young Miles in "The Turn of the Screw." "As I so barbarously and roughly jot the story down," Henry wrote, "I seem to feel in it the stuff of a play, of the particular limited style and category that can only be dreamed of for E[dward] C[ompton]."

After Christmas, and until the new year, Henry attacked a large mass of correspondence. He wrote a long letter to William describing the Daly episode, and discussing the visit of the Bourgets in America. "London has been very still, very empty and of an air extraordinarily soft and clear. I have passed no more selfishly complacent Christmas—in the cheerful void left by the almost universal social flight to the country. The autumn has been wholly fogless, and even the mists, which have now at last gathered, are harmless and silvery." He told William he was working "heroically" at the drama, and announced he would do so for another year. However, he found it difficult to engage in such ventures, which produced for the time being no income. But he had begun, now that Alice was dead, to receive the rents from Syracuse which he had made over to her during her lifetime: and these sums, little more than $100 a month, did give him—after twenty-five years in which he had lived by his pen—a certain margin. Nevertheless his habits were expensive; and he worked still as one who had to earn his living. He was to do so to the end.

The Daly episode had been, he told William, "a horrid experience," but nothing that one might not expect "in the vulgar theatrical world." His own feeling was that he had escaped from a sinking ship. "It was none the less for a while a lively disgust and disappointment—a waste of patient and ingenious labour and a sacrifice of coin much counted on." However he was not giving up. Alexander would play him in due course. He would complete his experiment, that is make his determined attack on the theatre and not allow himself to be disturbed by occasional adversity. He wrote:

I mean to wage this war ferociously for one year more—1894—and then (unless the victory and the spoils have not by that [time] become more proportionate than hitherto to the humiliations and vulgarities and disgusts, all the dishonour and chronic insult incurred) to "chuck" the whole intolerable experiment and return to more elevated and more independent courses. The whole odiousness of the thing lies in the connection between the drama and the theatre. The one is admirable in its interest and difficulty, the other loathesome in its conditions.

"I have come," he told William, "to *hate* the whole theatrical subject."

On the last day of 1893 he wrote a letter to Venice, to Mrs. Bronson. As in his other letters, he described the Christmas quiet that had descended on London, and the peaceful days he had spent. "I like the dusky London holiday-making, and the shopfronts flaring in the damp afternoons," he wrote. Elsewhere in this letter he asked: "Do you see anything of my old friend Miss Woolson? I am very fond of her and should be glad if there was any way in which you could be kind to her."

MISS WOOLSON

IN THE EARLY MORNING HOURS OF JANUARY 24, 1894—A LITTLE after one o'clock—two men walking in the *calle* beside the Casa Semitecolo noticed, in the dark, a white mass on the cobbles. One of the men thrust at it with his stick. This evoked a startling unearthly moan. The frightened men began to shout. Lights appeared and servants emerged: a nurse came running out of the building. Miss Woolson was carried back into the Casa. She had been ill with a new bout of influenza and had had a high fever. A few minutes before the men came upon her, she had sent her nurse to get something from one of the drawing rooms. While the nurse was gone, she had apparently opened the second-story window of her bedroom and thrown herself—or fallen—into the little street.

The grand-niece of James Fenimore Cooper was placed in her bed; there she lay peacefully, with no sign of pain and little sign of life. The doctor was summoned. She was, however, beyond recall. By the time the wintry dawn broke over the little canals and the lagoons, and over the Alps she had so recently contemplated, the solitary, shut-in life of Constance Fenimore Woolson had come to an end.

The American consul was promptly informed and cables were dispatched to Miss Woolson's sister, Clara Benedict, in New York. A cousin, Grace Carter, who was in Munich was summoned. Miss Woolson had died on a Wednesday; on Thursday the 25th the cousin arrived and took charge. From the nurse she gathered that Fenimore had spoken of wanting to be buried in Rome. On instructions from America, the servants were dismissed, and the Casa locked up under consular seal to await the arrival of the sister. Miss Carter accompanied the body to Rome, where John Hay, friend of Fenimore and of Henry, happened to be on a holiday. He took charge of the final arrangements.

I

Henry received the tidings of Miss Woolson's death from Mrs. Benedict in a cable from New York. She asked him whether he might find it possible to leave for Venice. Shocked and mystified, he assumed that Miss Woolson, like Lizzie Boott, had died of natural causes; an exchange of telegrams with friends in Venice and word from John Hay gave him the facts about the funeral in Rome, which had been set for Wednesday, the 31st, but no other details. He accordingly went, on the Saturday afternoon, to Cook's and made his travel plans. On returning to De Vere Gardens, he found a note from Constance Fletcher, who lived in the Palazzo Capello in Venice, and who was at that moment in London. She enclosed a clipping from a Venetian newspaper which gave a circumstantial account of the manner in which Miss Woolson had met her end.

It was now that Henry experienced the full shock and horror of the occurrence. That Fenimore should have chosen to do away with herself struck him as beyond belief. He had always known of her tendency to melancholy; he had recognized the solitude of her life; he had done what he could, when he was with her, to mitigate it. That she should have resorted to this extreme to release herself from her loneliness baffled him, and he searched his memories in his despair to discover clues that might help. By the next day, Sunday, he had made up his mind that he could not face the ordeal of her funeral. Before the "horror and pity" of the news, he wrote to John Hay, "I have utterly collapsed. I have let everything go, and last night I wired to Miss Carter that my dismal journey was impossible to me. I have, this morning, looked it more in the face, but I can't attempt it. I shall wire you tomorrow morning—one can do nothing here today; but meanwhile I must repeat to you that with the dreadful *image* before me I feel a real personal indebtedness to you in the assurance I have of your beneficent action and tenderness—in regard to offices that you will scarcely know how to make soothing and pitying enough." He went on to say that "Miss Woolson was so valued and close a friend of mine and had been so for so many years that I feel an intense nearness of participation in every circumstance of her tragic end and in every detail of the sequel. But it is just this nearness of emotion that has made—since yesterday—the immediate horrified rush to personally *meet* these things impossible to me."

Difficult as it is to speculate on the motives of Henry's decision, one thing is clear: he had been quite resigned to going to Rome when he had thought Fenimore had died of natural causes. From the moment that he learned that she had taken her own life—as the *Times* finally reported the next day—he had been "sickened and overwhelmed," not only by grief and, as he said, horror and pity: but also—as his later words and works were to show—by a feeling that in some way he too had some responsibility for her last act. To be sure, he could not be held accountable for a suicidal decision. Nevertheless what struck him now, with full force, was the pathetic suffering of this middle-aged, deaf woman, who worked so hard and led so cloistered an existence. "What a picture of lonely unassisted suffering!" he wrote to Hay. "It is too horrible for thought."

He wrote to Mrs. Bronson much in the same vein. He had been determined to go to Italy even though Dr. Baldwin had tried to dissuade him; it had been when he heard "for the first time, of the unimagined and terrible manner of her death" that he had lost heart to go. "So I have been kept away from you," he told her, "and I can't, while the freshness of such a misery as it all must have been, is in the air, feel anything but that Venice is not a place I want immediately to see. I had known Miss Woolson for many years and was extremely attached to her—she was the gentlest and tenderest of women, and full of intelligence and sympathy."

His decision not to go to Rome was apparently an instinctive act of self-protection: it came out of the mixture of emotion, the confusion of feeling, which he experienced at this moment. In recent months he had mourned the passing of many who were close to him; his personal altar of the dead was now crowded with votive candles. He could have faced the dead Fenimore if she had died as his sister had died. It was the brutality, the violence, the stark horror, the seeming madness of Fenimore's last act which struck him—and that he should have been so mistaken in a person for whom he had shown so much affection. In doing violence to herself, she had, so to speak, done violence to him and he sought now some shield behind which he could withdraw and take care of his deep wound. "Fearfulness and trembling are come upon me, and horror hath overwhelmed me," the Psalmist had sung. "Oh that I had wings like a dove! for then would I fly away, and be at rest." In the coming months James may have read this psalm; for in it he probably found his deepest feelings of this terrible moment in his life; and in it he found the title of the novel that he would ultimately write about a death in Venice.

The evolution of his feelings are documented for us in the letters he wrote during the ensuing days, and throughout this year—1894—which he had thought he would consecrate to the drama, but which was devoted much more to a spiritual altar of the dead that was being set up now in the gloom of his soul. Writing on the day after his decision not to go to Rome, to his friend Margaret Brooke, the Ranee of Sarawak, who was in Italy, he could not avoid pouring out to her his inner grief:

For the last two days it has seemed to me probable that I might see you very soon, in consequence, I grieve to say, of some terrible sad personal news from Italy. I was all prepared up to last night to start this morning [he was writing on January 28th] for Rome. Circumstances, at the eleventh hour, have made it impossible— and the reprieve, *in* these circumstances, is only an extreme relief. A close and valued friend of mine—a friend of many years with whom I was extremely intimate and to whom I was greatly attached (Miss Fenimore Woolson, the American novelist, a singularly charming and distinguished woman), died last Wednesday, in Venice, with dreadful attendant circumstances. Ill with influenza, aggravated by desperate insomnia, she threw herself out of the upper window of her house and died an hour later! It is too horrible to me to write about it—and I mention it really only to tell you that for the present I *can't* write.

He had never quite expressed it in this way— "with whom I was extremely intimate." Fenimore had always been his "admirable" friend, his "distinguished friend." But the Ranee had not known Miss Woolson, and he could speak to her, perhaps, more freely. In his telegram to John Hay he asked that some flowers be laid in his name beside Fenimore's grave. "The only image I can evoke that interposes at all," he wrote to Hay, "is that of the blest Roman cemetery that she positively *desired*—I mean in her extreme love of it and of her intensely consenting and more than reconciled rest under the Roman sky. *Requiescat.*"

II

On the day of the funeral, Henry wrote to Francis Boott:

I feel how, like myself, you must be sitting horror-stricken at the last tragic act of poor C. F. W. I can't *explain* it to you—it is with my present knowledge too dreadfully obscure—and I am tired with the writing and telegraphing to which I have had to give myself up in consequence—especially with the exhaustion of a second letter to poor Mrs. Benedict (258 Fourth Avenue, New York). Besides, I am still too sickened with the news—too haunted with the image of the act—and too much, generally, in darkness.

Henry, seeking explanations, reasons, motivations suggested to Boott that the event demanded absolutely "the hypothesis of sudden *dementia* and to admit none other.

Pitiful victim of chronic melancholy as she was (so that half one's friendship for her was always anxiety), nothing is more possible than that, in illness, this obsession should abruptly have deepened into suicidal mania. There was nothing whatever, that I know of, in her immediate circumstances, to explain it—save indeed the sadness of her lonely Venetian winter. *After* such a dire event, it is true, one sees symptoms, indications in the past; and some of these portents seem to me now not to be wanting. But it's all unspeakably wretched and obscure. She was not, she was never, wholly sane—I mean her liability to suffering was like the *doom* of mental disease. On the other hand she was the gentlest and kindest of women—and to me an admirable friend.

Fenimore was buried in a corner of the Protestant Cemetery in Rome, not far from the Roman wall and near the point where the pagan pyramid of Gaius Cestius thrusts its sharp diagonal beside the Christian ground. "We buried poor Constance W. last Wednesday laying her down in her first and last resting place," Hay wrote five days later to Henry Adams. "A thoroughly good, and most unhappy woman, with a great talent bedevilled by disordered nerves. She did much good and no harm in her life, and had not as much happiness as a convict."

She lies under the tall cypresses, not far from the graves of Shelley and Trelawny, and a short distance from the graves where Keats and his friend Severn are placed side by side. In death, as in life, Fenimore was companioned by great literary figures. A modern visitor among these clustered tombstones cannot but be struck by the fact that she also had chosen to be buried—and fate so arranged it—almost in the very spot where Henry James had tenderly laid to rest one of his most famous heroines, with whom Miss Woolson had identified herself and who, she felt, had been misunderstood and rejected by the Jamesian hero. Here, Daisy Miller had been interred, after she had died of the Roman fever, on an April morning long before, "in an angle of the wall of Imperial Rome, beneath the cypresses and the thick spring-flowers." It was still winter when the earth covered Miss Woolson's coffin. But John Hay caused the plot to be filled with perpetually blooming violets, and in due course a wide marble coping was placed around the flower bed and a Celtic cross of stone laid within it. On the coping there is simply the name "Constance Fenimore Woolson," and the year of her death, 1894.

CASA BIONDETTI

I

"THERE IS MUCH THAT IS TRAGICALLY OBSCURE IN THAT HORROR OF last week—and I feel as if I were living in the shadow of it," Henry wrote to Edmund Gosse, who read the paragraph in the *Times* and questioned him about his friend. To Mrs. Bronson Henry also spoke of "the strange obscurity of so much of the matter" and said that it had the "impenetrability of madness." He added: "Nothing could be more incongruous with the general patience, reserve and dainty dignity, as it were, of her life. Save her deafness, she had absolutely no definite or unusual thing (that I know of) to minister to her habitual depression; she was free, independent, successful—very successful indeed as a writer—and *liked*, peculiarly, by people who knew her." The weeks passed and Henry was unable to penetrate the obscurity. He could only offer himself certain consoling thoughts. He learned that Miss Woolson had been delirious; he was aware of the deep depression that often accompanies influenza; he reminded himself of all the accompanying circumstances of solitude and melancholy. Gradually certain comforting thoughts asserted themselves. If Miss Woolson's life had been a life of chronic melancholia and loneliness, then all that he had done had helped to provide a measure of happiness—had helped even to keep her alive. "My own belief," he wrote to William (who had met Fenimore in 1891 during his final visit to his sister), "is that she had been on the very verge of suicide years ago, and that it had only been stood off by the practical interposition of two or three friendships which operated (to their own sense) with a constant vague anxiety." To Lily Norton he wrote: "Isolation she sought and liked, but it was not the right thing for her and I can't help thinking that, given the condition she had long been in, the event might have been averted by an accidental difference of circumstance—as it was precipitated by the catastrophe of her illness." Again and again, to his inquiring friends, he repeated the sentence that "half one's friendship for her was always anxiety"; and he thereby discerned in his relationship with Fenimore those elements that had made for disquiet and uneasiness in himself. There had been, from the first, when he had known her in Florence, the obstacle of her deafness. Communication with her had never been of the easiest; and doubtless it had been at its best in their correspondence. Had they really understood one another? Had her act been a partial consequence of frustration—of frustrated love for Henry? The promise of an annual visit was thin support for an elderly devoted spinster otherwise living in a comparatively soundless world. We do not know whether Henry entertained such thoughts; nor can we say what measure of responsibility he may have felt—if he felt any at all. What is clear is that in time he took comfort in the thought that Fenimore had been seriously ill; and that she had not been altogether responsible for her actions.

He expressed this to Mrs. Bronson: "It was an act, I am convinced, of definite, irresponsible, delirious insanity, determined by illness, fever, as to its form, but springing indirectly out [of] a general depression which, though not visible to people who saw her socially, casually, had essentially detached her from the wish to live." This was also his answer to William James, who wrote to him that on the one occasion he had met Fenimore he had found her carefree, happy, lively and showing no sign of melancholia. Henry told him that it could not be visible to persons who saw Fenimore in a casual social situation.

There was another question, of a practical kind, which must have been a deep source of anxiety to the novelist. This was his correspondence with Miss Woolson. The author of "The Aspern Papers" was all too aware of the hazards of what Dr. Johnson called "The Great Epistolick Art." One of the first entries in his notebooks, after his sister's death, had been a worried paragraph about "the idea of the *responsibility* of destruction—the destruction of papers, letters, records, etc. connected with private and personal history." This had led him to write a little tale, "Sir Dominick Ferrand," about a young man who finds a desk with a secret drawer in it containing scandal-provoking letters of a famous statesman; the young man, in his impoverished state, is faced with the conflict of selling the letters or upholding privacy. In the end the letters are burned with "infinite method" and the hero is happy to see the pages turn to illegible ashes.

Henry could make "the private life" triumph in his fiction; but was it possible to do so in real life? He was all too aware how many trunks Fenimore possessed; he had seen her constitutional difficulty in extricating herself from the clutter of her days. He could imagine—he who always mercilessly cleared the approaches to his own privacy—what piles of paper, notebooks, possibly even diaries, there might be lying at this moment in the rooms of the temporarily sealed Casa Semitecolo. Fenimore had spoken of a will, shortly before her death, but none was found. She had even —Henry learned later—told Francis Boott that her last testament would contain a "surprise." When Boott told Henry this, he replied it was "just one of those numerous strangenesses that illustrate (as one looks back) her latent insanity." In the absence of a will, Clara Woolson Benedict, in New York, Fenimore's sister, fell heir to all her possessions. And Henry, in his correspondence with Mrs. Benedict, suggested that he would meet her when she came abroad, escort her to Venice and give her all the assistance she might need in taking charge of Fenimore's belongings. He would, in this fashion, perform a generous act of piety; and his good offices would be of great help to the bereaved woman, particularly since she spoke no Italian. At the same time there would be the comforting practical certainty that he would be in Venice when the Casa was opened, and at hand to cope with whatever privacies might require safeguarding among the dead woman's papers. His task was the opposite of that of his narrator in "The Aspern Papers." To make away with, rather than preserve, certain documents, must have been a part of his goal in undertaking what at best was an irksome and lugubrious task for a busy man of letters deeply involved in the theatre at this moment and not directly involved in Mrs. Benedict's affairs—save as a sympathetic and interested friend of her dead sister.

He went thus unwillingly. Without divulging why he was coming to Venice, he wrote to Mrs. Bronson asking her to find him some rooms. He had reached the age, he explained, when he no longer could tolerate hotels, and the sight of rows of international shoes lined up outside bedroom doors at night. And he went on to suggest that if possible she obtain for him Miss Woolson's rooms in the Casa Biondetti—those she had occupied before moving into the Casa Semitecolo. "A combination of circumstances, some of which I would have wished other, but which I must accept, make it absolutely necessary I should be in Venice from the first of April," he explained. He remembered, he said, that Miss Woolson had found these rooms particularly comfortable; and that the woman in charge had cooked for her. This would be ideal for the work he had in hand. He did not add that the rooms were ideally located in relation to the

Semitecolo, and he made no mention of Miss Woolson's sister. He asked Mrs. Bronson to try to get the place for a month. She sent him a wire very promptly to say that the apartment had been secured.

II

By the time he had made his arrangements to go to Italy at the end of March, the novelist had become accustomed to the idea of Fenimore's death; and the letter he wrote to Mrs. Benedict was a pouring of balm on his own wounds as well as on those he imagined to be hers.

Almost by this you will have heard from me that I will meet you at Genoa—be there when you arrive. I am sure Rome will be a very soothing, softening impression to you—that after a little the horror of the weeks you have been living through will be lost in the simple, assenting, participating tenderness with which (in regard to her memory and deep exemption now from everything that is hard in life) you will find yourselves thinking of her—till at last you will feel almost at peace in your acceptance. Meanwhile, only live, and think of living, from hour to hour, and day to day; it is perfect wisdom and it takes us through troubles that no other way can take us through. Have no plan whatever in advance about Venice. There is no need for any. The whole question will simplify itself, settle itself, facilitate itself, after you get to Italy.

He reached Genoa five days before she arrived; and was on the pier on March 29, 1894 when the *Kaiser Wilhelm II* docked. Mrs. Benedict was accompanied by her daughter Clare. Henry helped them through the customs and took them to the Hôtel de Gênes, where he himself was staying. The Benedicts had planned to proceed first to Rome, to visit the grave. Henry went directly to Venice, there to await their coming in the Casa Biondetti. "I found this pleasant little apartment quite ready for me and appreciably full of the happy presence of your aunt," he wrote to Clare Benedict in Rome. He urged her and Mrs. Benedict to stop in Florence on their way to Venice, to meet Dr. Baldwin whom Fenimore had known. Baldwin was a devoted and faithful friend and "it will be such a comfort and relief to him—a very great good indeed. I can well believe that the run from Pisa to Rome was dreary. But the worst dreariness passes and ebbs inch by inch. It is only a question of patience."

It was probably while he was waiting for the Benedicts that Henry visited, by himself, the little street behind the Casa Semite-colo and looked at the window from which Fenimore had jumped. Her relatives had done their best to conceal this fact, and to suggest that in her weakness and probable dizziness she had fallen. Henry however seems to have had no doubt. "The sight of the scene of her horrible act is, for that matter, sufficient to establish utter madness at the time. A place more mad for her couldn't be imagined." He wrote in this fashion some months later to Francis Boott, and he added, "I don't know why I remind you of these things, which only deepen the darkness of the tragedy."

The Benedicts arrived in Venice from Rome within a matter of days. Henry, Grace Carter, the two gondoliers and the dog Tello (who had been cared for by the gondoliers) met them. On the morning after their arrival the seals were removed and the silent rooms were entered, "a heartbreaking day, followed by many weeks of a task beyond words hard," Mrs. Benedict wrote in her diary. To a friend she wrote later that "Henry James met us at Genoa, and never never left us until all her precious things were packed and boxed and sent to America." Mrs. Benedict distributed mementos to Fenimore's friends. Henry recovered such of his letters as were found and was invited to take such books of Fenimore's as he wished. He took eleven volumes of her Turgenev in French, bound in half morocco ("You are now our Turgenev," she had once written to Henry); her personal volume of Rodman the Keeper, containing the place and date of each sketch, inserted in her own hand. He took also a bound copy of Fenimore's most popular novel, Anne, and Howells's Venetian Life inscribed to the authoress. Clare Benedict kept the books which Henry had given to her aunt, silent witnesses of their various meetings. He regained possession, however, of his *Essays in London*, asking for it perhaps for sentimental reasons, since there was a note written in it in Miss Woolson's hand, at the end of his essay on Mrs. Kemble. In this note Miss Woolson recalled the evening in which she had gone to the theatre in London to see Salvini and there encountered Henry with Mrs. Kemble, and Henry had surrendered to her his seat beside the aged actress. Mrs. Kemble had turned to Miss Woolson and said, in her deepest tragic tones: "I am *sorry* Mr. James has introduced you to me. I shall be obliged to tell you, *now*, that I shall not *speak* to you, or *look* at you, or be conscious of your existence even, during the entire evening." The volume remained in Henry's library. Miss Woolson's name, which had been written in it in pencil, was erased, and Henry wrote his own name over the erasure. On the title page "C. F. Woolson from H. J.," also written in pencil, had been erased, but the "H. J." remains legible. Henry also took as a memento a small painting by an artist named Meacci which years later he still had hanging in Lamb House. Eventually Mrs. Benedict asked him to return it to be placed in a little memorial room she had constituted to her sister in Cooperstown.

III

As Henry had suspected, the literary remains were voluminous. The impression one gets from the diary of Mrs. Benedict is that the novelist had ample opportunity—and doubtless would have been encouraged—to look through Miss Woolson's various miscellaneous literary papers. There were the notes she had been taking on the lagoons and islands of Venice. There was a commonplace book filled with comments on her readings. There were notebooks containing her reflections on art, music and literature, most of them of a distressing banality. Occasionally however an interesting thought crept in, a passage of singular insight. If Henry read these pages he must have come on a passage such as:

Many women, good women, think scenes in certain novels and plays "So untrue to nature!" These are the women who live always in illusion! They believe in all sorts of romances which have never had the least actual existence. They think in their secret hearts that all men are more or less in love with them; they go swimming through life in a mist of romantic illusion. Ibsen, for instance, is to them horrible. Though they may have Noras in their own family, and Heddas too.

or a note such as:

"He is interested in indexes," said H. with profound stupefaction.

There were jottings of remarks she had heard; comments in drawing rooms; ideas for stories. Many of her notes seemed to have been inspired by Hawthorne's notebooks, and were set down in his form:

To imagine a girl (or woman) doing some extraordinarily brave and heroic action, and then immediately afterwards being afraid of a mouse.

To imagine an American business man seeing "the late" prefixed in a newspaper to the name of some one he had known, and suddenly trying to imagine *himself* "the late."

To imagine a haunting face for years. Then to meet the person in real life.

The themes that haunted her, stated at greater length, were themes of women misunderstood and scorned:

To imagine a person (woman) always misunderstood; considered shy, sullen, cold, etc.—simply because she has never had about her people who really like her. To show the change—the gradual outburst, bloom and glow, even beauty—that follows an atmosphere of admiration, regard, sympathy and love.

A love story . . . It tells how she loved him. He did not think of her at all; in fact he never noticed her.

To imagine a woman obtaining all the romance and sentiment of her life in distant and wholly imaginary lovers. She has one at every corner!

Imagine a man endowed with an absolutely unswerving will; extremely intelligent, he *comprehends* passion, affection, unselfishness and self-sacrifice etc. perfectly, though he is himself cold and a pure egotist. He has a charming face, a charming voice, and he can, when he pleases, counterfeit all these feelings so exactly that he gets all the benefits that are to be obtained by them.

An American who has lived so long abroad that he is almost denationalized, and *conscious of it fully*; which makes him an original figure.

There was one note above all which Henry may have seen and which, remaining in his memory, might have been the source for an entry in his own notebook:

To imagine a man spending his life looking for and waiting for his "splendid moment." "Is this my moment?" "Will this state of things bring it to me?" But the moment never comes. When he is old and infirm it comes to a neighbour who has never thought of it or cared for it. The comment of the first upon this.

Henry's note, written seven years later:

. . . a man haunted by the fear, more and more, throughout life, that *something will happen to him*: he doesn't quite know what. . . . Yet "It *will* come, it will still come," he finds himself believing—and indeed saying to some one, some second-consciousness in the anecdote. "It will come before death; I shan't die without it." Finally I think it must be *he* who sees—not the second consciousness. . .

This was the germ from which Henry James ultimately developed "The Beast in the Jungle."

IV

For five weeks Henry, Mrs. Benedict and her daughter lived with the ghost of Constance Fenimore Woolson. Early in May, Mrs.

Benedict sent off to America twenty-seven boxes containing the effects accumulated during her sister's literary life abroad. James, she recorded in her diary, "came every day to see and help us—we could not have gone through it without him." Apparently, once he had satisfied himself about Miss Woolson's literary remains, he reverted to his usual working hours, spending his forenoons and early afternoons at the Casa Biondetti. He would arrive at tea-time at the Semitecolo, and the three would go out for a couple of hours in the gondola. On most evenings he dined with the Benedicts.

"I have had to plunge into a melancholy mass of preoccupations and a tangle of worrying business, consequent on the recent death here, under circumstances of great sadness, of an intimate friend," he wrote to Francis Palgrave. "Venice is obscured and saddened by it—and seems to me moreover not yet (at this early stage of the spring) to have its characteristic warm glow—its pink and gold. It is hard and white and *blafard*. However, it's the same sweet old Venice." A few weeks later, when the Venetian episode was over, he wrote to William from Ravenna of "the great hole bored in my time and my nerves by the copious aid and comfort I couldn't help giving to poor Mrs. Benedict—Miss Woolson's sister—who, staying there five weeks, made daily demands of me to help her in the winding-up of Miss W's so complicated affairs, all left, so far as Venice was concerned, at sixes and sevens. This proved a most devouring, an almost fatal job."

To Francis Boott he said that "all of my first weeks in Venice were populated with the dolorous *detail* of the two poor Benedicts, who occupied Miss Woolson's sad death-house and took elaborate possession of her immensely accumulated effects." He added that all the knowledge Mrs. Benedict collected of Miss Woolson's last weeks "tended directly to confirm the conviction she had already formed that an unmistakable lapse from sanity had occurred sometime before her death—that some cerebral accident had been determined the previous summer." This is questionable; certainly the notes on the lagoons and the diary entries of Fenimore's last Christmas show no lapse from her usual ability to observe and to record. Henry's earlier hypothesis of chronic depression seems to fit the circumstances of Miss Woolson's death much more accurately.

The novelist's own role in aiding Mrs. Benedict seems to have occupied his first fortnight in Venice. A notebook entry of April 17, 1894, brief and pointed, suggests the term of his principal funereal duties, but suggests also the inner outrage he had suffered. He wrote:

Here I sit, at last, after many interruptions, distractions, and defeats, with some little prospect of getting a clear time to settle down to work again. The last six weeks, with my two or three of quite baffling indisposition before I left London, have been a period of terrific sacrifice to the ravenous Moloch of one's endless personal, social relations—one's eternal exposures, accidents, disasters. *Basta.*

Exposures, accidents, disasters. The mounting strength of the three words, suggests the full force of his Venetian experience. There had been danger of exposure; there had been accident; there was the disastrous inroad on his working time: there was the greater disaster of his personal hurt. We may guess that by April 17, when he made this note—that is two weeks after the work at the Casa Semitecolo began—Henry had settled all the questions that concerned him in Fenimore's death and he could relax. The most difficult part was over. As for the rest—*basta!*

v

Early in May the Benedicts surrendered the Casa Semitecolo to General de Horsey and left for further travels in Europe. The Curtises were in India and the Palazzo Barbaro was let. Few of Henry's friends were in Venice, and he could now settle down to work that had been delayed. He had promised Henry Harland a long tale for the *Yellow Book.* One of the reasons he had been attracted to this hard-cover quarterly, of which he did not altogether approve, was that he would be allowed to write his *nou-*

velles without regard to a word-count. The first issue, earlier that year, had contained his tale of "The Death of the Lion." That sardonic tale had been the first he had written after Fenimore's death, and it masked, in its moments of savage wit, all the anguish of the time. Its picture of an elderly, neglected man of letters, unread and unknown, who becomes a "lion" because a newspaper finally takes notice of him, was one of the bitterest—and most amusing—of the "tales of the literary life" which Henry now began to write. The "lion" is taken up by a sympathetic young man who constitutes himself his protector and virtually his "manager." But he cannot protect him from the draughts at the home of Mrs. Weeks Wimbush, the "lion" fancier. She collects celebrities and at her home a precious manuscript of the great man's is lost, as it is passed from hand to hand—unread. The "lion" dies in complete unawareness of the fuss around him.

The tale which James set down in Venice, and which ran to great length, was "The Coxon Fund," built around his recent reading of a life of Coleridge by James Dykes Campbell. He was struck by the personality of the poet-critic, "wonderful, admirable figure for pictorial treatment." Thus emerged his portrait of the gifted Saltram, who had magic in his talk, and lived his life freely with unconcern for the Philistines around him. The story is perhaps the first in which James's "later manner" begins to emerge: and one has the impression that he struggled in the writing of it to express in a bolder way than ever before his belief in the supremacy of the artist whose vagaries and idiosyncrasies society must learn to tolerate. Some of the story's force is smothered in verbal extravagance; nevertheless its ironic message is sufficiently clear. The artist must be given full freedom: he must be forgiven his sins against the social body. He must be allowed his transgressions—his illegitimate children, his sublime ignorance of daily routine or method, his sexual irregularities—but it must also be recognized that if he is too well endowed, he might cease to struggle altogether. When finally an American fund is established for the gifted Saltram, he lapses indeed into benign indifference. "The very day he found himself able to publish, he wholly ceased to produce." His wife says he has simply become "like everyone else." Saltram draws his income "as he had always drawn everything, with a grand abstracted gesture. Its magnificence, alas, as all the world now knows quite quenched him." If James was thus re-imagining an endowed Coleridge, he was prophesying certain aspects of an endowed James Joyce. The more personal message of "The Coxon Fund" was avowed by James in his later prefaces to this and other stories about writers—that they had gathered their motive from "some noted adventure, some felt embarrassment, some extreme predicament, of the artist enamoured of perfection, ridden by his idea or paying for his sincerity." And he also said that they proceeded from "the designer's own mind" and were fathered "on his own intimate experience." These were but ways of saying that the "tales of the literary life"—including "The Figure in the Carpet" and "The Next Time," written shortly afterwards—expressed James's own disappointment in the marketplace as well as in the world of letters. He felt that his work was misread—when it was read—and more often discussed without having been read at all. James was at last beginning to say that he did not care; that he had followed rules and conventions too long, and that he would go his own way, publicly and privately and—*que diable!*—take from life what he could get from it. In the Casa Biondetti, that gruesome summer, he began to find the light by which he would work in his later years.

This did not mean that the old ingrained puritanism in him foundered at this moment. The obverse of "The Coxon Fund" was still an individual carrying his bundle of guilt on his shoulders. And in the Casa Biondetti he set down the idea for a tale he would not write for many years: that of a young man carrying some unspecified burden, who seeks to find someone to tell it to, that he may be eased of it. The young man has "a secret, a worry, a misery, a burden, an oppression." In our time, James probably would not have pondered such a story too long, and the young man would have eased himself of oppression and worry on the psychoanalytic couch. However, in Venice in 1894, James could spin this personal idea, suggestive of the burden he himself carried, and of the young man's round of visits in which no one wants to listen to him: everyone has his own private worries, or is selfishly indifferent. As he planned the story, he finally would have someone else unload a burden on the already-burdened young man. "He is healed by doing himself what he wanted to have done *for* him." And "the charm and interest of the thing must necessarily be in the picture—the little panorama of his vain contacts and silent appeals." The tale "A Round of Visits" was not written until 1910, by which time it underwent some modification. But the notation of it in Venice, at the time of the writing of "The Coxon Fund," indicates to us the polarities of James's ambivalence.

While he thus worked in the Casa Biondetti, the hot weather came and with it something he had never before experienced in his beloved Venice. The ships had begun to ply directly from New York and Boston to Genoa and Henry James discovered that this summer the Grand Canal was transformed into Marlborough Street and Back Bay. Venice became, "if I may be allowed the expression, the mere *vomitorium* of Boston." He had never seen such an Americanized Venice, all mixed up with the Germans and other European tourists who annually flooded the Piazza. "They are all 'our' people—yours and mine," he wrote to Morton Fullerton, "and they dis-Italianize this dear patient old Italy till one asks oneself what is at last left of its sweet essence to come to, or for. The accent of Massachusetts rings up and down the Grand Canal and the bark of Chicago disturbs the siesta." Late in May he decided to leave and to make a pilgrimage he had promised himself. Even as, years before, he had read William's letter to his father, over the newly-dug grave in Cambridge, so now he would stand beside this other grave, in Rome. He would pay his visit to Fenimore; he would keep his solemn promise to her—and to himself.

PILGRIMAGE

WHEN HENRY LEFT VENICE, CROWDED WITH HIS COUNTRYMEN, HE felt like "Apollo fleeing the furies." On his way to Rome he stopped in Florence and climbed the hill of Bellosguardo. Fenimore's Villa Brichieri seemed to stare down at him "with unspeakably mournful eyes of windows." He visited friends in the Castellani. The place was for him "a cemetery of ghosts." He went to the Allori Cemetery, outside the Roman Gate, and for the first time saw Lizzie Boott's bronze tomb. "Strange, strange it seemed, still to see her only so—but so she will be seen for ages to come."

By comparison with Venice, Rome seemed empty and at that season it happened still to be cool. He had not been there for some years; his recent visits to Italy had been confined to Venetia and Tuscany. The city spoke to Henry "with its old most-loved voice as if a thousand vulgarities perpetrated during the last fifteen years had never been." It too had its phantoms. He went to the Barberini and called on William Wetmore Story. He found him "the ghost of his old clownship." He, who had talked so well of old, was now "very silent and vague and gentle." And Henry thought of the great unsettled population of statues in his studio which he knew Story's children did not like. Soon they would be turned "loose upon the world." Well, he mused, Story, fortunate man, had had fifty years of Rome.

Count Primoli invited Henry to luncheon in his picturesque palace in the Via Tor di Nona near the Tiber and here Henry found himself sitting next to the "she-Zola" of Italy, Matilde Serao, "a wonderful little burly Balzac in petticoats—full of Neapolitan life and sound and familiarity." There were other strange Roman types, male and female, present. Madame Serao told Henry the astonishing news that Paul Bourget had just been elected to the Academy—had arrived comparatively young among France's "immortals."

When he stood before Miss Woolson's grave for the first time it had already received its marble coping. It was purple with Roman violets; veins of newly-planted ivy crept around its base. Henry had always been deeply moved by the Protestant Cemetery. He never spoke of it without alluding to the pyramid, the ancient wall, the cypresses. We have no record of the day on which he paid his visit, or of the silent hour of communion he spent alone with the dead. But there may be echoes of this and of a later visit in his description of John Marcher at the grave of May Bartram in "The Beast in the Jungle." There he speaks of Marcher's standing "powerless to turn away and yet powerless to penetrate the darkness of death; fixing with his eyes her inscribed name and date, beating his forehead against the fact of the secret they kept, drawing his breath, while he waited as if, in pity of him, some sense would rise from the stones. He kneeled on the stones, however, in vain; they kept what they concealed."

He described the grave to Boott as "beautiful—in a beautiful spot—close to Shelley's. It was her intense desire to lie there." Thirteen years later, on his last visit to Rome, he made the pilgrimage again, for he wrote to the Benedicts: "The most beautiful thing in Italy, almost, seemed to me in May and June last, the exquisite summery luxuriance and perfect tendance of that spot. I mean, of course, that very particular spot below the great grey wall, the cypresses and the time-silvered pyramid. It is tremendously, inexhaustibly touching—its effect never fails to overwhelm." If he used the word overwhelm in 1907, we may believe that he was overwhelmed when he saw the grave in all its violet-sprinkled newness in 1894. "I echo your judgement of her life and fate—they are unmitigatedly tragic," he wrote to Boott. "But to have seen something of her unhappiness is to find in her extinction something like one's knowledge of the cessation of a horrible pain." For Fenimore too there had come a "divine cessation."

THE INVADED ALTARS

I

THE REMAINDER OF HENRY'S STAY IN ITALY THAT SUMMER OF 1894 was rather a scramble, and a continual heartache. He had a few days in Naples; he returned to Rome briefly; he went to Florence and stayed with Dr. Baldwin. Under his roof he contracted influenza, and the doctor quickly pulled him through. He went to Bologna, where it was quiet, and he had a few peaceful days. He didn't want to go back to Venice. He wondered whether he would ever go back to it in the future. Finally, at the end of June, he journeyed there just long enough to pick up some luggage, and even then he withdrew to visit Mrs. Bronson at the uncomfortable La Mura. There were tourists everywhere. To this had his great Americano-European legend come: he, who had been its veritable historian, now was to be the spectator of a great invasion: "Europe"—from now on he began to put quotation marks around the word—had been the great adventure of his youth and of his generation. The continuing American discovery of it had been the substance of all the comedy and irony and tragedy in his fiction. And now it was losing all that he treasured in it: its peacefulness and its sacredness, as a shrine of civilization: it had become as commonplace as the buttons on one's coat, or the noisy numbered streets of New York. One Mrs. Jack, bestriding Europe, could be a source of amusement; a thousand Mrs. Jacks was a catastrophe. He was to write in his notebook a year later—of "the chaos or cataclysm toward which the whole thing is drifting," and to speak of

the deluge of people, the insane movement for movement, the ruin of thought, of life, the negation of work, of literature, the swelling, roaring crowds, the 'where are you going?', the age of Mrs. Jack, the figure of Mrs. Jack, the American, the nightmare—the individual consciousness—the mad, ghastly climax. . . . The Americans looming up—dim, vast, portentous—in their millions—like gathering waves—the barbarians of the Roman Empire.

From Bologna he wrote to Henrietta Reubell that he dreamed of "some Alpine pasture—some high hillside, under the great chestnuts, where I can hear the plash of a torrent and the tinkle of cattle bells." As he paused in Venice he wrote to William, "I am demoralized and my spirit [is] broken by the most disastrous three months' attempt I have *ever* made to come 'abroad' for privacy and quiet. . . . These three months have been simply hell!" and he added he would get off to "some lone Swiss hillside and then I shall be better." Early in July he went to the Splügen: he found the little river that girdled the hotel at Chur not as copious or pellucid as he had thought; it was thin and brown, "and the voice of the compatriot rings over it almost as loudly as over the Grand Canal. For the compatriot is here in her hundreds (excuse the gender) on her way to the Engadine and this first brush with the dreadful Swiss crowd takes the heart out of my disposition to linger by the way." His great temple had been desecrated; others were in possession of his altars. The decades-long quiet and peace of his personal "Europe" was shattered. He had planned to stay away from London until August. He was back in De Vere Gardens on July 12.

Although he did not know it, he had left the Continent, almost, for life. He would cross the Channel but three times during his remaining years, and at very long intervals. At this moment, all he felt was a relief to regain England, to turn his back on the rape of Europe.

Shortly after his homecoming, Walter Pater died, and Henry, writing to Edmund Gosse, envied him the way in which he had hidden himself from sight behind his work. He had had "the most exquisite literary fortune" and had achieved "the mask without the face." Henry added almost exultantly that there wasn't an inch in the total area of "pale embarrassed, exquisite Pater," not even "a tiny point of vantage for the newspaper to flap his wings on." There spoke a writer who that summer had had to protect himself from "exposures, accidents, disasters," and who had only recently written his brother at length expressing fear lest Alice's journal fall into the hands of relatives: "I seem to see them showing it about Concord—and talking about it—with the fearful American newspaper lying in wait for every whisper, every echo."

There were eddies of importuning Americans in London as well; Mrs. Jack herself was on the horizon, and Henry left to pay rural visits. He could rely on tranquillity in the countryside. He spent some days at Torquay with W. E. Norris, a minor novelist of the time whom he had come to know, and whom he rather liked. He had a night and a morning with Rudyard Kipling, who "spouted to me many admirable poems—but all violent, as it were—and all about steamers and lighthouses." The *Jungle Book* was "thrilling, but so bloody." In mid-August he went to St. Ives, in Cornwall, to stay near the Leslie Stephens. He had long been a friend of the taciturn Stephen, and an admirer of the beautiful Julia, his wife. Henry put up at the Tregenna Castle Hotel; and every day he went for long walks with his former editor at the *Cornhill*, "the silent Stephen, the almost speechless Leslie," paying occasional visits to Talland House, the Stephen summer home. The world knows that house today and its personages not as Henry saw them, but through the eyes of Virginia Woolf, then the young Virginia Stephen, whose delicate beauty struck Henry from the first. The time had come when James was encountering the living substance of future novels as had been the case when he met, before their time, the characters of Marcel Proust. For a fortnight Henry moved (as we now know) in the landscape of *To the Lighthouse* and among its people; and went striding over the moors with the future Mr. Ramsay. Although he had known Stephen since 1869, they still met and walked in great intervals of silence. Henry found this kind of English "dumbness" almost a relief after the chattering tourists of the Continent. And the vigorous walks on moor and coastline, always of great length, gave him the physical exercise and fresh air he had hoped to get in Switzerland.

11

At the end of the summer, and quite without design, but by circumstances not altogether coincidental, he found himself housed once more with the ghost of Fenimore. The Bourgets had come to England to spend a brief holiday while their new apartment was being prepared for them in Paris. They went to Oxford and put up at the Randolph. Henry joined them, deeply curious to hear about their recent American tour. To be in Oxford was to be in the very spot where Fenimore had spent her last months in England and where, on many occasions, he had visited her. "Disturbing as it was to enter the house," Henry nevertheless went to No. 15 Beaumont Street to call on Fenimore's former landlady, a cultivated woman who had been a schoolteacher and of whom Miss Woolson had been very fond. This lady, Mrs. Phillips, was on her side devoted to Fenimore. "She would have done anything for her and I wish she might have been free to do more," Henry wrote to Clare Benedict. "I was much moved by the spectacle of her emotion."

Henry did not spare himself this re-encounter with a recent past; he not only invited it, but ended by taking lodgings in the same house. His letters during most of September 1894 and several of his entries in his notebook are dated "15 Beaumont Street, Oxford." He saw much of the Bourgets. He and his confrère would spend the day at their work and meet in the late afternoon for long strolls through the college gardens and the cloisters in the waning light. Bourget, for all his success, was deeply depressed; his election to the Academy, which would have gratified most writers, seemed to him one burden the more, and his biographer speaks of his poisoning "the very real joy" he felt in revisiting Oxford by conjuring up the memories of the Oxford dead—men such as Mark Pattison and Walter Pater. The image comes to us of the two novelists, both rather short and stout, walking solemnly through the ancient town and its historic colleges, haunted by their private phantoms, yet turning them into brilliant talk. This was the background for the theme James entered in his notebook one day in Beaumont Street, after the Bourgets had left. He wanted to write a tale called "The Altar of the Dead." The name, he felt, was happy, and he hoped the "story may be half as much so." At its inception the idea for the tale was simply a "conceit" that would take the form of "a man whose noble and beautiful religion is the worship of the Dead." The story he wanted to write was that of an individual who cherishes for "the silent, for the patient, the unreproaching dead" a tenderness which finally takes the form of some shrine—some great altar in which a candle is lit for each person who is gone. "He is struck with the rudeness, the coldness, that surrounds their memory." Henry emphasized that the altar was "an altar in his mind, in his soul." Later in working out the tale he gave it material form: his hero, Stransom, actually arranges to establish the altar in a church and even finds the Bishop, with whom he works out the details, "delightfully human" and "almost amused." This tale, sketched in Beaumont Street, was completed very rapidly in De Vere Gardens.

What James did not sketch out was the drama—the conflict—with which he endowed it. It is an eerie tale, flimsy in its materials, yet written in great soaring organ tones, and evocative in its symbolism: for it embraces the universal relation between the living and the dead; and it contains within it also the force of Christ's sermon:

Therefore if thou bring thy gift to the altar, and there rememberest that thy brother hath ought against thee; Leave there thy gift before the altar, and go thy way; first be reconciled to thy brother, and then come and offer thy gift. [Matthew 5:23, 24]

Stransom, lighting candles for all his dead, cannot bring himself to light one for Acton Hague, the friend who had once wronged him. He has forgiven Hague; but he will not include him in his particular shrine. Presently Stransom discovers that a woman is also regularly worshipping at his altar. By a series of circumstances he comes to know that for her the entire altar is but a single candle, lit for the very man he has excluded. Acton Hague had wronged her, also. She had forgiven, and she worshipped his memory. In this fashion, she takes symbolic possession of the altar; and Stransom, who had expected that the last missing candle would be lit for himself, finds her insisting that it be lit for Hague.

There is, however, another side to the tale. This is the power-struggle between a man and a woman, each participating in the same obsession, and each determined to have his way. Like Isabel and Osmond, and so many other of James's characters, the struggle here is between mirror-images of power. In effect, the woman in this tale takes from the man his "altar of the mind," and there is no room for truce between them. She will have it only on her terms. At the very outset, when they begin to speak to one another, they admit "they did not care for each other." Presently Stransom recognizes that "she used his altar for her own purpose." If she had given him a worshipper, "he had given her a splendid temple"; and again "she was really the priestess of his altar." In these circumstances, he loses all taste for his creation. He feels his candles have been extinguished by her; there has been "a dire mutilation of their lives." There is little left for him to do. One day he dies before the invaded altar. She is contrite at the last moment; but she may well be. For, finally, he has yielded, and she has her triumph. *She* has been unyielding. In the tale Henry made her into a writer who publishes her works under a pseudonym. Neither her name nor her pseudonym is given.

What we may read in "The Altar of the Dead" is that there had been between Henry and Fenimore a strange matching of personalities, and strange distortions in their mutual vision of one another. Henry had hitherto ruled out women and, in his bachelor state, had no desire to become involved with them. He had thought that in Fenimore he had found a disinterested devotion —as distant as was consonant with his own sense of freedom and sovereignty. Then, apparently, in some way, Fenimore had made him feel that she had claims on him—claims he had not been prepared to meet. The "it won't do" of "The Aspern Papers" suggested at the time what he may have experienced at the Villa Brichieri; and the final "arrangement" that he would once a year visit Fenimore in Italy had been apparently an ultimate compromise. Yet in the end she had performed an act of horror. His altar was spattered with her blood. And the mystery of her grave was intolerable to someone like Henry, who sought total vision and total insight. Had she died a normal death Henry would have taken possession of her, and been able to light a candle for her within the altar of his soul as he had lit candles for his near ones of Quincy Street; for Minny, long ago; for Lizzie; for his great confrères; for Turgenev; and for the young dead of his recent years. How light a candle for Fenimore, when he could not possess her? She had possessed herself: she had arbitrarily cut herself off from him *by her own act*. Fenimore had asked for too much. And if he had yielded, this would have been the loss of his sovereign self.

The old and long-buried equations of Henry's life had been acted out in Fenimore's death: in the struggle between man and woman, in many of his tales, one or the other had to die. It was impossible for two persons to survive a passion—and in this case, had it been a passion? Certainly not on his side. But on hers, apparently, it had. These were the unfathomable mysteries which now began to haunt Henry, and were to haunt him for years to come, until he would find a partial answer—a decade later—in the tale of "The Beast in the Jungle." But other experiences would intervene to offer him illumination for that tale. An entry in his notebooks late in November of 1894 suggests the phantoms with which he was struggling, and his feelings about the conflict of will that had prevailed between him and Fenimore. He envisaged a story in which "a man of letters, a poet, a novelist" discovers after years "of very happy, unsuspecting, and more or less affectionate, intercourse with a 'lady-writer'" that she has been anonymously "slating" his books in certain periodicals to which she contributes. He pondered "the situation of the two people after the thing comes to light." The reviewer had had one attitude to the writer —as a writer—and another to him as "a friend, a human being." From this fantasy, so close to the mysteries of his relationship with Fenimore, he went on to an analogous one—it was the last of this fatal year—"a small drama, in the conception of the way certain persons, closely connected, are affected by an event occurring, an act performed" which results in "the contrasted opposition of the two forms of pride," the pride that stiffens the heart, and the pride that suffers. Decidedly Fenimore's act had stirred up in Henry James a sense of personal betrayal. He never wrote these tales, but they are variants of the situation he had imagined and worked out in the muted yet vivid language of "The Altar of the Dead."

For the moment all he had was the silence of the grave in Rome, and the malaise that something had happened in his life that was like a great barrier, thrown across its roadway. In the past, he had always "taken possession." And in his tales of artists, it was always someone else who makes the sacrifice for the great man. In "The Middle Years" the admiring young doctor had given up his post; in "The Death of the Lion" the dazzled young journalist had thrown up his job. In "The Coxon Fund" the young woman had given up her dowry to subsidize the genius. And years before—twenty-five years before—he had felt, when his young cousin Minny Temple had died of tuberculosis, that she had surrendered her life to give him the strength to live and fulfill all that she had been unable to do. At the end of his "untried years," facing the English countryside as he received the news of the extinction of this bright young flame, he had rejoiced that she lived on as a "steady unfaltering luminary in the mind." Her image would "preside in my intellect." It had been "almost as if she had passed away—as far as I am concerned—from having served her purpose." And this purpose had been that of "inviting

and inviting me onward by all the bright intensity of her example." Minny had been locked away in the "crystal walls of the
past."

His taking "possession" of the dead is fully expressed by Stransom in the tale of the Altar. "There were hours at which he almost caught himself wishing that certain of his friends would
now die, that he might establish with them in this manner a connection more charming than, as it happened, it was possible to enjoy with them in life." The Henry James who had difficulty establishing full and charming connections with people in life could
do so when they were dead and locked within the crystal walls of
his imagination. Fenimore had evaded this. She had died on her
terms, not his. He could find no crystal walls for her.

THE TERRIBLE LAW

I

MINNY TEMPLE HAD DIED AT THE END OF HENRY JAMES'S TWENTY-
seventh year, when he stood on the threshold of his literary life.
Constance Fenimore Woolson had destroyed herself when he was
in his fifty-first year, and a famous man. And now, before the
long-burning candle of Minny, and the unlit candle of Fenimore,
Henry found himself dreaming of a novel in which a young
woman, with all of life before her, an heiress of the ages, is
stricken and must die. In the year of Fenimore's death he returned to his memories of Minny. Early in November, shortly
after writing "The Altar of the Dead," he set down his first notes

for the large fiction that would become, almost a decade later, *The Wings of the Dove*.

This novel has always been regarded as Henry's attempt to recapture the drama of Minny's untimely end. He named his heroine Milly Theale, thereby echoing Minny's name; and in his autobiographies he spoke of having sought "to lay the ghost in the beauty and dignity of art." However when he set down his first notes for the novel the figure of Fenimore also stood beside him. We can glimpse her in his search for a place where he would assemble his characters. "I seem to see Nice or Mentone—or Cairo—or Corfu—designated as the scene of the action." This is a curious ranging about the Mediterranean. James had never been in Cairo or Corfu; but Fenimore had, during her Eastern tour with Mrs. Benedict, chronicled by her in the magazines and published posthumously as a book, *Mentone, Cairo, and Corfu*. In the end Henry chose neither Cairo nor Corfu, nor Mentone, where Fenimore long ago wrote her poem about love. Her death in Venice, that for the time had changed the aspect of his days, became the death in Venice of *The Wings of the Dove*.

In that novel there would be the same struggle as in "The Altar of the Dead." It would be embodied in the unyielding spirit of Kate Croy who bends Merton Densher to her wishes, and to her scheme to have him make love to the dying girl so that they may inherit her riches. It is a sinister and cruel plot. The novel belongs to the later time, to the same period as "The Beast in the Jungle." And at its end the image of the dead girl dominates the living, and changes the course of their lives. In *The Wings of the Dove* Henry thus incorporated the two women whose deaths he had faced at the beginning and at the end of the middle span of his life—Minny, the dancing flame, who had yielded everything and asked for nothing and whom he possessed eternally; and Fenimore, the deep and quiet and strong-willed, who had given devotion and "intensities of fidelity" but had yielded nothing and had disturbed the altar of his being.

11

The struggle for the altar was ended. In his tale, his hero had died of it. In life, Henry had endured. What remained now was a dull ache and an unresolved, unanswerable mystery. The altar itself, that of art, still shone, high and pure, and if the candles had momentarily dimmed, time would restore their luminosity. Standing on the edge of the winter late in 1894, Henry turned from his contemplation of the dead to the problems of his life. George Alexander shook him out of his Oxford reverie. The play that was to have further delayed *Guy Domville* had had a short run. Suddenly the actor-manager was asking for more cuts and announcing rehearsals. Henry threw himself into the revisions, feeling as if the stage were exacting flesh from him every time he altered a scene. He had written to his brother that he would wage his theatrical war for "one year more." The year was running to its term. Presently rehearsals began, and early in 1895 the costume play would be produced on the stage of one of London's best theatres, and by one of London's best companies. Perhaps Henry would have his *revanche:* he would retrieve the lost ground, recover the old victories, find again a reasonable show of fame and perhaps a modest show of fortune.

"Ah the terrible law of the artist," he had written when he had begun his theatricals, "the law of fructification, of fertilization, the law by which everything is grist to his mill—the law, in short, of the acceptance of all experience, of all suffering, of all life." Henry had long ago bowed to that terrible law. He bowed now knowing that the genius residing somewhere within his gouty and aging body still had courage and force and will. "To keep at it— to strive toward the perfect, the ripe, the only best; to go on, by one's own clear light, with patience, courage and continuity, to live with the high vision and effort, to justify one's self—and oh, so greatly!—all in time: this and this alone can be my lesson from *anything!*"

His words might be weak, but "the experience and the purpose are of welded gold and adamant. The consolation, the dignity, the joy of life are that discouragements and lapses, depressions and darknesses, come to one only as one stands *without*—I mean without the luminous paradise of art. As soon as I really re-enter it—cross the loved threshold—stand in the high chamber, and the gardens divine—the whole realm widens out again before me and around me—the air of life fills my lungs—the light of achievement flushes over all the place, and I believe, I see, I *do*."

Such was his flight, his invocation to his muse and to the powers by which he lived. He was ready once again to confront the world. The period of his mourning was over. The recently-installed electric lights on the St. James's Theatre burned like some twinkling mundane altar, lit in the Mayfair marketplace, where his newest work, on which he had spent so much energy and lavished so much affection, would find its public. He knew that this time he had created with all the experience of his dramatic years and the accumulated resources of middle life. In his tale of "The Middle Years" he had talked of a new chance, a new style, a "later manner." Perhaps *Guy Domville* would be his new chance. At Christmas of 1894, when one of the most tragic years of his life approached its end, he waited for the rising of the curtain on his new play—and on his future.

NOTES AND ACKNOWLEDGMENTS

My principal debt in this volume is to Constance Fenimore Woolson's literary executor, Miss Clare Benedict, who generously gave me permission to use the letters of Miss Woolson to Henry James and who in a series of letters to me gave me such recollections as she had of the friendship of her aunt with Henry James. I am also indebted to Mrs. Robert H. Bishop for giving me access to Miss Woolson's letters to Samuel Mather, and to Professor Lyon N. Richardson for making known to me the existence of this archive. I wish to express my thanks to Mr. John James for allowing me the same access to the James papers which his father, the late William James, and his uncle, the late Henry James of New York, gave me long ago. In addition to my debt to Harvard, and in particular to the librarian and staff of the Houghton Library, signalled in the preceding volumes, I owe particular thanks to Mr. Norbert Heermann for the photograph of the Bootts-Duveneck at the Villa Castellani, which he

allowed me to use in anticipation of his own work on Duveneck.
I am grateful to him also for certain details of Duveneck's life.

In Florence, early in 1962, I was generously given access by the
Marchesa Nannina Fossi Rucellai and her brothers, Conte Ber-
nardo and Conte Gian Giulio Rucellai, to the letters of Henry
James written to their grandmother, Katherine De Kay Bronson
and to their mother, the late Contessa Edith Bronson Rucellai,
now in the Rucellai archive. These, with the Curtis letters in the
Baker Library at Dartmouth, made available to me through the
agency of Professor Herbert Faulkner West, have enabled me to
reconstruct certain of James's later Italian visits. I wish also to
thank Mr. Ralph Curtis of Paris and Venice for replying to certain
of my inquiries. The correspondence with Elizabeth and Francis
Boott is in the James Collection at Harvard. I am indebted to
Colby College Library and Professor Carl J. Weber for some of
the Vernon Lee material, and my thanks are due to the following
institutions and persons for documents furnished or assistance
given:

The Bodleian Library; the Columbia University Library; the
Edward Lawrence Doheny Memorial Library, St. John's Semi-
nary, Camarillo, California; The Library, University of Glasgow;
the University of Illinois Library and Dr. Gordon N. Ray; the
Humanities Research Center, University of Texas; Janet Adam
Smith; Dr. Octavia Wilberforce and Mr. Dan H. Laurence.

I also wish to thank Professor Mario Praz and Professor Marcello Spaziani, of the University of Rome, for assistance given me
in examining the materials in the library and museum of the
Fondazione Primoli. Professor Kenneth B. Murdock, co-editor of
Henry James's notebooks, generously allowed me to quote from
them and, as first director of the Harvard University Center for
Italian Renaissance Culture in the Villa I Tatti, gave me access
to the Biblioteca Berenson.

Unless otherwise indicated, the documents mentioned in the
notes below are in the James Collection or other collections in

the Houghton Library at Harvard. In the interest of concision the following abbreviations are used in the notes:

AJ = Alice James
AK = Aunt Kate (Catherine Walsh)
Barrett = Barrett Collection
CEN = Charles Eliot Norton
CFW = Constance Fenimore Woolson
Curtis = Mr. and Mrs. D. S. Curtis
FB = Francis Boott
Gardner = Isabella Stewart Gardner
GN = Grace Norton
HJ = Henry James
HJ Sr = Henry James (father)
Hoppin = William J. Hoppin, *Journal of a Residence in London*
JF = F. O. Matthiessen, *The James Family* (1947)
KB = The Bronson (Rucellai) papers
LB = Elizabeth (Lizzie) Boott
Lubbock = *Letters of Henry James* (1920)
Mrs. HJ Sr = Mrs. Henry James (Mary Walsh, mother)
N = *The Notebooks of Henry James*, edited by Matthiessen and Murdock (1947)
NSB = *Notes of a Son and Brother* (1914)
NY Ed = New York Edition
NYPL = New York Public Library
R = Henrietta Reubell
RJ = Robertson James (brother)
RPB = Ralph Barton Perry, *Thought and Character of William James* (1935)
SBO = *A Small Boy and Others* (1913)
SW = Sarah Butler Wister
TS = Typescript
TSP = Thomas Sergeant Perry
WDH = William Dean Howells
WJ = William James (brother)

WMF = William Morton Fullerton
Vaux = Vaux Papers (Robertson James papers)

BOOK ONE: *Terminations*

Homecoming: N 23-24, 32-36. "The Point of View," and "A Bundle of Letters." AK to Mrs. RJ 14 Nov. 81 (Vaux); GN 13 Dec. 81.

The Dome and the Shaft: "The Point of View." *The American Scene.* NY Ed, XIV. Ward Thoron, *Letters of Mrs. Henry Adams* (1936); GN 10 Jan. 82; R 9 Jan. 82; Godkin 15 Jan., 22 Jan. 82. Lewis and Smith, *Oscar Wilde Discovers America* (1936). Gardner 23 Jan. 82; Mrs. HJ Sr 22 Jan. 82.

Mary James: N 39-40. RJ 27 Jan. 82 (Vaux); Mrs. HJ Sr 29 Jan. 82; Gardner [3?] Feb. 82; Mrs. Francis Mathews 13 Feb. 82.

An Exquisite Stillness: N 40-42. Daniel Frohman, manager of the Madison Square Theatre, communicated to me his comments on "Daisy." Hoppin 9 Feb. 82; R 9 Feb. 82; Mrs. Kemble TS 5 Apr. 82; "Emerson" in *Partial Portraits.* HJ Sr to HJ 9 May 82.

A Little Tour in France: Godkin 5 June 82; N 42-43; WJ *Letters,* to his wife, 24 Sept. 82; AJ 6 Aug., 16 Oct. 82. Account by WJ's son Henry, in WJ *Letters* I 209-10. Turgenev to Ralston, *Revue Mondiale,* Jan. 1925: "*Henry James m'a fait une visite. Il est toujours aussi aimable. Il a beaucoup grossi; il est presque aussi gros qu'Albert Turgenev, avec qui il est venu me voir.*" LB 7 Oct. 82; WDH 15 Oct. 82.

November Parting: "Turgenev" in *Partial Portraits.* Gardner 12 Nov. 82; Hay 26 Nov. 82 (Brown); WDH 27 Nov. 82.

A Winter Summons: WJ 26 Dec., 28 Dec. 82; RJ 30 Dec. 82 (Vaux); AK's notes on HJ Sr's last remarks in Vaux. Macmillan 26 Dec. 82.

A Blessed Farewell: WJ *Letters* I 218-220. WJ 1 Jan. 83.

Son and Brother: Godkin 3 Mar. 85; WJ 8 Jan., 11 Jan., 23 Jan., 5 Feb., 7 Feb., 11 Feb. 83. "A New England Winter." Macmillan 27 Jan., 9 Apr. 83; Mrs. Kemble TS 1 Feb. 82; letters of J. R. Osgood, Yale University Library, Barrett and Colby College. Osgood 19 Apr. 83 (Yale). Carl J. Weber, *The Rise and Fall of James Ripley Osgood* (1959). Professor Weber kindly furnished TS of two letters used in his book. Osgood 5 Aug. 1887; C. F. Woolson to Osgood 30 Dec. [87]. Reading in Boston: N.Y. *Tribune* 9 May 1883. Laurence Hutton, *Talks in a Library* (1905). N 42-43. HJ's letters to Emma Lazarus in Columbia University Library, where I saw them through courtesy of Professor Ralph L. Rusk. GN 28 July 83. "The Patagonia." Aldrich 20 Sept. 83. Daudet on Turgenev, and HJ translation: both mss. are in Barrett. LB 14 Oct. 83.

BOOK TWO: *The Art of the Novel*

The Lost Freshness: LB 11 Dec. 83; GN 14 Oct., 29 Oct. 83; Miss Dorothy Ward gave me access to the letters to Mrs. Humphry Ward, now in Barrett.

Letters to Sir George and Lady Lewis were seen by courtesy of the late Miss Katherine Lewis. The Du Maurier letters, now at Harvard, were made available to me in 1937 through the kindness of Miss Daphne Du Maurier. There are hundreds of letters to Sir Edmund Gosse. The largest collection is in the Brotherton Library, University of Leeds. Other Gosse letters were made available to me in Barrett, Berg, and Colby collections, the Duke University Library, and in the collection of Robert H. Taylor. There are some also in the Houghton. HJ to his godson, communicated to me by C. C. Hoyer Millar. See his *George Du Maurier and Others* (1931). Sir Osbert Sitwell, *Noble Essences* (1950). Sir Evan Charteris, *Life and Letters of Edmund Gosse* (1931). Mrs. Humphry Ward, *A Writer's Recollections* (1918). Godkin 3 Mar. 85.

Castle Nowhere: The four letters from Miss Woolson to HJ are dated: Hotel Bristol, Sorrento, 12 Feb. and resumed 23 Feb. 82; Dresden 30 Aug. 82; Venice 7 May 83; Venice 24 May 83. Miss Clare Benedict, by whose permission the excerpts are here published, informed me of the agreement between her aunt and HJ to destroy each other's letters. WDH 21 Feb. 84.

The Besotted Mandarins: Child's letter to Goncourt 5 Feb. 84 is in the Bibliothèque Nationale, Paris. I am indebted to Professor R. Ricotte, an editor of the Goncourt journals, for communicating to me the data here used prior to publication of the journals which enabled me to identify the anonymous *Atlantic* article in the Contributors' Club of May 1884 (724-727) as by Child. Aldrich 13 Feb. 84; Gosse 7 Feb. 84. WJ 20 Feb. 84; WDH 21 Feb. 84; GN 23 Feb. 84; WMF 29 Feb. 96; TSP 6 Mar. 84; Mrs. Ward 21 Feb. 84; R 16 Sept. 84, 5 July 85. William Rothenstein, *Men and Memories* (1931-32). In a later letter from HJ to Howard Sturgis HJ actually refers to Miss Reubell as Etta Barrace, one of the rare instances in which he identified an "original."

An Insolence of Talent: WJ 20 Feb. 84; GN 23 Feb., 2 Aug. 84; AJ 28 Mar. 84. I wish to thank David McKibbin of the Boston Athenaeum for helping me to find information concerning certain of Sargent's subjects who were also friends of HJ. Sir Evan Charteris, *John Sargent* (1927); Charles Merrill Mount, *John Singer Sargent* (1957). Mr. Mount provided certain details from his own researches. LB 2 June 84. GN 28 Mar. 84.

Matrons and Disciples: GN 2 Aug. 84, 24 Jan. 85. Albert Feuillerat, *Paul Bourget* (1937). General Daille, Bourget's executor, gave me access to HJ's letters to the novelist. *Vernon Lee's Letters,* with a preface by her Executor (Privately Printed 1937); see also Carl J. Weber, "Henry James and His Tiger Cat," and Burdett Gardner, "An Apology for Henry James's 'Tiger-Cat,'" in *PMLA* LXVIII (Sept. 1953); see also Leon Edel, "Henry James and Vernon Lee," *PMLA* LXIX (June 1954). Edith Wharton, *A Backward Glance* (1934); TSP 28 Sept., 12 Dec. 84.

Atmosphere of the Mind: R 10 Sept., 16 Sept. 84. *Henry James and Robert Louis Stevenson,* edited by Janet Adam Smith (1948), contains the two essays and all of the letters between the two writers available at the time of publication, as well as Stevenson's poems to HJ. Since then 15 more letters have turned up; I have used these from the Lubbock TS in the Harvard Collection.

The Two Invalids: TSP 14 Sept. 79; AK 11 Nov., 17 Nov., 24 Nov. 84, 12 May, 18 May 85; WJ 5 Oct., 4 Dec. 84, 29 Jan., 18 May 85; GN 6 May, 3 Nov. 84, 25 Jan., 9 May 85; LB 24 Apr., 4 May 85; Mrs. Godkin 2 Oct. 84; WDH 23 May 85. The inscription in *Kidnapped* is dated 21 July 1886.

A Very American Tale: Caroline Ticknor, *Glimpses of Authors* (1922); Miss Rosamond Gilder gave me access to certain of HJ's letters to her father, Richard Watson Gilder; Gilder 31 July 84; N 47. GN 9 Dec. 85; WJ 5 Oct. 84, 14 Feb. 85, 9 May, 13 June 86; WDH 23 May 85; Hay 23 May 85 (Brown).

BOOK THREE: *A London Life*

The Naturalist: TSP 12 Dec. 84.

The Peacock and the Butterfly: Sargent to HJ 29 June 85; R 5 July 85; Miss Boughton, 3 July 85 (Barrett); George D. Painter, *Marcel Proust, I* (1959); *Memoirs of Léon Daudet* (1926). Marcel Proust, *By Way of Ste. Beuve* (tr. Warner) (1958). *Letters of Marcel Proust,* edited by Mina Curtiss (1949).

Picture and Text: E. V. Lucas, *Life and Work of Edwin Austen Abbey* (1921); Gosse's account is in Lubbock I, 88-89. LB 13 Nov. 85; R 18 Nov. 85; WJ 10 Sept. 86. Dr. John A. P. Millet gave me access to HJ's letters to his father.

Clover: LB 7 Jan., 6 Feb. 86. CFW to Hay 26 Dec. 85 (Brown). Godkin 6 Feb. 86.

34 De Vere Gardens: I pieced together the description of the apartment from allusions in a series of letters to his friends and from his preface in which he speaks of the west window. Also from Urbain Mengin's unpublished memoir made available to me. GN 9 Dec. 85, 7 Feb., 16 July 86; LB 7 Jan. 86; Godkin 6 Feb. 86; WJ 9 Mar., 10 Dec. 86.

Politics and the Boudoir: GN 24 Jan. 85; 27 Feb., 16 July 86; WJ 13 June 86. Roy Jenkins, *Sir Charles Dilke* (1958); TSP 26 Sept. 84.

A Lion in the Path: Francis Steegmuller, *Maupassant* (1949). Professor Marcello Spaziano of the University of Rome supplied excerpts from Maupassant's letters to Primoli, and Professor Mario Praz kindly conducted me through the Palazzino Primoli. See Spaziani's *Joseph-Napoléon Primoli, Pages Inedites* (1959); also "Lettere inedite di Maupassant al Conte Primoli," in *Studi in Onore di Vittorio Lugli e Diego Valeri* (Venice [1961]). FB 15 Aug. 86. The Wilde anecdote stems from Vincent O'Sullivan. WMF 14 July 1893. RLS 2 Aug. 86.

The Divided Self: NY Ed, V. N 68-69. G. Du Maurier to HJ 1 Nov. 86. *The Princess Casamassima.* Lionel Trilling, *The Liberal Imagination* (1950). Irving Howe, *Politics and the Novel* (1959); Woodcock and Avakumovic, *The Anarchist Prince* (1950); Nellie Sanchez, *Life of Mrs. Robert Louis Stevenson* (1920).

BOOK FOUR: *Bellosguardo*

The Lonely Friends: CFW to Hay 26 Dec. 85 (Brown); LB 22 Feb., 18 Oct. 86; R 11 Mar. 86; FB 22 Feb., 15 Aug., 4 Nov., 26 Nov. 86.

The Two Villas: AK 30 Oct. 86; LB 18 Oct. 86. KB 6 Dec. [86]. Hay 24 Dec. 86 (Brown). Miss Mercede Huntington kindly allowed me to inspect the Villa Castellani, now Villa Mercede. The Villa Brichieri now contains a series of apartments.

A Polyglot Society: AK 26 Feb. 87; GN 25 Jan., 27 Feb. 87; SW 27 Feb. 87; CFW to Hay 10 Jan. 87 (Brown); WJ 23 Dec. 86, 18 Feb., 7 Apr. 87. KB 5 Feb., 15 Feb., 18 Feb., 23 Apr., 3 May 87. Janet Ross, *The Fourth Generation* (1912); WDH 25 Feb. 87; FB 15 Mar. 87; Mrs. Sands 26 Feb. 87. The letters to Mrs. Sands were made available to me by the late Miss Ethel Sands; Gosse 24 Apr. 87; Laura Wagnière, *From Dawn to Dusk* (Privately printed), contains an account of the Castellani and the Florentine fetes. Mrs. Kemble TS 20 May 87.

The Aspern Papers: KB Monday [87]. N 71-72. Charteris, *Sargent.* NY Ed, XII. The palace James had in mind for this tale is the Capello on the Riva Marin near the railway station, "the old pink-faced, battered-looking and quite homely and plain (as things go in Venice) old Palazzino. It has a garden behind it, and I think, though I am not sure, some bit of garden wall beside it." The palace still stands. (From an HJ memorandum to Alvin Langdon Coburn kindly made available to me by Mr. Coburn.)

Palazzo Barbaro: NY Ed, X. AK 16 June 87; GN 23 July 87; SW 7 Oct. 87; NY Ed, XIII. N 83-85. Dr. Gloria Glikin kindly searched the files of the *World.* KB 21 Jan., 26 Jan. undated letter, Florence, Saturday [87] and 17 Sept. 87.

BOOK FIVE: *Art and the Marketplace*

A Massing of Masterpieces: SW 7 Oct. 87; WJ 29 Oct. 88; CEN 6 Dec. 86; "An Animated Conversation," reprinted in *Essays in London.* WDH 2 Jan. 88. *Harper's New Monthly Magazine* (Oct. 1888).

Elizabeth Duveneck: R 1 Apr., 5 Apr., 24 May 88; FB 3 Apr., 21 Apr., 15 May 88; Mrs. Curtis 2 Apr., 15 May 88. R 18 Dec. 87, 1 Apr., 5 Apr., 24 May 88.

A Meeting in Geneva: Aldrich 3 Mar. 88; R 29 Oct. 88; WJ 29 Oct. 88; FB Oct. 88; Curtis 30 Oct. 88.

The Expense of Freedom: NY Ed, VII. Mrs. Ward's novel, *Miss Bretherton* (1885). R 21 Apr. 88. Lady Battersea, *Memoirs* (1922). GN 7 Dec. 86, 23 July 87. N 90-92.

A Chastening Necessity: Macmillan 28 Mar. 90; WJ 16 May 90; Mrs. Edward Compton described to me the circumstances of HJ's dramatization. The documentation for HJ's play-writing years will be found in *The Complete Plays of HJ*, edited by Leon Edel (1949). In the present volume I have been able, thanks to new documentation, to explain more fully than I did hitherto HJ's financial reasons for turning to the stage.

The Gallo-Romans: Jusserand gave me his reminiscences of HJ in 1930. I also talked with Mengin in the 1930's and later corresponded with him. His son, Robert, has aided me in my documentation of these friendships. I also gained insight into them in talks with Mary Robinson (Madame Duclaux). M. Mengin gave me access to the letters to him. They are now in the Harvard collection. Jules Jusserand, *What Me Befell* (1933). R 24 May 88. N 101. *Life and Letters of E. L. Godkin,* edited by Rollo Ogden (1907).

The Private Life: Mrs. Bronson 12 Jan. 90; FB 11 Jan. 90.

BOOK SIX: *The Dramatic Years*

Theatricals: Complete Plays. Arthur Waugh, *One Man's Road* (1931). CFW's Bellosguardo story was "Dorothy," *Harper's* (March 1892). FB 11 Jan. 90; WJ 16 May 90; WDH 17 May 90. Dr. Octavia Wilberforce gave me access to HJ's letters to Mrs. Bell and also details concerning Elizabeth Robins. The Humanities Research Center, University of Texas, gave me access to the HJ letters to Miss Robins published by the actress in *Theatre and Friendship* (1932). FB 20 July 91. Lowell 30 Dec. 90, 8 June, 20 July 1891.

A Divine Cessation: AJ *Journal.* WJ 2 March, 5 March, 8 March, 9 March 92; WJ to HJ 7 Mar. 92; RJ 8 Mar. 92; FB 9 Mar. 92; R 15 Mar. 92. N 181-83.

The Wheel of Time: Nadal, see *The Conquest of London.* Tennyson, CFW to Samuel Mather, 14 Oct. 92. I am indebted to Mrs. Robert H. Bishop for access to this correspondence. Fullerton: I had some of these details from WMF himself in the 1930's and in Paris toward the end of the war. Leon Edel, "Jonathan Sturges," *Princeton University Library Chronicle* (Autumn 1953). I talked with Logan Pearsall Smith in the early 1930's. Henry C. Brewster, "Henry James and the Gallo-American," *Botteghe Oscura* (Spring 1957). Mr. Brewster gave me access to the correspondence before he published it. CFW to Samuel Mather, 29 Apr. 1893.

In Siena: Curtis 6 June, 11 June 92; KB 11 June 92; Mrs. Palmer 10 June 92 (Barrett); R 21 June 92; Gardner 26 June 92; WJ 19 Dec. 93.

The Two Queens: Gardner 3 Sept. 92; GN 23 Aug. 92; Betty Miller, *Robert Browning* (1952). KB 27 Sept. 92. Mr. Stout and the Gardner Museum gave me access to Mrs. Bronson's letters to Mrs. Gardner. The late William James told me the anecdote of his uncle's remarks on natural affections.

Mrs. Kemble: Complete Plays. SW 20 Jan., 13 Mar. 93; Daly 25 Jan. 93; Bentley 20 Jan. 93 (Illinois).

Episode: WMF 16 Jan. 93; WJ 20 Jan. 93; WJ to Vernon Lee 11 Mar. 93. HJ pocket diary 29 July 1912 records motoring to have tea with the Ranee of Sarawak at Ascot, "Vernon Lee there with whom I had a good deal of talk." Weber, Gardner, *op. cit.*

In the Marketplace: WJ to HJ 17 Mar. 93. GN 20 Aug. 93. Lucien Daudet, before his death, generously gave me HJ's letters to his father and his recollections of the 1890's. N 133-34.

Rehearsal: Complete Plays.

BOOK SEVEN: *The Altar of the Dead*

A Venetian Christmas: Curtis 14 July, 19 Sept. 93; FB 21 Oct. 93. KB 31 Dec. 93. *Complete Plays.* N 139-41.

Miss Woolson: Cables in Mather papers. Angelina Milman [26 Jan. 94] (Barrett); Hay 28 Jan. 94 (Brown); TS Ranee of Sarawak, 28 Jan. 94; Gosse 30 Jan., 3 Feb. 94; FB 31 Jan. 94; Hay to Adams 5 Feb. 94, William Roscoe Thayer, *Life of John Hay* (1915). Lily Norton, 8 Feb. 94; WJ to HJ 25 Feb. 94; KB 2 Feb. 94; N.Y. *World*, 28 Jan. 94.

Casa Biondetti: Clare Benedict, *The Benedicts Abroad* (Privately printed), contains an account of HJ's meeting with Mrs. Benedict in Italy and excerpts from HJ's letters to Mrs. Benedict and her daughter. Miss Benedict informed me that HJ's letters were returned to him. The books which HJ took remained in his library up to the time of its dispersal. KB, Genoa undated [Mar. 94]; TS Palgrave 16 Apr. 94. N 17 April 94. WMF 30 June 94. WJ 25 May, 29 June 94.

Pilgrimage: FB 9 Oct. 95. Brewster 24 June 94.

The Invaded Altars: Gosse [?] Aug. 94. "The Altar of the Dead." HJ: *The Untried Years,* final chapters.

The Terrible Law: N 169-74. 111. *Complete Plays.*

Index

401